The Ancestry of
Our English Bible

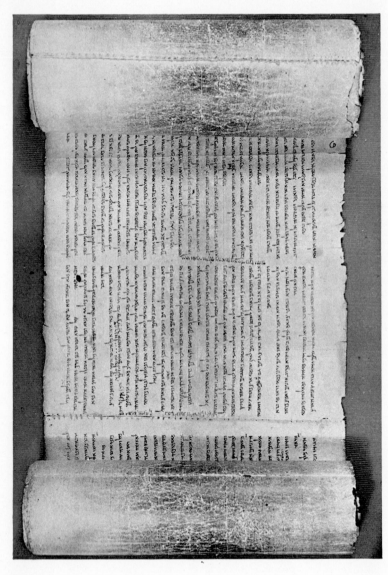

Scroll of Isaiah found near the Dead Sea, showing 40:2-28 (By permission of the American Schools of Oriental Research.)

The Ancestry of
Our English Bible

AN ACCOUNT OF MANUSCRIPTS, TEXTS, AND VERSIONS OF THE BIBLE

BY IRA MAURICE PRICE, PH.D.

LATE PROFESSOR OF THE SEMITIC LANGUAGES
AND LITERATURES IN THE UNIVERSITY OF CHICAGO

THIRD REVISED EDITION BY

WILLIAM A. IRWIN

ALLEN P. WIKGREN

PROFESSORS IN THE UNIVERSITY OF CHICAGO

Harper & Brothers, Publishers
NEW YORK

To

JUDGE WALTER BURGES BEALS

Judge and Chief Justice of the Supreme Court of the State of Washington, retired, whose generosity through lectures in the churches of his State, with rare exhibits from his large and valuable collection of ancient manuscripts and early Bibles, has added much to the general knowledge of the ancestry of our English Bible.

Library of Congress catalog card number: 55-11644

Contents

Illustrations

Diagrams

[In the diagrams the broken lines indicate, in each case, the period prior to our oldest manuscript.]

Preface

OUR English Bible is the descendant of a long line of ancestors. It is the gathering up, the focalization, of the best that is found in all the manuscripts and versions extant. It is the result of the best efforts of about seventy-five of the leading scholars of the last quarter-century.

How did these scholars produce our English Bible? What were the sources of their materials? Where were these materials found? What is their character? Where are they preserved? How were they used by scholars in the production, for example, of our Revised Version? These are a few of the questions that arise in the minds of every earnest, thoughtful student of the Bible. They can be answered only by a somewhat extended description and by references to many books and articles.

These questions were discussed in a popular vein in a series of eleven articles in *The Sunday School Times* during the first three-quarters of the year 1904. Their publication in book form was announced for the autumn of the same year. But long, distressing, and fatal illness in the family of the writer, and the decision to expand the material to more than twice its original size, necessitated the postponement of its publication.

The purpose of this volume is to present in as concise and popular form as possible a description of the principal versions and texts of the Bible, from the earliest known translations and manuscripts down through the Middle Ages, even to modern times. Now and then a version or manuscript is prefaced by a statement of the historical background, where such is required to bring out more sharply the characteristics of such document. This has been done especially in the discussion of the early versions of the English Bible, for the Bible work is best understood if we appreciate the historical conditions of those days.

The division of the book into three parts is natural, though it may, at first, seem to need justification. The earliest versions and manuscripts do not all contain both the Old Testament and the New. The fact that the originals of the two were written in different languages is sufficient ground for treating them in two parts. Then the existence of some versions, such as the Samaritan Pentateuch, in the Old Testament alone calls for such a division of the theme. It soon becomes apparent, however, that the line between Parts I and II cannot always be sharply drawn; for, as in the case of the Vulgate, both Testaments are included. There is consequently some almost unavoidable overlapping, where the version is discussed in both Parts I and II. This disadvantage is partly overcome in the case of the Vulgate by devoting the chapter in Part I to early Latin Old Testament manuscripts and the Vulgate down to the ninth century, and that in Part II to early Latin New Testament manuscripts and the Vulgate down to modern times. In Part III, "The English Bible," no division is made between the Old Testament and the New, both being treated in each chapter.

Some portion of each chapter descriptive of a version is given to an account of the principal manuscripts. Only such facts are mentioned as serve prominently to distinguish those documents in the history of the text. Of some of the great manuscripts, such as the Sinaitic, a few essential facts regarding its discovery are given, that we may the better know the cost of some of our most valued treasures.

The illustrations are designed to set vividly before the eyes of the reader facsimile specimens of some of the earliest and most important texts and versions now in the possession of the great libraries of the world, and of some private collections. These have been gathered from a large variety of sources, as is indicated in the List of Illustrations. Full acknowledgment is here made to the firms and individuals who have so generously granted permission to reproduce them for this volume. The names of such grantors appear in full in the List of Illustrations.

The Bibliography gives merely a selection of the literature that will prove most helpful in further investigation of the theme of each chapter.

The diagrams illustrative of the relations of the versions and transcripts present to the eye some patent facts that should be remembered.

The author acknowledges his indebtedness to many writers and authors from whom the material of this volume has been gathered and reconstructed. The Bibliography cites almost in full the sources employed in its production.

The thanks of the author are due his colleague, Professor Ernest D. Burton, for his kindness in reading the manuscript of Part II, "The New Testament," and for making valuable suggestions; and to Professor C. W. Votaw for reading the proofs of the same and for indicating points of improvement in the matter and forms of statements. The author, however, is alone responsible for the method of treatment.

To the publishers, who have spared no pains in making the volume attractive in form and make-up, there is also due a debt of thanks.

IRA MAURICE PRICE

The University of Chicago
New Year, 1907

Preface to First Revised Edition

THE output of published documents on the Bible during the last thirty years has been enormous. Discoveries of MSS, their publication, and the discussions of their character alone embrace many volumes every year. Comparative textual studies to evaluate their contents and classification are tightening the lines toward the recovery of the original text.

In revising this edition the aim has been to retain as far as possible the plates and the original pagination, and at the same time to add to the appropriate chapter distinctly new material. Such additions are made to Chapters VI, X, XIV, and XVII. To Chapters V, IX, XII, XIII, XVI, XVIII, XX, and page 319 just a "Note" is added.

Of these additions, that to Chapter VI gives several sections on the marvelous new finds of MSS touching the Greek of the Septuagint; and that to Chapter X mentions especially valuable Coptic MSS on the Old Testament. Chapter XIV carries seven sections on the momentous discoveries of New Testament MSS, and the divisions of the New Testament on which they throw light. Chapter XVII adds three sections on some items of the textual significance of the finds of the last thirty years.

The Biblical MSS discovered and studied during the last half-century have been a constant stimulus to new translations of the Bible. This has been notably true since the turn of the century. In response to repeated requests a chapter is given to Recent and Modern-Speech Translations (XXIV).

The Bibliography of nearly thirty years ago has been entirely recast. Selections only of the numerous available works are named. Even so, the list contains more than fifty titles of new works that have appeared since 1907. Instead of arranging them under chapters as in the old list, thus requiring much repetition, they are now placed under the three Parts (I, II, and III) of the book, thus reducing the repetition to a minimum.

Some few additions are found in the Chronological Table and the Personal and Topical Index.

The gratitude of the author is hereby expressed to those who are using this volume as a textbook for their practical suggestions touching the revision; also to Dr. Kenneth W. Clark for furnishing the number and classification of New Testament MSS as catalogued today.

The author also gladly acknowledges his indebtedness to other writers, especially to Dr. F. G. Kenyon, whose works on MSS, their estimate and treatment, are so replete with sound learning.

The generosity of Professor H. A. Sanders, of the University of Michigan, in contributing to the author's equipment his Old Testament volumes of the Freer Collection, is gratefully acknowledged.

To the members of the New Testament department of the University of Chicago for their interest and active encouragement, especially to Professors Edgar J. Goodspeed and Harold R. Willoughby, who read the MS of the additions on New Testament texts and problems with helpful suggestions, the author extends sincere thanks.

To the publishers for their skill in putting together this revised edition in such usable and serviceable form the author is truly grateful.

IRA MAURICE PRICE

Ferncroft,
Olympia, Washington
August, 1934

Preface to Second Revised Edition

N O BOOK means so much to religion as the Bible." So Professor Edgar J. Goodspeed begins the introduction to his edition of the original preface to the King James Version. And he goes on, "It has more to teach the modern world about religion than even its strongest advocates have realized. Few of them have fully explored the wealth and depth of its contribution to modern religious attitudes." His words have far wider relevance than a mere casual reader will detect. The culture of the Western world has been molded by the Bible. This was its great book, its inspiration, the source of its wisdom and thought for a thousand years. Missionaries carried it to savage tribes that were our ancestors, and by its teachings shaped their evolving civilization. Then with the Protestant Reformation it came to new importance and centrality. The spring and source of the great impulse of these Protestant centuries has been, in deepest analysis, the Bible with its profound understanding of human life and its words of matchless beauty. Allegedly "emancipated" folk of today dismiss it as obsolete; they suppose that modern scholarship has reduced it to a jumble of primitive traditions and ignorant superstitions. But in reality critical Biblical scholarship has, instead, served to reveal the amazing character of this ancient literature that has come down the centuries to us as the priceless bequest of the ancient world. Those who have any comprehension of the older cultures of the Near Orient are compelled to sheer astonishment at the profundity and beauty of the Biblical words and concepts, coming as they did out of such environment. But the wonder does not stop there. The Bible is the effectual hope of our troubled age, threatened as it is with horrors far surpassing those we have so recently endured. This opinion calls for little demonstration. It is the emphasis of all sorts of persons who wrestle with the problem of peace for our time and who hope for the success of that unparalleled venture, the United Nations; notwithstanding many of them, it would appear, pay but unconscious tribute to ancient seers who fought for human rights and equal opportunity for all classes and races of men. One of these Biblical thinkers, some twenty-seven centuries ago, startled his age with a rhetorical question that could well land one behind bars even at this day in some parts of our own land, "Are you not as the Ethiopians to me? says the Lord." And another envisaged a time when the nations would flow up—to the point of attraction!—to the mountain of the house of the Lord, to learn his ways; then they would beat their swords into plowshares and their spears into pruninghooks and learn war no more.

But the Bible can serve its function in the modern world only if it is understood. And one part of such understanding is a knowledge of the course of events through which it has been preserved for us, remote as we are in time and culture from its original writers. It was to this purpose that Dr. Price's book was dedicated. How well it has served its function is testified by its successive reprintings and its continuing popularity. Its author was constantly on the alert to enlarge and improve it with the newer knowledge which came so richly through the decades after the book was first published. His additions and changes down to the time of his passing from us in 1939 are well known to the many who have grown familiar with the volume through these many years. It is, we believe, in a spirit comparable with his own faith and hopes that the present revision has been carried through; for the story of the Bible is never complete, and our knowledge of its ancient course is steadily enlarging. Yet how much there is that still lies obscured from our vision will be apparent in every chapter of this book. The volume, then, in this current edition, is issued as a sort of interim report on an activity that will never come to finality. Our sincere hope is that in some not unworthy way it may continue to serve the needs of students of the Bible, and through them the profound searchings of our distressed age.

The measure of revision that we have carried through has been dictated by relevant facts. Dr. Price wrote originally in response to the deep stirring of interest aroused by publication of the American

Standard Version. Considerable material in his early chapters has thus lost the relevance it possessed at that time. The changes we have made will be most apparent at this point. Yet those familiar with the work in its earlier form will recognize the impulse of Dr. Price's thought throughout, and they will not read far until they come to his authentic wording. It is still Dr. Price's book, in his characteristic presentation. The course of scholarship has, however, called for new chapters on textual criticism. Also progress in the work upon the Revised Standard Version has conduced to expansion of the former brief note, adequate though it was originally, into a full chapter; and even so, it is obvious, the account is not yet complete.

Our debt to all who have gone before will be evident to those competent to judge. In keeping with the character wisely imposed upon the volume at the first, we have not burdened our pages with footnotes; our bibliography will make general confession of our indebtedness. It is a pleasure to acknowledge also the assistance we have received from our colleagues in the Oriental Institute and in the Federated Theological Faculty of the University of Chicago. They have greatly enhanced what value this edition may possess. For its faults and deficiencies we must ourselves bear responsibility.

We are happy also to make grateful acknowledgement of the courtesy we have met at the hands of publishers and their generous permission to make use of material which we have incorporated: to the Lutterworth Press for extracts from their *Codex Sinaiticus*, Tischendorf's own account of his epochal find; to the Macmillan Company and Cambridge University Press for a quotation from H. B. Swete's story of Codex Cottonianus in his *Introduction to the Old Testament in Greek*; to the University of Chicago Press for excerpts from *The Translators to the Reader*, edited by Edgar J. Goodspeed; to Princeton University Press for the photograph of a page of the Greek papyrus published in *The John H. Scheide Biblical Papyri*; *Ezekiel*, edited by Johnson, Gehman, and Kase; to the Trustees of the late Sir Henry S. Wellcome for the photograph of a letter from *The Lachish Letters*, edited by H. Torczyner; to Mr. A. Chester Beatty for the photograph of a page from the Beatty papyri; to the University of Michigan Press for the photograph of a page from the *Facsimile of the Washington Manuscript of the Four Gospels in the Freer Collection*; to the

Oriental Institute of the University of Chicago for photographs of a Biblical text on a clay stamp, of a Biblical fragment from the geniza, and of a page from a Coptic Book of Proverbs. Especially we are indebted to the staff of Harper & Brothers for their assistance and many valuable suggestions. Their patient understanding through the many months of preparation of this revision is a grateful memory.

ALLEN P. WIKGREN
WILLIAM A. IRWIN

University of Chicago
May, 1949

Preface to the Third Revised Edition

Although adjustments to the constantly advancing story of the Bible were made in each of the two reprintings since publication of the Second Revised Edition in 1949, once again more extensive changes are called for. In addition to numerous lesser matters, these in the main relate to two topics.

Here for the first time, we believe, the story of the Revised Standard Version has been carried through its publication and the varying reactions of the public during these three years. As well, attention has been given to the finds near the Dead Sea, which were related in their incipient stage in the edition of 1949. The brief account in Chapter I has been revised; in the more ample space of an appendix the perplexity and debate of scholars has been recounted, and their pursuit of one clue after another in a wrestle with the mystery of the age and significance of documents which so astonishingly forced themselves upon attention.

A. P. W.
W. A. I.

September, 1955

INTRODUCTION

THE Bible has come down to us through thousands of years of adventure and devotion. All sorts and conditions of people have given of their thought and toil and care to its preservation. They have passed it on age after age, sometimes at great price, until at length it serves for our edification today. As one sits in the beauty, and indeed the luxury, of a modern church and listens to the reading of a passage from the Gospels telling of Jesus' ministry among the quiet hills of Galilee, or follows, entranced, a fragment of the lyric beauty that is the poetry of Israel, a sense of awe must come over him; after all these ages and in spite of the upheavals the world has witnessed, we still have the very words written or spoken in those far-off days! All round the world, in lands of which Israel never dreamed, peoples today hear, each in his own tongue in which he was born, the simple stories of rural Palestine, the raptures of the Psalmists, the threats and warnings of prophet-poets on fire with a sense of the divine righteousness; or, it may be, they read letters written by the great apostle to churches gone and forgotten long ages ago except for his share in them. There is mystery and wonder in it. This modern world, seemingly engrossed in its pursuit of pleasure and property, proud of its mastery of forces that made a plaything of man in days gone by, enjoying luxuries and bounty such as would have shamed the pride of kings, yet cherishes as its greatest book and most prized possession a collection of stories and poems and laws and letters that slowly grew up through a thousand years of a culture largely rustic. But that book was preserved while empires fell, while persecutions raged, and through the wearing length of the ages, by men and women unknown and unhonored, who found in these simple words their greatest joy. An uncritical age could lightly explain that this literature was the Word of God; and yet today our richest and deepest spirits, after meeting the questions and uncertainties which the scientific temper properly arouses, still bow their heads in reverence and affirm that it is so!

The long story is vivid with color and romance: with the royal purple of monarchs, for whom great manuscripts were slowly indited and illuminated, and the somber tones of simple folk who gave up their lives rather than their treasured Book; with the pomp of priests in the temples, and the pageantry of churchmen; with the devotion of scholars. There we meet, too, Jewish scribes toiling through the years, wearing out their lives in minutiae that weary us to contemplate but for them were glorious with a great devotion. They copied and checked manuscripts, counting the words and even the very letters, finding the middle word of a book and indeed of the whole Bible—and all in order that the sacred Scripture might be preserved in truth. We are indebted to hosts of Christian monks who likewise had no better way of copying the Bible than by tedious labor of hand. Often they embellished the pages, and doubtless brightened their own labor, with gorgeous rubrics or quaint illustrations. Later came the great achievement that through five centuries has changed man's life more than any other single invention since the stone ages: the art of printing. Appropriately, the first important book so produced, as everyone knows, was a Bible, a Latin Bible, since that was then the great Bible of all Western Christendom. And fittingly in the sequel the printing press has served to scatter Bibles in a thousand tongues to the remote ends of the world. But the story tells, too, of adventure that has thrilled many a modern scholar and often with him the whole Bible-reading world: the discovery of old copies of parts of the Bible in one of the languages of the ancient world. They have been found in all sorts of places—in the libraries of remote monasteries, in rubbish heaps and wastebaskets. A recent find was in the stuffing of an Egyptian mummy case; another was an old clay stamp that is thought to have been used in sealing wine jars. They have been gifts to kings and museums. They have been found in the hands of dealers in antiquities. Strangest of all, they have come to light in the downtown areas of modern American cities where they were carried by families migrating from Europe. The romance of discovery is like that of discovery of hidden treasure; and indeed such it is, for a Biblical writer has spoken in truth of the Word of God, "The return from it is better than the return from money, and its profit than fine gold."

Yet these ancient manuscripts in dead languages may perhaps seem no more than interesting curios or, at best, items for book collectors. The truth is far other. They are the materials and tools of scholars' inquiries. They are means for a better knowledge of what the writers of the Bible actually said. For strange as it must appear to many a devout student, slips and errors and omissions have marred the Bible through the long course of its recopying and reprinting. Yet a word of reassurance to those for whom this fact may be new or disturbing: there is nothing in any or in all such errors to affect the great realities of our faith, or our basic responsibility to do justly and to love mercy and to walk humbly with our God.

The story of the Bible is not alone one of preservation, for actually in its original languages it is today known to relatively few outside the limits of special scholarship. Its translation has been and continues to be of the highest importance; by this means it has been spread afar and its words have become the treasures of countless millions from every class of society. The process began even before Christian times, when the Jews of the city of Alexandria translated their Scriptures from Hebrew, which had become unfamiliar, into the Greek of their every-day conversation. In this they were pioneers in more than the Biblical field, for while translation of single documents was practiced even early in the far history of Babylonia, nothing on a scale comparable with this had ever before been undertaken. These Egyptian Jews in their response to the religious needs of their people were thus the first in the long succession of men who have translated whole bodies of literature into languages foreign to their authors. But also they began the process which, first through certain great Biblical versions of the ancient world and in recent times by means of the hosts of modern translations, has for its object the giving of the Bible to every people in its own tongue.

High among these Bibles of the modern world stands the English Bible. It, too, has a notable history, within the greatness of the story of the Bible as a whole. Early in the seventeenth century, however, after nearly eighty years of intensive labor in translation by English scholars and on the background of an earlier activity reaching back into Anglo-Saxon times, there was produced that version which even yet is honored and beloved throughout the English-speaking world. The English Bible holds a pre-eminent position in the realms of religion and literature. For more than three centuries it has easily and gracefully held its place in the esteem of those who use our language. Its power and influence today permeate our culture. Macaulay is reported to have written, "The English Bible is a book which, if everything else in our language should perish, would alone suffice to show the extent of its beauty and power."

The importance of the Bible requires that it command the best scholarship, and that it contain the best possible expression of the thoughts which the original writers set forth in words that now are for most people unintelligible. This has been the impulse in the various versions of the English Bible that have continued to be produced, notably in recent years. Some of these enjoy high use and popularity. The existence of so many different renderings all claiming to be the Bible is not an unmitigated evil. For apart from the merits of each in illuminating or explaining the scriptural words, the diversity serves to remind readers of the long history of the Bible; by revealing the difficulties that translators face, these versions serve to draw attention away from the mere words, beautiful as they are, and to center it instead on the Bible's transforming truth. Some of these translations, found in every community, in addition to the "Authorized" or King James Version first published in 1611, are the Revised Version of 1885 (though better known in England than in the United States), the American Standard Version of 1901, the Jewish Version of 1917, and the Revised Standard Version of the Bible of 1946 and 1952. These are in a sense official translations; they stand in direct succession to the great original translations of the sixteenth century, a stream of tradition so interwoven in our culture as to be considered, in a special way, *the* English Bible. In addition there are several translations which have been produced either through private enterprise or by Bible societies. Deserving mention among these are Spurrell's *A Translation of the Old Testament Scriptures from the Original Hebrew,* Fenton's *The Bible in Modern English,* and the translations of the American Bible Union. More widely known are James Moffatt's *The Bible: A New Translation*; the several editions of the New Testament, then of the Old Testament, and finally of the Apocrypha, published by the University of Chicago Press, and at length issued in a single volume entitled *The Complete Bible: An American Translation,* translated by J. M. Powis Smith, with three other scholars, and Edgar J. Goodspeed. There are also editions which have for their purpose the presentation of the Authorized or Revised Versions in an improved literary form, sometimes with introductions and notes. Notable are the Temple Bible, an arrangement of the Authorized Version and Moulton's *The Modern Reader's Bible,* a literary distribution of the matter of the Revised Version of 1885. A more recent publication which has attracted considerable attention through its excellence is *The Bible Designed to Be Read As Living Literature: the Old and New Testaments in the King James Version,* edited by Ernest Sutherland Bates. However, it gives less than the full text of the Bible, consisting rather of somewhat lengthy passages selected on the grounds of their literary excellence. It is thus an example of the "shorter Bibles" of which there are now a considerable number. All of them possess merit in that they offer a compact selection of notable Biblical passages; and all serve a good purpose. Yet persons familiar with the Bible will doubtless find them disappointing by reason of their omission of one or another much-loved passage.

This activity in production of new versions or editions is a mark of the unflagging interest in the Bible which is one of the less spectacular but profound features of modern times. For the Bible is *the* great Book of the modern world, upon which in very large measure our Western culture is founded. But there is also a more technical reason for these numerous Bible translations that is revealed by examination and comparison of them. Briefly, the translators have been actuated by the hope of presenting more truly the meaning of the Biblical writers.

Those who would translate into English the Hebrew of the Old Testament, or the Greek of the New Testament, face a difficult task. They undertake to render a literature that was copied over and over again for many hundreds of years. Mistakes inevitably were made, and many of them have never been corrected. No one of us could copy by hand ten pages of manuscript without making some errors. We would at least forget to dot some *i*'s or to cross some *t*'s; most of us would leave out words, write some words twice, omit some lines, repeat others, and make various other blunders. Just these things have happened to the manuscripts of the Bible.

Fortunately we possess many copies, partial or complete, of ancient translations, by the help of which we can often detect, and sometimes correct, a scribal error. For in hosts of passages they diverge in greater or less measure from our accepted Biblical text. To the total of such variant readings, as they are called, must be added the differences existing among Hebrew manuscripts of the Old Testament, and among Greek of the New Testament. The problem thus created is a considerable part of the subject matter of what is known as the textual criticism of the Bible, that is, the study that seeks to determine precisely what words the Biblical authors originally wrote. The handling of such problems is one of the basic issues in a translation of the Bible.

Many editions of the Bible take account of these variants in a series of marginal notes, while providing in them other explanatory material as well, notably alternate translations where the Hebrew or Greek is ambiguous. A few examples chosen from the American Standard Version will be of interest. In Genesis 6:3 we find, "My spirit shall not strive with man for ever"; the marginal rendering for "strive" is "Or, rule in"; "for that he also is flesh" has as its alternative in the margin, "Or, in their going astray they are flesh." Genesis 49:10 reads, "Until Shiloh come; And unto him shall the obedience of the peoples be," while the margin renders, "Or, till he come to Shiloh; having the obedience of the peoples." Isaiah 23:13 reads, "this people was not; the Assyrian founded it for them that dwell in the wilderness"; the margin reads, "This people is no more; the Assyrian hath appointed it for the beasts of the wilderness."

The New Testament carries on its margins scores of important variations of a similar character. In Matthew 25:41 we find, "Depart from me, ye cursed"; but in the margin, "Or, Depart from me under a curse." Luke 1:35, last half reads, "The holy thing which is begotten shall be called the Son of God"; but the margin has: "Or, that which is to be born shall be called holy, the Son of God." In John 1:9 we find, "There was the true light, even the light which lighteth every man, coming into the world"; but in the margin, "Or, the true light, which lighteth every man, was coming"; and still another marginal rendering is, "Or, every man as he cometh." Paul's epistles likewise provide striking variant renderings: I Corinthians 2:13, "combining spiritual things with spiritual words"; in the margin, "Or, interpreting spiritual things to spiritual men." II Corinthians 2:17, "corrupting the word of God"; but in the margin, "Or, making merchandise of the word of God."

And here are some genuine variants noted in the margins, as distinct from mere alternate translations. The difficult passage in which Elisha sends word to Benhadad, King of Syria, through Hazael (II Kings 8: 10), saying, "Go, say unto him, Thou shalt surely recover; howbeit Jehovah," etc., has a marginal note that says, "Another reading is, say, Thou shalt not recover, for Jehovah, &c." In Isaiah 9:3 "thou hast increased their joy" has a marginal note, "Another reading is, thou didst not increase the joy." Isaiah 52:2, "loose thyself from the bonds of thy neck," has in the margin, "Another reading is, the bands of thy neck are loosed." In the Lord's prayer, in Matthew 6:13, there is a marginal note which says, "Many authorities, some ancient, but with variations, add, For thine is the kingdom, and the power, and the glory, for ever. Amen." To Mark 16:9 f. there is this marginal remark, "The two oldest Greek manuscripts, and some other authorities, omit from ver. 9 to the end. Some other authorities have a different ending to the Gospel." In John 3:31b, 32a, "he that cometh from heaven is above all. What he hath seen and heard, of that he beareth witness" has a note in the margin, "Some ancient authorities read, he that cometh from heaven beareth witness of what he hath seen and heard." Examples of this class of readings might be multiplied indefinitely to show that there are variants of the Hebrew and Greek manuscripts which are worth careful study on the part of every diligent student of the Bible.

A few passages where ancient versions are cited by name will suffice to conclude this brief glimpse of a very important aspect of Bible translation. In I Samuel 14:18 Saul is represented as saying, "Bring hither the ark of God. For the ark of God was there at that time with the children of Israel"; but the margin reads, "Some editions of Sept. have, Bring hither the ephod. For he wore the ephod at that time before Israel." In II Chronicles 1:13 the translators adopted the reading of three ancient versions as against that of the Hebrew, as seen in the marginal note, "So Sept., Vulg. and Syr. The Heb. has, to." This same policy was adopted in Psalm 22:16, "They pierced my hands and my feet," since the margin says, "So the Sept., Vulg., and Syr. The Hebrew text as pointed reads, Like a lion, my, &c."

Acceptance of such variants constitutes one of the striking features of the "modern speech" translations, such as Moffatt's and the *American Translation*. Readers must often be amazed at the divergence of these from the Bible with which they have been familiar. In part this is due to different English style, Moffatt in particular having translated very freely, whereas the King James Version was extremely literal; but also much of the difference is due to translation of a different original. The editions of the Moffatt Bible have given little guidance toward understanding this, but the first edition of the Old Testament in the *American Translation* had over ninety pages of "textual notes" a large number of which were references to ancient readings that the translators had considered superior to the Hebrew and had adopted. A few illustrations will serve the present purpose. In Genesis 4:8, the translation reads, "Then Cain said to his brother, Abel, 'Let us go off into the country'"; on this the note is, "So Vrs. [versions]; Heb. om. [omits] 'let us go off into the country.'" Genesis 18:22 reads, "While the LORD remained standing before Abraham," which is annotated, "So original text, the Jewish scribes having transposed 'Abraham' and 'the LORD.'" A particularly striking illustration is provided by I Samuel 14:41, where the American Standard Version says briefly, "Therefore Saul said unto Jehovah, the God of Israel, Show the right. And Jonathan and Saul were taken"; but the *American Translation* reads, "Therefore Saul said, 'O LORD, God of Israel, why hast thou not answered thy servant this day? If the guilt be in me or in Jonathan my son, O LORD, God of Israel, give Urim; but if it is in thy people Israel, give Thummim.' Then Jonathan and Saul were taken." A note explains this astonishing discrepancy: "So LXX [Septuagint] thus giving the complete formula of casting the lot, found only here, Heb. omitted an entire clause, probably owing to repetition of a word." The familiar reading of Amos 8:14 gives us, "As the way of Beer-sheba lives," but the *American Translation* says, "As thy Dod lives, O Beersheba."

The marginal readings classified in the preceding sections bristle with questions concerning the "whence" of our English Bible. They point to scores of manuscripts which do not agree among themselves in all respects, and to ancient versions that frequently diverge some-what widely from the commonly accepted text of the Old and New Testaments. If the books of the Old and New Testaments each had its beginning in a single manuscript, such as, for example, the letter which St. Paul wrote to any one of the churches he addressed, how could all these variations arise? How could there be such a vast collection of variants as that found, for example, in the Variorum Teachers' Bible? This question is easily answered. As we know, before the invention of printing, books were multiplied solely by the fallible method of copying by hand. A slip of the pen, an error of sight, or of hearing, or of memory, on the part of a copyist, finding its way into the text would then be perpetuated in subsequent manuscripts with the same care as that exercised in preserving the best text. Later copyists added their own mistakes to the growing total, and thus for centuries the process of deterioration went on. How serious the situation became is attested by a famous comment about the Latin Bible in the fourth century A.D.; it was charged that there were as many different texts as there were manuscripts. But at various points in the long history of the Bible, scholars set themselves to correct this situation and, if possible, to improve the methods of copying and so forestall blunders as far as was possible.

These efforts provide a part of the engrossing narrative that lies before us. But obviously they have meaning only in relation to the whole long story of the writing and copying of the Bible, and of its translation. The study of this takes us back into Palestine to a starting point many centuries B.C. where we ask how the Hebrew people learned to write, and when and how they began to record their religious experiences and later to collect these writings into a sacred literature. The entire story, though of a bulk that defies more than outline treatment, will confront us with many aspects of Jewish history and religious belief, with the rise of Christianity and its spread through the world, with ancient efforts to give the Bible to peoples in their own languages, with some of the great scholars of remote times and their successors in the medieval and modern world, until at length it brings us to our own days and the labor of Biblical specialists to discover so far as is possible the original text of the Bible and to translate it accurately in words worthy of its great theme.

PART ONE

The Old Testament

CHAPTER I

The Hebrew Bible:
Writing, Text, and Manuscripts

WRITING is very old in Palestine. Students of the Bible used to comment with interest on the mention of "the marshal's staff" in the song of Deborah (Judges 5:14), as providing a lone fragment of evidence that writing was practiced in Israel's land through long previous ages; for the words in Hebrew really mean, "the staff of the writer." But all astonishment is gone out of the phrase; the work of archaeologists has given us many examples of Palestinian writing long prior to the age of Deborah. In fact we know of not less than five, perhaps six, different systems used there before the Hebrew conquest. Still more remarkable, the Canaanites were a literary people, and we possess a considerable body of their poetry!

Among the numerous inscriptions in their well-known hieroglyphic writing which the Egyptians left on the rocks near their mines in southern Sinai, there were found others also, in a totally different script which for many years baffled the ingenuity of scholars. At length considerable progress was made in decipherment, and the astonishing result emerged that the writing was alphabetic. The letters were, most if not all of them, very primitive, pictographic forms of what became later the Hebrew consonants. The language was likewise a Semitic dialect closely related to Biblical Hebrew. A few samples of the same sort of writing have come to light in Palestine itself, revealing that the original system, whatever its origin, came to be employed in greater or less measure by the Canaanites. But Canaanite writing is most famous now in the form of a cuneiform alphabet. Some scholars think it was evolved from the "Sinaitic," but certainly the method of writing was borrowed from the age-old writing of Babylonia. It was in this cuneiform alphabet that the Canaanite religious poems had been written, which first were found at Ras Shamra in northern Syria in 1929 and have since constituted one of the fruitful subjects of Biblical investigation; for this Canaanite literature carries large numbers of remarkable parallels to the Old Testament. Clearly the Israelites were deeply influenced by these poems.

Besides these two somewhat indigenous systems, numbers of documents in both the hieroglyphs of Egypt and the cuneiform writing of Babylonia have been uncovered in Palestine. This is not at all remarkable, since the land lay right across the highroad between these two great centers of ancient civilization. But as though these four were not enough, ancient Canaan—if for the moment we may use the name to designate the entire land of the Canaanites—employed two further systems. Of one of these we possess ten documents of varying length found in the excavations at Byblos. They contain one hundred fourteen different characters, a number which apparently precludes their being strictly alphabetic, but instead suggests a syllabary. The other system occurs only in a single document, found at Balu'a in Moab. It has only four lines; its script is quite unknown. Syria-Palestine was surely a land of writing; its genius overflowed in three unique systems, which through the refining of centuries of use presently gave to the world the letters that were carried to Greece and the Western world, in one direction, and to Arabia and the East, in the other, and so have made one of the most profound contributions to human culture of all the long story of man's upward climb.

Numbers of documents of various length and intrinsic interest have been found that reveal the gradual development of the "Sinaitic" system into what our interest would lead us to call the Hebrew alphabet, although the term "Phoenician" also would be appropriate. Three letters on a potsherd found at Gezer, a few short texts from Lachish dating apparently before the middle of the second millennium B.C., a limestone plaque from Shechem bearing seven alphabetic signs, an ostracon from Beth Shemesh said to be of the fourteenth century, the inscription on the sarcophagus of King Ahiram of Byblos, a strange little text of perhaps the tenth century called the "Gezer Calendar" that lists the appropriate agricultural activities for successive months, the Moabite Stone of about the middle of the ninth century, the ostraca from Samaria rather less than a hundred years later, then the inscription in the conduit of the pool of Siloam, and, most remarkable of all, the letters on potsherds found in the excavation of ancient Lachish written in the time of Jeremiah: these with numerous smaller finds such as seals and stamped jar handles provide, in the main, the fixed points by which we can trace both the steady use of Hebrew writing in Syria-Palestine, from Canaanite times to the fall of the Hebrew kingdoms, and also its gradual evolution into the form of letters with which most of the Old Testament was written. Subsequent developments also are somewhat generously documented.

However, for the pre-exilic period the ostraca, in particular, merit brief comment, for the distribution of their finding—in Samaria of the eighth century, in Lachish of the sixth, and on the hill of Ophel of an unknown date—shows clearly that the practice of writing with a pen on broken pieces of pottery was widespread and continuous during the times of the Hebrew kings. Nor did it then terminate; excavations at the head of the Gulf of Akaba have yielded similar documents in Aramaic dating from the fifth century. The facts quicken a hope that archaeological work may yet be rewarded with still other, and perhaps more remarkable, written materials from ancient Israel. The Ophel document is so badly weathered that its reading has provided basis for lengthy debate; apparently it contains a list of names. Those from Samaria were found in the excavation of the remains of the Israelite palace and consist of receipts for payment of oil and wine, apparently taxes in kind. The group of eighteen found in the ruins of a Jewish guardroom on the site of the Biblical city of Lachish constitute our most remarkable body of documents, to date, from ancient Palestine. On several of them little more than a few disconnected letters or words can now be read, but nine are more or less well preserved. Their contents relate to activities at the time when Nebuchadnezzar's armies were advancing to the invasion of Judea. Even yet their words have power to stir one with some strange vicarious excitement, as they relate that the watchmen in Lachish can no longer see the signal fires of Azekah—evidently the foe had already overrun the city and was now advancing against Lachish and all the cities of Judah. But for the Biblical student there is a scarcely less marked emotional reaction as he reads words and phrases and linguistic constructions familiar from the Hebrew Old Testament and realizes that he is thus permitted a moment's experience of the common life of Judah in the days of Jeremiah and Ezekiel, and to hear, as it were, the very words of common communication of the people who listened to the public preaching of the prophets and later under Jehoiachin were carried into exile in far Babylonia.

The Moabite Stone, found in 1868, was for long our one notable document from the time of the Hebrew kings. It is an inscription of King Mesha of Moab, who is mentioned by name in II Kings 3:4 and apparently referred to elsewhere; it celebrates his successful revolt from Ahab of Israel, and mentions also King Omri; but most remarkable, it speaks of Yahweh, the God of Israel. The inscription in the entrance of the tunnel to the Pool of Siloam records the completion of the tunnel when the two groups of workmen, hewing from opposite ends, somewhere deep in the heart of the rock each heard the sound of the other's tools and so cut through to meet. It is believed to date from the time of King Hezekiah who, as related in II Kings 20:20, constructed a conduit, presumably this very one.

The beginnings of the literature which we now call the Old Testament carry us far back in the nation's history. Certain scraps of poetry are apparently as old as the time of the wandering in the wilderness, and the hero tales in the Book of Judges must have originated not long after the events they describe. But all this was at first an oral literature, carried in memory and repeated by one narrator to another. No one can tell when it began to be set down in written form. Clearly, the account of David's reign given in II Samuel 9–20 was written by someone who himself took a part in the events he describes; hence, its date cannot well be later than the middle of the tenth century. It is entirely plausible that the tales of the Judges began to be written about the same time under the impulse of the notable cultural advance of Solomon's reign. It has been claimed that the oracles of Balaam were likewise put in writing about this same time. The following centuries were rich with a growing literature of Israel. The earlier books of the prophets are of uncertain origin, but Jeremiah's clearly began with the roll which he himself dictated to his secretary, Baruch, in the year 604 B.C. (Jer. 36:32). There is evidence also of the existence of a collection of Isaiah's oracles early in his active career (Isa. 8:16).

The Old Testament, as we know it, is a collection of these and other diverse bodies of literature. As such it came into being through three major steps of "canonization," that is, of acceptance by the Jewish people as of divine origin and authority. We know little of the discussions and developments, official or private, by which this was attained, except at their very end, but the commonly accepted view is that the Pentateuch was canonized sometime during the fourth century B.C. The canon of the Prophets consisted of the Earlier Prophets —Joshua, Judges, Samuel, and Kings—and the Latter: Isaiah, Jeremiah, Ezekiel, and The Twelve (minor prophets); its acceptance is dated about 200 B.C. The rest of the books comprised a collection called, by the Jews, the [Sacred] Writings. It was finally acted upon in the second century A.D. There were eleven of these books: Psalms, Proverbs, Job, Song of Songs, Ruth, Lamentations, Ecclesiastes, Esther, Daniel, Ezra (including Nehemiah), and Chronicles. The striking fact is the inclusion here of the Book of Daniel instead of among the prophets as in the English Bible. But also it deserves note that the books in the above list from Song of Songs to Esther were known to the Jews as the Five Rolls. The whole number of Old Testament books was twenty-four according to usual reckoning, but Josephus and some others, by combining Ruth with Judges and Lamentations with Jeremiah, made them twenty-two—the same number as the letters of the Hebrew alphabet.

The materials and methods of the early writing of these books are likewise unknown to us. It is not impossible, in view of the discoveries mentioned above, that some smaller fragments of what was to become the Old Testament were written with a pen on potsherds. But rolls are mentioned in the Old Testament, specifically in connection with Jeremiah's earliest book. Later usage would make it possible that these were of leather or, in course of time, of parchment, but a more plausible guess would be papyrus. The form of the writing, happily, is now clear to us from the ostraca of Samaria and of Lachish. It was quite different from that of the Hebrew alphabet used today, which is commonly spoken of as employing "squared characters," whereas the old Hebrew was of a somewhat cursive form. We possess documents that show the gradual evolution from the form of the letters used in the times of the kings, through that of certain Aramaic documents of the fourth and following centuries, onward to the final development of the "squared" alphabet. A single word found inscribed in a cave at Araq el Amir, near Heshbon in Transjordan, shows the change nearing completion. Very significant evidence is provided by a business document in Aramaic written on papyrus in Egypt, probably near Thebes, about 300 B.C.; in it we have our earliest example of that distinction of medial and final forms of certain letters which presently became a uniform feature of the developed alphabet. However, Biblical manuscripts obviously fall into a separate class; the conservatism of religious practices would probably result in their being written in older characters for some time after the newer forms were in common use. But in reality we know little about this. It has been argued that the Nash Papyrus, shown among the illustrations of this book, is to be dated in Maccabean times, rather than at the end of the first century A.D. as hitherto believed. If that is so, we have evidence of the writing of Biblical passages in the square characters in the second century B.C. Apart from this, we can only speculate that the change was taking place in the last two centuries before our era.

The Hebrew alphabet consists of twenty-two letters, all of them consonants. Obviously vowels were pronounced—speech would be impossible otherwise—but the ancient Hebrews, like many other Semites, did not feel it necessary to write them. However, in early Christian times, when the Hebrew language was no longer in general use, the lack of them became an occasion of embarrassment, and after certain preliminary attempts the system of vowel symbols now familiar in Hebrew Bibles was developed along with two others that did not attain comparable popularity. The direction of the writing was not yet established in the Sinaitic and certain other early inscriptions, but otherwise the language has always been written from right to left, in lines descending the column or page. In the Moabite Stone and the Siloam inscription the words are separated by a dot, a practice followed also in the Lachish letters, although somewhat inconsistently. Later it was abandoned, and separation of words was indicated only by spacing. Since in crowded writing this might not always be apparent, and because the letters of a word were not joined together as in our cursive writing, occasions could well arise when it was not clear whether a certain consonant belonged to the preceding or following word—and Hebrew is of such character that the shift of one consonant can sometimes deeply alter the sense.

From an early time Hebrew scribes were charged with the responsibility of reproducing more or less considerable bodies of a growing literature that was destined to be of extraordinary interest; and from the fourth century B.C. onward they labored with the copying and multiplying of manuscripts of sacred collections that comprised in course of time the three great sections of the Hebrew Bible. The dispersion of the Jews, more especially after the time of Alexander's conquests, with the consequently growing demand for more and ever more copies of the Scriptures for both private and synagogue use, must have placed the copyists under a sense of pressure that aggravated the inevitability of error.

In addition to the normal difficulties which the scribes faced, the ravages of war and persecution very greatly endangered these Hebrew rolls. There were at least three events which threatened the very existence of the cherished records of the Jews. The first and most critical of all was the destruction of Jerusalem by Nebuchadnezzar, in 586 B.C., though at this time it is probable that some portions of the Old Testament had been carried to Babylonia by the exiles eleven years before. Again, when Antiochus Epiphanes (in 167 B.C.) ordered all the copies of the law to be destroyed (I Macc. 1:56, 57), his decree did not reach to Babylonia, where Ezekiel and Ezra had been busy in earlier centuries instructing their people, and where doubtless copies of the Old Testament books were again preserved from the disaster that swept Palestine. Nor did it reach to Egypt, where, about one hundred years before, translators had busied themselves to put into Greek some at least of the sacred books of the Jews.

The destruction of Jerusalem by Titus in A.D. 70 was a third disaster that threatened the life of the Old Testament. According to the Babylonian Talmud, Titus destroyed copies of the law. Josephus (Wars 5:5, 7) states that one single copy of the law occupied a prominent place in the victory of Vespasian. This is the earliest mentioned manuscript of the Old Testament, and was said to have shown just thirty-two variations from the received text. This document was later deposited in the royal library at Rome, and later, in A.D. 220, was handed over to the synagogue of Severus, probably by the emperor, who was a good friend to the Jews.

These perils did probably extinguish much Hebrew literature. For we find today, mentioned in the Old Testament, the names and titles of twenty-four books that have perished. By far the largest number of these is found in Kings and Chronicles. It is not impossible that some of those works, if extant, would be found in our Bible, but they were probably blotted out by the dire disasters that befell Jerusalem and the Jews between 600 B.C. and A.D. 100.

What stories of heroic devotion cling about the survival of the Old Testament through these times of severe trying we cannot tell. The fact that Antiochus Epiphanes made it a capital crime to possess copies of the sacred books reveals as in a sudden flash of illumination something of the adventure and danger of those days when the Jews chose to give up their own lives rather than their religion or their Scriptures. Yet the devotion of quieter times must not be overlooked; and a study of the Old Testament as it now is must of necessity give more attention to the continuing work of the scribes, the mark of whose activity is discernible on almost every page of the Hebrew Bible. We have said much about their errors and are going on to say more, for the study of the text of the Old Testament—"textual criticism" it is called—is a continuing requirement for a proper understanding of the meaning of Scripture. Nonetheless, the great feature of the work of copyists is rather the success they attained in accurate preservation of these books. Respect for our traditional Hebrew text of the Old Testament, and for the scholars to whom we owe its excellence, has steadily grown in recent years as we have repeatedly found that at points where the accepted reading seemed difficult and suspect, it is in actuality entirely correct, and the trouble has lain rather in our own ignorance. This does not mean that we are going back to an uncritical traditionalism, but it does mean that scholars are much more wary of proposed "emendations" of the text, even though these seem to be supported by some ancient version, than they were fifty or more years ago.

A striking illustration of the high accuracy attained by the Jewish scribes is provided by an examination of the old manuscript of the Pentateuch preserved in the British Museum, to which more extended reference will be made shortly. It is believed to date from the tenth century A.D., yet its text is practically identical with that of recent printed Hebrew Bibles which depend on the great rabbinic Bible of Jacob ben Chayim of 1525. Though the manuscripts of which ben

Chayim made use are not known, it has long been recognized that they cannot have been old; hence the spread of more than six centuries between these dates need be reduced only a little for our present purpose. The comparison, then, of these two sources of the Pentateuch serves well to dramatize the perfection to which the scribes had brought their methods of accurate transmission of the text of the Bible. We are, every one of us at this day, profoundly indebted to the devoted care of hosts of unknown men through many centuries, who gave their whole lives to the seemingly tiresome minutiae of the Biblical text, inspired by the faith that it is the Word of God and in every small detail of transcendent importance in His purposes.

Still we fail to understand our Bible of today if we do not take full account of the many passages where, in spite of all the care of the scribes—rather, should we say, occasionally because of such care?—changes did find their way into the text. For the astonishing fact is that in some cases deliberately and with full knowledge they altered the text they had received. They did this for a number of reasons, the most famous of which was the desire to remove excessive anthropomorphisms or to maintain propriety or reverence. According to tradition, there are eighteen such alterations. A good illustration is provided by Job 32:3, which reads, "and yet had condemned Job"; the original text was, "and yet had condemned God." A much more apparent class of such changes, although not generally recognized, consists of the very numerous cases of introduction of the Hebrew word for Lord alongside the name of the God of Israel. This is most evident in the Book of Ezekiel, where the phrase "the Lord Jehovah" (according to the rendering of the American Standard Version) occurs to the point of tedium. This was evidently intended as a guide to the reader to avoid uttering the sacred name; later, when the system of vowel signs had been devised, the scribes had another means of accomplishing this end. Comparable with this is the insertion of the word *bosheth* (shame) in place of the name Baal in a number of cases, for example in the personal name Ish-bosheth, which certainly was originally Ish-baal.

The unintentional changes introduced by the scribes—in more crass language, their mistakes—are more numerous. The following classification of them is in general use:

1. Failure to see the sense of a passage. In some cases this has meant that words were incorrectly divided. A good example is found in Amos 6:12, "Shall horses run upon the rock? Will one plow there with oxen?" The word for "oxen" should doubtless be divided into two words, and then it will read, "Will one plow the sea with oxen?" Another good illustration is Psalm 73:4, "For there are no pangs in their death; but their strength is firm." Simply by separating the word translated "in their death" we can translate, "For they have no pangs, sound and firm is their strength"—a meaning that better fits both the thought in the context and the parallelism.

2. Errors due to the eye: (a) Repetitions: in Leviticus 20:10, we should omit the five Hebrew words repeated (in the English translation, the first clause); I Chronicles 9:35-44 has been repeated, doubtless through an error, from I Chronicles 8:29-38. (b) Omissions: as where, in Proverbs 10:10b, the omission is made up from verse 8b; but the Septuagint and the Syriac read for 10b, "He that rebuketh boldly is a peacemaker." (c) Transposition of letters or words: II Chronicles 3:5 represents the porch of the temple as one hundred and twenty cubits high. The Septuagint reads twenty cubits, as the Hebrew will also by a transposition of two letters and then of the two relevant words; this is certainly the original reading. Psalm 35:7 reads, "For without cause have they hid for me their net in a pit, without cause have they digged a pit for my soul." By simply transposing the words "pit" and "net," we read: "For without cause have they hidden their net for me, without cause have they digged a pit for my life." There are also numerous cases where one letter has been mistaken for another by the copyist. A good illustration is provided by the familiar name Nebuchadnezzar; it ought to be Nebuchadrezzar, but by a confusion of the two Hebrew letters *n* (נ) and *r* (ר) this now almost universal, but erroneous, form arose. Another error of the same kind is that "Hadadezer" has been erroneously read "Hadarezer," by mistaking the Hebrew *d* (ד) for *r* (ר). In Isaiah 39:1, we find "Merodach-baladan," but the parallel in II Kings 20:12 has "Berodach-baladan" —which arose by a confusion of two Hebrew letters *m* (מ) and *b* (ב).

3. Errors due to the ear, resulting in the use of one Hebrew word for another of almost the same sound. It is apparent that in the effort to expedite the production of manuscripts the practice was sometimes

followed of employing a reader for a group of scribes who then would write from his dictation. A good example of such errors is found in Psalm 100:3, where "and not we ourselves" should be "and we are his." In II Chronicles 10:18, "Hadoram" corresponds to "Adoram" in I Kings 12:18.

4. Errors of memory, evidently occasioned by the scribe's having remembered the thought, rather than the exact words of his exemplar. Thus the Hebrew verb *to call* in II Samuel 22:7 is replaced in the parallel passage in Psalm 18:7 by the verb *to shout*. Probably it was through a lapse of memory also that the name Jehoiakim is given in Jeremiah 27:1, where the context shows clearly it should be Zedekiah, as in verse 3.

5. Errors due to carelessness or ignorance. Of this type there are many examples. In I Samuel 13:1 we find "Saul was — years old," where apparently some copyist carelessly neglected to put down the number. In II Samuel 3:7, "Ish-bosheth" is missing, although it is found here in the Septuagint, Syriac, and Vulgate. II Samuel 11:21 has "Jerubbesheth," which may possibly represent a careless writing of "Jerubbaal" (Judges 6:32). In I Samuel 27:8, "Girzites" is read in some manuscripts "Gizrites," which is evidently correct. I Samuel 12:11 has "Bedan," but according to the Septuagint, the Syriac, and the original narrative as the story is told in the Book of Judges, chapter 4, the name should be "Barak."

Such errors as these crept into the text gradually and were transmitted by copyists from one manuscript to another continuously down through the centuries. Many of them are ancient. Indeed, comparison of the Hebrew text with the older versions shows that the period prior to the making of the Septuagint translation, that is, before the middle of the third century B.C., was the time of worst corruption. In other words, the scribes gradually awoke to the necessity of greater care, and developed methods of insuring a higher degree of accuracy. One of these was the practice of counting the verses (though these did not yet bear numbers) and even the letters in the various books, and then of making note of the middle verse, the middle word, and the middle letter of each book. These notations are still found at the end of each book in our Hebrew Bibles. The middle verse of the Pentateuch is Leviticus 8:7; the middle verse of Joshua is Chapter 13:26; of Judges,

Chapter 10:8. The middle verse of the Hebrew Bible is Jeremiah 6:7. If a scribe, after he had finished his work, could not make his count tally with these notations, it was evident some error had been made which must then be corrected or the copy discarded.

Some time after the exile, the Law, or, as we know it, the Pentateuch, was arranged to be read in regular course. In Acts 15:21, we read that, "Moses from generations of old hath in every city them that preach him, being read in the synagogues every sabbath." This custom has continued to the present day. In Palestine it was read through in three and one-half years, but in Babylonia, in one year. To facilitate this plan the law was early divided into sections, called parashahs, or, in Palestine, sedarim. The Babylonian usage presently prevailed because of the greater authority of the Babylonian Talmud, with the result that the Torah in Hebrew manuscripts and printed editions is now divided into fifty-four parashahs, and since the thirteenth century an annual reading of the whole Pentateuch has been the universal practice of Jews. But it is apparent that there are only fifty-two, or once in seven or eight years fifty-three, Sabbaths in a year. Hence there exists a dual division of several sections with longer or shorter passages for adjustment of this discrepancy.

After the Law was read in the synagogue a corresponding, or appropriate, passage was read from the Prophets. An example of this is to be recognized in the incident in the synagogue at Nazareth (Luke 4:17 f.) when Jesus read from the prophet Isaiah (61:1 f.). However, the sections into which the Prophets were divided are not definitely known.

Some of the poetical portions of the Old Testament—such as the Song of Moses, Exodus 15, the Song of Deborah, Judges 5, the Psalm of David in II Samuel 22 (Psalm 18), as also the list of names in Esther 9:7-9—are written in a peculiar form, to represent some phantasy of the scribes. In the Septuagint the Psalms are arranged in a form corresponding to the parallelism of the Hebrew original.

There was no early division into chapters, but a division corresponding closely to our verses is ancient, although numbers were not attached to these successive passages until medieval times. When a reader in the synagogue in the time of Christ, or for centuries thereafter, had read a short passage, an interpreter would translate it into Aramaic, which was the language of the times (compare Nehemiah 8:8). The practice indicates that there were regularly recognized divisions in the text.

About the beginning of the second century of our era, we have seen, the Jewish scholars took final action upon the contents of the canon, or, in simpler words, decided what books belonged to their Bible—the Old Testament we call it. Somewhere in this lengthy period, of which we know very little in a precise way, another very important step in the history of the Hebrew Bible appears also to have been taken. Already the manuscripts had been copied for centuries and all of them had become corrupt, with the perplexing result that no one could say with certainty what were the exact words of Scripture. But the Bible had grown in importance as a divine rule of life and conduct, and also the methods of exposition that were coming into vogue placed great emphasis upon minute features of the manuscripts, such that words and particles and even peculiarities of writing were believed to convey some mystic revelation. Thus the question pressed for solution: what was the true text of the Bible. Yet the original manuscripts of centuries before could not be invoked. They had long since disappeared. Equally it was out of the question for the orthodoxy of the time to depend upon the Septuagint translation as a basis for correction; and anyhow it also was corrupt. A story has come down to us that the authoritative text was determined by comparing three manuscripts (apparently of the Torah) that were found in the Temple; the method followed was that in cases of differences of reading, the agreement of two was accepted against the third, and thus a text was attained to which finality was attributed. We shall readily believe that the story does less than full justice to the scholars concerned, for a procedure so clumsy as this would today be disdained —and the ancient Jewish text critics were able scholars. However, there must be a kernel of historic truth in the account, for the Latin Vulgate, translated just about A.D. 400, evidences a Hebrew text very close to ours of today. But on the other hand, such scraps of Biblical Hebrew as we possess from the first seven or eight centuries of the present era still manifest considerable diversity. The precise meaning of these facts is not obvious. It has been suggested, however, that a final authoritative text was actually determined somewhere about the beginning of Christian times, but, lacking official monopoly or over-sight of manuscript reproduction, older and inexact types of text con-tinued to be used for centuries. Even when the official text had attained undisputed supremacy, scribal errors continued; they are found even in relatively late manuscripts. Nevertheless, the high precision of the work done by the copyists through ten centuries, till the art of printing reduced the probability of error, constitutes striking evidence of the care exercised by the school of textual scholars that arose in the early Christian centuries, and of the excellence of the methods they devised.

This most famous school of Jewish text critics we know as the Mas-soretes; it is a name derived from a Hebrew word meaning tra-dition: they were the scholars charged with the responsibility of pre-serving the traditional text. The counting of the words in the Biblical books, and the rest of such minutiae mentioned above, was part of their work. They accumulated a vast body of notes on the occurrence of words, features of writing, directions for pronunciation, variants in their sources, and the like. These constitute what is known as "the Massorah." It was written in the margins of their manuscripts and at the ends of the books of the Bible and, according to its location and bulk, is called Massorah magna, Massorah parva, or Massorah finalis. In some of this the Massoretes were heirs of earlier scribes, but their own work was distinctive and epochal. Beginning, as they apparently did, about A.D. 600, their great age of activity extended from the latter part of the eighth century to the first half of the tenth. Massoretic work was carried forward in many centers; we hear of it in Nisibis, in north-ern Mesopotamia; the Jewish schools of Babylonia were prominent; but the most famous center was Tiberias, in Palestine, of whose scholars the names of several have been preserved, in particular of five genera-tions of the ben Asher family. The last of these, and apparently the greatest, Moses ben Asher, and his son Aaron, who flourished just be-fore and just after A.D. 900, brought to conclusion the line and the work of the Massoretes. Their results have become authoritative for the Hebrew Bible, for it is in very large measure the system of ben Asher that is employed in printed Hebrew Bibles. A rival system goes under the name of ben Naphtali; a few of its readings are preferred by modern critical editors of the text. Of ben Naphtali little is known, in fact the extreme view has been suggested that the name represents no individual at all, but is only a sort of personalizing of the system or of the group that produced it. A more reasonable position is that ben Naphtali (whose personal name is not known) was a contemporary of the latest ben Ashers and lived also in Tiberias, the great center of Massoretic activity. Some would locate him in Babylonia, but this is quite improbable; his system is definitely Tiberian. A number of manuscripts and fragments have in recent years been identified as of the ben Naphtali school; consequently, we are no longer dependent on ancient lists of divergences but can study at firsthand these differences from the standard ben Asher reading. Tradition tells of a total of 875 such disagreements. However this may be, our newer information does not alter the former understanding that these were, in the vast majority of cases, matters of vocalization and accentuation, which affect not in the least the meaning of the text. Trivial as debate over such matters may perhaps seem to us, the serious disagreement of the two schools is evidence of the meticulous care expended by the Massoretes in the proper preservation of the Bible.

However, at this point we are confronted with the most striking part of the work of these ancient textual scholars. They created a system of vowel signs and accentual marks which they inserted into their manuscripts, above or below, and to a less extent in the body of the consonants of the traditional text. It was pointed out above that the Hebrew alphabet, in common with most Semitic alphabets, consists of consonants alone. This was a reasonably satisfactory method of writing so long as Hebrew continued to be the common language of the people—modern Hebrew likewise seldom writes the vowels, yet encounters little embarrassment in reading—but by early Christian times Aramaic had made heavy inroads into the prevalence of Hebrew. It was doubtless in considerable measure due to this situation that the Jewish scholars, apparently about A.D. 700, found it desirable to undertake a system of written vowels. The impulse expressed itself in Palestine, and there a group of symbols was evolved that is similar to the vowel signs found in a few Samaritan manuscripts. This vowel system is known as the Palestinian. The meager knowledge which we had of it a little while ago has in recent years been greatly enlarged by the famous discovery, in 1897 and following years, in the rubbish room (the genizah) of the old synagogue in Cairo, of half a dozen fragmentary Biblical manuscripts in which it is employed. The scholars of Babylonia were similarly active, but they had the stimulus and guidance of Syrian literary men, their neighbors, who were evolving a system of vowel signs and other guides to reading, based primarily on a simple diacritical point. The influence of the developed Syrian system is apparent in at least one fragmentary Hebrew manuscript found in the genizah. But not content with this, the Jewish scholars went on to create a complex series of signs based in considerable part on conventionalized representations of weak letters, some of which had been sporadically used for centuries to indicate the correct vowel in cases where doubt might arise. The Babylonian and the Palestinian vowels were written above the relevant consonants, but the third of these systems, which is correctly called the Tiberian, although clearly developed out of the Palestinian was written, in general, below the consonants. Yet more important was the precision and detail to which the representation of the pronunciation of the Hebrew words was developed in this system, differentiating the quality of even the slightest vocal elements. This is the system that in course of time became universal in the west and is now familiar through its use in all printed editions of the Hebrew Bible.

But the Massoretes of Tiberias and of Babylonia went yet farther in their written guides to the correct reading of the Bible. They evolved complex systems of accentual marks; indeed in the Tiberian tradition there is actually a second system which is employed for the poetic books of the Bible only. These "accents" serve the need that is met in modern writing by use of punctuation, and thus they frequently become guides to the correct meaning, as the Massoretes understood it. But it is clear that the original purpose was to give direction for the proper inflection of the voice in public reading in the synagogue. They are thus not unlike musical notations.

An acute problem is how far the Massoretic system of vowels represents the actual pronunciation of Biblical Hebrew in ancient times, for, we would recall, the insertion of all these diacritical marks took place more than a thousand years after the writing of considerable parts of the Old Testament and many centuries subsequent to the latest of it. The question is of more than passing importance, for it will be realized that all subsequent systems of Hebrew grammar are built upon the Massoretic punctuation. Yet uncertainty has been felt for many years. On one hand, the care with which anomalous features of vocalization are recorded and the use in certain cases of vowels other than those required by the rigid rules of the system would seem to indicate that the Massoretes were recording an actual living pronunciation. But over against this, proper names in the Greek translation made about 250 B.C. diverge notably from their vocalization in the Massoretic text. To a lesser extent this is true of the Vulgate also, although its translation took place only a few centuries before the great activity of the Massoretes. However, definitive evidence was not available until the discovery by Cardinal Mercati about 1895 of a palimpsest (rewritten) manuscript of part of the famous work of the great Christian scholar, Origen, known as the Hexapla; the manuscript contains considerable passages of the Psalms transliterated into Greek letters. Since the Hexapla dates from approximately A.D. 250, the manuscript provides thus our earliest record of the pronunciation of Hebrew. And the astonishing fact is the divergence here apparent from what the Massoretes were to decree a few centuries later. There seems no escape from the conclusion that the Massoretic system is not a faithful record of the language of the eighth century A.D. but is in considerable part an artificial creation. These men, under whatever influence, decided how the Bible ought to be read, developed their complex and precise system, and diverted the course of the natural evolution of the Hebrew language. Their success in Palestine is clearly intelligible, for Tiberias was through those centuries the intellectual center of the land; but in time their system overcame and displaced the Babylonian also.

A strange fact in the history of the Hebrew Bible is the late date of extant manuscripts—in view of the antiquity of certain portions of the Old Testament one is justified in saying the *very* late date. The great majority of them are subsequent to the ninth century A.D. Our surprise is heightened by the contrast of the Greek Bible, of which important manuscripts date all the way from the early centuries of our era, with certain fragments still older. The explanation, apart from the exigencies of Israel's ancient history to which reference in this connection has already been made, appears to lie in the Jewish practice of destroying worn-out manuscripts to save them from impious hands. How far this devout procedure was expedited by the Massoretes, desirous of eradicating all record of systems rivaling their own, we do not know. An old fragment of Biblical Hebrew is the Nash Papyrus, which has been commonly dated about the end of the first century A.D.; but more recently argument has been presented that it ought to be ascribed to the second half of the second century B.C. It is a fragment of a single column of a papyrus manuscript written with ink, in the square characters, apparently by some Jew in Egypt. The extent of the complete work we have no means of estimating, nor yet its purpose, although the suggestion has been advanced that it was a lectionary. The view seems somewhat plausible in view of the contents, which are the Decalogue and the single verse Deuteronomy 6:4, known as the Shema, which is introduced with some Deuteronomic phraseology. A clay stamp in the Oriental Institute of the University of Chicago containing the one verse Jeremiah 48:11 evidently comes from some date within the first four centuries of the present era. The meager information available as to its origin points to Babylonia. A number of bowls, also from Babylonia, inscribed with incantations, contain as part of their magic formulas brief quotations of Biblical Hebrew; a favorite passage was Zechariah 3:2. They were written apparently before the fifth century A.D.

The varying worth of these fragments, however high, is now eclipsed through a discovery announced in two brief press releases in April, 1948. About a year before, it appears, a group of Bedouin had found in a cave near the northern end of the Dead Sea, on its western side, a number of pottery jars containing leather manuscripts wrapped in cloth. These they took to Bethlehem; and from there, after some negotiations, part of them came into possession of St. Mark's Syrian Orthodox Convent in Jerusalem, who presently submitted them to representatives of the American Schools of Oriental Research for study and publication. The rest were secured by the Hebrew University. Both groups issued preliminary discussions in the autumn of 1948.

Most remarkable of the documents is a copy of the Book of Isaiah, complete except for a few words. Considerable attention has been attracted also to a commentary on the Book of Habakkuk, which, it is of some worth to note, concludes with chapter 2. Parts of the Book of Daniel were found too; one fragment was from the Aramaic section, and another covered the transition from Hebrew to Aramaic in our present chapter 2. There were "several apocryphal books never known to exist in Hebrew, but in Greek translation only." A mysterious document deals with "the war of the sons of light and the sons of darkness." Most of the manuscripts are in Hebrew, but one (in addition to Daniel) is in Aramaic. Argument about the date and significance of the manuscripts soon became heated. From the first it was claimed that they were of the second century B.C.; but other scholars dismissed them as early medieval and of little importance.

When conditions permitted, the cave was visited by archaeologists who reported that the pottery fragments were mainly of the Hellenistic age. They found fragments of several more manuscripts of Biblical books and of other, apparently apocryphal, works. All told it is calculated that parts of not less than twenty manuscripts have come out of that amazing cave. Presently it became apparent through further finds by the Bedouin that the entire region should be carefully searched. Early in 1951 an expedition from the Jordan Department of Antiquities and the École Biblique in Jerusalem, guided and assisted by Bedouin, excavated four caves in the Wadi Murabba'at, three kilometers from the Dead Sea. Two of the caves were some fifty meters in length and five meters high. One had been periodically occupied from Chalcolithic to Roman times. Manuscripts were found written in Hebrew, Aramaic, or Greek, mostly of the second century A.D. Their contents are various. Incredible as it may seem, there are actually letters from Bar Kochba, the leader of the great revolt against the Romans A.D. 132-135. A few Biblical texts were discovered, also of the second century. In March of 1952 the Department of Antiquities and the Ecole Biblique, assisted by members of the American School of Oriental Research in Jerusalem, investigated the area extending for some eight kilometers north and south of the famous cave that had first attracted attention to the region. Remarkable discoveries were made: two rolls of thin copper into which a Hebrew inscription had been impressed, but of much greater importance, a group of manuscript fragments of varying sizes. The Biblical materials far exceed the great treasures of the first cave. Almost every book of the Old Testament is now represented, with greater or less portions preserved.

But this is not all of the astonishing results of research in this hitherto neglected region. In three seasons of work, those of late 1951, and of the winters of 1953 and 1954, a site near the Wadi Qumran was excavated. It turned out to have been the headquarters of the Essene sect, of which our knowledge had formerly been based mainly on brief accounts in Philo and Josephus. Excavation showed that the Essenes had used the place from the second century B.C. until the great revolt of A.D. 68-70. Then it was taken over as a Roman military post; and later, in Bar Cochba's revolt, it was similarly used by the Jewish troops. These findings corroborate the opinion that has been developing from a study of the manuscripts, that they come from the Essene library. The major debate about their date is now concluded; it is recognized that they come from a period extending from perhaps the third century B.C. to the second A.D.

The contributions of these discoveries to the study of the text of the Old Testament will become fully realized only through years of scholarly work. Already it is apparent, however, that while the Isaiah scroll from the first cave contained some, but relatively few, variants from our common Hebrew text, the later finds depart notably; they are closer to the tradition represented by certain manuscripts of the Greek Bible. We are still very far from the autographs of the Biblical authors, and it would seem foolish to suppose that we shall ever find them; but the discoveries since 1947 have carried us back well over a thousand years closer to them. It is a result that justifies superlative adjectives. Here it will suffice to comment that the fondest dreams of former students of the Old Testament never rose to the height of what is now established fact. (See Appendix, p. 321, for further discussion of the Dead Sea Scrolls.)

The treasures of the Cairo genizah have enriched us with a considerable number of fragments of Biblical manuscripts from the sixth and following centuries A.D. Their high value is evident in that before their discovery we were compelled to begin with the completed work of the Massoretes, as evidenced in manuscripts subsequent to the time of ben Asher. But the genizah fragments permit us a glimpse behind the scenes, as it were, to observe the evolution of the Massoretic work, in the way hastily sketched just now, and the character of the consonantal text through those finally formative ages. An important example of these genizah fragments contains more than three chapters of the Book of Daniel (Dan. 9:24-12:13); it is believed to date not later than the seventh century. Some other notable fragments contain Isaiah 53:4-58:8; Jeremiah 26:19-29:31; Ezekiel 13:11-16:31; Psalms 69:28-71:2.

Not less notable among the revolutionary changes of recent years in our knowledge of Hebrew manuscripts has been an improved understanding of the place and significance of some which have long been known. This has come about in the first instance through the research of the eminent German scholar, Professor Paul Kahle, greatly expedited, if not actually determined, by the remains in the Cairo genizah. Indeed, much of the account of the work of the Massoretes given above is based upon Kahle's findings.

Manuscripts of Biblical Hebrew total a large number, although not rivaling the immense bulk of those in New Testament Greek. Their age extends all the way from the very old documents just now mentioned down to the present, for it is important to recognize that Hebrew scrolls are still written by hand for synagogue use. The manuscripts are sometimes classified according to geographic origin—German, Spanish, Italian, etc.; but apart from such interest as may inhere in chirography, these distinctions have little value. For many centuries the text has been conformed to a rigid pattern.

Fortunately we have older materials. The genizah manuscripts, though fragmentary, are priceless, for they provide a clue to evaluation of subsequent material. The significant classification of manuscripts is Babylonian, Yemenite, and Western, or perhaps one should say Tiberian. The Babylonian and Yemenite stand close together for Yemen was a sort of geographic pocket that preserved the Babylonian tradition uncontaminated by Tiberian influence, but yet with distinctive features of its own. These two groups stand apart from the Western in their vowel system and in their Massoretic tradition. But also there are in places significant differences in their consonantal text. A famous example of the Babylonian manuscripts is the codex, i.e., a book, not a roll, of the Latter Prophets (Isaiah, Jeremiah, Ezekiel, and The Twelve) preserved in Leningrad and bearing a date corresponding to A.D. 916. It is at the same time a striking illustration of the triumph of the Western tradition, for its vowel system departs from the true Babylonian, as evidenced in the much older fragments from the genizah, and actually it has in places Tiberian instead of its proper "supralinear" vowels.

It is in the field of Western manuscripts that recent developments have been most spectacular. Attention has long been drawn to a codex of the Pentateuch in the British Museum, bearing the number Or. 4445. Of its 186 folios, 55 were added in A.D. 1540, but the remains of the original manuscript are much older. On paleographic grounds it was formerly ascribed to the ninth century. It is a beautifully written manuscript, fully pointed with vowels and accents, and supplied with Massorah magna and parva. Its merits have justly impressed all students of the Hebrew text, and it has been regarded as the oldest extant manuscript containing an approximation to the complete text of any large part of the Hebrew Bible. This and the Leningrad Prophets have taken priority among Hebrew manuscripts. But serious attention has been accorded also to a codex of the Former and Latter Prophets in the Karaite synagogue in Cairo, dated A.D. 895 and claiming to be the work of ben Asher, as also to the great treasure of the synagogue of the Sephardim in Aleppo which, it is asserted, comes from Aaron ben Asher. These claims have in the past been dismissed, however, as more or less deliberate deceptions, and attention has centered rather on a manuscript of the entire Old Testament, numbered 19a, in the Public Library in Leningrad, and bearing a date equivalent to A.D. 1008 or 1009; it has commonly been said that this is the oldest known manuscript of the entire Old Testament.

But Kahle altered all this, and set our knowledge of the history of the Hebrew Bible on a new basis. He has demonstrated the validity of the claims for the ben Asher origins of the Cairo and Aleppo manuscripts. Further he has shown that Leningrad 19a contains a true text of Aaron ben Asher, as does also British Museum Or. 4445. This latter is an earlier recension, hence is to be dated early in the tenth century, somewhat later, it will be observed, than was formerly believed. The succession seems to be this: The Cairo codex is the work of Moses ben Asher; it was written in Tiberias in A.D. 895. British Museum Or. 4445 comes from his son Aaron ben Asher. But Aaron continued to develop his system; the Leningrad and the Aleppo manuscripts, in this order, represent his maturing position on Biblical accentuation. The Leningrad manuscript is not original, yet its source is such as to inspire complete confidence. It was copied in Cairo in A.D. 1008 or 1009 by Samuel ben Jacob, as he has recorded, "from the corrected clear books prepared by the master Aaron ben Moshe ben Asher." It is immense gain to realize that the completed work of the Massoretes as crystallized in the Bible codices of its greatest exponents is, in their own genuine formulation, actually in the possession of modern scholarship. Upon this solid basis all study of the later history of the Hebrew text of the Old Testament must proceed.

The Jews were quick to realize the immense importance of the art of printing. While many regarded the achievement with suspicion, and efforts were presently put forth to suppress the practice by royal fiat, the Jews, on the other hand, in their first printed book in 1475 extol it as wise, and the crown of all wisdom which the heroine Deborah might well have put on her head. Two years later the first printed Biblical Hebrew came off the press. It was a Psalter interspersed, verse by verse, with the commentary of Rashi. The typographical difficulties were so great that only the first few Psalms were printed with vowel points. The work was full of errors of many kinds. During the next ten years (1477-87) at least four editions, covering all the Old Testament, were printed in as many different cities. The entire Hebrew Old Testament with vowel points and accents was first published at Soncino, February 14, 1488. It was printed next at Naples, 1491-93; and a third time in the Brescia Bible in 1494—the text used by Luther. A fourth edition appeared at Pesaro in 1511-17. All these editions were issued under Jewish sponsorship.

The first edition of the Hebrew text to be published under the direction and authority of Christian influences was that found in the so-called Complutensian Polyglot. This great work carried in three parallel columns the Hebrew text, the Septuagint, and the Vulgate, the latter between the other two, like Jesus crucified between two thieves, as the editor quaintly explains! Through the Pentateuch the Polyglot carried also the Aramaic translation called the Targum of Onkelos. It was edited by Cardinal Ximenes and printed at the University founded by him at Alcalá, Spain, 1514-17. The magnitude of this undertaking may be partially understood when it is said that the Cardinal had to cast all his own type before he began the printing. The edition consumed more than fifteen years of labor, cost fifty thousand ducats, and was completed only a few months before the Cardinal died at the age of eighty-one.

The first Hebrew Bible with full vowel points and the Rabbinic material for interpretation of the text, including a small selection of Massoretic material, was printed by Daniel Bomberg at Venice, 1516-17. This was the first Hebrew text to divide Samuel, Kings, and Chronicles each into two books; and the book of Ezra into Ezra and Nehemiah. The so-called *editio princeps* of the Hebrew Bible, with all Rabbinic helps, was Bomberg's second edition, edited by Jacob ben Chayim, a Jew of Tunis, 1524-25. This became the standard edition of the Massoretic text. Its influence upon all later editions of the Hebrew Bible, with the exception of the third edition of the Kittel Bible to be discussed later, has been great. This fact enhances the importance of ben Chayim's text. But we know little of the sources he employed, beyond the edition of 1516-17. His manuscripts were certainly late, and he himself complains of their errors. He tells in his preface of his assiduous toil for the sake of accuracy. It would seem though that this was directed primarily toward the Massorah, of which his edition has been the great source until recent times.

The great Paris Polyglot, found today in a few of our large libraries, was edited by Le Jay and printed in 1628-45 in ten folio volumes. A rival of this stupendous work was the London Polyglot, edited by Brian Walton and published in London in 1657, in six folio volumes. They are impressive works, the London Polyglot, by virtue of the planning of its pages, perhaps slightly the more so. On each opening of the first volumes there appear side by side or conveniently arranged the Hebrew text with interlinear Latin translation, the Latin Vulgate, the Septuagint, the Aramaic Targum, the Syriac, the Arabic, and through the Pentateuch the Samaritan and the Samaritan Targum also, the six latter each paralleled with a Latin translation. Through the New Testament, where obviously there was no Hebrew text, the pages have the Greek with interlinear Latin, the Vulgate, Syriac, Arabic, Ethiopic, and through the Gospels the Persian also, each of these four latter likewise given an accompanying Latin translation. The work is a tribute to the interest of the seventeenth century in the text of the Bible, and to the scholarship of the time that had already discovered and had come to value such relatively unfamiliar Oriental versions as the Samaritan, Ethiopic, Syriac, Persian, and Arabic.

The Hebrew Bible of today is divided into chapters and verses. This chapter division had its origin in the Vulgate and is accredited to Lanfranc, Archbishop of Canterbury, who died 1089; to Stephen Langton, who died 1228; and to Hugo de Sancto Caro in the thirteenth century. The divisions began to be used in the Hebrew Bible in the thirteenth century, but the first edition to introduce the chapter numbers into the text was that of Arius Montanus in 1571, a Hebrew Bible with Latin interlinear translation. The first purely Hebrew Bible so printed appeared in 1573-74; verse numbers began with the Athias Hebrew Bible of 1559-61.

Naturally the printing of so large a number of Hebrew Bibles at so many places, and based on the readings of so many different manuscripts, occasioned confusion in interpretation and anxiety regarding the true text of the Old Testament. This led to the practice now exemplified in the margins of our English Bibles of collecting the variants or differences in the readings of the known manuscripts. It is sufficient here to say that the first great collector and publisher of variants was an English scholar, Benjamin Kennicott. He employed a number of scholars and spent nine thousand pounds sterling in carrying on his work. It was a major task of a lifetime. One finds his preface deeply moving, where he devoutly gives thanks to God that twenty-five years of toil have drawn to a conclusion. In brief summary, he had effected the collation of 694 manuscripts, besides many editions of the Hebrew Bible. The variants he notes are of the consonantal text only. His results were published at Oxford in two folio volumes in 1776-80.

Giovanni de Rossi, professor of Oriental languages in Parma, Italy, collected the variants of 310 printed editions and 732 manuscripts, of which latter Kennicott had used only 80. His work was published in four volumes at Parma, in 1784-88, with a supplementary volume in 1798.

Kennicott and De Rossi thus collated a total of 1,346 Hebrew manuscripts and 342 editions, altogether 1,688 different sources for the Old Testament text. Their immense labor contributed much less than they hoped toward an authentic text of the Old Testament, for it revealed relatively few variants among all this mass of material. Many of them are to be ascribed to scribal carelessness; a few deserve consideration. But the entire undertaking stands under the judgment, now fully apparent, that all the sources employed are much too late to be of significance. Nevertheless, we must concede that the work was necessary; all subsequent study is under obligation to the labor of these men, for textual study could not proceed with confidence if deprived of the information which they made available. Their results, though negative, yet constitute a positive contribution of high importance.

The growing interest in textual problems of which these two great works were a symbol continued through the following century, and even to the present, stimulated by an increasing bulk of old manuscripts steadily coming into the possession of the scholarly world. In Old Testament study it manifested itself in intensified activity in textual criticism and, in particular, in new editions of the Hebrew Bible. The first of these calling for mention here is that edited by Baer and Delitzsch and issued in a succession of volumes from 1869 to 1895. Complaining of the inaccuracies which marred the best current editions, the editors undertook to remedy the situation with a dependable publication of the text of the Rabbinic Bible of Jacob ben Chayim of 1525. They gave footnotes also and, at the conclusions of the volumes, long lists of Massoretic notes as well as their own observations on the testimony of manuscripts and editions in cases of uncertain readings. Similar was the objective of Christian D. Ginsburg in his *Massoretico-Critical Edition of the Hebrew Bible* published in 1894. He found occasion to criticize the accuracy of the Baer and Delitzsch volumes, notably in matters strictly Massoretic. For his work he collated and employed the readings of seventy-three manuscripts and nineteen editions, so that the copious footnotes in which these are summarized constitute a valuable conspectus of the later tradition of the text. Ginsburg's Bible is, in this respect, a sort of subsidiary to the great projects of Kennicott and De Rossi. Both these editions are subject now to disparagement on the ground of their basic assumption that the ben Chayim text is authoritative. In addition, Kahle points out that Baer's approach to the Massorah was completely erroneous. However, the primacy of the ben Chayim text was maintained also in the first and second editions of the Hebrew Bible which has become almost standard scholarly equipment in recent years, Rudolph Kittel's *Biblia Hebraica,* first published in 1905. Its distinctive feature is an ample critical apparatus accompanying the text in the form of a series of footnotes on each page. In large measure these consist of citations of variants in the versions, but numerous conjectural emendations are suggested as well. But Kittel's third edition, which after preliminary publication of separate fascicles appeared in 1937, was a completely new work. It signalized a revolution in Hebrew Bibles, for it abandoned the ben Chayim tradition and instead printed the text of the Leningrad manuscript 19a, discussed above. The critical apparatus of the edition, while developed beyond that of the other editions, was of the same sort; but a striking new feature was the inclusion of ben Asher's Massorah, printed in the margins beside the several passages to which it refers. Jacob ben Chayim had printed Massorah also in his great edition, but it was a composite mass of notes gleaned by the editor from various manuscripts as though of universal validity; whatever its merits, even this conglomerate had largely ceased to attract the attention of editors, the Baer and Delitzsch edition being an exception, though of a dubious sort. But here in Kittel's third edition, for the first time the student of the Hebrew Bible is given a printed record of the "Masora added on the margins of his Biblical text with the greatest exactness and care by the most famous Masoretic authority"—so it is described by Professor Kahle, who supervised this aspect of the edition. Altogether the Kittel *Biblia Hebraica,* notably in this third edition, has established itself as indispensable equipment for the serious student of the Hebrew Old Testament.

CHAPTER II

The Samaritan Pentateuch

THE doleful story of the decline and fall of the Hebrew kingdoms is known to every student of the Old Testament. The rampant social iniquities and religious perversions through which the northern kingdom was sinking ever lower to its eternal ruin are revealed in the prophecies of Amos and Hosea as also in some passages of the Book of Isaiah. The culmination of the tragedy came in 722 B.C. when the Assyrians after a lengthy siege captured the nation's one remaining fortress, the capital city Samaria, and extinguished Israelite nationality. The records of King Sargon tell that at this time 27,290 Israelite captives were carried off by him into exile in Assyria. And so begins the famous riddle of "the lost ten tribes"; for these uprooted Hebrews never returned as a body to their land, but on the contrary they disappeared presently from history. A few traces of their presence are to be discerned in the Assyrian literature; also stories like that in the Book of Tobit imply their survival in Mesopotamia and contiguous lands. But we lack clear record of what happened to them. Nonetheless, the answer to the problem is fairly apparent. We may regard it as practically certain that Sargon used the captives as slave laborers on his great building works, where doubtless hosts of them died under the hardships imposed. Many others were apparently overtaken by the fate that the Assyrians intended: they mixed with the native population and lost their identity. The few who clung stubbornly to their Hebrew distinctiveness seem to have amalgamated with the Jews when they in turn were carried into captivity more than a century later.

But the story of the Samaritan community and of their Pentateuch takes us back to the land of Israel. The Old Testament historian relates that after the destruction of Samaria, "the king of Assyria brought men from Babylon and from Cuthah, and from Avva, and from Hamath and Sepharvaim, and placed them in the cities of [the province of]

Samaria instead of the children of Israel, and they possessed Samaria, and dwelt in the cities thereof" (II Kings 17:24). Sargon himself in his own inscriptions which were found in the ruins of his old palace at Khorsabad, just north of Nineveh (Annals, 95-97), says: "The tribes of the Tamud, Ibadid, Marsiman, Chayapa, the distant Arabians who inhabit the desert, whom no scholar or writer knew, who had paid tribute to no king, I smote in the service of Asshur my lord; the remaining inhabitants I carried away and settled in Samaria." In other words, Sargon and II Kings agree on the general policy that was carried out regarding the repopulating of the northern kingdom from which captives had been carried to the East.

Taken together, the two records give the names of ten different nationalities, including the Jews already there, who were settled together in the same territory. To this conglomerate, other peoples were added at a later time, as seen in Ezra (4:2), where the Samaritans say to the Jews: "Let us build with you for we seek your God, as you do, and we have been sacrificing to him since the days of Esarhaddon, king of Asyria [681-668 B.C.], who brought us here." In the formal protest against the building activities of the Jews, sent to Artaxerxes, king of Persia, the Samaritans give this astounding list of foreign peoples who made up their populace, imported at a still later date (Ezra 4:9, 10): "Then wrote Rehum the chancellor, and Shimshai the scribe, and the rest of their companions, the judges, the rulers, the officials, the Persians, the people of Erech, the Babylonians, the people of Susa, that is the Elamites, and the rest of the nations whom the great and noble Assurbanipal [king of Assyria, 668-626 B.C.] brought over, and set in the city of Samaria, and in the rest of the country beyond the River."

Out of this composite group arose the Samaritan community. But its diversity from the people of Judah has been exaggerated. We err if we regard the Samaritans as a conglomerate of foreigners intruded into Palestine in the eighth and seventh centuries B.C. It is apparent that the Assyrian conduct at this time ran true to the ancient practice of deportation in general. The total of 27,290 people whom they carried off does not in the least represent the whole population of north Israel. Present-day Palestine numbers about a million and a half persons. Recognizing that this includes the people of the territory that comprised both the ancient kingdoms of Israel and Judah, admitting also that the peopling in antiquity may have been more sparse, it is yet certain that north Israel numbered its population not in tens, but in hundreds, of thousands. The exiles taken to Mesopotamia when Samaria fell constituted only a small fraction of the whole. When Jerusalem fell in 586 B.C., Nebuchadnezzar "carried away Jehoiachin to Babylon, and the king's mother and the king's wives and his officers and the leading men of the land . . . and all the men of substance to the number of seven thousand, and the craftsmen and smiths numbering one thousand: all of them capable of making war" (II Kings 24:15-16). Just so at Samaria, the conqueror took into exile only persons of the responsible classes, men who might conceivably constitute a nucleus of leadership for sedition against Assyria. But the peasants on the land, and the common folk—in fact the great mass of the population—remained. Israel's land was still populated by Israelites. The medley of intruded foreigners failed to alter this basic fact, for at the most they represented only an accentuation of the infusion of foreign blood that had been a continuing circumstance of Hebrew history.

It is in the light of this situation that we must read the Biblical account of royal sanction for the worship of Israel's God by the immigrants, as well as the stories of relations between the Samaritan and the Jewish communities after the exile. When the former approached the Jews with an offer to co-operate in the rebuilding of the temple, claiming, "We seek your God just as you," they were, we have every reason to believe, speaking literal truth. A plaintive lament regarded by some expositors as having originated in the Samaritan community when rebuffed by the Jews expresses this same sense of participation in the Hebrew heritage:

> Thou art our father
> though Abraham know us not
> and Israel will not recognize us.
> Thou art the Lord, our father;
> our redeemer; from of old is thy name.
> Why dost thou make us err from thy ways?
> Why dost thou harden our heart from fearing thee?
> Return, for the sake of thy servants,
> the tribes of thine inheritance (Isa. 63:16-17).

But this estimate of the Samaritans does not tell all. There were sound reasons, whether or not adequate, why the Jews should have been unwilling to mingle freely with them. Nonetheless, the two groups merely perpetuated a situation existent since their earliest days in the land. Though intimately related by blood, they continued to regard each other with suspicion and animosity. As time went on the breach widened, owing partly to repeated insults offered by the Jewish group under pressure of leaders recently come from Babylonia. Presently the rift became complete in the famous "Samaritan schism," apparently sometime in the fourth century B.C.; and thus when Alexander of Macedon came to Palestine in the course of his victorious campaigns, the Samaritans, we are told, sought and secured permission to build their own temple on Mount Gerizim. And so it came about, as described in the Gospel of John, that the Jews had no dealings with the Samaritans. It is of interest to realize that the community has persisted to the present. Its center has always been in the heart of Palestine, and now its sole location is there, in the city of Nablus. But the population has shrunk to little more than a hundred persons so that, unless present tendencies can be reversed, its extinction within measurable time is unavoidable. In the meantime, to witness its annual celebration of the Passover on Mount Gerizim, according to the ancient ritual prescribed in Exodus 12, is one of the rewarding experiences for the visitor so fortunate as to be in Palestine in the springtime.

It is the common belief that the final breach with the Samaritans occurred sometime after the editing and canonization of the Pentateuch. Such seems the most plausible explanation of the fact that this is sacred Scripture for them also. It is, indeed, the only portion of the Bible that they recognize. The strange fact is that our Book of Joshua, glorifying a northern hero as it does, is not in their Bible. And the rest of the Jewish canon of the prophets, as also that of the Writings, does not command their devotion. They are a striking example of a people whose religious thinking crystallized in ancient times and has made but slight advance since.

The Samaritan Pentateuch is not a translation of the original Hebrew, and so is not properly a version. It is a Hebrew text, which has been maintained largely in independence of the Jewish tradition since the fourth century B.C. but written in a script similar to the old Hebrew characters. Hence it reaches back farther in its origin than any other Biblical text except the Hebrew itself. Its adoption by the Samaritans may have been attended by certain changes in the text conformable to their peculiar beliefs. One of the striking differences is the reading, in Deuteronomy 27:4, of "Gerizim" instead of "Ebal" as in the Hebrew text, thus pointing to the pre-eminence of Mount Gerizim, the location of their temple. However, the Samaritans have a real "version" of the Pentateuch. It is the so-called Samaritan Targum, a translation into an Aramaic dialect apparently made in early Christian times. It also is written in the old characters of their Pentateuch, so that examination is required to show whether a manuscript is the Samaritan Pentateuch or the Samaritan Targum. They have also an Arabic translation that seems to have originated about the eleventh century A.D.

The chief value of the Samaritan Pentateuch is that it is an independent text which has had its own transmission by copyists who were, it is supposed, uninfluenced by the Jewish textual tradition. It is important thus as a check on the errors and corruptions that may have crept into the Hebrew text through its numerous copyings down to the time of the printing of the Hebrew Old Testament. This worth is qualified, however, by uncertainties as to the history of the Samaritan text; yet when it is in accord with other ancient authorities, it is recognized to be cogent evidence.

The existence of the Pentateuch, as the Bible of the Samaritans, was known to European scholars in the sixteenth century. Joseph Scaliger, the famous linguist, complained that Christians traveling in the East took no pains to secure a copy of it. The first specimen of it to be seen in Europe was brought by the Italian traveler, Pietro della Valle, in 1616. He spent twelve years visiting the East and published the best information then extant about Turkey, Persia, Egypt, and India. The Samaritans consisted in his day of several small communities, located at Gaza, Cairo, and Damascus, in addition to the group at Nablus. At the urgent request of the French ambassador in Constantinople, Della Valle attempted to secure a copy of the Samaritan Bible. After failure at three of the places, he finally succeeded in buying two copies in the Samaritan community in Damascus. One of these contained the Hebrew text of the Pentateuch in Samaritan characters on parchment; this he presented to the ambassador. The second, a copy of the Samaritan Targum, he kept for his own library. But in a few years both had found their way into the Oratoire, and they were published in 1632 as the fifth volume of the Paris Polyglot. Since that time scholars and travelers have secured a goodly number of these sacred documents; they are now found either as private possessions or in various libraries of Europe and America.

The most sacred copy of the Samaritan Pentateuch is in the synagogue at Nablus, so carefully guarded that few have seen it and no one has been permitted to handle it. It is written on parchment, which now is in very bad condition. It carries a colophon, not at the end of the manuscript but in the body of several columns by the device of giving special prominence to selected letters in the successive lines, and thus reads vertically down the page. It says in part, "I, Abishua, son of Pinehas, son of Eleazar, son of Aaron the priest—on them be the favor of the Lord and his glory—wrote this holy book at the door of the Tent of Meeting on Mount Gerizim Bethel, in the thirteenth year of the settlement of the Children of Israel in the land of Canaan. I give thanks to the Lord." While the form of the colophon precludes that it was written later than the completion of the manuscript, yet no scholar gives any credence to its excessive claims. By some it has been confidently ascribed to the first century A.D. or earlier, but the general opinion is more conservative. It was "rediscovered" by the Samaritans in the fourteenth century; its prior history is unknown except that evidently its origin is several centuries earlier. Apart from this uncertainty, the older manuscripts of the Samaritan Bible date from the thirteenth century A.D., although a few may be still earlier. The John Rylands Library, Manchester, has one bearing a date corresponding to A.D. 1211-12, which is said to be the oldest, practically complete, Samaritan Pentateuch outside Nablus. In recent times there has been some activity among the Samaritan community in preparing manuscripts for sale to tourists, so that considerable parts or the entire Pentateuch, written on paper scrolls, or smaller portions in crude book form, have become not uncommon in this country.

The Samaritan Pentateuch quickly made an impression upon the scholarly world. Sixteen years after Pietro della Valle's discovery, we have seen, it was published in the Paris Polyglot. Then later it was included along with the Samaritan Targum in the London Polyglot. It was published, but in Hebrew characters, by Blayney of Oxford in 1790. Kennicott and De Rossi collated it in their studies of manuscript sources of the Hebrew text. In 1868 Petermann published a grammar of the language, including in the volume the whole of Genesis. The most recent publication of the text is that by von Gall in 1914-18. This is a work in five volumes, giving the text in Hebrew characters, with appended critical notes. The editor tells that in the undertaking he collated about eighty manuscripts, including fragments. Most of these are of the fourteenth and fifteenth centuries, several are of the thirteenth and sixteenth, and one is as late as the nineteenth. One bears a date in the seventh century, but von Gall expresses grave skepticism of its authenticity. This has been the first undertaking to deal extensively with variants in the Samaritan text, and von Gall's text must be regarded as the best we possess. It has been objected that he overlooked a number of important manuscripts; further, he took no account of Samaritan inscriptions, most of which are Biblical, and one at least is not later than the sixth century A.D. However, their total bulk is not large.

But the history of the Samaritan Targum, subsequent to its publication in the two great Polyglots, is less gratifying. De Rossi took account of two manuscripts that included it along with the Samaritan Pentateuch; one of them had the Samaritan translation into Arabic as well. In 1875 Brüll republished the Polyglot text, but in the square characters. Petermann and Vollers believed a better text was available in a manuscript brought by the former from Nablus, which accordingly they published in the Samaritan characters in 1872-93. But the need of a dependable publication of the Targum is still acute. The most recent study, published by Lea Goldberg in 1935, emphasizes this point while at the same time arguing that the Targum was never an artistically conceived work carried through as a unity, but arose in the religious practice of the people; in other words, the differences manifest in present-day manuscripts are ultimately due not to textual corruption but rather to diverse original translations. In the course of time these were considerably influenced by the Jewish Targums and by the Arabic translation, and suffered, as well, considerable textual deterioration, as is the fate of all texts subject to hand copying. The far-reaching contributions of the genizah fragments, discussed in a previous chapter, are felt here likewise. Certain documents from the seventh to the ninth centuries A.D. contain Aramaic translations of passages of the Pentateuch, sometimes alternating with the Hebrew text. This translation resembles both the so-called Targum of Pseudo-Jonathan (of which more must be said presently) and also the Samaritan Targum. It is a tempting deduction that both of these are alike derived from an Aramaic translation of the Pentateuch current in Palestine in the early centuries of our era. If so, we would have in this fact demonstration of the superficiality of the common belief that through all the centuries subsequent to the great schism the Samaritans had no cultural relations with the Jews.

The unfinished character of the Samaritan Targum reflects the history of the community; for after the success of Islamic arms Palestine became increasingly Arabized and slowly the Samaritans found themselves in an Arabic-speaking environment, and then they themselves accepted the language of the country. Aramaic ceased to have meaning, and the Targum fell into disuse before it had ever attained a fixed and official form. Its place was taken by an Arabic translation. And the nature and source of this translation provides astonishing corroboration for the conjecture offered just now of Samaritan-Jewish interrelations through these centuries, for this Arabic version was nothing other than the famous work of the great Jewish scholar Saadya, of which more will be said below. It was written in Samaritan characters; and such old manuscripts are among our best evidences of the original of Saadya's translation. In course of time it underwent alteration; in the thirteenth century it was revised by a certain Abu Sa'id, and from this time was written in Arabic script. The older translation is clearly marked off by its form as well as its source.

The Samaritan Pentateuch differs from the text of the Hebrew in about six thousand items. A large proportion of these consist of insertions of "vowel letters," insertion or omission of conjunctions, and such other minor variants. But there are more than a thousand different readings that may not be dismissed. Without prejudging their meaning or origin, they may be arranged in the following classes:

1. Explanatory additions to the text, as in Genesis 7:3; to the

Hebrew, "of the birds also of the heavens," the Samaritan adds, "which are clean." In Genesis 44:31, to "the lad is not," the Samaritan adds "with us."

2. A difference of a letter or two, which either improves the sense or avoids some difficulty, as in Genesis 49:10, "The sceptre shall not depart from Judah, nor the ruler's staff from between his feet"; by the change of a single letter (*r* to *d*) the Samaritan reads, "from amidst his standards."

3. Corrections to agree with some parallel passage. In Genesis 11:10 f., "and he died" is added to what is said of each patriarch, as in Genesis 5. In Exodus 4:18, for the Hebrew "Jether," the Samaritan reads "Jethro," as in Exodus 18:1.

4. Differences that relieve some supposed historical difficulty; thus in Exodus 12:40, the 430 years are said to cover the whole period of wanderings by reading "in the land of Egypt and in the land of Canaan" instead of simply "in Egypt." The most notable variation of this kind is found in the genealogical tables of Genesis 5 and 11. The Samaritans seem to have assumed that no one would have been more than 150 years old at the birth of his first son; when this number is exceeded, as in the case of Methuselah and Lamech, 100 years or more are taken from it. If the remaining years of the patriarch's life stood as in the Hebrew text, he would survive the flood; so changes were made to allow each individual to die in the year of the flood.

5. Differences that represent Samaritan ideas. The chief passage is Deuteronomy 27:4, where "Ebal" is displaced by Gerizim"; but also after Exodus 20:17 and Deuteronomy 5:23 a command is given to build an altar. In Genesis 49:7, Jacob's rebuke of Simeon and Levi, "cursed be their anger," is changed to read, "noble was their anger."

The importance of all such variants and the worth of the Samaritan text as a whole were matters of keen scholarly debate for many years. It is apparent that one may take the view that these readings are all corruptions or deliberate changes made by the Samaritans; it is equally possible to argue that many, if not all, represent actual original readings from which the Hebrew text diverged. In 1815 the great Hebraic scholar Wilhelm Gesenius came out with a disparagement of the Samaritan variants, which he held were in almost every case inferior to the Hebrew. His view had great influence. But in recent years an increasing respect for Samaritan readings is making itself felt. Everyone recognizes that the probability of some deliberate alteration for doctrinal purposes is very high; but still much evidence of a high value remains. In particular when the Samaritan agrees with the Septuagint, or with other ancient versions, against the Hebrew, its testimony must be regarded as very cogent. An illustration of this situation is supplied by Deuteronomy 32:35, where the Hebrew says, "Mine is vengeance, and I will repay," but the Samaritan with the Septuagint indicates an original reading, "At the day of vengeance, I will repay."

CHAPTER III

The Greek Bible: The Septuagint

THE military campaigns carried into western Asia and Egypt by Alexander the Great opened the door for a cultural conquest. Alexander's troops were unconsciously missionaries of Greek civilization, and he himself was impelled by an ambition to spread the Greek way of life. Wherever his invincible battalions beat down the enemy, there the Greek language secured a foothold. Its conquests, however, were most marked and permanent on the shores of the Mediterranean Sea. Here the Greek language displaced the native tongues in some countries as the language not only of culture but of commerce and religion. Greek literature also secured a firm place, and prepared in a most remarkable manner for the advent and expansion of Christianity several centuries later.

Alexander's conquest of Egypt expedited the process of penetration into that country by Greek settlers, commerce, culture, and religion which had already been in operation for several centuries. His magnificent foresight led to the founding of Alexandria, soon to become the most important port in the eastern Mediterranean. It quickly attracted a large Greek population that presently made it a great center of Greek culture and creative scholarship. But it became also a cosmopolitan city. Its commercial advantages drew to it tradesmen from all Oriental lands, who brought, along with their wares, their customs and religions also. In turn they themselves fell under the spell of Greek civilization.

The geographic relationships of Egypt and Palestine are such that communication between them has been close and frequent throughout history, and still earlier remains reveal similar intercourse far back into the stone ages. References to such contact are numerous in the Old Testament, most famous being the Joseph story and the account of the oppression of the Hebrew slaves by Pharaoh. But on several other occasions individuals or groups went down to live in Egypt. Famines, wars, commerce, and politics all alike stimulated these migrations. In the days of Jeremiah a group settled in the eastern Delta. A few decades later a Jewish garrison was established at Assouan; whether related to the previous immigrants we do not know, but the community was still there at the end of the following century. However, it was the liberal policy of Alexander and his successors that laid the basis for the great development of the Jewish community in Egypt which came about in the late pre-Christian centuries.

It is reported that in the times of the Ptolemies one-third of the population of Alexandria was Jewish. Obviously they were deeply influenced by the Greek civilization. They spoke the Greek language and adopted some Greek methods of thought and systems of belief. But among this multitude of Greek-speaking Jews there were many who held tenaciously to the beliefs of their fathers. They believed in the God of Abraham, Isaac, and Jacob although they were steeped in the language and culture of a foreign people. Their religious needs brought about an event of great importance to Bible students—the translation of the Hebrew Old Testament into the Greek language. Nothing of the sort had ever happened before. And in the sequel it was to prove of far greater significance than its authors had dreamed. For by early Christian times the translation had entirely outgrown its purpose as the Bible of the Jews of Alexandria and was in use by Jews in all the lands around the eastern part of the Mediterranean Sea. It was the Old Testament of Paul and of the apostles, and was in constant use by the church fathers in the first few centuries of the Christian church. It was the text, too, from which several other important translations were made that will be examined farther on in our discussion, and it has been the Bible of the Greek church from its organization to the present day.

A good story has come down from antiquity to explain the origin of this remarkable work; it is contained in an alleged letter of a certain Aristeas to one Philocrates. Ptolemy Philadelphus (285-247 B.C.), so the account goes, desiring a copy of the Jewish literature for his great library, sent an embassy to the high priest in Jerusalem with a letter in which he reviewed his practice of freeing Jewish slaves who had come into Egypt under the Persians and under his own father, and requested that the high priest therefore send down accredited scholars to translate the Jewish law for him into Greek. In due course these arrived, seventy-two scholars chosen by the high priest, six from each of the tribes of Israel. They were magnificently entertained by the monarch and then set to work in a quiet house by the seashore, where in exactly seventy-two days they completed their translation of the Pentateuch. It was read before the assembled Jews of Alexandria and approved; then it was read to the King, who was greatly pleased and, as a good story would demand, sent the scholars home with princely gifts. A later variant of the account has the group working in pairs, in thirty-six separate cells—which a Christian writer half a millennium later claims to have seen still extant in Alexandria! Then these thirty-six separate translations, the situation demands, when examined were found word for word identical! It's a good story—even if it hasn't a word of truth in it! Its fictitious character has been fully demonstrated. But it is *symbolically* true; it is an excellent commentary on the place that this translation came to take in Jewish life in the subsequent centuries, a place so high that miraculous elements and almost divine inspiration were invoked to account for it.

Scholars uniformly concede that the translation of the Pentateuch was made in Alexandria about the middle of the third century B.C.; hence, about the latter part of the reign of Ptolemy Philadelphus. However, the impulse to its creation, it is highly probable, came not from the monarch but from the Jewish community itself, which had through these few generations of life in a foreign land forgotten its ancestral tongue, and so required the Scriptures in a language it could understand. The Aristeas story is rendered still more dubious by a consideration of the apparent origins of other early translations of the Bible, where opinion now inclines steadily toward regarding them as corporate achievements of their communities. It has indeed been hotly debated whether or not there was a single original Greek translation or whether the version as it came to be known gradually evolved out of a number of independent efforts to give a rendering of the Hebrew.

Since antiquity the translation has been uniformly known as the Septuagint (often designated by the symbol LXX); it is an abbreviated Latin word meaning "seventy"—it is the translation of the seventy. It was the first of vernacular translations of the Bible, of which the modern world has produced immense numbers. Yet why should it be called Septuagint when Aristeas' story tells of seventy-two translators? Various answers are given: that there were seventy members of the Alexandrian Sanhedrin; that the Jews believed there were just seventy languages in the world, hence this was symbolically a universal translation. But all that is clear is that we do not know; and most persons go on supposing the name refers to the translators.

It is now certain that the Old Testament was not all translated in the time of Ptolemy Philadelphus, nor by the same persons. The work was done by different men, through a period approximating 150 years; we cannot be sure that it was complete by the beginning of the first century B.C. It is of diverse character and uneven merit. The Pentateuch is a creditable translation, especially of Leviticus and Deuteronomy. Ecclesiastes is so slavishly literal that it is little more than a Grecized Hebrew. Daniel was considered so unsatisfactory a translation that the church ruled it out and substituted for it the Greek translation of Theodotion. As a result the Septuagint of Daniel came close to being lost. Until recently it was known only in a single Greek manuscript that is not earlier than the ninth century A.D. The Book of Esther has a note attached to it stating that it was translated by Lysimachus of Jerusalem and taken to Egypt in the fourth year of Ptolemy Philometer (185 B.C.). The prologue to the Book of Ecclesiasticus implies that the whole Old Testament was completed before 132 B.C. In some of the books, notably Proverbs and Jeremiah, sections are transposed, sometimes in a complicated pattern. For example, immediately after Jeremiah 25:13, Chapters 46-51 are introduced in the following order: 49:34-39; 46; 50; 51; 47:1-7; 49:7-22; 49:1-5, 28-33, 23-27; 48; then the Hebrew order is resumed from Chapter 25:15 to Chapter 45:5. In I Samuel the Septuagint either cut the Hebrew text so as to relieve it of difficulties or had a different original as the basis of its translation.

These liberties taken with the Hebrew text may be due in large part to the purpose for which the translation was made. The aim was to cast the Hebrew thought of the Old Testament into Greek molds, so that it might be plain to ordinary Jewish readers of Greek. Therefore fidelity to sense was more essential than fidelity to form. The translators seemed to be perfectly ready to make such slight changes or additions as were necessary to clear up the sense of any passage. Indeed it has

been claimed that the work belongs properly with Biblical interpretations, not with translations. Occasionally the translators substituted
literal for figurative expressions. They inserted or omitted words and
clauses, and added or changed clauses as they saw fit. But many of
the variants show that the text used was different from ours of today.
In some cases this means little more than the use of different vowels;
frequently, too, the relation of the two texts can be explained on the
grounds of a confusion of two or more Hebrew consonants. But other
differences are wider, raising at times a difficult problem as to the true
relation of the Hebrew and Greek readings. In II Samuel 6:5, instead
of "with all manner of instruments made of fir wood," the translation
reads "with all (their) might and with singing." In Jeremiah 15:19,
the clause, "bring thee again," is read in the Septuagint, "give thee a
habitation." Ezekiel 23:42, "and the voice of a multitude being at ease
was with her," is read in the Septuagint, "And with a loud noise did
they sing therein." The Septuagint omits, in Ezekiel 32:31, "even
Pharaoh and all his army, slain by the sword." In Ezekiel 34:16, "but
the fat and the strong I will destroy," is made to read, "and I will
keep the fat and the strong." These few examples are but illustrations
of the multitude of variations that this, our oldest translation of the
Hebrew Old Testament, presents. The proper evaluation of their
evidence and then the use of them in a search for the original text of
the Old Testament are matters of great skill and delicacy. Indeed the
study of the Septuagint has become a highly specialized enterprise,
with certain scholars giving practically their working lifetime to it.

The Septuagint, as it has come down to us, embodies a translation
not simply of our Hebrew Bible but also of many of the so-called
apocryphal books. This may be due to the fact that the Jews of Alexandria took a more liberal view of what constituted their sacred literature than did the Jews at Jerusalem. These apocryphal books are
distributed among the other books. To assist in locating them we give
their order as appearing in the Septuagint. The so-called historical
books, while differing from the order in the Hebrew Bible, proceed in
the same succession as in the English Bible, until II Chronicles is
concluded. From this point the apocryphal books appear among the
canonical books. We follow here the order found in the best manuscripts and identify the apocryphal books with successive numbers:

Immediately after II Chronicles we find (1) Esdras, followed by Ezra (called II Esdras and including Nehemiah). Then follow, in order, Psalms, Proverbs, Ecclesiastes, Song of Solomon, Job, (2) Wisdom of Solomon, (3) Wisdom of ben Sira (or Ecclesiasticus), then Esther with (4) The Rest of Esther, (5) Judith, (6) Tobit, followed by Hosea, Amos, Micah, Joel, Obadiah, Jonah, Nahum, Habakkuk, Zephaniah, Haggai, Zechariah, Malachi, Isaiah, Jeremiah, (7) Baruch, then Lamentations, (8) Epistle of Jeremiah, followed by Ezekiel, Daniel, which opens with (9) Susanna; after Daniel 3:23 comes (10) The Song of the Three Children, and after the close of Daniel comes (11) Bel and the Dragon, then (12) I Maccabees, (13) II Maccabees, (14) III Maccabees, and in some manuscripts (15) IV Maccabees. II Maccabees was not a Hebrew book; but when the orthodox Jewish canon was completed even those written in Hebrew were omitted. This fact deprived them of the regard given the canonical books, and they practically ceased to be copied by the Biblical scribes. Thus we know them almost exclusively in translations. One of the thrilling bequests of the Cairo genizah consisted of several fragmentary remains which gave us the text of a considerable part of the Hebrew original of the Book of Ecclesiasticus. It had been unknown since the twelfth century, and the Greek text, a none too happy translation, had been the best surviving authority. Some years ago a prominent scholar had undertaken to restore the Hebrew text on the basis of the Greek, but his results, as tested by the genizah finds, were not impressive.

We have already noted the late date of our oldest Hebrew manuscripts. Although they preserve a literature in parts long antedating the making of the Septuagint, yet there are extant manuscripts of this version much older than any document of Biblical Hebrew that we possess, except a few fragments and the Isaiah scroll; and comparison of the age of the great manuscripts of the two traditions gives an advantage to the Greek of six or, perhaps we should say, of eight centuries. This fact makes the Septuagint of high importance for the study of the early text of the Hebrew Old Testament.

It is our good fortune that manuscripts of the Septuagint are somewhat numerous in the great libraries of Europe. They are written in two kinds of script: in large separate letters, really capitals, and in a small running hand; the former is called uncial, and the latter, appropriately, cursive or minuscule. The uncial manuscripts date in general from the third to the tenth century A.D., and the cursives mainly from the ninth to the sixteenth, although some very important cursives are as early as the second century, and some fragments are actually from the second century B.C. Scholars refer as a rule to the uncials by capital letters, as A, B, D, etc., and to the cursives by Arabic numerals. There are about thirty known uncials, none of them complete and some more or less fragmentary, and more than fifteen hundred cursives, of greater or less extent, besides some thirty manuscripts containing lections (readings for religious services) from the Septuagint. It is apparent that the uncials are of high importance, such that the greatest of them call for brief description.

The oldest of these preserved to modern times, so far as is now known, consists of several fragments of papyrus that together make up two parts of a single leaf which originally contained II Chronicles 24:17-27. The manuscript was a codex, which on paleographic grounds has been dated about the middle of the third century A.D. Only slightly later, dated indeed "between the middle and end of the third century A.D.," is a manuscript of the minor prophets belonging to the Freer collection in Washington, D. C. Its much greater bulk raises it in importance far above the fragments of Chronicles; it contains some parts of Hosea and almost the complete text of the rest of the books of the minor prophets. Professor Sanders, who published it, assigned it the symbol W; he describes its writing as "a sloping uncial of the oval type with a decided leaning to the cursive." The material of this manuscript also is papyrus, some of which was badly broken when found. Another papyrus manuscript of the minor prophets is several centuries younger. It was acquired by the library of the University of Heidelberg, and was published by Professor Adolf Deissmann in 1905. There are preserved of it twenty-seven mutilated leaves, about 9½ x 4¼ inches, with twenty-eight lines to the page, that contain the text of Zechariah 4:16 to Malachi 4:5. The script is a large and coarse uncial not earlier than the seventh century.

The most complete known manuscript of the Greek Bible, including both Old and New Testaments, is Codex Vaticanus (referred to by the symbol B), which, as the name implies, is preserved in the Vatican Library. It was brought there by Pope Nicholas V in 1448 and listed in the first catalogue of the library in 1475. Its earlier history is mere conjecture. Its real character and value were unknown for centuries because it was not accessible to scholars. The Roman church guarded it so closely that no Protestant scholar of ability was allowed to study it for any adequate length of time until the middle of the nineteenth century. The codex was first made known in 1533, when Sepulveda called the attention of Erasmus to it. It was the major source of the mixed text of the Septuagint published by Pope Sixtus V in 1587. In 1669, Bartolocci, librarian of the Vatican, made a collection of some of its variant readings, which remained unpublished. Abbate Mico collated it for Richard Bentley in 1720 (published in 1799) and Andrew Birch, of Copenhagen, again collated it in 1781 (published in 1788, 1798, 1801). Napoleon took this treasure to Paris, where Hug carefully examined it in 1809 and was the first to make known its great value and supreme importance (1810). In 1815 it was restored to Rome and became practically inaccessible to scholars. Tischendorf in 1843, after several months' delay, was permitted to look at it for six hours. In 1844, De Muralt was allowed nine hours to examine it. In 1845, the English scholar Tregelles, even with Cardinal Wiseman's introduction, was not allowed to copy a word. His pockets were searched and all writing material taken from him. If he looked too intently at any passage the two attendants would snatch the volume from him. Other scholars, who had traveled far and were thoroughly competent to estimate its value, suffered the same disappointments in their efforts to examine it.

In the meantime, Cardinal Angelo Mai printed this manuscript (Rome, 1828-38), but it was not published until 1857 (in five volumes). The inaccuracies of the edition discounted its value from the first. In 1866, Tischendorf made a third attempt to see it, this time applying for leave to edit the document. He secured permission to study it under the supervision of C. Vercellone for three hours a day. By the end of the eighth day he had, contrary to the conditions on which he was to use the manuscript, copied out bodily twenty pages. His permission was revoked, but upon entreaty he was given six more days. As a consequence of this opportunity, Tischendorf was able, in 1867, to publish the best edition of the text up to that time. Vercellone and his successors published a very complete edition in six folio volumes

(Rome, 1868-81). But the best edition of all was a photographic fac-simile of the entire work, prepared by Abbate Cozza-Luzi and issued in 1889-90, by which the manuscript itself is now made accessible to the scholars of the world. Another photographic facsimile was published by V. Hoepli, 1904-05.

Codex Vaticanus (B) is written in uncials on 759 folios of fine vellum, three columns (of about forty-two lines each) to a page 10 inches wide by 10½ inches high. The character of the writing is plain and simple, such as leads scholars to locate this manuscript in the first half of the fourth century. It contains no enlarged letters, no pauses, no divisions into chapters or sections. Tischendorf thought that the scribe of the New Testament was the same one who wrote a part of Codex Sinaiticus. This supposed identity of one of the scribes is evidence of contemporary character. There are corrections by several hands, some of which are of real value.

This codex originally contained the whole Greek Bible. In its present state, after all the ravages of time and use, it lacks Genesis 1:1 to 46:28; Psalms 106-138; all of Hebrews following chapter 9:14; the Catholic Epistles; and the Apocalypse.

Another very famous manuscript, actually rivalling the importance of Vaticanus, especially in the Old Testament, is the one preserved in the British Museum and known as Codex Alexandrinus (designated A). It has 773 leaves of parchment, each 10½ inches wide by 12¾ inches high, with two columns of writing. It was originally a manuscript of the entire Bible; but the following passages are now lacking from the Old Testament: Genesis 14:14-17; 15:1-5, 16-19; 16:6-9; I Kings 12:20 to 14:9; Psalms 50:20 to 80:11. From the New Testament there have been lost Matthew 1:1 to 25:6; John 6:50 to 8:52; and II Corinthians 4:13 to 12:6. But in addition the manuscript contains the four Books of the Maccabees; the "Epistle of Athanasius to Marcellinus on the Psalter"; the "Argument of Eusebius"; and a summary of the contents along with directions for reading, ascribed to this same author. All of this material on the Psalter is immediately prefixed to it; and at its close there stand the apocryphal 151st Psalm and certain canticles or chants from other parts of the Old Testament. According to the Table of Contents, the manuscript also contained originally the Psalms of Solomon. The New Testament section contains remnants of the two Epistles of Clement; from the first, one leaf is lost, but of the second only a fragment remains.

The manuscript came to England as a gift from Cyril Lucar, Patriarch of Constantinople, to King James I. It was given in 1624, but was not actually sent until a couple of years later. In the meantime King James had died; but in any case the gift was several years too late for use as a source in the preparation of the famous English version of the Bible that bears his name. Of the prior history of the manuscript little is known, but such evidence as is available, including the character of the writing, indicates that it was written in the first half of the fifth century A.D. An Arabic introductory note signed by "Athanasius the Humble," believed to be Patriarch Athanasius III of Alexandria, who died in 1308, claims that the manuscript had been presented to the patriarchal office there. A statement in Latin dates the gift 1098. Cyril Lucar stated that he had himself carried the manuscript to Constantinople. He claimed also that it had been written by Thecla, a devout woman of Egypt who, it seems, died early in the fourth century soon after the Council of Nicea (A.D. 325). However, not much weight can be placed on this statement.

Apart from work in preparation of the Complutensian Polyglot, of which more must be said presently, this was the first uncial manuscript to be used by modern Biblical scholars, a collation of its principal readings in the Pentateuch and the New Testament being included in Walton's Polyglot of 1657. Publication of the manuscript was undertaken promptly. Job was printed in 1637, a few short passages later, and then the Psalter in 1678. The great edition, however, was delayed until the following century, when John Ernest Grabe's publication of the Old Testament part of the manuscript in four volumes was issued at Oxford in the years 1707-20. Grabe's death occurred in 1712, when only Volumes I and IV, the Pentateuch and the poetical books, had appeared, and the remaining volumes were brought out by Francis Lee and William Wigan. Like the Sixtine edition of Vaticanus, this was not an exact copy of the manuscript but was emended from other ancient manuscripts, in particular by the use of fragments of the Hexapla. But it has the immense advantage that all such alterations are clearly marked; a system of notations was employed not unlike the diacritical marks of Origen. An edition of the entire Old Testament in facsimile type was published in three folio volumes, 1816-28, by H. H. Baber. Then in 1859 a new edition of Grabe's work was brought out by Frederick Field. The New Testament portion was issued at London in 1786 by C. G. Woide, and in 1860 by B. H. Comper. The entire manuscript in photographic facsimile, edited by E. Maunde Thompson, was published by the British Museum in three volumes in 1881-83, and again in reduced photographic facsimile in four volumes in 1909-36.

Third in importance among the great uncials is Codex Sinaiticus (designated by the Hebrew letter *aleph*, but also commonly referred to as S). Though this document ranks in age with the Vatican manuscript, its fragmentary character reduces its value. Its discovery provides one of the famous stories of the romance of manuscript hunting. In April, 1844, a young German scholar by the name of Tischendorf sailed from Leghorn for Egypt and the East in search of manuscripts. In his two years of study in Paris he had become convinced of the need of a better text of the New Testament, and this he hoped to find through unearthing authoritative old manuscripts of the Bible. Some time in May he came to the Convent of St. Catharine at the foot of Mount Sinai, and it was there, he says, "that I discovered the pearl of all my researches. In visiting the library of the monastery . . . I perceived in the middle of the great hall a large and wide basket full of old parchments; and the librarian, who was a man of information, told me that two heaps of papers like these, mouldered by time, had been already committed to the flames." Imagine his excitement when he saw among these discarded sheets a number of pages of a very old Greek manuscript of the Bible! But his eagerness betrayed him, for the monks realized that this supposed refuse was actually of great value; they permitted him to take only "a third of these parchments or about forty-three sheets" which on examination proved to contain several chapters of I Chronicles, some of II Esdras, all of Esther, part of Tobit, most of Jeremiah, and about half of Lamentations. He brought them away with him, and after his return to Europe published them in 1844, entitling the volume *Codex Friderico-Augustanus,* in honor of the king of Saxony. But he concealed carefully the place of their discovery, since he hoped yet to secure the rest of the manuscript.

With this in mind he made a second visit in 1853, but succeeded in finding only a fragment containing eleven verses of Genesis which he discovered in a roll of papers. It served, however, to show that the great manuscript had originally contained the entire Old Testament; yet by this time he had resigned himself to the conviction that most of it had long since been destroyed. Contemplating the high reverence in which the Emperor of Russia was held in Eastern monasteries, he made an appeal in the autumn of 1856 to the Russian government for assistance in a plan of systematic research in the East. In spite of bitter opposition and consequent delay, the proposal was eventually approved and funds were placed at Tischendorf's disposal. Toward the end of January, 1859, he was once more at the Convent of St. Catharine, where he was received cordially. However, several days' search among manuscripts failed to reveal what he most sought. Then on the afternoon of February 4, to employ his own vivid account,

I was taking a walk with the steward of the convent in the neighborhood, and as we returned, towards sunset, he begged me to take some refreshment with him in his cell. Scarcely had he entered the room, when resuming our former subject of conversation, he said, "And I, too, have read a Septuagint.". . . And so saying he took down from the corner of the room a bulky kind of volume, wrapped in a red cloth, and laid it before me. I unrolled the cover and discovered to my great surprise, not only those fragments which fifteen years before I had taken out of the basket, but also other parts of the Old Testament, the New Testament complete, and in addition, the Epistle of Barnabas and a part of the Pastor of Hermas. Full of joy which this time I had the self-command to conceal from the steward and the rest of the community, I asked, as if in a careless way, for permission to take the manuscript into my sleeping chamber to look over it more at leisure. There by myself I could give way to the transport of joy which I felt. I knew that I held in my hand the most precious Biblical treasure in existence.

He spent the night copying the Shepherd of Hermas (in his own account above called the Pastor of Hermas), of which no Greek copy was previously known.

Next morning he requested that he might take the manuscript to Cairo in order to have it completely transcribed there; but the prior, who alone possessed the authority to permit this, had himself set out for Cairo two days before. Tischendorf followed in haste, secured the prior's consent, and in a short time was once more in possession of the manuscript, to the task of copying which he then set himself. In the course of the following weeks he determined to ask the monks to send the manuscript as a loan to the Emperor of Russia. Obstacles arose; but in the course of the summer he had opportunity to be of service to the convent in connection with certain negotiations in Constantinople. On September 24 he returned to Cairo, and next day the grateful monks gave him the manuscript to be taken to Russia on loan and there copied accurately. It was on November 19 that he presented to their Imperial Majesties in the Winter Palace at Tsarskoe Selo his "rich collection of old Greek, Syriac, Coptic, Arabic, and other manuscripts, in the middle of which the Sinaitic Bible shone like a crown."

When the facsimile copy of the manuscript in four volumes was published by Tischendorf at St. Petersburg in 1862 it made a profound impression upon the Christian world. Oxford and Cambridge universities conferred honorary degrees upon the noted scholar, the Pope sent an autographed letter of congratulations, and an eminent British scholar, whom Tischendorf does not name, is reported to have said, "I would rather have discovered this Sinaitic manuscript than the Koh-i-noor of the Queen of England."

It remains to add that in 1869 the loan of the manuscript was changed into a gift; the Archbishop and the monks presented it to the Emperor, who gave them in acknowledgement nine thousand rubles. The Archbishop wrote Tischendorf on July 15, 1869, "You know that this famous Bible manuscript has now been presented to the exalted Emperor and Autocrat of all the Russias as a testimony of our and the Sinai Monasteries' eternal gratitude." The manuscript remained in St. Petersburg (now Leningrad) until 1933, when it was sold by the Soviet government for £100,000 to the British Museum, where thus two of our great uncials are now prized possessions. In the meantime, it had been published by Oxford University Press in a great photographic facsimile edition prepared by Kirsopp and Helen Lake; the New Testament appeared in 1911, and the Old Testament in 1922.

Codex Sinaiticus consists of 346½ leaves of vellum, made from the finest and best quality of antelope skins. The leaves are 15 by 13½ inches, which, in making the codex, were gathered into quires of four. Each page has four columns, except in the poetical books, where there are only two, written in large uncials with twelve to fourteen letters to a line. Much discussion has centered about the dating of the manuscript, but without changing notably the conclusion reached by Tischendorf himself. He assigned it to the middle of the fourth century, or about the time of the death of Eusebius in A.D. 340. He thought it entirely possible that this might have been one of the fifty copies of the Bible which Constantine ordered for the churches of Constantinople, and that two centuries later it might have been sent by the emperor Justinian to the convent at Mount Sinai, which he founded. In the New Testament Sinaiticus is the most nearly complete among all the older Greek manuscripts that we possess. But of the Old Testament only pitiful fragments remain from the earlier part, although happily complete books are preserved from the later part. In total we have fragments of Genesis 23 and 24, and of Numbers 5-7, then I Chronicles 9:27 to 19:17, Ezra 9:9 to 10:44, but also Nehemiah, Esther, Tobit, Judith, I Maccabees, IV Maccabees, Isaiah, Jeremiah, Lamentations 1:1 to 2:20, Joel, Obadiah, Jonah, Nahum to Malachi, Psalms, Proverbs, Ecclesiastes, Song of Solomon, Wisdom of Solomon, Wisdom of ben Sira (Ecclesiasticus), and Job.

The fourth important manuscript of the Septuagint is the Codex Ephraemi (marked C), written in the fifth century, now in the Bibliothèque Nationale in Paris. It is a palimpsest; that is, a reused manuscript: the Biblical text was partly erased, and over it was written, somewhere about the twelfth century, the Greek version of a treatise composed by St. Ephraem of Syria. It is with great difficulty that some parts of the underlying Biblical text can be made out. With quickening interest we learn that it was Tischendorf who in his student days at Paris first succeeded in reading the complete text. Apparently this was originally a complete Bible; it would have ranked with our greatest manuscripts if it had not been defaced and largely destroyed by some medieval individual in need of writing material. As matters stand, however, there remain of the Old Testament portion only sixty-four leaves. They contain parts of Job, Proverbs, Ecclesiastes, Wisdom of Solomon, ben Sira, and the Song of Solomon. Of the New Testament 145 leaves have been preserved, out of an original total of 238; they contain parts of every New Testament book except II Thessalonians and II John. The manuscript is written in medium-sized uncials on pages 12¼ inches by 9½, a single column of 40-46 lines to the page.

Its modern history is interesting. Brought to Europe by Johannes Lascaris, it was probably purchased, along with the rest of his library, at his death in 1535, by Pietro Strozzi, and later by the Medici family. Catherine de Medici carried it with her to Paris in order to read the sermons of St. Ephraem. There it presently found its way into the Royal Library, and thus is now preserved in the Bibliothèque Nationale. Near the end of the seventeenth century a student thought he could detect traces of writing under the Ephraem text. Careful examination proved him correct; a few pages were deciphered, and their readings actually used in Mill's Greek Testament of 1710. But not until 1834 was important progress made, and then later, as already noted, Tischendorf succeeded in 1840-41 in reading practically every word of the Greek text, and even in discovering notes of several correctors of the text. In 1843-45 he published at Leipzig the first complete edition of the manuscript.

From the same century come two other manuscripts of the Freer collection. One of these which Professor Sanders designates by the symbol Λ he dates "certainly" in the fifth century, and is "inclined to refer it to the first half." It contained the entire Psalter; the parchment, however, was found in very bad condition, but the editor's skill has deciphered a large portion of the text. The other manuscript (designated Θ) contains only Deuteronomy and Joshua, although originally it began with Genesis; the other four books of the Pentateuch have been lost, as also a few leaves from this part.

Codex Cottonianus (D), a charred manuscript of the fifth century, containing the Book of Genesis, is now in the British Museum. Of it Professor H. B. Swete has written, "No other uncial codex of the LXX of which any portion remains, has suffered so lamentable a fate. Brought to England from Philippi in the reign of Henry VIII . . . it remained in the royal library till the reign of Elizabeth, who gave it to her Greek tutor . . . , and from his hands after several vicissitudes it found its way into the Cotton collection. In 1731 . . . it was reduced by fire to a heap of charred and shrivelled leaves." It was originally written in a beautiful uncial character, and furnished with 250 illustrations that carry the evidence of close relation to the mosaics of

San Marco in Venice. Had not the text been carefully collated before the fire, its value now would be slight.

The Bodleian Genesis (E), at Oxford, was written in the tenth century. It contains in a good state of preservation Genesis 1:1 to 14:6; 18:25 to 20:13; 24:55 to 42:17. Codex Ambrosianus (F), at Milan, was written in the fifth century. It carries three columns to the page and is fully punctuated, accented, and supplied with breathings. Its contents are Genesis 31:15 to Joshua 12:12, with a few lacunae here and there; also fragments of Isaiah and Malachi. The Vienna Genesis (L), of the fifth or sixth century, contains the whole of Genesis. The manuscript is famed for its beauty; it is written in silver letters on purple vellum, and is illustrated with a large number of miniatures painted in water colors. Codex Basiliano-Vaticanus (N), at Rome and Venice, belongs to the eighth or ninth century. It consists of two volumes, somewhat mutilated, and is written in sloping uncials. Its special importance is that it was used with the Codex Vaticanus (B) as the basis of the Roman edition of the Septuagint issued in 1587. Codex Sarravianus (G) was apparently written at the end of the fourth or the beginning of the fifth century. It consists of rather more than 150 leaves of parchment containing disconnected portions of Genesis to Judges. Most of the leaves are in Leiden, some are in Paris, and one is in Leningrad. Its high interest is that it contains critical marks that Origen inserted into his Hexapla, of which more will be said below.

The cursive manuscripts are in general of a later date than the uncials; consequently their value will commonly be proportionately less. However, it is apparent that some of them have been copied from good manuscripts, perhaps early uncials, so that they take a place of importance only slightly less, if at all, than that of certain of the uncials. Certain "families" of these late manuscripts are recognized by scholars, just as in the study of manuscripts of the New Testament.

Yet the worth of all these is now transcended by the remarkable papyrus documents, written in cursive script, that have been discovered in recent years. Most famous of them are a group known as the Chester Beatty Biblical Papyri. They were purchased from dealers in Egypt by Mr. A. Chester Beatty, of England, in 1931, and embrace parts of twelve distinct manuscripts, of which eight contain portions of the Greek Old Testament and one has an apocryphal book and Christian homily. Eight different books of the Old Testament are represented. They are Genesis, Numbers, Deuteronomy, Isaiah, Jeremiah, Ezekiel, Daniel, and Esther. Two manuscripts contribute to the text of Genesis. One of these is in reality an uncial, hence would properly have been discussed above, but it is more suitably included here; it has forty-four leaves with two columns on each page, and contains about two-thirds of the book. It was written in the fourth century. The other manuscript, of twenty-two single-columned leaves, contains about one-quarter of Genesis, written in cursive script probably at the end of the third century.

Numbers-Deuteronomy is a beautifully written document, two-columned, in a small book hand. It is thought by Kenyon to be certainly of the second century, and thus he adjudged it "the earliest extant manuscript of any part of the Greek Bible." Though somewhat mutilated, the best part of thirty-three leaves have been preserved, and twenty-two more can be identified. Isaiah is in bad shape, with remnants of twenty-seven leaves, only about one-half intact. It was charmingly written, and has a few marginal notes, some in Coptic, all dating from about the third century. Jeremiah is represented by a part of one leaf—of about the same date. Ezekiel and Esther, written by different hands, are a single codex of probably the second half of the third century. The manuscript became divided in some unknown way, and part of it, containing a large section of Ezekiel, came to this country and has been published under the title *The John H. Scheide Biblical Papyri: Ezekiel.* Daniel has thirteen leaves, one-half of each gone. Its writing locates it in the first half of the third century. We have mentioned above the unique feature that this is a true Septuagintal text of Daniel. Ecclesiasticus has one leaf and part of another, in a coarse hand of the fourth century. These Chester Beatty papyri are a prize contribution to our textual material for the study of the Septuagint. Their importance is to be judged, not alone by their age, but also by another circumstance that will become clear when we go on presently to discuss the work of Origen.

This group of papyri includes three manuscripts of the New Testament that contain greater or less portions of fifteen books in uncial hands of the third century. These significant documents will be described in connection with the discussion of the New Testament text (Chapter XII). They also include a manuscript containing the last ten chapters (97:6-107:3) of the apocryphal Book of Enoch, hitherto known only in Ethiopic, and a homily on the Passion by Melito, Bishop of Sardis, which was previously unknown except through allusions in early Christian writers. Professor Campbell Bonner, who published this University of Michigan papyrus (See Bibliography), has indicated that the Enoch 106-107 passage is from an apocryphal book of Ezekiel, and with this judgment Kenyon in his publication of the total collection is in agreement.

Paralleling in date some of the Chester Beatty papyri is a cursive that was published in the same volume with the Freer manuscript of the minor prophets. It was, when last heard of prior to the war, in the Stadtsbibliothek of Berlin. It had been bought in Egypt in 1906 by Professor Carl Schmidt, and was edited jointly by him and Professor Sanders and published in 1927. It consists of sixteen leaves of papyrus, nine written in double columns and seven in single columns. The writing measures about 8½ x 6¾ inches, and the lines on a page vary between twenty-eight and thirty-seven. The writing resembles papyrus documents of the end of the third or beginning of the fourth century. The text contains Genesis 1:16-35:8, where the codex breaks off.

But most sensational of all is a pathetic group of papyrus fragments, all that remains of two great manuscripts of the Book of Deuteronomy —whether or not they contained the entire Pentateuch we do not know. The first of these were discovered in the cartonnage of a mummy along with certain other literary scraps, the most important of which is a fragment of the *Iliad*. The nondescript character of the group tell their story; they were waste "paper" that found a last use in stuffing mummy coverings for some nameless Egyptian undertaker. Some years ago they came into the possession of the John Rylands Library, in Manchester, England, and there they were studied and were eventually published by C. H. Roberts. The Biblical materials consist of fragments of at least four columns of a roll of Deuteronomy; they contain parts of Deuteronomy 23:24-24:3, 25:1-3, 26:12, 26:17-19, 28:31-33, besides three scraps with only a few letters on each. They are dated about 150 B.C.—not more than a single century after the Pentateuch was translated! How one wishes that Egyptian undertaker had

been more addicted to the use of the Bible! This manuscript, if anywhere nearly completely preserved, would have been far and away
the most astonishing document in the whole history of the Biblical
text. No one knows where this waste material was stuffed into a decent
memorial for some departed Egyptian, but such evidence as is available points to Upper Egypt, probably the Fayum. In contrast to all
the other manuscripts and fragments of the Greek Bible surveyed
above, this was a Jewish Bible; it is of interest to observe then that
within a hundred years after the translation was made, the Septuagint
was carried by Jews from Alexandria into Upper Egypt, and probably
used there in some long-forgotten synagogue.

The other fragments are in the possession of the Société Royale de
Papyrologie du Caire. Their origin likewise is unknown but they too
are believed to come from the Fayum and are dated "in the 2nd to
the 1st century B.C."; but indeed it is admitted that their closest affinities
are with known writing of about 160 B.C. The manuscript has been
assigned the notation P(apyrus) Fouad no. 266. The extant fragments
contain in beautiful rounded uncials part of the Greek text of Deuteronomy 31:28 to 32:7. A notable feature of the manuscript is that it
did not render the name of the God of Israel by some Greek equivalent
or transcription, but retained the original Hebrew consonants of the
word YHWH, written in clear Aramaic form. The scribe was conscious of the problem of changing from the left-to-right writing of
the Greek to the reverse direction for this Hebrew word, and carefully
measured off his space with dots that still stand in the manuscript.

Meager as are the remains of these two manuscripts, they are rich in
information about the history of the text of the Bible through the
period from which they come. They are positively thrilling in their
testimony that parts of the Greek Bible from pre-Christian times have
actually been preserved, and in the tantalizing hope they encourage
of yet further exciting discoveries.

The first printing of the Septuagint was in the Complutensian
Polyglot, completed under the supervision of Cardinal Ximenes in
1514-17 but not published until 1522. The Aldus edition, based on
manuscripts in Venice, appeared in 1518, and thus actually antedated
the publication of the Complutensian. But the great edition of the
Septuagint in these centuries was that published under the patronage

of Pope Sixtus in 1587. It is in the main the text of Vaticanus, though with divergences that are estimated to total four thousand. The Codex Alexandrinus, likewise emended and supplemented from other manuscripts, was published in 1707-20 by an Oxford scholar, John Ernest Grabe. Surpassing all these in importance was the work of Robert Holmes and James Parsons, published at Oxford in 1798-1827. It is a great edition of the Septuagint in four folio volumes. Its text is that of the edition of 1587. But the new feature of the work was its comprehensive critical apparatus; it gave variant readings of about 325 manuscripts, together with much patristic evidence, and the readings of the previous editions. In 1850 Tischendorf published a revision of the Roman texts with variants from S, A, and C; four editions appeared before 1867, and three others after Tischendorf's death. However, the most common edition of the Septuagint today is that published by Henry Barclay Swete at Cambridge, England, in three volumes in the years 1887-1894. It employs the text of the best extant manuscript of each part of the Old Testament—most commonly Vaticanus—but notes the variants of a few others of most importance. Yet Swete's edition was only a preliminary publication of the great Cambridge project on the Septuagint. The final results have been in process of publication under the names of Alan E. Brooke and Norman McLean since 1906, when Volume I, *The Octateuch,* began to appear. To the present, publication has progressed as far as the Book of Tobit (in the order of Septuagintal books listed above); that is, in the order of our English Bible everything prior to the Book of Job, along with several books of the Apocrypha, is now published. The work differs from Swete's only in the greater scope of its critical apparatus. It has attempted an exhaustive examination and presentation of the evidence, and thus it gives the evidence, not alone of Septuagintal manuscripts, but also of quotations by church fathers, of versions related to the Septuagint, and of whatever else may bear upon the problem of the original reading of this Greek translation. The printed text, it is to be observed, is that of the Swete edition—in other words, mainly the text of Vaticanus —and where this is lacking, then of the best other manuscript available. The critical material is arranged in a great series of footnotes.

At the same time, a group of German scholars under the direction of Professor Alfred Rahlfs of Göttingen were at work likewise on an edition of the text of the Septuagint. But they aimed at a "critical" text. That is, instead of presenting the evidence and leaving it to each individual scholar to make his own decision as to the correct reading, as is the principle of the Cambridge group, the German scholars undertook to appraise the evidence themselves and to give what they believed to be the correct text. They have printed, thus, not the text of any known manuscript, but a "made text" arrived at by their use of the evidence. Whether the Cambridge or the Göttingen is the better procedure remains an open question. Both have advantages and disadvantages; each person must decide for himself which serves him best. Professor Rahlfs also published a preliminary edition; it appeared in 1935 with the title, *Septuaginta, id est Vetus Testamentum Graece juxta LXX.* The text is based mainly on a collation of the manuscripts A, B, and S. In 1922 Rahlfs had published a study of Ruth that is particularly significant by reason of its discussion of method. The final results of the Göttingen group began to be published in 1926, first Genesis, then other parts at intervals of years.

Two other "Septuagintal projects," though left incomplete at the death of their authors, demand mention because of the high quality of the methods employed in them. The first in point of time is that of Paul de Lagarde, to whom, it has been remarked by a well-known scholar, "living students of the Septuagint must look up as the leader of modern progress." We shall have occasion shortly to point out that it was he who identified the Greek text of a certain manuscript as Lucian's recension of the Septuagint. He conceived the plan of reconstructing the three great recensions of this version as a preliminary step toward establishment of its original reading. Unfortunately, he was able to carry through this undertaking only for the Lucianic text of the books Genesis to Esther. This he published in 1883 under the title, *Librorum V. T. Canonicorum, pars prior, Graece.* The other project was that of the late Max Margolis. He published in 1931-38 *The Book of Joshua in Greek,* but only as far as Joshua 19:38. However, in the excellence of critical principles and the meticulous care exercised the edition is a model for critical study of the Septuagint.

The immensity of the scholarly work upon an old translation here sketched, and the high value set upon manuscripts and fragments of varying degrees of antiquity from the second century B.C. to the sixteenth A.D., may well astonish one. On closer examination, it seems like the work of the Massoretes, who spent their lives in tedious examination of details of the Hebrew text. And indeed the two are intimately related; both alike have been based on a conviction of the high worth of the Bible for contemporary life, and a realization that problems of text come first in the task of expounding it. Consequently it is the purpose of scholars in their work on this old Greek translation (1) to determine as nearly as may be, by a study of all the manuscripts and whatever other evidence is available, the text of the Septuagint as it was originally translated from the Hebrew; (2) to discover by this means approximately the text of the Hebrew Old Testament from which the Septuagint translation was made; (3) to learn, by a comparison of this text with the Massoretic text, so far as is possible the original words of the Old Testament books. The value of the Septuagint expands as one studies it; from several points of view it is an immensely important body of ancient literature. For the Biblical student its study brings rich rewards in fresh insights into the thoughts of the writers of the Old Testament, as well as glimpses of the life of Jewish communities in Egypt in the immediately pre-Christian centuries, and of the thought of the early Christians, for whom it was the first Bible.

CHAPTER IV

Rival Greek Bibles and
Revisions of the Septuagint

THE Septuagint was the Bible of the Greek-speaking world in the times of Christ and the apostles. From its pages the New Testament writers usually quoted. The early Christian church all about the shores of the Mediterranean Sea adopted it. By its words they proved that Jesus was the promised Messiah, and all the law and the prophets were fulfilled in him. Their success in such debates naturally aroused antagonism among the Jews and a growing skepticism toward their formerly cherished Greek Old Testament. Often in these arguments the Jews fell back on the assertion that there was something wrong in the translation. Finally they repudiated the Septuagint as being a Christian Bible and sought a translation that would not betray their doctrine. And in fact, it was not long before there were several rival Greek translations, each bidding for favor as the most faithful rendering of the Hebrew original.

The first of these was the translation made by Aquila. According to the scanty information we possess, he was a proselyte to Judaism who came from Sinope in Pontus, Asia Minor. Epiphanius tells that he lived about A.D. 128. He is reported by Jerome to have been a pupil of Rabbi Akiba between A.D. 95 and 135. Such training would account for the excessive reverence for the very letter of the text which his work manifests. His translation is slavishly literal, seeking to render every word and particle, regardless of literary form, the requirements of the Greek language, or the demands of clear expression. He often follows Hebrew idioms contrary to Greek usage, casts new words to suit his convenience, carries Hebrew words bodily over into Greek spelling, and generally violates principles of grammar and syntax to put the Hebrew into a cold, literal Greek. Such renderings have some value for the study of etymology, lexicography, and the text, but are far from being helpful to the common reader. Aquila's translation soon came to the front among the Jews and became their official Greek version of the Old Testament. Its wide use is apparent in a mention of it by the Christian leader, Irenaeus, about A.D. 177. Some writers identify Aquila with Onkelos, the author to whom the principal Targum, or Aramaic translation, of the Pentateuch is ascribed. But the evidence is not conclusive.

This Jewish translation aroused the Christians of the second century, among whom a new translator appeared in the person of Theodotion, believed to have been an Ebionite Christian of Pontus, or of Ephesus. His translation is located between A.D. 180 and 192, in the reign of Commodus. It was based on the Hebrew, and in style and character in some parts closely followed the Septuagint. In fact, it is called by some scholars rather a revision of that venerable version than a new translation. It is clear that its purpose often seems to have been to make a correction of that work. Theodotion, in contrast with Aquila, gave a free rendering of the Hebrew and had due regard to correct and idiomatic Greek. He inserted the postscript to Job, and the additions to Daniel, viz.: Susanna, Song of the Three Children, and Bel and the Dragon. His translation soon won its way in the Christian church for its fidelity to the Hebrew and its improvement on the translations of some of the books of the Septuagint. Indeed, it attained such favor that it came to exercise a large influence upon further revisions of the Septuagint. Also, Theodotion's version of Daniel was so much superior to that of the Septuagint that it presently became the standard rendering in Septuagintal manuscripts. As a result, the true Septuagint of Daniel almost disappeared; it is known today in only two Greek manuscripts. The book of Job in the Septuagint lacked about one-sixth of the matter found in the Hebrew text. These gaps likewise have been filled out from Theodotion's translation.

The third great translator of the Hebrew into Greek in this period was Symmachus, who, on the authority of Eusebius and Jerome, was an Ebionite. His activity as a translator apparently is to be dated near the reign of Severus, A.D. 193-211. His translation, of which only fragments survive, is remarkable for its fidelity to the original Hebrew, for its pure and even elegant Greek, and for its display of literary skill.

Like Jerome, he had a worthy conception of a translator's duty; and Jerome held the translation in high regard and used it in his own great work. He gave this description of the three versions "Aquila translates word for word, Symmachus follows the sense, and Theodotion differs slightly from the Septuagint." Symmachus' influence on our English Bible came by way of Jerome's Vulgate, with which the translators of the Authorized Version were familiar.

The greatest Biblical scholar of the early Christian centuries was Origen. He was born at Alexandria, A.D. 186, and was surnamed Adamantios because of his untiring energy. His early life and training, his skill as a teacher, and the broad scope of his scholarship were famed and lauded all down the Christian centuries and are an inspiration to us of later days. His tremendous energy and skill in Biblical lines of research laid the foundation for critical Biblical study. Indeed, the first half of the third century marked an epoch in the history of Biblical textual study. Origen found in use in his day, besides the Old Testament in Hebrew, also the Septuagint and the three Greek versions noted above. He complained that every manuscript contained a different text from every other. He conceived the idea of carefully comparing all these different versions and manuscripts, and of producing therefrom the best possible manuscript or version. In order to accomplish this, not only for himself but for all who should study the Scriptures, he planned a stupendous work, called the "Hexapla," upon which he, with helpers, occupied twenty-eight years of his life. It was the arrangement in six parallel columns of (1) the Hebrew text then current, (2) this same Hebrew text put into Greek letters, (3) the Greek translation of Aquila, (4) the Greek translation of Symmachus, (5) the Septuagint, revised by himself, and (6) the Greek translation of Theodotion. These versions were arranged so carefully and adjusted so nicely that the ordinary Bible student who could read Greek could make use of this Hexapla.

The purpose of Origen's Hexapla was not to restore the original text of the Septuagint but to make it correctly and adequately represent the Hebrew original. But also, seminary teacher as he was, he hoped to stimulate an interest in Hebrew scholarship among Christians. For the notable fact is that as Christianity developed beyond its Jewish origins, a knowledge of the Hebrew language within the church fell

Hebrew	Heb.Transliterated	Aquila	Symmachus	LXX.	Theodotion
לַמְנַצֵּחַ	λαμανασση	τῷ νικοποιῷ·	ἐπινίκιος·	εἰς τὸ τέλος·	τῷ νικοποιῷ.
לבני קרח	λαβηνκορ	τῶν υἱῶν Κόρε	τῶν υἱῶν Κόρε	ὑπὲρ τῶν υἱῶν Κόρε	τοῖς υἱοῖς Κόρε
על עלמות	αλ·αλμωθ	ἐπὶ νεανιοτήτων	ὑπὲρ τῶν αἰωνίων	ὑπὲρ τῶν κρυφίων	ὑπὲρ τῶν κρυφίων
שיר	σιρ	ᾆσμα.	ᾠδή.	ψαλμός.	ᾠδή.
אלהים לנו	ελωειμ·λανου	ὁ θεὸς ἡμῖν	ὁ θεὸς ἡμῖν	ὁ θεὸς ἡμῶν	ὁ θεὸς ἡμῶν
מחסה ועז	μαςε·ουος	ἐλπὶς καὶ κράτος,	πεποίθησις καὶ ἰσχύς,	καταφυγὴ καὶ δύναμις,	καταφυγὴ καὶ δύναμις
עזרה	εζρ	βοήθεια	βοήθεια	βοηθός	βοηθός
בצרות	βσαρωθ	ἐν θλίψεσιν	ἐν θλίψεσιν	ἐν θλίψεσι	ἐν θλίψεσιν
נמצא מאד	νεμσα μωδ	εὑρέθη σφόδρα.	εὑρισκόμενος σφόδρα.	ταῖς εὑροῦσας ἡμᾶς σφόδρα.	εὑρέθη σφόδρα.
על כן	αλ·χεν·	ἐπὶ τούτῳ	διὰ τοῦτο	διὰ τοῦτο	διὰ τοῦτο
לא נירא	λω·νιρα	οὐ φοβηθησόμεθα	οὐ φοβηθησόμεθα	οὐ φοβηθησόμεθα	οὐ φοβηθησόμεθα
בהמיר	βααμιρ	ἐν τῷ ἀνταλλάσσεσθαι	ἐν τῷ συγχεῖσθαι	ἐν τῷ ταράσσεσθαι	ἐν τῷ ταράσσεσθαι
ארץ	ααρς	γῆν,	γῆν	τὴν γῆν	τὴν γῆν
ובמוט	ουβαμωτ	καὶ ἐν τῷ σφάλλεσθαι	καὶ κλίνεσθαι	καὶ μετατίθεσθαι	καὶ σαλεύεσθαι

THE FORM OF ORIGEN'S HEXAPLA

to negligible proportions. This situation Origen sought to remedy. Hence he gave the Hebrew text the place of prominence on the page of his Hexapla. To assist elementary students of the language, he put beside it, in the next column, a transliteration of the Hebrew into Greek, and next to that, the excessively literal version of Aquila that thus could serve almost the functions of an interlinear translation. Then Symmachus followed, as an accurate, but literary, rendering of the Hebrew. Theodotion was given sixth place since his translation was related to the Septuagint, rather than immediately to the Hebrew original. However, in the sequel, the fifth column of the Hexapla proved the most important. It was Origen's revision of the Septuagint, which he carried forward by the following method:

Where the manuscripts of the Septuagint differed, he chose the reading which gave the best translation of the Hebrew original. In case there were words in the Hebrew that had no adequate representation in the Septuagint, he inserted in the Septuagint text such translation of these words as was found in one of the other three Greek versions, preferably from Theodotion. Such insertion was marked by an asterisk (※ or ⁜) at the beginning, and a metobelus (⸕) at the close of the passage. A passage which was found in the Septuagint but had no equivalent in the Hebrew was marked in Origen's Septuagint at the beginning by an obelus (—), or a horizontal line, and at the end by a metobelus, but it was not expunged. These are the more important of the critical marks introduced by Origen to specify the sources and variations of his version of the Septuagint.

Origen's Hexapla was one of the great achievements of early Christian scholarship, besides being an epochal point in the whole history of the transmission of the Bible. The magnitude of the work can be conceived only when we realize that the whole Old Testament written according to Origen's plan would have filled, so it has been calculated, more than six thousand leaves, or twelve thousand pages of carefully copied and critically worked over Hebrew and Greek manuscripts.

Our knowledge of the Hexapla was for a long time dependent upon descriptions by the early historian of the church, Eusebius, and by Epiphanius, by Jerome, and by a few others, besides some brief specimens occurring as notes in Biblical manuscripts. However, as was mentioned in our discussion of the Massorah, Giovanni Mercati found in 1896 a palimpsest manuscript of the tenth century, in the Ambrosian library in Milan, that gives the first continuous passages of the Hexapla known in modern times. It contains parts of the Psalter, and provides a vivid realization of the tremendous amount of close critical work necessary to finish even a single page. Also, in 1898, there was found in the genizah collection of palimpsests brought to Cambridge from Cairo, Egypt, a Hexaplar fragment of Psalm 22, dating probably from the eighth century A.D. Though this double leaf, containing 105 lines of Hebrew, is badly worn, enough remains to make it plain that Origen's method was to put one Hebrew word, or at most two in a line, in the first column, and its exact equivalent in the Greek column. This plan is exemplified in both the Milan and the Cairo palimpsests. The entire Psalter, containing some 19,000 words, when written as these lines were, would cover about 450 leaves.

The Hexapla was completed about A.D. 240 or a little later, at Caesarea in Palestine, where Origen spent the last twenty years of his life. And there the manuscript remained, a prized treasure of the Christian community. Its immense bulk precluded that it should be frequently copied; indeed, apart from the fragments mentioned above and some uncertain deductions from the readings of some other versions we are ignorant of the existence of any copies whatever of the work in its broad scope. But the high regard for the person and scholarship of Origen, resulting in a belief that he had successfully restored the text of the Septuagint, led some parts of the church to accept the fifth column of the Hexapla as authoritative, and so to have it copied as the valid Greek Old Testament. The original Hexapla was seen and studied in Caesarea by Jerome about A.D. 400, and by other owners or copyists of manuscripts, who have noted certain facts in their margins. Early in the seventh century, too, apparently it was studied by Paul, Bishop of Tella in Mesopotamia, for he made a translation of the fifth column into Syriac, copying carefully Origen's critical signs, so that this "Syro-Hexaplar" version is one of our most valuable sources for these. The date given for this translation is 617-618. On this basis, the Bishop was the last person (of whom we have any record) to have seen the great work. Only fourteen years later Caesarea was captured by the Saracens. The fate of the Christian library and of its treasured Hexapla we do not know, except only that both alike disappeared and have never been heard of since.

A part of Bishop Paul's translation, copied in the eighth century, is now in the Ambrosian library in Milan. This contains the prophets and the most of the Hagiographa. The Codex Sarravianus (G) in Leyden, Paris, and Leningrad, as already mentioned, is a manuscript of Origen's fifth column, partially provided with his critical symbols. Its date is not later than the fifth century—less than 200 years after Origen laid down his work. The Codex Coislinianus (M) in Paris, from the seventh century, covering Genesis to I Kings 8:40, with some breaks, contains a Hexaplar text and has numerous Hexaplaric signs in the margins.

The interest in problems of the Biblical text that manifested itself in the sixteenth and seventeeth centuries turned, naturally, to these old Greek renderings and expressed itself in the work of Flaminius Nobilius, who in 1587 brought out his collection of readings of Aquila, Symmachus, Theodotion, and others. Then in 1622 Johannes Drusius published *Veterum Interpretum Graecorum in totum vetus Testmentum Fragmenta, collecta, versa & notis illustrata*. But the first to claim specific publication of the remains of the Hexapla was a Benedictine monk, Bernard de Montfaucon, who in 1714 published at Paris two volumes entitled *Hexaplorum Origenis quae supersunt multis partibus auctiora, quam a Flaminio Nobilio & Joanne Drusio edita fuerint ex manuscriptis & ex Libris editis eruit & notis illustravit*. These works were, however, superseded by Frederick Field's publication already referred to; in 1875 he brought out in two large volumes the extant fragments of the Hexapla. Notwithstanding subsequent discoveries and developments this is yet the standard work.

Origen failed in his excellent purpose of establishing a single authoritative text of the Old Testament in Greek. His work may, however, have had influence in reducing the chaos that existed formerly, for by the early part of the following century there were in circulation three dominant types of Septuagintal text corresponding to the three countries, Palestine, Syria, and Egypt.

It was natural that the Christians in Palestine, particularly at Caesarea, should have treasured the memory of Origen, whose great scholarship seemed their own possession because of his long residence among them. Not many years after his death Eusebius, who became the great historian of early Christianity, was associated with the church there. Presently we find him, along with a presbyter named Pamphilus, engaged in an effort to bring the results of Origen's work on the Greek Bible to the service of the churches, instead of lying secluded in the library in Caesarea. Specifically, the project was to copy and circulate Origen's fifth column, containing the critical marks, in a separate manuscript and with alternate readings from the other columns noted in the margins. We do not know the plan of co-operation of the two men, but part of the work was done while Pamphilus was in prison awaiting the martyrdom that came to him in A.D. 309. Apparently then Eusebius finished the task and issued it as the correct text of the Septuagint. It attained large success in Palestine; the Emperor Constantine ordered fifty copies for use of the churches. But it will be apparent that the critical marks when divorced from the accompanying Hebrew text lost their meaning. As time went on they were copied more and more carelessly, and presently were omitted entirely. In the history of the text of the Septuagint, the result was disastrous, for to the extent to which Eusebius succeeded in making his version popular, evidence of Septuagintal readings prior to the time of Origen has been confused or lost.

About the same time, a Christian of Samosata in Asia Minor by the name of Lucian was busy on a similar undertaking. He had studied in the great Christian school at Edessa in Mesopotamia, and later coming to Antioch quickly established a reputation for scholarly proficiency. In course of time we find him associated with a Hebrew scholar in a revision of the Septuagint that was far more thorough than that of Eusebius. He introduced divergent readings, emended expressions, and corrected the translation. But an important advantage he possessed was the use of Hebrew manuscripts that differed from those known to Origen. The result is that his revision supplies us frequently with readings otherwise unknown, but intrinsically superior. Especially through the books of Samuel and of Kings the "Lucianic recension" is a most valuable resource of the modern text critic. His revision was adopted throughout Asia Minor from Antioch to Constantinople. Lucian fell a martyr to the persecution of Maximus in 311.

A third reviser of the Septuagint was Hesychius; but unfortunately we know little about him. He is thought to have been the martyr-bishop mentioned by Eusebius, who fell under the persecution that destroyed Lucian. His revision was adopted as the Septuagint in Alexandria and Egypt, for he was one of the Alexandrian school of learned men.

The manuscripts that can be identified with these revisions of the Septuagint are not numerous. There is in Trinity College, Dublin, a palimpsest, Codex Dublinensis Rescriptus (o), similar to the Codex Ephraem, consisting of only eight leaves of Isaiah. It was written in Egypt in the sixth century and is credited with relationship to the revision of Hesychius. The finest manuscript relative to this group of revisions is the Codex Marchalianus (Q), in the Vatican Library at Rome. It was written in Egypt in the sixth century and contains the books of the prophets. Dr. Ceriani, who edited the manuscript, has shown that it was originally the text of Hesychius, which is preserved also in a few cursive manuscripts. Its value is greatly enhanced by marginal readings taken from a text of Origen's Hexapla, with initial letters indicating the source of the readings.

Notes in the Syro-Hexaplar version of Paul of Tella and a statement of Theodoret provided the clue by which Frederick Field was able to identify the text of Lucian. Working independently, the German scholar, Lagarde, reached similar results, so that a certain group of cursive manuscripts are now recognized as Lucianic.

But it has been a much more complicated matter to identify the Hexaplaric text of Eusebius, that is, eventually of Origen. We have noted how Eusebius' well-intentioned work resulted in a confusion of the text, such as it may have been in the third century A.D., by the inclusion of considerable blocks of material intruded by Origen in his Hexaplaric scheme. Some of this could be identified through the sources which Field so ably collated, but actually no more than fragments of information about the Hexapla have survived, as he indicates freely in the title of his work, *Origenis Hexaplorum quae supersunt ... Fragmenta.* And thus it is that until recently a basic uncertainty has hung over a very large part of the Septuagintal text which we possessed; we had no means of determining what part of it was original, deriving from the pre-Christian translators, and what was to be

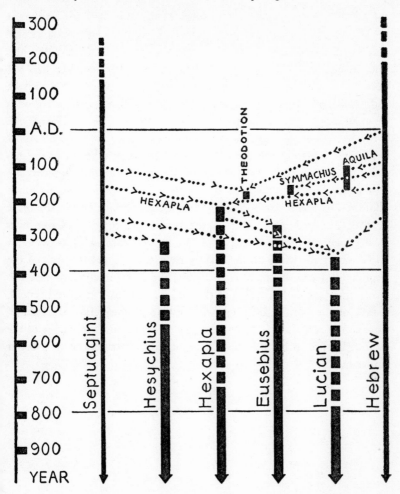

DIAGRAM SHOWING THE RELATION OF THE RIVAL GREEK BIBLES
AND REVISIONS TO THE SEPTUAGINT

ascribed to Origen in the third century A.D. The acute problem was how to attain a pre-Hexaplaric text. It has been our good fortune in recent years to have secured authentic samples of this early form of the Greek Bible.

This is part of the high significance of recent papyri and manuscript discoveries. It will be apparent from the dates assigned that some of the Chester Beatty papyri, not to speak of the John Rylands fragments of Deuteronomy, were written prior to Origen's work; and careful study of the others, as of the Freer manuscript of the Minor Prophets also, reveals that even if later than the time of Origen they had not been influenced by the Hexapla. We have thus an objective basis of judgment and are in a position to decide the claims of certain groups of manuscripts which had formerly been identified as pre-Hexaplaric.

Study of the Septuagint and the use of it as a tool for recovery of the original text of the Hebrew Bible have thus taken a great step forward. But there is no occasion for complacency; the problems are still acute. The John Rylands fragments are too brief to tell us much about the text as it was a century after its translation; and in the three or four hundred years that elapsed before the copying of our next earliest sources of the Greek Bible an untold number of corruptions had found their way into the text. Even if the original readings of the Septuagintal translators were available, the interpretation of this evidence into terms of criticism of the Old Testament text would remain a task of the highest delicacy, with always a considerable margin of uncertainty remaining. Nonetheless, advances in our knowledge of the Septuagint are to be welcomed as important contributions to a better understanding of the Bible.

CHAPTER V

The Latin Bibles

THE official language of the Roman Empire was Latin. Yet it was never in general use throughout all the provinces of the Empire. In countries nearest to Rome it gradually became the language not simply of officialdom but of all important public institutions. But the Christian church in the first century, and well along into the second, doubtless owing to its Eastern origin seems to have preferred Greek. The books of the New Testament were written in Greek, and Paul's preaching and writing were done in the same tongue. Even the early bishops of Rome spoke Greek. One of the oldest manuscripts of the New Testament—the Codex Alexandrinus—contains an epistle of Bishop Clement of Rome, written in Greek to the Corinthians. In fact, the Scriptures of the early Christian church were Greek through and through; it used the Septuagint for its Old Testament, and the Greek Gospels and Epistles as its New Testament.

But the constantly increasing influence of Rome gradually overcame the predominance of Greek. The Christian church in the West, like all other institutions, finally adopted Latin as the language of its ritual and services. This soon led to the need either of an interpretation in Latin by the leader of the church services or of a translation. Thus gradually a Latin Version came into being and through some process of editing reached a form that was commonly accepted as correct, if not official. That is, the "Old Latin" was a growth, rather than the fruit of an organized project of translation. However, we must recognize that in the Old Testament its beginnings may be even older than here suggested. Certain features point to a Jewish origin; it is entirely possible that the Jews in or about Carthage, like those in Alexandria a few centuries before, served the religious needs of their synagogues by producing a Bible in the local language. Then in

course of time, it would appear, the Christians adopted this translation for use in their churches.

The current Latin Bible of today is the Vulgate, translated by
Jerome at the close of the fourth century A.D. But the Old Latin was
of much earlier origin; also it was of different genius. There is abun-
dant evidence in the church fathers, in manuscripts, and in some other
sources, that a variety of Latin versions were current before Jerome's
day. Augustine (353-430) says that "those who have translated the
Scriptures from Hebrew into Greek can be numbered, but the Latin
translators cannot, for every one into whose hands a Greek manuscript
came in the first periods of the Christian faith, and who fancied that
he had some skill in both languages, ventured to translate." It is now
generally conceded that at the latest a Latin translation of the entire
Bible was in circulation at Carthage by 250 A.D. It is entirely probable
that portions of the Bible, particularly the New Testament for its immediate value to the Christian church, were extant in Latin before
A.D. 200. Of course, the New Testament was translated immediately
from the original Greek, but in the Old Testament the Old Latin
versions were made from the Septuagint—a translation of a translation of the Hebrew Bible.

It has been claimed that the Old Latin version had its origin in
Syria or Asia Minor, probably at Antioch, that powerful literary and
religious center in the early Christian centuries. Its faithfulness in
some places to the Hebrew text, and its resemblances to Lucian's
readings, as well as the certain knowledge its translator reveals of the
administrative arrangements of Palestine in this period, are some of
the many evidences for the view. This Old Latin version made in
Syria would then have been carried to Rome, to the countries of
Europe, and to North Africa, in the region of Carthage. However,
the theory has failed to command adherence; instead, the version is
believed to have originated in Africa, its agreement with Lucian then
being due to the use of "pre-Hexaplaric" Septuagintal sources by both.
In any case Cyprian (about A.D. 200-258) quotes freely from the Old
Latin, and apparently always from the same type of text. Tertullian,
Cyprian's teacher, likewise quotes Scripture in his writings, but in a
manner that strips his quotations of value for text criticism. He apparently paraphrases, quotes from memory, and so uses the matter as to

lead one to suspect that he discounted the authoritative value of the text he quoted.

Two types of text of the Old Latin version are recognized, distinguished as the African and the European recensions. The historic relations between these is not known, but a third type, called the Italian, is believed to be a revision of the European. No complete manuscript of the Bible, or even of the Old Testament, in the Old Latin translation has survived to the present; indeed, after piecing together all our sources, there remain still large sections for which we have nothing. The Old Latin version of Wisdom of Solomon, Ecclesiasticus, Baruch, and Maccabees, are in the Vulgate. Jerome did not revise them, consequently the old version was taken over into the later Latin Bible. But for the rest we must have recourse to other sources. By means of various ancient manuscripts, generally fragmentary, and of quotations in the works of certain church fathers, we can piece together other parts, so that we have the Old Latin of Numbers, Deuteronomy, Joshua, and Judges to the middle of Chapter 20, Ruth, Esther, Tobit, the Psalms only slightly revised, considerable fragments of Genesis, Exodus, Leviticus, and of the prophetic books, but only a little of Samuel and Kings, and of Ecclesiastes, Job, and Proverbs.

The major importance of the version for us lies in its value as a source for the study of the Septuagint. Since it was translated prior to the time of Origen, or in any case from sources independent of his work, it provides very significant evidence on the pre-Hexaplaric text. Its agreement with Lucian's readings in many passages, although he lived much later than the time of its translation and certainly was not influenced by the Old Latin, is further evidence of the pre-Hexaplaric character of the text employed by both.

The standard edition of the Old Latin remains that of Pierre Sabbathier, *Bibliorum Sacrorum latinae versiones antiquae seu vetus italica,* which came out in three volumes, 1743-49. Actually Sabbathier's death occurred in 1742, but the work was carried to completion by Vincent de la Rue. It was based partly on manuscripts of the version and partly on citations in the church fathers. The work was republished in 1757. Numerous studies of the Old Latin have appeared in recent years, and several texts of greater or less extent have been published. The need of a comprehensive edition has been keenly felt, yet Sabbathier has remained our one great resource. Fortunately this situation is now being rectified by the monks of Beuron, who are bringing out a superb edition that employs all known manuscripts and editions. They published an introductory volume in 1949, and began issuing the text in 1951.

The existence of several Latin versions, differing greatly in their texts, occasioned either by careless copying or translating or both, soon aroused complaints and shook the faith of the church in the authoritative value of the manuscripts. Jerome, a most accomplished scholar, who was born at Stridon on the borders of Dalmatia and Pannonia about 340-342, came "to the kingdom for such a time as this." His parents were wealthy and he had the best school advantages of his day. His early training, his four years of travel in the East, his five years (374-379) spent in the desert of Chalcis in self-discipline, and finally a thorough study of the Hebrew language under a rabbi who had been converted to Christianity, prepared him for his great task. In this period, through correspondence and explanation of Scripture terms, he formed a close friendship with Pope Damasus. In 379 he moved to Antioch, where he was ordained presbyter. Later, at Constantinople, he became thoroughly imbued with the expositions of Gregory Nazianzen. In 382 he went to Rome, where he spent more than two years in close association with Pope Damasus.

At the request of the Pope, who had displayed large interest in the Scriptures, Jerome undertook a revision of the Old Latin version on the basis of the Greek text. He began with a revision of the Gospels, which appeared in 383. This was followed very soon by the Acts and the rest of the New Testament. For while there are difficulties in ascribing the non-Gospel books to Jerome, there is no completely satisfactory alternative explanation of their origin. In the Gospels the revision is very painstaking and thorough, based on the European Old Latin and a Greek text of the Alexandrinus type; but in the rest of the New Testament the work becomes progressively limited to making revisions only where compelled by the original text.

Jerome's first work on the Old Testament, it is supposed, was a revision of the Old Latin Psalter, done on the basis of the Septuagint and making only such changes as the sense required. This very mild revision is called "The Roman Psalter." However, Jerome's connection with it is now called in question. But by a decree of Pope Damasus it became the official version of the Psalter in the churches of Rome and Italy and so remained until Pius V (1566-72). It is still the official Psalter in St. Peter's at Rome, and at Milan, and is employed in part in the Roman missal, and in one place in the breviary in the Invitatory Psalm 94 (95).

About the end of A.D. 384 Pope Damasus died, and in 385 Jerome left Rome for Palestine. After a prolonged study of its topography and cities, and a tour of Egypt, he, with his associates, settled in Bethlehem. Here in 389 he founded two religious houses, over one of which he presided for at least fifteen years. Over the other, founded for nuns, Paula, a devout widow, was in charge until her death.

Somewhere during these years, probably about A.D. 387 in response to requests, Jerome again revised the Psalter. In this work he used, in addition to the Septuagint, the Greek text of Origen's Hexapla, together with some of his critical symbols. This revision became known later as "the Gallican Psalter," for it was first adopted in Gaul. It was finally accepted and decreed to be the official version of the Psalter in the Latin church, where it remains today as the version of the Psalms embodied in the Vulgate. Jerome also translated or revised other books of the Old Testament on the basis of the Septuagint, but only the Psalter and Job of this revision have been preserved.

More and more Jerome came to see that a Latin version of the Old Testament would accord better with the original Hebrew if it were a new translation instead of merely a revision of a version based on the Septuagint. In his controversies with Jews, he came to realize the futility of appealing to the Septuagint, for they denied that it truly represented the original Hebrew. Jerome's friends, too, were urgent that he undertake a new translation direct from the Hebrew. In response to these requests, as he says in his prefaces, he began little by little to translate the separate books, and to send copies of them to his friends. Thus the great Biblical scholar was led gradually and almost casually into doing piecemeal what later became his great lifework.

He first translated (A.D. 390) the easier historical Hebrew of the Old Testament, the books of Samuel and Kings. These he prefaced with the "helmeted prologue" (*prologus galeatus*), so called because in it Jerome assumes the role of one armed to meet antagonists of his version. It is practically an introduction to his whole work of translation.

The next task that he set himself was a new translation of the Psalter, although he had already twice revised it. The prophets and Job followed in order, then Ezra and Chronicles—all these translations falling within the years A.D. 390-396. For two years he had to lay aside the work because of severe illness. He was able to take up his task again in 398 and translate Proverbs, Ecclesiastes, and Song of Songs; it is said that he did Ecclesiastes as a sort of diversion during his convalescence. The Pentateuch followed in order, and in A.D. 404 Joshua, Judges, Ruth, and Esther. The death of Paula, head of the convent, occurred in that same year; soon thereafter appeared the apocryphal parts of Daniel and Esther, and later the books of Tobit and Judith translated from the Aramaic. These completed Jerome's translation of the Old Testament from the original text. He neither revised nor translated Wisdom of Solomon, Ecclesiasticus, the Maccabees, and Baruch.

Jerome's personality as reflected in the prefaces to his translations is extremely interesting. His profound scholarship did not deaden his sensitiveness to criticism and opposition. For fourteen years (390-404) he had labored almost incessantly to produce a faithful rendering of the Hebrew, but he met, in the main, only keen criticism and the antagonism of churchmen all about him. He defended his position in his prefaces, which fairly ring with denunciations of his ignorant, superstitious critics. He wielded a sharp pen, possessed a hot temper, and did not fail to combine them in cutting and caustic retorts; one of the famous epithets hurled at his critics was "two-legged asses"! He gives us, besides, in these prefaces, an idea of how he worked, what difficulties he encountered, features of the Hebrew text of his time, and how he finally succeeded in a task that gave to the church such a reliable translation of the Hebrew text. Jerome asserted his reverence for the Septuagint but at the same time said that his effort was only to render clearly from Hebrew passages that were obscure in the Septuagint and the Old Latin. The conservatives of that day, as of this, clung to the older versions because long use and familiarity had cast a halo of sanctity about them. But the wisest of the church-men soon began to recognize the superiority of Jerome's work. Augus-tine, who had expressed fear of its consequences, now wisely turned to praising it. But poor Jerome saw only contention and strife to the time of his death at Bethlehem in A.D. 420. He never had the satis-faction of seeing his all-important service to the cause of Biblical learn-ing publicly recognized for anything like its true worth. Yet its merit insured it a hearing and gradually won for it a place of utmost impor-tance in the progress of Christianity. It became the Bible of all Western Christendom; for a thousand years it was practically without a rival. It was carried throughout western Europe; it was the authoritative Scripture of Christian missionaries and teachers; from it vernacular versions were made by scholars who knew little of Hebrew or Greek. And even after the acceptance of local translations by the Protestant bodies, the Vulgate continued to be the Bible of Roman Christianity. In the entire history of Bible translations, the importance of the Vulgate is rivaled only by that of the Septuagint.

Jerome did not live to see his success. But that century, the fifth, did not pass by without public recognition of his real service to the understanding of the Bible. Then Pope Gregory's commentary on Job (about A.D. 580) accepted Jerome's translation as on a par with the Old Latin. In the next two centuries the church fathers quoted both the Old Latin and Jerome's version, the latter gradually gaining the priority. The use of the two versions side by side led to the correction of one by the other and finally to the mixing of the texts. Even by the sixth century, this corruption had gone so far that Cassiodorus took steps to correct the current versions by the best old manuscripts. But like other Biblical texts, Jerome's translation was subject to in-creasing corruption through succeeding centuries until the age of printing. Notable revisions were undertaken from time to time. Of them an account will be given in Chapter XIII.

The "Vulgate," as Jerome's translation came to be called, is dis-tinguished from the Septuagint notably in that, apart from the books taken over bodily from the Old Latin and the passages confused or corrupted in transmission, it is the work of a single translator. This provides a much greater unity of style and method than in the Greek Bible, so that one can with safety make certain generalizations about the version. Jerome's acquaintance with the Jewish scholarship of his time was a valuable resource, providing numerous insights that enhance his translation. His work, too, possessed a literary quality that was to prove of significance in the history of Western Christendom. Also, his principles of translation were excellent; his effort was, not to equate word for word, but to render the thought of the original in graceful and idiomatic Latin. However, the freedom of his translation has proved a disadvantage for the modern textual critic, for it gives less precise evidence of the wording of the original than a version such, for example, as Aquila's. This critical deficiency of the Vulgate is further aggravated by its late date. By Jerome's time the Hebrew text of the Old Testament, corrupt as it had become, was long since officially fixed and was approximating the form in which we know it today. So it is that, as compared with the Septuagint, the passages are few where the Vulgate provides clear evidence for correction of an error in the Hebrew text. Nonetheless, it is one of our great ancient versions, whose testimony may not be neglected.

There are thousands of Old Latin and Vulgate manuscripts in the public and private libraries of Europe. Professor Samuel Berger, of Paris, examined more than eight hundred in the libraries of Paris alone. It is thought that the total number will not be less than eight thousand. Most of them are late thirteenth- or fourteenth-century documents that possess slight critical value. A large percentage of them are Gospels. All told, the manuscripts are grouped in ten classes: (1) Early Italian texts; (2) Early Spanish texts; (3) Italian texts transcribed in Britain; (4) Continental manuscripts written by Irish or Saxon scribes, showing a mixture of two types of text; (5) texts current in Languedoc; (6) other French texts; (7) Swiss manuscripts; (8) Alcuinian revision; (9) Theodulfian revision; and (10) medieval texts. We mention in particular only three of the oldest and most valuable of the manuscripts of the Old Testament: (1) One of the earliest of the Spanish texts is the "Ashburnham Pentateuch," now in the Bibliothèque Nationale at Paris (Nouv. acq. Lat. 2334), a beautiful Vulgate manuscript of the seventh or eighth century, with pictorial illustrations. (2) Codex Complutensis, in the library of the University of Madrid, Spain, a complete Latin Bible of the ninth or tenth century, of which, however, Ruth, Esther, Tobit, Judith, and I and II Maccabees are from the Old Latin version. (3) Codex Amiatinus of the whole Bible, in Florence, dating from the beginning of the eighth century; it was copied in England, either at Wearmouth or Jarrow, and carried by Abbot Ceolfrid in A.D. 716 as a gift to the Pope.

The first edition of the Vulgate, as everyone knows, was also the first printed book of importance, the Gutenberg Bible published between 1452 and 1456. The greatness of the achievement cannot be readily exaggerated. Yet as a presentation of the text of the Latin Bible it is very erroneous—Gutenberg had enough to do without undertaking an intensive course of textual criticism! This, then, was the problem bequeathed to subsequent scholarship. The story of the efforts toward an authoritative text of the Vulgate must be left for a subsequent chapter, where more appropriately the entire Bible comes under consideration. Here we must be content with two episodes of the long process. The Latin Bible published in 1590 at the Vatican press by Pope Sixtus V and then, slightly altered, again issued in 1592 by Pope Clement VIII has remained to the present the standard text of the Vulgate as also the authoritative Bible of the Roman Catholic church. But the textual criticism of the sixteenth century is not adequate for today. The need has long been felt for a better collation of all important evidence. In 1907 Pope Pius X assigned to a commission of the Benedictine Order headed by Cardinal Gasquet the task of preparing a critical edition of the Vulgate. With Dom H. Quentin as editor, the following volumes have already been published by the Vatican press: Genesis in 1926, Exodus and Leviticus in 1929, Numbers and Deuteronomy in 1936, Joshua, Judges, and Ruth in 1939, Samuel in 1944, Kings in 1945, Chronicles in 1948, I-II Esdras, Tobit, and Judith in 1950, Esther and Job in 1951, and Psalms in 1953. Since Quentin's death in 1935 the work has been carried on at the Roman monastery of St. Jerome.

CHAPTER VI

The Syriac Bibles

SYRIAC, it is apparent, is the language of the Syrian people. But at this point an inconsistency enters the explanation, for Syria is the land lying northerly from Palestine along the coast of the Mediterranean Sea; yet this is not the homeland of the language we know as Syriac, nor of the Syriac Bibles. Instead Syria in ancient times was inhabited by Arameans, and only relatively late was the now familiar name applied to it. The Arameans, by virtue of the advantages of their location between the great commercial centers of hither Asia on the one hand and the Mediterranean as a highroad to Europe on the other, became the great traders of the ancient world. Through this means their influence spread afar. They were known at the court of the Assyrian monarchs, and with the destruction of the empire their peaceful penetration became one of the significant cultural facts of all this region through succeeding centuries. It is to the language of this eastward extension of the Arameans that the name Syriac is applied; in fact, it is sometimes termed Eastern Aramaic.

But there were Israelites in these lands as well. Disaster brought them in floods. When Samaria fell in 722 B.C. and the northern king-dom was destroyed, the Assyrian conqueror carried off, we have noted, 27,290 captives whom he settled in the lands about the middle Tigris. The ruin of the Jewish state brought similar deportations of thousands of exiles to the plain of Babylonia in 597 and 586 B.C. Less spectacular was the relentless pressure of economic need which through all the centuries entailed unrecorded migrations, much as is related of the family of Elimelech in the Book of Ruth. It appears that by Christian times many of the cities of Syria and Mesopotamia had each a Jewish group in its population. And presently the same impulse which we have noted as operative in the wealthy Jewish quarter of Alexandria must have manifested itself; the Jews needed a translation of their

Scriptures into the intelligible tongue of daily intercourse, that is, into an Aramaic dialect.

The origin of the Syriac Old Testament has been a matter of prolonged debate, for the Syriac Bible, as long as we have known it, has been a Christian book. It contains the New Testament as well as the Old, has come to us through Christian hands, and has been the grounds of Christian exposition and homily. Nonetheless, the possibility of a Jewish origin of the Old Testament translation has been entertained for many years, with scholars ranging themselves on one side or the other of the argument. But many features of the translation, a striking one of which meets the reader in the very first verse of Genesis, have steadily inclined opinion until now it is freely recognized that the Christian church, in possession as it was of a Syriac Old Testament before the third century A.D., had accepted the Jewish translation and made this its own.

The city of Edessa in northern Mesopotamia, situated as it was on the great highway from east to west and destined to be of foremost cultural significance in succeeding centuries, has been considered in the past as the place where this work of translation was carried through. But Kahle argues vigorously that we are to look, instead, to Adiabene, the region lying east of the Tigris River between the two Zab tributaries. There about the middle of the first century A.D. a King Izates and his mother Helena became proselytes to Judaism. Helena is celebrated for her piety and her gifts to the Temple in Jerusalem; and Izates, so it is claimed, in loyalty to the religion of his choice inspired the translation of the Hebrew Bible into the language of his kingdom. The task was relatively easy, for the translators leaned very heavily on the old Aramaic translation then current in Palestine. Indeed, some passages are little other than transliterations of this western Aramaic into the script of the Syriac Jews; and elsewhere interrelations are frequent.

This account gives clarity and meaning at once to our earliest information about the Peshitta, as the translation is called. Theodore of Mopsuestia, in the fifth century, did not know where or when it had been made. Ephraem Syrus, who died A.D. 373, made it the basis of an elaborate commentary. He mentions the Syriac Old Testament as widely circulated in the churches of Syria in his time. It had been

translated at so distant a day that some of the words had already become obscure to him, and required extensive comments. Aphraates, a
churchman at Mosul, about the middle of the fourth century, quotes
passages out of all the canonical books of the Syriac Old Testament,
with the exception of Song of Songs, though he gives none from the
Apocrypha. Then still farther back, just after the middle of the second
century, Melito of Sardis cites "the Syrian" in discussing the sacred
books. It is not certain, however, that he refers to the Syriac Bible.

Our ignorance of the actual origin of the Peshitta is complicated
with yet one further difficult question. It has long been recognized
that the translation at many points agrees with the Septuagint as
against the Hebrew text. Yet this is not the whole situation; often
Septuagint and Hebrew agree against the Peshitta, or Hebrew and
Peshitta against the Septuagint. Nonetheless, the situation is such as
to have prompted the serious question whether the Syriac translation
was not made from the Greek rather than direct from the Hebrew.
But the evidence is of varying force in different parts of the Old
Testament. Besides, similarities may have arisen through the work of
copyists in the long and ill-regulated course of transcription of the
Syriac Bible. Or again, the relationships may in considerable part be
due to official revisions that took place in the centuries when the
prestige of the Greek Bible was very high among Oriental Christians.
In any case, there is in all this no refutation of the view that would
make the Syriac originally a Jewish translation.

Fortunately there is, however, a phase of the origin of the Peshitta
on which we can be reasonably confident. It is commonly agreed that
the translation was not done by a single individual. Just as in the
Septuagint, differences of style and of translator's procedure reveal
beyond doubt the hands of different workers. And indeed such a view
is neither novel nor radical; it was already advanced by Ephraem
Syrus, and by Jacob of Edessa, who lived through the second half of
the seventh century A.D. From such diverse beginning, then, the translation received in course of time the imprint of the scholarship of yet
other workers. Early in the fifth century, just about the time when
Jerome in Palestine was wrestling with the problems of the Latin
Bible, a noted Syrian scholar by the name of Rabbula, then Bishop
of Edessa, labored to bring out of the growing confusion of variant

Syriac texts one authoritative Bible for his people. More than two centuries later, Jacob of Edessa spent nine years in revising the Peshitta Old Testament with the help of the Greek versions.

Of the Septuagintal origin of one Syriac translation there is no doubt whatever. That is the so-called Syro-Hexaplar version, already mentioned. Bishop Paul of Tella on his way to Egypt examined Origen's Hexapla, which after the lapse of more than three centuries since the death of its author was still in the library in Caesarea; then in the course of the two following years, A.D. 616-617, he made a Syriac translation of its fifth column—that is, it will be recalled, of Origen's revised text with his critical marks inserted. These marks Bishop Paul copied carefully into his Syriac version; further, his translation was very literal. For both reasons, it is of immense value to present-day scholars in their study of the Hexapla.

The contents of the Syriac Old Testament cover about the same ground as the Hebrew text. Its number of books is twenty-two; but their arrangement varies considerably in different manuscripts. The version current among the Nestorian branch of the Syrian church lacked Chronicles, as did that among the Jacobites at Edessa. But this book is found in the manuscripts of the sixth century, though with a division in most of them at II Chronicles 6:1. Esther is not found in the Nestorian version, nor is Ezra-Nehemiah in that of the Jacobites. In this latter, too, Esther, Judith, Ruth, and Susanna form "the Book of the Women." The order of books resembles that in the Septuagint more than that in the Hebrew Bible. One is thus led to suspect that here as well as in the text as we now have it, Septuagintal influence was operative. In addition to the regular books of the Septuagint and the Hebrew, complete Syriac manuscripts, like the Codex Ambrosianus, contain the Apocalypse of Baruch, IV Esdras, and IV and V Maccabees.

Manuscripts of the Peshitta fall into two great classes, eastern and western, corresponding to the great schism that rent the Syrian church in the sixth century. The eastern, or Nestorian, manuscripts are in general more valuable, since their text has been less influenced by the great popularity of the Septuagint in Mediterranean lands. The total extant manuscripts of the version, of both classes, are of considerable number. One of the finest collections is in the British Museum; it was obtained mainly in 1842 from the monastery of St. Mary Deipara, which is situated in the Nitrian desert in Egypt. In this collection there is a manuscript of Genesis, Exodus, Numbers, and Deuteronomy which bears a date corresponding to 464 A.D.; it is the earliest date on any known manuscript of the Bible. There is also a manuscript from the sixth century containing Isaiah, the Psalms, and other important books. The large number of other manuscripts in the collection, of both eastern and western Syrian origin, together cover practically the entire Old Testament and the Apocrypha. Cambridge University has several manuscripts of high importance, among them the great "Buchanan Bible" of the twelfth century that was brought from India, although apparently its ultimate origin was somewhere near Syria. It is a complete Bible; it has both Old and New Testaments and the Apocrypha, although the manuscript is much damaged by the course of the years. An Italian treasure is the Codex Ambrosianus, of Milan as the name implies; it dates probably from the sixth century, and contains the entire Old Testament. It was published in a photo-lithographic edition in 1876-78. A competent scholar has adjudged it our most valuable authority for the Peshitta text of the Old Testament. The Preface to the Psalter in this manuscript says that the Psalms were translated from the Palestinian language into Hebrew and thence into Greek, from which the Syriac translation was made. It is of interest that a British Museum manuscript, Codex Rich, makes the same claim in regard to the entire Syriac Old Testament, adding, however, that the Greek text employed for the translation of the Psalter was that of Symmachus. In this connection it may be remarked that one of the notable features of the Syriac Psalter is the freedom with which the superscriptions are omitted or changed—owing, it is thought, to the influence of Theodore of Mopsuestia, a very original and vigorous scholar of Asia Minor about the early fifth century A.D. There are several Peshitta manuscripts in this country also, notably in Union Theological Seminary and in Harvard University, where among others, it is said, there is "an old and excellent manuscript of the Historical Books and the Wisdom of the Old Testament." The Oriental Institute of the University of Chicago possesses a fragment of the Pentateuch from the sixth or seventh century that contains Exodus 14:21 to Leviticus 25:48.

The critical value of the Peshitta is not small. It was an original translation from the Hebrew, and, even though later worked over and edited in the light of Septuagintal readings, its basic quality as an independent translation persists. It is of uneven value, however, since different books were the work of different translators; still it maintains a somewhat median level. It does not reach the high standard of excellence of the Septuagint in its best parts, nor does it fall to the depths of some of the poorest parts of that version. Its readings almost always give good sense, which, if not found in the original, have been touched up from tradition or some other source. The freedom of the translators in the changing of suffixes and paradigm forms violates a modern critic's ideas of exactness. The dependence of the Peshitta on the Septuagint is often a difficulty in textual study. Where both of them are against the Hebrew, it may be that the Syriac is merely a transcript of the Septuagint, and thus the weight of authority of the two readings is greatly reduced.

The Syriac Pentateuch, like that of the Septuagint, is a fair translation of the Hebrew text. Ruth is a paraphrase, Job is quite literal, while Chronicles is expository. Almost all the separate books of the Old Testament have been carefully studied, and their critical value has been estimated in monographs published by various scholars of modern times.

Nonetheless, basic critical work on the Peshitta still waits to be done. In brief, we do not possess a dependable text of the version. The known manuscripts differ, as is the way of manuscripts; and most printed editions are quite uncritical, and misleading in that their fixity attributes to them an authority which they in no way merit. Publication began in 1625, when the Psalter was brought out by Gabriel Sionita, a Maronite, who while widely read in his own native Syriac literature was seriously lacking in qualifications demanded for his difficult task. Although his work has been variously evaluated—it is even charged that he did not take the task seriously, and that he was careless —yet it should be borne in mind that methods of handling ancient texts have greatly developed since the seventeenth century. Unfortunately, however, he based his work upon a manuscript which has been adjudged "the worst of all known manuscripts of the Peshitta"; it has been described as "unfortunate both in its birth and in its bringing up. From the first it contained more errors due to homoioteleuton than any other manuscript here cited; and it was afterward revised by an editor who made corrections in the text and supplied omissions in the margin on a large scale often without any manuscript authority whatever." Decidedly a bad beginning for our printed texts of the Syriac Bible! For the fact is that until recently all subsequent editions of the Peshitta have used but slightly revised recensions of Sionita's text.

However, in this same year Thomas Erpinius of Leiden likewise completed a text of the Psalms which he says he edited from "two very ancient manuscripts." Only one of these has been since identified; it is not at all "very ancient," but only of the fourteenth century. Nonetheless, Erpinius' text has received commendation for its "goodness."

Sionita's Psalter was republished in the Paris Polyglot, for which he edited the complete text of the Peshitta Old Testament; it appeared in volumes six to nine, 1632-45. Then Brian Walton took it over in his London Polyglot of 1657. Several important Syriac manuscripts had in the meantime come into the possession of English scholars, but for some strange reason Walton did not employ them to make a thorough revision. He published a sort of excursus containing a lengthy critical apparatus for the Syriac, but the real contribution of working this into the printed text was not made. Indeed, it is said that Walton's text is really worse than Sionita's, having introduced a number of fresh errors.

And so the matter stood until 1823, when the British and Foreign Bible Society brought out a new edition, the work of Professor Samuel Lee. By this time a wealth of good manuscripts was available; in addition the works of Syrian church fathers were known, and Lee recognized their value as evidence on the Peshitta text. But the result has proved disappointing. He showed uncritical judgment in his use of the Syriac fathers, notably of Barhebraeus. Still worse, he employed the Polyglot text as the basis of his work, and left the worst of Sionita's mistakes uncorrected. Competent scholars have accordingly dismissed his results as "essentially a reprint of the text of the Paris and London Polyglots."

In 1852 another edition appeared, the work of an American missionary, Reverend Justin Perkins. It was printed at Urumia in Iran. For his text he made use of materials collected during his missionary work in the East, and in many points it is an improvement on previous editions. In particular the Psalter is excellent; "the text is not perfect, but it seems to be as near perfection as that of the best MSS." But elsewhere the text is heavily dependent on Lee's; in fact Chronicles has been taken over *in toto*. As a general judgment, then, the Urumia Peshitta is not regarded more highly than Lee's text and that of the Polyglots.

In 1861 P. de Lagarde issued an edition of the Apocrypha. Then twenty-six years later the Dominicans of Mosul published a Peshitta containing both the Old and New Testaments. It had however a sectarian, rather than a scholarly, purpose; the Catholic missionaries wished to free their communicants from dependence upon the Urumia Bible with its Protestant origin. Nothing has been made public as to the sources employed, and no claim is made for a critical value in the edition. Its purposes are purely "practical." In 1877 an edition of the Psalter had been issued, likewise at Mosul, by Bishop Joseph David. Presumably it was incorporated into the complete Peshitta of 1887 and merits the same comment.

In 1892 an "apparatus criticus to Chronicles in the Peshitta version" was published by W. E. Barnes, who likewise brought out in 1904 an edition of "The Peshitta Psalter according to the West Syrian Text," which was the first critical printing of any part of the Syriac Bible. Barnes does not claim to have done exhaustive work with his sources. "So great, indeed," he says, "is the mass of material that a selection had to be made." Accordingly, he chose ten manuscripts that seemed best suited, and checked occasional readings in four others. Nonetheless, the edition is of very high importance as the first really critical text to be published. Yet we must note that Barnes did not aim at establishing the original text of the Syriac Psalter; it was only the West Syrian recension of that text which he published. It will doubtless be of great value to the editor who undertakes the larger task, but in itself it is but a step toward that end. Barnes's text was republished with slight alterations by the British and Foreign Bible Society in 1914. In the same year they brought out also an edition of the Pentateuch, based on the Lee text but re-edited by Barnes, Charles W. Mitchell, and John Pinkerton. Whether the Old Testament will now be completed in the difficult conditions of postwar days remains to be seen.

A unique publication of the Peshitta was undertaken by the Jewish scholar, Chaim Heller; he set himself to bring it out in Hebrew characters for the use of Jewish readers who do not know Syriac. Genesis was published in Berlin in 1928 and Exodus in 1929, but unfortunately nothing further has appeared. Heller has used the Lee text but claims to have taken account of "all the different readings in other types of the Peshitta." In the copious notes appended on each page he has adduced also the evidence of the Samaritan sources, the Jewish Targums, the Greek versions, the Vulgate, the Arabic, and the Kennicot and De Rossi collations of the Massoretic text.

Then the Oriental Institute of the University of Chicago, some few years after its founding, initiated a "Peshitta project" conceived on an ample scale. Critical texts of the Syriac fathers were first to be determined, and the evidence of these was then to be added to that of the best manuscripts of the Syriac Bible so as to establish a really authoritative critical text of the Peshitta. Much work was done on Barsalibi and Barhebraeus. In 1931 an edition of *Barhebraeus' Scholia on the Old Testament; Part 1, Genesis-II Samuel* was published, with critical apparatus. But there the project encountered obstacles, and presently it came to a standstill before ever the problem of the text of the Peshitta was reached.

But the need of a dependable text of the Peshitta continued a prime issue of critical Old Testament study. It found expression in the Congress of the International Organization of Old Testament Scholars in Copenhagen in August, 1953. A committee was appointed, with Professor D. Winton Thomas of Cambridge as chairman, to consider plans, and to make a beginning on the undertaking prior to the following meeting of the Congress three years later.

CHAPTER VII

The Targums

THE peoples of Syria in pre-Christian times, we have seen, were Arameans, and their language is known as Aramaic; it was closely related to Hebrew. The Arameans had migrated out of the Arabian desert sometime before the middle of the second millennium B.C.; they settled wherever they could establish themselves all around the Fertile Crescent, and by the eleventh century were in the process of building up important states in Syria. The Arameans with whom we are most familiar in Old Testament story are those who had their center in Damascus; in our common translations they are inaccurately called Syrians. Aramaic written material of one sort or another takes us all the way back to the eighth century B.C. A couple of Aramaic words are quoted in Genesis 31:47, but the earliest Old Testament mention of the language by name is in the story of Sennacherib's attack on Jerusalem, when the Judean officials requested the Assyrian emissaries to speak in Aramaic (II Kings 18:26).

With the passing of the great empires of Mesopotamia, Aramaic spread rapidly, and the Jewish exiles there in course of time found themselves obliged to adopt it as their native tongue. In Palestine the Aramaic triumph was slower, yet it made headway, in part, no doubt, through the influence of Babylonian Jewry but partly also because the Hebrew-speaking community had been dealt a very heavy blow in the catastrophe of 586 B.C. It is difficult to say how largely the language had become the common speech of Palestine at any point in the last centuries B.C. The public reading of the law by Ezra (Nehemiah 8:1-8) is sometimes cited as evidence that Hebrew had passed out of general use; for it is related that as Ezra read, interpreters moved about among the audience explaining the meaning of the words, that is, supposedly, translating the Hebrew into Aramaic. But in reality the account may mean no more than that these men acted as Biblical expositors; they explained and applied the passages that were read. However, the prevalence of Aramaic among the common people, by the first century A.D., is apparent from the number of words and passages in this language quoted in the Gospels, as well as from Jewish sources representative of the usage of that time.

Still, Hebrew lived on in Palestine as a language of common communication. The fact that the Book of Daniel, dating in large part from the second century B.C., has a large Aramaic section in an otherwise Hebrew book is typical of the whole mixed situation. We remember that when Paul addressed the mob in the Temple after his arrest he "spoke in the Hebrew language"; yet whatever one might wish to deduce from this phrase is qualified by the consideration that the word *gabbatha* is described in John's Gospel as "Hebrew" (John 19:13). The matter is clarified rather from the Jewish sources, which show that Hebrew continued as a living language, not merely a literary relic in the schools, until the final disaster to Jewish national life in the collapse of the revolt of Bar Cochba. But side by side with it, Aramaic was also a colloquial tongue dominant in Galilee and among Babylonian Jews whose pilgrimages to Jerusalem had considerable influence in advancing the language. These facts provide a clue to the astonishing events of the Day of Pentecost: "Parthians and Medes and Elamites" and the rest—they were all Jews, and would readily understand Aramaic even when spoken with a Galilean accent (Acts 2:7-12).

This centuries-long process carried an inevitable consequence. Just as in Egypt and elsewhere, the Jewish communities came gradually to need a translation of their Scriptures into the vernacular tongue. There is every reason to believe that such translation came about unofficially, and even sporadically, various small communities falling naturally into the habit of interpreting and of orally translating Scripture passages into the common language. These Aramaic translations are called Targums (a late Hebrew and Aramaic word meaning translation; there is a sense in which it would not be inaccurate to speak of the Septuagint as the first of the Targums). In the nature of the situation, it is idle to attempt a dating of the beginnings of these Aramaic translations, but certainly they lie well back in the pre-Christian centuries.

The Targums, then, were at first extemporaneous renderings employed in the synagogue services along with the Hebrew scriptures. Much homiletic material would obviously be included, and so the Targums as we know them are a combination of real translation with a considerable bulk of exegetical paraphrase and other matter aimed at religious instruction. Rules were presently evolved for the guidance of the translator; in the synagogue service only one verse of the Pentateuch was to be read from the Hebrew before its Aramaic rendering, but in the Prophets three verses might be so read. It is apparent that these extemporary renderings would presently fall into somewhat fixed form and, through the course of years, by their repetition as the appropriate Sabbath came round would become stereotyped into a somewhat uniform, if still only oral, Targum.

It is not known when the translations were first committed to writing. Certain traditions would push the process back into pre-Christian times. It is notable that some quotations in the New Testament, e.g., Matthew 27:46 citing Psalm 22:1, accord with readings of the Targums, yet this may indicate no more than the persistence of the oral tradition. The first mention of a written Targum is found in a report (Bab. Shab. 115:1) that a Targum of Job was confiscated in the first century A.D. The Jewish authorities would not permit the use of written Targums at that time for synagogue services, but there was no ban on them for private study. The Targum of Job was evidently of this latter sort. It is thought that Job could not have been the first of all the important Old Testament books to appear in this form, and hence that there must have been written translations of other books long before this time. But the Targums in their present form are of much later date; notwithstanding a large part of their total represents an ancient tradition. Formerly the view prevailed that the fourth or fifth century A.D. is the earliest date to which they can be ascribed. But more recently attention has been drawn to genuine ancient features and historic allusions indicative of a much greater age and rendering it highly probable that the Targums as we know them are to be linked up with pre-Christian written translations, themselves in turn the crystallization of a very long oral tradition. The written Targums continued to receive accretions through many centuries until their text was at length officially determined, as that of the

Hebrew Scriptures had been long before. It is this later material that is commonly cited in support of the usual dating, which however relates not to the original writing but to the final form of the text. A fact of importance is that fragments of a Palestinian Targum that date from as early as the sixth century A.D. were found among the genizah documents; but obviously these are far from original copies, hence have little relevance for the problem of the beginnings of the written Targum.

The great Targums, on the Pentateuch and on the Prophets, attained final form in the Babylonian academies not before the fifth century A.D., and became the officially approved translations. But acceptance in Palestine was slow, partly because of the rivalry between the Babylonian and the Palestinian schools and partly because Palestinian Jews had already their own Targum, sanctioned by centuries of use. Not until the ninth century did these Babylonian Targums establish themselves in the West; and the astonishing fact is that by that time they had lost their original *raison d'être*, for the success of Islam had made Arabic the language of the land. Their belated recognition was a part of the larger triumph of Babylonian Judaism in its contest through several centuries for intellectual and religious leadership of Judaism. The Babylonian Talmud and these Babylonian Targums stand together as symbols of a profound evolution in Judaism. Indeed, the Targums came into Palestinian life, not primarily as translations, but as the crystallization of correct interpretation, as it had been determined in the Babylonian academies.

There are several Targums. They group themselves according to the divisions of the Hebrew Bible: Targums on the Pentateuch, on the Prophets, and on the Writings.

The Pentateuchal Targums are three; in order of importance they are the Targum of Onkelos, the Jerusalem Targum (also known as the pseudo-Jonathan Targum), and the Fragmentary Targum. The Targum of Onkelos is that to which reference was made just now; it is sometimes called quite properly the Babylonian Targum. The identity of this Onkelos has long been discussed; the similarity of the name to that of Aquila, the author of the very literal Greek translation of the Old Testament, has repeatedly inspired attempts to equate the two individuals. And indeed tradition would lend support to the view, for according to the Babylonian Talmud he was a proselyte who lived in the first century A.D. But this is of little significance. We have already seen the source of this Targum; the name is certainly a Hebraized form of Aquila, attached to it by the Babylonian scholars apparently with full intention of relating the translation to Aquila's Greek. As part of its official status, the Targum of Onkelos was equipped with a Massorah of its own, paralleling that for the Hebrew text. Commonly the translation is beautifully literal and simple. When the meaning is obscure some explanatory word or clause is interpolated. It is, as stated above, the official interpretation of the Hebrew text.

The Fragmentary Targum consists of only about 850 verses. Its language is the Aramaic of Palestine, and its form is paraphrastic. Formerly scholars believed it had originated in someone's intention to interpolate these verses into the Targum of Onkelos. But once again the genizah finds have contributed to the solution of a debated issue; the Fragmentary Targum, it becomes clear, is a remnant of the old Palestinian Targum.

The Jerusalem Targum is also called the Palestine Targum; this is a natural contradistinction to the epithet of the Targum of Onkelos, but also it indicates the real origin of the work. For the Jerusalem Targum has evolved out of the old Targum of Palestine. It has preserved much of the expository material that characterized the latter, while the actual translation is close to that of Onkelos—apparently substituted for an older rendering. Thus the text is replete with popular stories and marginal notes that have grown up around the text in the course of centuries. The Targum is practically complete, lacking only about a dozen verses. It is sometimes referred to as the Targum of Jonathan on the Pentateuch, that is, pseudo-Jonathan, since the real Targum of Jonathan is the well-known translation of the prophets. The source of the confusion is apparent. The abbreviation "Targum J." was erroneously read "Targum Jonathan" by reason of the familiarity of the latter name.

The Targum of Onkelos was first published, without vowels, at Bologna in A.D. 1482, and with vowels in 1491. The first edition of the Fragmentary Targum was issued in Venice in 1517, and the first printing of the Jerusalem Targum appeared in Venice in 1591.

The Targum to the Prophets is attributed to Jonathan ben Uzziel, a pupil of Hillel in the first half of the first century A.D. But this again is only window dressing. As pointed out above, it continues the Targum of Onkelos and was produced by the Babylonian schools; like Onkelos it came to an official fixity not before the fifth century. A subtle relation to the Onkelos translation has been pointed out in that the name Jonathan is the Hebrew equivalent of Theodotion; the Jewish scholars in Babylonia apparently by this means undertook to tell their public that these two Aramaic translations stood in the same relation to the Hebrew text as the familiar Greek versions of Aquila and Theodotion. These relationships serve to characterize the Targum. It resembles that of Onkelos but is more free. Especially in the poetic books it commonly avoids difficulties by paraphrase. Occasionally a passage like Hosea 1:3 is turned wholly aside from its proper meaning and is devoted to moralizing on Israel's career. Likewise Isaiah 5:1 f. is not translated at all, but is interpreted. Ancient geographical names are sometimes changed into those in use in the translator's time; thus Shinar becomes Babel, No (or No-Amon) is changed to Alexandria, etc.

This Targum was first printed at Leiria, Portugal, in A.D. 1494, with the Hebrew text and a rabbinical commentary.

Most of the Targums on the Hagiographa are comparatively late in origin. Some of them seem to have arisen even after the need for such paraphrases had ceased, their earliest mention being in the eleventh century. But the tradition of the existence of a Targum of the Book of Job in the first century A.D. has already been mentioned, and one on the Psalms also was known then, for Jesus quoted from it as he hung on the cross (Matt. 27:46; Mark 15:34). These two books are much alike in their translation. But about fifty verses in Job and a lesser number in Psalms have a double translation, and half a dozen of these in Job have actually a third rendering. These additional translations were apparently added by some interpolator in the eighth or ninth century for his language is late and artificial and his style imitative. Proverbs stands alone among the Targums, with a strange mixture of Aramaic and Syriac. It is thought to have been made, not entirely from the Hebrew, but in large part from the Syriac version, for about one-third of it is almost identical with the latter.

The Targums on the Megilloth ("Rolls," that is, Song of Songs,

Ruth, Lamentations, Ecclesiastes, and Esther) are, in varying degrees, paraphrases rather than translations. They abound in citations of historical parallels, reasons are given for the occurrence of certain events, words are philologically explained, etc. Ecclesiastes, Esther, and Song of Songs almost touch the limits in paraphrastic freedom. There are indeed two Targums on Esther, consistent with the high popularity of the book among the Jews. Both are highly "midrashic," but more than half of the first of them is taken up with legends about Solomon, the Queen of Sheba, etc. All these Targums were probably the work of different men.

Targums on Chronicles were unknown until after the publication of the Polyglot Bibles. Two very imperfect texts were discovered and published, one in 1680-83, the other in 1715; they are believed to have originated in the eighth and ninth centuries. Of Daniel, Ezra, and Nehemiah no known Targums exist.

Much work has been done in investigation of the Targums in recent years, and editions of some of them have been published. Paul de Lagarde printed the Reuchlin manuscript of the Targum of the Prophets in 1872, and the following year the Targums of the Hagiographa. In 1884 Abraham Berliner brought out the Targum of Onkelos with notes; in 1899 Moses Ginsburger did the same for the Fragmentary Targum, and in 1903 for Pseudo-Jonathan. Alexander Sperber has been engaged for some years on preparation of an edition of the Targum on the Prophets. He has as yet, however, published only specimens of his work, in 1927 and 1945. With the latter of these he expressed the confident belief "that as soon as the world returns to normalcy again" he would be "in a position to publish the Targum and even on a broader basis than hitherto planned, covering the entire Bible." But for the present, the most convenient source for a complete, if uncritical, text of the Targums still remains the various editions of the "rabbinic" Bible, *Mikra'oth Gedholoth*.

The study of these ancient translations yet offers large scope for investigation; in certain cases not even basic questions have been settled. Or to put it the other way, our ignorance of the Targums is still impressive! The homiletic motivation in their creation, the seeming looseness in their methods of translation, and the late date commonly attributed to their origin seem to rob them of much of their value for text criticism. Yet such disparagement can be carried too far. We have already spoken of the long period covered by their evolution, so that their older parts must be conceded a considerable antiquity. Further, to dismiss them as loose paraphrases is a course more cavalier than the obvious facts will support. For the worth of Targumic testimony to the Hebrew text is freely recognized in a large number of passages. What is needed is a sound understanding of the methods of these ancient paraphrasing translators and a discerning application of their evidence to our textual problems. But apart from this the Targums merit a wider knowledge than they now enjoy, for they are a rich storehouse of Jewish religious thought and Biblical exegesis through many centuries.

CHAPTER VIII

Other Eastern Versions
of the Old Testament

CHRISTIANITY was not limited in its adherents to the peoples who bordered on the Mediterranean seacoast. Many important races whose boundaries lay next the coast peoples' embraced the teachings of this growing, new religion. One result was that soon there came a need for the Bible to be translated into the various native tongues of the believers. Local scholars soon arose to perform this important task, so that each people sooner or later possessed a copy of the Bible in its own language. Most of these translations were made from the Septuagint, which, we have seen, was the great Bible of the ancient Mediterranean lands. The vigorous activity in our own day of translating the Bible for peoples who have never had it provides a vantage point from which to understand the great importance of all these ancient Bibles for their original readers. Without disparaging this, we use such versions more prosaically for the evidence they offer in textual criticism. With this objective we estimate their worth on the basis of several questions, such as: Who was the translator? How well equipped was he for that great work? From what version of the Bible did he translate? How faithfully has he translated the text before him? Did he use more than one version as the basis of his translation? Did he take undue liberty with the text before him? We can scarcely expect an answer to all these questions, but enough can usually be found to help us estimate, at least approximately, the value that we are to attach to these versions relative to the English Bible of today.

Christianity came early to Egypt. The story of the Ethiopan eunuch (Acts 8:27-39) carries an implication of the spread of the new faith to the lower, not less than the upper, valley of the Nile within the early days of the apostolic preaching. Eusebius indeed reports a belief current in his time that St. Mark preached in Alexandria. In any case, the geographic proximity of Egypt to Palestine, with intercourse that had continued from remote antiquity, renders it probable almost to the point of certainty that Christian groups were established in Egypt in the first century. Yet we lack definite record of this. The Book of Acts, except for a very few minor allusions, is concerned with the spread of the church north and west. And authentic sources of the Egyptian church itself take us no farther back than the fourth quarter of the second century, by which time the church in Alexandria was a strong and thriving body, and Christianity had spread into Upper Egypt at least as far as the Fayum.

This omission by the official record of the apostolic age is the more astonishing in view of the greatness which the Egyptian church presently attained. Ptolemy Philadelphus in the third century B.C. "builded better than he knew" when he established the famous library and museum at Alexandria, for by this means he assured an intellectual leadership by the city of Alexandria that was to continue for nearly a thousand years and to provide a broad base for the achievements of the Christian church there. The Christian catechetical school, Clement and Origen, who were successively its leaders, Athanasius, Cyril, Monophysite Christology, the copying of the great Vaticanus and Sinaiticus manuscripts—these are just a few terms of various categories that suggest far-reaching implications as to the vast contribution of the church in Egypt to the history of Christianity.

Yet these names imply, and correctly, a sort of foreign intrusion into Egyptian life for which again we must give credit or blame to the dynasty of the Ptolemies; for they were Greek-speaking Macedonians. Greek became the language of officialdom and of the intelligentsia in Alexandria. And the early Egyptian church was Greek. This is apparent from its use of and critical work upon the Septuagint, from the writings of Clement and of Origen, and perhaps more "romantically" from the Christian papyri unearthed about the beginning of this century at Oxyrhynchus, of which possibly the most famous are the fragments containing the "Sayings of Jesus."

But Christianity did not remain a prerogative of the educated classes. A vigorous native church presently arose; of such simple Christians we have archaeological evidence from the second century. Greek was their language likewise, but native Egyptians were soon found within the church. Especially in the third century the movement spread notably among them. And it was this indigenous Christianity that made one of the distinctive contributions to the character of the whole movement through many centuries. That was the practice of asceticism and the development of the monastic life. The geography of Egypt gives a clue to this feature, as to many others in the long history of the country. The proximity everywhere of the desert provided a refuge to which apparently fugitives could flee, and in which Christians, as historic fact, did find sanctuary during some of the severe persecutions that befell the church in the early centuries of its history. The names of Antony in the latter part of the third century, prominently associated with the first impulse to Christian monasticism, and of Pachom a little later, who was the first to organize these solitary ascetics into incipient monastic orders, will suffice for our present purpose. Of these names, Pachom is certainly Egyptian; but of the linguistic composition of these earliest monastic groups we know little. It is related, however, that a certain Alexandrian journeyed "up into the Thebaid" to visit Pachom, but since he knew only Greek he found it necessary to learn "the Theban tongue." We hear of the activities of the ascetics, both the solitary and the communal, in reciting Psalms and other religious literature, but to our disappointment nothing is said of the version of the Bible employed. It is better than a guess, however, that for a considerable time they used the Septuagint. Yet the pressure for a vernacular rendering of the Scriptures which we have had occasion to remark many times already was felt here also. In particular, the monastic organization of Pachom implies strongly the existence of a native version, for he lays emphasis on Bible reading; yet the location of his group, well to the south in Upper Egypt, renders it highly probable that a considerable number of his monks knew no Greek. And actually there has been preserved a Coptic (i.e., Egyptian) Biblical codex which is dated "not later than the middle of the fourth century A.D.," that is, well within the lifetime of Pachom; and the scope of its contents—Deuteronomy, Jonah, and Acts—indicates clearly that the version was already of some age. Indeed, competent scholars date the translation into Coptic about the middle of the third century, and some would even draw it back into the second.

Coptic was not linguistically uniform. The long, narrow valley of the Nile favored the evolution of dialects, and of these, five have been distinguished; they are Akhmimic, sub-Akhmimic, Sahidic, Fayumic, and Bohairic. The two first are of minor relevance. Of the others, the Biblical remains in Sahidic are the most important, in part because of their bulk but still more because of their greater antiquity and of the study they have received at the hands of modern scholars. The date given above for the Coptic translation refers to the Sahidic. The importance of a vernacular translation at this early date gave prestige to the dialect and favored its spread through the valley. But apparently in reaction against this, other translations, notably Akhmimic, were produced sometime about the fourth century. Their duration, however, must have been brief. It is said that in the fifth century Sahidic had established itself as the literary language throughout Upper Egypt and presumably was making notable headway as the spoken language also. In any case, by the eleventh century, according to the testimony of Athanasius of Kos, the minor dialects had disappeared, for he knows of only Sahidic and Bohairic.

The translation of the Bible into this latter dialect was later than the Sahidic by an undetermined period variously estimated from one to four centuries. However, its position as the speech of the Delta, in its western part at least, and the growing importance of the church in Alexandria gave it an immense advantage. But in A.D. 641 the Arabs conquered Egypt and thereby sealed the doom of the native dialects. Increasingly Arabic became the common language of the land, and Coptic receded slowly but inevitably into the role of a religious tongue. Apparently this process had become complete before the eleventh century, when the patriarch, long since cut off from communion with the church of the west by the Egyptian Monophysite heresy, removed his seat from Alexandria to Cairo. He carried southward with him the translation into Bohairic, which presently became established as the sacred language of the Coptic church and has so continued to the present. Indeed it remained a living speech even into the nineteenth century and is understood and slightly used by small groups to the present. Sahidic also survived the Arabic conquest for several centuries in the relative seclusion of southern Egypt that offered sanctuary for the Christian church. By a strange caprice of history these groups made use of the ruins of the ancient Egyptian temples for their Christian worship, and have left their graffitic inscriptions on walls and pillars where centuries before the might and glory of Amon had been piously celebrated. The Coptic church still lives, with significant promise for a land once again experiencing one of the cultural revivals that have marked its long history. But Coptic has ceased as a living tongue.

Bohairic attracted scholarly attention in the seventeenth century. Walton ignored it in his comprehensive survey of Oriental versions, but Psalm 1 in this dialect was published in 1663 at Leiden. The Pentateuch was issued at Oxford in 1731, and the Psalter at Rome in 1744. But the first notice of Sahidic was the publication of a grammar in 1778. Eleven years later a fragment of John's Gospel in middle Egyptian appeared. All these were followed by an interest, and an activity in publication that continue to the present.

Sahidic manuscripts in varying degrees of fragmentary condition date all the way from the fourth century to the twelfth or thirteenth. The bulk of them discovered and published in recent years constitute an important contribution to Biblical textual study. A remarkable feature of these manuscripts is the accuracy of their preservation. It is pointed out that the remains of Deuteronomy, Jonah, and Acts which we possess from the fourth century are "in precise agreement" with texts of eight centuries later. Notwithstanding the relatively large number of known manuscripts, practically all more or less incomplete, however, we do not possess the entire text of the Sahidic Old Testament. Most of the Pentateuch has been preserved, the larger part of Joshua, Judges, and Ruth, the Books of Samuel, fragments of Kings, the greater part of Isaiah, smaller parts of the other prophets, but practically complete texts of Psalms, Proverbs, Job, Ecclesiastes, Esther, and Song of Songs. Only fragments of Lamentations are known, and of Chronicles and Ezra-Nehemiah nothing at all. The textual evidence of the Sahidic version is most notable in the Book of Job, where it omits some 376 lines or half-lines now in our Hebrew text, and in Hexaplaric recensions of the Septuagint. But the meaning of this situation is not easily discerned. Some would say that these passages are thus shown to be late intrusions into the Hebrew; others take the position that the Sahidic has been conformed to Origen's results by omission of material that he marked with an asterisk. The issue is complicated by the features of Hebrew poetry which seem to demand the presence of some at least of these suspected passages in the original poem. Altogether the evidence of the Sahidic has bestowed upon us a first-rate textual problem!

In the Bohairic dialect more complete manuscripts have been preserved. The Pentateuch, the Prophets, Job, the Psalms are practically complete, and fragmentary materials of other books are known. But Biblical texts in the middle Egyptian dialects are very few and in general fragmentary. It has indeed been suggested that a complete Bible never existed; the prevalence of Greek through the region rendered a native Bible unnecessary until after the rise of Monophysite theology in 431. The most important extant materials are of the minor prophets and Proverbs, though some fragments of Exodus also are known.

The beginnings of Christianity in Ethiopia—now called Abyssinia —are obscure. For the date of its introduction, the source whence it came, and the identity of its earliest evangelists we are dependent on native traditions. These point, on one hand, to the vigorous Christianity of Antioch as the mother church of Ethiopian evangelism, a theory that receives considerable corroboration from certain features of the Ethiopic Bible; on the other hand, the Ethiopic Book of Saints tells of two brothers "from the country of the Greeks" who were taken captive in Ethiopia and remained there for many years preaching and teaching Christianity. When at length they departed, one of them, by name Frumentius, went to Alexandria where he was ordained bishop by Athanasius and sent back to continue his work. His memory is piously preserved in the title Abba Salama. But in reality there is no contradiction in the two accounts. Earliest knowledge of Christianity may well have come from Syria, but then Frumentius could well have done essentially the work attributed to him, in particular the organization of the Ethiopic church.

It seems clear, however, that a Christian king ruled in Ethiopia in the middle of the fifth century; indeed there is evidence that he became a convert in the course of his reign. Soon, if not immediately, Christianity was established as the state religion of the land, and the monarchs made themselves vigorous champions of the faith. Through the centuries prior to the rise of Islam, close relations were established with the church in Egypt and by this means the monastic organization of Pachom spread into Ethiopia, as well as considerable Egyptian Christian literature. Most important of this, and obviously one of the first books to be introduced, was the Bible. This was apparently the Septuagint version, which in spite of the existence already of some parts of the Sahidic translation was still the Bible of Egypt. Such seems to be the best interpretation of our evidence, confused and contradictory as it sometimes is. Some scholars have advanced the opinion that the translation was made from Origen's Hexapla; some claim a direct dependence on the Hebrew text. But whatever its source, an Ethiopic translation was begun in the latter part of the fifth century, apparently promoted by the zeal of the new royal converts. We know nothing of the order and course of the work of translation, but only that it seems to have been completed by A.D. 678, the date ascribed to the version of Ecclesiasticus.

The upheaval of the entire Near East resulting from the spread of Islam entailed in Abyssinia a period of confusion and disorder lasting from the seventh to the thirteenth century. Little is known of the history of the land through this time, but a negative result of the chaos is important for the Biblical student. No early manuscripts of the Ethiopic Bible have survived; the oldest known to us are of the latter part of the thirteenth century. Unfortunate as this may well be regarded, the value of the Ethiopic Bible for textual criticism is still further discounted by the fact that a number of revisions were carried through at various times subsequent to the cultural revival of the land about the fourteenth century. Naturally the unnamed scholars charged with this task made use of the available foreign versions of the time, notably the Peshitta and the Arabic translation; it is to their credit that they had recourse to the Massoretic text as well. But what was commendable for practical religious purposes has become for the critic a serious loss; for the resultant Ethiopic text is scarcely more valuable, as evidence of the Greek text from which the original translation was made in the fifth century A.D., than is Origen's Hexaplaric Septuagint for the Hebrew text of the third century B.C.

The languages of Abyssinia are more confusing than are the Coptic dialects. Old Ethiopic is known as Ge'ez. It is the language into which the translation we have been speaking about was made. But by about the tenth century it had become extinct as the medium of common intercourse; it lived on, even to this day, only as a sacred liturgical language. In its place the languages of northern Ethiopia are Tigré and Tigriña. Nonetheless Amharic, from southern Ethiopia, has become the national language. But along with it there are four other southern languages: merely to list their names, Harari, Guragué, Argobba, and Gafat. The last of these has now also become extinct, but several of the others subdivide into an incredible maze of dialects. Of Guragué it is said there are about twenty! Several of the languages have Biblical translations, of greater or less extent; in Gafat, for example, there is, so far as we know, nothing but a highly corrupt recension of the Song of Songs. Practically all these translations appear to have been made from the old Ethiopic, the most notable exception being the Gafat, which is a translation of the Amharic.

The Ethiopic canon differed from the Jewish. It omitted the Books of Ezra and Nehemiah, as well as the two Books of the Maccabees from the Apocrypha. On the other hand it included several apocalypses, some of which find no place even in the more liberal Jewish canon of Alexandria. It is to this fact that we are indebted for the recovery of the Book of Enoch, known for several centuries only in very imperfect Greek and Latin fragments, and the third Book of Baruch which apart from the Ethiopic has not survived at all.

It is estimated that outside of Abyssinia there are today about twelve hundred manuscripts of various parts of the Ethiopic Bible. Most of them are in Europe. The British Museum has a large collection acquired mainly at the time of the Abyssinian war in 1867. They give, however, the text of the late revision mentioned above. A considerable number of manuscripts also are in this country. How many there are in Abyssinia itself no one knows, but it seems probable that the number is large.

No complete Ethiopic Bible has ever been printed. The earliest edition of any part was a Psalter printed by Johannes Potkin in Rome in 1513; a second edition followed in 1518. The Psalms were included in the London Polyglot, as also the complete text of the New Testament. The first attempt at a critical edition, however, was the publication of the Octateuch by August Dillmann in 1853 and of Samuel and Kings in 1861-71. Another edition of the Octateuch, being the text of the Paris Codex with the variants of five other manuscripts, was brought out by J. Oscar Boyd in 1909-11. Oscar Löfgren has contributed two carefully collated editions, one of Daniel in 1927, the other of the minor prophets in 1930. S. A. B. Mercer's critical edition of Ecclesiastes appeared in 1931. The Gafat version of Canticles was published by Wolf Leslau in 1945, but whether it can be regarded as a critical edition, eminent though its scholarship obviously is, remains an open question; for its text is that of a single manuscript —but no other in this language is known to exist!

The Gothic Version: The Goths of Dacia in Europe invaded Cappadocia in the third century. Among the captives carried away were some Christians. Ulfilas was born in Dacia, of captive Christian parents, about A.D. 310. His sturdy, aggressive Christian character pushed him to the front, so that about 340 he was consecrated bishop either at Constantinople or at Antioch. After maintaining his bishopric in Dacia for seven years he was driven to Moesia, which was the region now included in Bulgaria and part of Yugoslavia. In this country Ulfilas translated the Bible into the language of the Goths, the captors of his parents. He is said to have invented the alphabet in which to write his translation, and thus the version takes on additional importance as the first written literature of the Goths. Indeed, it is "by several centuries the oldest specimen of Teutonic speech." Ulfilas' work was certainly done about the middle of the fourth century, for he died by 383.

A contemporary, Philostorgius, states that Ulfilas translated "all the books of the Scripture with the exception of the books of the Kings, which he omitted because they are a mere narrative of military exploits, and the Gothic tribes were especially fond of war." Only fragments of the Old Testament remain among the dozen or so known manuscripts of the Gothic version. These fragments include parts of Genesis 5, Psalm 52, and Nehemiah 5-7.

A study of the version shows that it is most closely related to the Lucian text of the Greek. This is as we would expect, since that recension of the Greek was current in Asia Minor during the century of Ulfilas' activity.

The Georgian Version, like the Gothic version, arose in the fifth or sixth century on the outskirts of Christianity. Armenian tradition ascribes it to the work of Mesrop, who is said to have invented the

Georgian alphabet. In the monastery at Mount Sinai there is a papyrus Psalter of this version from the seventh or eighth century, and a copy of the Gospels and a Psalter dated in the ninth century. A manuscript of the whole Bible, with some omissions in the Pentateuch, is now preserved in two volumes in the Iberian monastery on Mount Athos. Also a manuscript of the prophets at Jerusalem is ascribed to the eleventh century. The best printed edition seems to have been that issued at Moscow in 1743, in which, however, certain gaps in the Georgian original were filled by translation from the Slavonic Bible. Comparison of the different manuscripts shows that there have been frequent revisions and additions. This version, like the preceding, was doubtless made from the Greek, with possibly some influences from the Syriac. However, the lack of a critical edition prevents final decision upon such questions.

The Slavonic version was the Bible of one of the great races contiguous to the centers of Christianity in the early centuries. Its origin is not traced back of the ninth century. The work is attributed to two brothers, Cyril and Methodius, sons of a Greek nobleman, whose relations to Slavonic neighbors gave them a knowledge of that tongue. Their first efforts are thought to have been bent toward translating such parts of the Bible into the tongue of the Bulgarian Slavs as would be of most use in church services. Later, the whole Bible was so rendered. Some Slavic scholars maintain that the original Slavonic translation was in a dialect closely similar to the old Bulgarian.

Some of the manuscripts of this version date from the tenth or eleventh century. But the oldest manuscript of the whole Bible is very late, 1499, and is now at Moscow, known as the Codex Gennadius. Of the Old Testament manuscripts, the oldest are of the Psalter, reaching back to the eleventh or twelfth century. Special studies of several Old Testament books have been published in recent years; the interest being shown by native Slavic scholars is particularly encouraging. It seems probable that many important manuscripts still await publication and study.

The value of this version differs in different books of the Old Testament. The Pentateuch (the Law), the "Prophets" of the Jewish canonical division, the Psalter, Job, Ecclesiastes, Wisdom of Sirach, and Song of Songs were translated from the Greek by different persons. The Book of Esther was translated from Hebrew; Chronicles, Ezra, Nehemiah, and some others were translated from the Vulgate, just before the date of the Gennadius Codex of 1499. When critically edited, the version will thus provide a measure of textual evidence upon all three of these ancient Bibles.

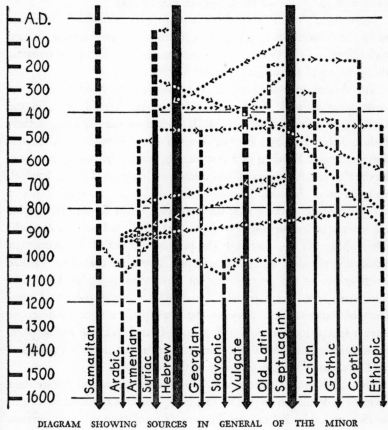

DIAGRAM SHOWING SOURCES IN GENERAL OF THE MINOR
EASTERN VERSIONS

The Armenian version was made for the Christian communities of eastern Asia Minor. An Armenian church is mentioned in the third century; apparently it was founded by Syrian Christians. The Armenian Bible seems to have been translated from the Septuagint somewhere about A.D. 400; but later revisers made use of the Syriac and perhaps the

Hebrew. It is noticeable that the chapters and verses of Jeremiah are arranged, not as in the Septuagint, but as in the Syriac and Hebrew. Where the Syriac and Hebrew differ, it usually follows the Hebrew. Such composite character of the Armenian version is thought to be due to the use of Origen's Hexaplar text, whose symbols now and then seem to find place in Armenian manuscripts.

It is claimed that this version is one of the most beautiful and accurate of all the versions. Its language is so closely allied, in grammar, syntax, and idioms, to the Greek that its renderings very faithfully transmit the meaning of the original text.

The Armenian Bible contains the books of the Septuagint in the same order up to I and II Esdras (where the latter is Ezra in the Greek); then Nehemiah (called III Esdras in the margin), Esther, Judith, Tobit, I, II and III Maccabees, Psalms, Proverbs, Ecclesiastes, Song of Songs, Wisdom of Solomon, Job, Isaiah, the twelve Prophets, Jeremiah, Baruch, Lamentations, Death of Jeremiah, Daniel, Ezekiel, and Death of Ezekiel. The following additional apocryphal books are found in the manuscripts: the Testament of the Twelve Patriarchs, the History of Joseph and his wife Asenath; and the Hymn of Asenath. These latter are not found in the printed editions of the Armenian Bible, nor are they in all manuscripts. There are also some further irregularities in the arrangement of these various books. Each Old Testament book has a preface containing an introduction and summary of contents. In addition to the usual preface some manuscripts have a special introduction, as a passage from David the Philosopher, from Athanasius, from Epiphanius of Cyprus. Daniel is a translation of Theodotion's version as found in the Septuagint.

Printed editions of the Armenian Bible appeared first at Amsterdam in 1666; in Venice in 1733. The first critical edition appeared in Venice in 1805, edited by Zohrab, on the basis of a collation of several manuscripts. A later edition appeared in Venice in 1860.

The great Arabic conquests of the seventh and eighth centuries A.D. entailed ultimately an Arabic Bible also. For while great numbers of the population bowed to the logic of events and became Moslems, the Jews remained faithful to their traditions, and the Christian churches lived on, though greatly depleted in numbers. In course of time the Arabic language established itself as the sacred tongue in a great belt of territory from the Atlantic eastward as far as India and the Malay archipelago; in varying dialects it became, and continues to this day, the vernacular speech of much of North Africa, of Egypt, Palestine, and Syria, and of Mesopotamia. In these latter lands the need of an Arabic Bible came to be felt. To some extent it may have been felt even before the triumphs of Islam, for there were Jews and Christians in Arabia before the time of Mohammed. Nevertheless, it was in the lands to which the language spread that the impulse toward an Arabic translation presently found expression. Indeed, the vitality of the impulse is evidenced by the diversity of such translations as came into existence. An Arabic translation from the Coptic version of the Septuagint is extant, and there are several manuscripts of an Arabic translation of the Samaritan Pentateuch. However, the Arabic Bible proper began in the tenth century. The Pentateuch was translated by Saadya, the Gaon, who was born in the Fayum in Upper Egypt in A.D. 892 but early removed to Babylonia, where he became head of one of the great Jewish schools and the most famous Jew of his time. His death occurred in A.D. 942. His translation was made, obviously, from the Hebrew, as was the Book of Joshua likewise. But Judges, Samuel, Kings, Chronicles, and Job were rendered from the Peshitta, and the prophets, Psalms, and Proverbs from the Septuagint. It was this strange mixture that was found by the editors of the Polyglots in an Egyptian manuscript of the sixteenth century and employed by them for their edition.

It will be recognized then that the Arabic version possesses little value for the textual critic. Even the translations direct from the Hebrew were made in a period long subsequent to the official fixing of the text, and indeed are almost contemporary with our great early Hebrew manuscripts. Still less do the Arabic Bibles current in recent times concern the critic. They possess many excellent qualities, their wide use throughout the lands of the Near East makes them cultural documents of high importance, but they fall completely within the class of modern Bible translations, of which the Bible societies now report a total well over a thousand. A translation from the Vulgate, made by Sarkis er Rizzi, Maronite Bishop of Damascus in 1620 and first published in 1671 in Rome, enjoyed a considerable popularity when it was adopted by the British and Foreign Bible Society and used by the first Protestant missionaries to Syria. Yet its defects became so apparent that in 1848 a new translation, direct from the Hebrew and Greek, was undertaken jointly by the American Mission in Syria and the American Bible Society. On August 22, 1864, the translation was finished, and on March 10 in the following year it was issued from the press. The Jesuit fathers in Beirut also realized the necessity of a modern translation; and on November 12, 1876, the first part of their Arabic Bible was authorized, to be followed shortly by the two remaining parts. A remarkable feature is that this, like the translation by the Protestant missionaries, was made direct from the Hebrew and Greek, although the editors claim that the Vulgate, as the authorized version, was carefully compared. Both translations also employed native Arabic scholars especially for guidance in Arabic idiom; and both, it is relevant to comment, in their published editions manifest beautiful typography. These are the Arabic Bibles of today.

CHAPTER IX

The Versions and the Practice of Textual Criticism

THE versions surveyed in the preceding chapters are obviously only a selection from the mass of Bible translations which have steadily grown in number, most notably within our own times. Two principles have dictated the selection. They have all been treated as "ancient" versions, although the distinction wears thin at the point of the Slavonic translation, for, as will become apparent later in this study, it was actually subsequent to the beginnings of the English versions. But further, these versions are all of greater or less importance as resource material for dealing with problems of the accuracy of the text of the Old Testament, in more technical language, for textual criticism. Another determining interest has been the ancestry of our English Bible; directly or indirectly these ancient translations contributed to the great stream of Bible transmission which in the course of the centuries gave us our several English versions.

The wide variety of temporal and geographic distribution of the ancient versions is an impressive feature of their story. They were produced, too, by many sorts of men in differing circumstances. Some were scholars of the first rank with a fine sense of the true nature of translation; others employed methods that can better be described as popular; but all alike were devout, and concerned to serve the religious needs of their people. Some translations were excellent; some rendered well the meaning of the original but through their freedom lost considerable of its literary flavor; others were slavishly literal to the point of obscurity; and yet others incorporated greater or less interpretative material. But whatever their merits and differences the versions as a whole are intensely interesting as religious documents. With them we follow the spread, first of Judaism, and then of Christianity through the ancient world; we look into small communities in the midst of an all-embracing paganism but bound together by a glimpse of unseen realities that lifted them out of the sordidness or actual misery of their common circumstances, and transformed all with the glory that they read in the pages of their supremely great Book. Sacred Scripture it was for them: holy writing; and only that faith and the reality on which it was and is based—let our critical views be what they may—can explain the amazing story of the spread and transmission of the Bible and the power it has been in the shaping of civilization.

Yet however attractive this aspect of our story may be, we must here deny ourselves more than an occasional reference to the deepest facts of the Bible and confine attention to narrower matters. For scholarly work, the versions have the specialized value already assumed in much of our discussion: they are priceless evidence upon the history of the Biblical text. In the long course of transmission errors of copying did as a matter of fact enter by various means into the tradition. These ancient translations enable us to cut back progressively behind the point where one after another of these foreign intrusions came into the text. For this purpose their testimony is of diverse relevance. Some are translations of previous translations, hence are a second step away from the original; several have been revised under the influence of other translations, and all without exception have themselves suffered through an extended process of transmission similar to that which created the problem in the original text. To seek to discover that original under such a mass of complicating and obscuring late recensions may well seem no more than an effort to correct one inaccurate tradition by means of others even more unreliable. And indeed there would seem to be much truth in such disparagement of the work of the text critic, even though touched with cynicism. For the restoration of the original text is an extremely difficult undertaking, such as commonly to defy success; in general one's best results are little better than a reasonable probability. However, one must guard against the easy assumption that the later increments which the critic seeks to identify are devoid of value. Sometimes, it is true, they are nothing but rather meaningless confusions of the original words; the advantage of correcting these is apparent. But a large bulk of "corruption" consists of intruded words or phrases or even considerable sections that are of the nature of commentary or expansion. Only an arbitrary conception of the process of revelation can deny to the devout men who wrote these words out of the reality of their own religious experience a share in the divine guidance which created the greatness of the best of the Biblical writers. Nonetheless, it is clear gain for us to be able to distinguish the words of the latter, as of the commentators also, and to understand somewhat accurately just what each said for the troubled needs of his own time.

Here then is the significance of textual criticism in the total of Bible study, and here the importance of the versions as the critic's prime resource, for we have seen that all our Hebrew manuscripts are too late to provide testimony upon the most acute problems of the corrupted text. There is, however, another bulk of important relevant material, to which no more attention has been given hitherto than a few allusions. It is the so-called "patristic quotations," although the term must be somewhat enlarged, as we shall see in just a moment. The leading figures in the church of early centuries, the "fathers," they are called, when writing on religious matters naturally quoted from the Bible of their time and region. The "fathers" of Africa near ancient Carthage quoted from the Old Latin Bible, those in the east used one or another of the Greek Bibles or of the local translations that arose in the course of time: Coptic, Ethiopic, Armenian, Syriac, etc. But a similar practice was followed by Jewish Biblical scholars. The *Midrashim*, for example, are full of Biblical quotations; indeed it will be recognized that the immense bulk of famous Jewish writing of those early centuries, Midrash, Mishnah, Talmud, was Biblically based and made large use of direct quotations. So to the Christian "fathers" we must add the great Jewish scholars of early times, as a source of evidence upon the Biblical text. It is obvious that such evidence is fragmentary; it is seldom if ever that a complete text of a Biblical book can be recovered from any one of these sources. Still the bulk of such quotations is impressive. The nature of the quotations raises problems. Did the "fathers" check their references in the interest of accuracy? Or did they quote freely from memory? There is good reason to suspect that often they followed the latter course, in which case their evidence must be correspondingly discounted. Further, the patristic quotations, as distinct from those by the Jewish scholars, are always from one of the versions, not infrequently a secondary one, hence are one or two steps away from the original. Yet all of their evidence is important and may not be neglected in the total of the critic's source material. The variety and relationships of these several strands of available material are graphically presented in the accompanying chart. It has the disadvantage of implying a greater precision in regard to dates than is possible; also the temporal spread of the patristic and similar Jewish materials does not lend itself to the scheme of the chart, and so only an approximate date for their beginnings is indicated. With these warnings the reader may find the diagram of help.

There are just two methods of textual criticism; for lack of better terms we may call them the objective and the conjectural methods. The latter is also called the rational; in any case it is not to be equated with guessing. By the former is meant the use of objective evidence such as manuscripts, versions, quotations, and even evidence preserved within the Old Testament itself, the most notable of which consists of double recensions of passages, for example II Samuel 22 and Psalm 18, Isaiah 2:2-4 and Micah 4:1-3, etc. The conjectural method is invoked when the critic employs other lines of evidence: grammatical considerations, poetic structure, the logic of the context, circumstances of the ancient writer's time, and the like, and finally his own best judgment in assessing the total diverse mass of testimony and deciding on a reconstructed text. It has been commonly held that the prevalent method of Old Testament text critics is that of conjecture, while in the New Testament, thanks to the wealth of manuscript evidence available, only the objective method is employed. But this is quite erroneous. Doubtless many readers will raise an incredulous eyebrow when told that both alike depend upon both methods; the ultimate recourse of the New Testament critic, not less than of the Old, is what we have just now called the conjectural method. It is apparent that the very wealth of the New Testament critic's objective resources compels him to differentiate and evaluate their conflicting testimony; in the end his decision rests, not on an irreproachable authority, but on his own best judgment as to what all the evidence really means in terms of an original text. At this point he is on common ground with his Old Testament colleague! The difference between them is not in method, but in relative bulks of available objective resources. The New Testament critic is compelled to perform an immense labor of classifying and sifting of materials before he comes to his real task of con-

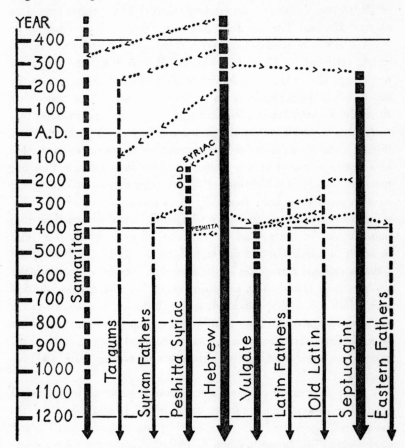

DIAGRAM SHOWING GENERAL RELATION OF THE ANCIENT VERSIONS
TO HEBREW

jectural criticism. In the Old Testament, the critic feels beggared, by comparison, and would gladly give a prince's reward for a tithe of his colleague's resources. But by a shorter path he comes presently to precisely the point where New Testament text criticism must also say its final word: he must exercise his best judgment upon his available evidence.

The first matter to be considered in a study of the text is its authenticity: Is, or is not, our present reading of a given passage identical with what the original author first wrote? It is a question partaking of all the complexity and uncertainty inherent in the entire procedure of text criticism. The resources just now mentioned are those to be invoked at this point also. Corruption is indicated by variants in manuscript, versional, or "patristic" sources; also by linguistic aberration or perhaps abnormality, by logical or chronological disconnection, by anachronism, by irregularity in literary structure, or by any other suspicious feature. He is a bold critic, however, who would claim that corruption is established by the presence of any or all of these marks, though obviously its probability rises with their increase. We have come to a chastened mood in this matter—we have been chastened by our mistakes! Readings which formerly were accepted as certainly wrong have in some cases been shown by the advance of knowledge to be quite correct; the error was ours who boldly charged textual corruption. Yet on the other hand the situation affirmed already must also be borne in mind. The Hebrew text of the Old Testament has beyond a doubt suffered corruption in the course of the centuries. Gradually we have been forced to an increasing respect for the care and success with which it has been preserved; but we must not run into an excess in the conservative direction as mistaken as that from which we have escaped. Even though the text merits profound respect, it contains, nonetheless, great numbers of corruptions of varying bulk and significance.

A ready illustration of our former errors is provided by I Samuel 13:21. The context relates the repression of the Israelites by the Philistines, who permitted no metalworking but required agricultural implements to be brought down to Philistine craftsmen for sharpening. One of our standard commentaries published at the turn of the century says, "The verse is admitted to be hopelessly corrupt." We may not deny that it contains difficulties, but of one disputed word there is now no question; that is the Hebrew word *pim*. The standard translations depend on the Targum in rendering it "file." The Authorized Version adds a note "a file with mouths"—whatever that can mean!

The note in the American Standard suggests the meaning "edges," which likewise presumes, apparently, that *pim* is the plural of *peh*, mouth. However, in recent years there have come to light nearly a dozen stone weights inscribed with this word *pim*. As a measure of weight, it served in early times also as a denomination of what we may loosely call money. This verse 21 tells in authentic Hebrew of the charge made by the Philistine metalworkers for sharpening the Hebrews' plowshares and mattocks. The fact that the text was accurately preserved for many centuries even after its meaning had been lost has salutary implications for the text critic, only second in importance to the sobering effects of a consciousness of his former error.

When the critic has satisfied himself that error has crept into his text, then his use of the versions toward a recovery of the original falls neatly into three definite steps.

First, he must come as close as is now possible to determining the original readings of the several versions in the passage being examined. The immensity and complexity of this task has already been indicated, particularly in regard to the greater versions. It has been pointed out how certain scholars have devoted their main energies through a working lifetime to the recovery of the original Septuagint, and in the end have attained only incomplete results. The work of Professor Max Margolis provides a sobering illustration. The excellence of his methods and results all workers in the field recognize. He worked with painstaking care for many years and completed less than the entire book of Joshua. Great progress has been made on the Septuagint, but no one would for a moment claim that we have reached even approximate finality. And in regard to the other versions the situation is far worse. Little more than a good beginning has been made.

The task confronting the critic is that of assembling and classifying the total evidence that we possess in the primary versions—that is, those that were translated direct from the Hebrew—and in those that provide reason for believing they were revised by comparison with the Hebrew and thus may contain testimony as to its readings; this evidence the critic will assemble for each version from manuscripts, patristic quotations, and secondary translations where they exist. Then he must evaluate the evidence in the light of the character and history of the source employed, and finally apply it to the delicate procedure of deciding what the version originally read. When it is realized that this must be done for all the versions, even for the secondary ones, before their testimony can be employed in appraising the text of their parent versions, it becomes apparent that the undertaking is quite beyond the abilities of any single critic, however able and learned. Yet without finality in this first step text criticism cannot be certain. And indeed that is just where we are and must remain for an indeterminate period while special studies push forward our knowledge of the several versions. What the critic does, and can only do, is to employ the best available information as to the correct reading of each of the versions —he will secure this from the most reliable manuscripts or from the work of dependable specialists—and then proceed to a conclusion which, if he is a competent scholar, he will recognize fully to be no more than approximately correct.

Having arrived at this point, the second step in the critic's use of each of the versions is to determine what Hebrew reading lay back of the translation. If we may employ a word that has come into general technical use at this point, the critic must decide what was the *Vorlage* of the version.

Now it may well appear that the answer here is tiresomely simple: All that is needed is enough knowledge of ancient Hebrew to re-translate the version, and presto, there it is! Comparison with the Massoretic text will then show the corruptions that have entered the tradition. But this is precisely what no competent critic will do. A complex bulk of relevant considerations must first be weighed. The critic must bear steadily in mind that interesting and important as are the version's renderings intrinsically and historically, he is concerned not with the ideas which the ancient translators drew from the text but only with the evidence they provide as to what the Hebrew was in their time. With this consideration many alleged variants will wither and disappear. Others will follow them when a little thought is given to the form of the Hebrew text in ancient times. It has already been pointed out that the practice of marking word separations fell into disuse somewhere in later pre-Christian centuries; the resultant uncertainty as to both words and sentences has often occasioned translations that seem remote but actually attest our present Massoretic text. The same conclusion relates to the insertion of vowel letters into the text sometime subsequent to certain of the versions; once again seemingly strange translation actually arose from the consonants of our text.

But further, a familiarity with the principles and problems of the art of translation is highly relevant. No one is competent to undertake the full task of criticism of the Biblical text until he has himself wrestled with the perplexing difficulties entailed in rendering it into a version acceptable for general religious use. The differences of structure and of modes of thought in any two languages, more especially in those so distinct as Hebrew and the European languages, not infrequently are such that true translation is impossible. And through considerable areas of less acute issues the rendering will of necessity lie a greater or less distance in the direction of paraphrase. The grotesque result that would be attained if one were to retranslate selected passages of one of our modern Biblical versions as evidence of the Hebrew text from which it was derived should prove a sobering consideration for the too literal critic. To make a proper use of the ancient versions, then, one must be familiar with the ancient practice of translation, and in particular with the characteristics of the individual translator of the passage under study. Translators differ as much as original authors; they have their favorite words and phrases and grammatical and logical constructions. In this fact lies the importance of the work that has been done toward identifying the several ancient workers who reveal themselves in certain of the versions, notably the Septuagint; it will not suffice to cite Septuagintal usage in general, the decisive matter is rather the tricks and habits and modes of the individual translator. Thus the Hatch and Redpath *Concordance to the Septuagint* becomes indispensable equipment to the text critic; unfortunately there is no Hatch and Redpath for the other versions. Translators differ widely in their freedom. We have already commented on the extreme literalism of Aquila's Greek version and, though less marked, of the Syro-Hexaplar; in the other direction one thinks of the freedom of Jerome's Vulgate and, still farther out, of the homiletical renderings of certain of the Targums. The effort to make a passage meaningful for the local group concerned sometimes dictated renderings that diverged from the literal words of the original. A modern version for equatorial Africa translates the phrase "whiter than snow" by the words "whiter than wool." A study of the Greek of the Book of Isaiah has revealed in it a comparable intrusion of local coloring.

The critic may well adopt, if not a rule, at least a feeling of "economy of variants" as he finds one after another alleged variant dissipating under considerations such as are here suggested. However, he will eventually arrive at renderings which defy explanation on grounds other than that the *Vorlage* of the version differed at this point from our present text. Here he comes to the third step in his use of the versions for recovery of the original Hebrew: What is the significance of this *Vorlage* in the history of the text? Even yet the problem is not a simple one of alternatives: the Massoretic text *or* the version's reading; it is rather to assess the process by which these two readings arose. At some point in the long history of the Hebrew text there was only one reading of this passage. How then did it separate into the two represented in the variant now present? Here again the Hatch and Redpath concordance will be of great assistance, for its listing of all the Hebrew words translated by any one Greek word will frequently indicate the probable original. It will sometimes reveal also the course of corruption. But in any case, the critic's next step is to evaluate the two readings in the light of their origins.

This is the final point to which the versions can carry the critic in his effort to recover the original text. Somewhere along his advance he must, however, exploit also the resources provided by conflations within the Hebrew text, in particular by certain phrases which are commonly recognized to be corrupt and confused. Careful examination will sometimes reveal that the scribe was himself uncertain; either he had two different readings between which he could not decide, or else his exemplar was in such condition that its reading was ambiguous. In either case he took the safe course of giving both readings—and there they are to this day, a confusion and perplexity to the reader. An illustration is found in Nahum 1:10, which seems to say something about entangled like thorns and drunken with liquor: two ideas that do not easily lie together. But the second phrase is, in the Hebrew, obviously a corrupt duplicate of the first; the scribe has included both! Recognition of such "corrupt conflations" will go far toward elucidating many difficult passages.

Much more important for the critic, however, are the duplicate passages to which brief reference was made above. But their number must not be limited to the well-known duplications entailing several verses or even a whole chapter or poem. Account is to be taken also of brief portions, not more than a verse, or a phrase, or even a single word, that are repeated in a context which renders them significant as evidence upon the primary reading. The Old Testament, in its several parts, bears many marks of its devout use as sacred literature. Some of these are spoken of as pious glosses, others are comprehended under the blanket term "editorial additions." But it is revealing to see both as deposits rather of a process of commentary upon the Scriptures, a process that expressed itself in one direction in the free translations of the Targums and in another in the immense Midrashic literature. In this latter the common form of treatment is, first, the quotation of a Biblical verse or phrase, followed then immediately by commentary, or sometimes by variant comments. Precisely this sort of pious commentary is found in considerable bulk within the Old Testament, notably in the Book of Ezekiel, but also though less frequently in other prophetic books, and with comparative rarity elsewhere. The comments are of high value as deposits of Jewish religious thought, but the quotations are the important matters for the text critic. In them he possesses direct textual evidence, which though fragmentary yet antedates all other objective evidence by an unknown period, certainly in many cases by several centuries. It will be apparent that this type of evidence requires the same cautious evaluation as was just now demanded for the handling of the approximate *Vorlage* of the versions. But in any case, arrived here, the critic has completed the "objective" side of his task and is ready to undertake the much more delicate procedure of "conjectural" criticism.

It is notable how few rules exist for his guidance: "In general the older reading is superior"; "In general a consensus of readings, or a majority, is to be preferred"—rules that concern the objective side of criticism and in Old Testament frequently beg the real question. More relevant are the observations that "The shorter reading is preferable," and "The more difficult reading is preferable." Yet it is obvious that these can be no more than suggestions for cautious consideration; for applied rigidly both lead to absurdity. The latter, for example, would mean that the Old Testament originally was nonsensical, or else written in cryptic terms such as to reduce it to near-nonsense. As guides, not as rules, however, the two suggestions are valuable. Slightly better is the observation that the reading is preferable which lends itself to simplest explanation. But the total of all rules will not take one far. Soon the critic is cast loose to make shift for himself, depending only on his own abilities. Far better than any formulation of methods is a wide scholarly facility in the languages concerned and in the history of the transmission of the Bible. Added to this one should possess a broad understanding to apply to the ways of scribes and translators, and best of all a fund of common sense that expresses itself in good judgment. Lacking these, the would-be critic should find some other field for the exercise of his talents: perhaps modern fiction!

It has been said that the final resource in textual criticism must be paleographic and contextual. If the terms are defined generously, they will serve. Certainly a knowledge of the history of the alphabets concerned, more particularly of the Hebrew, is indispensable. The similarities of letters in the successive stages of evolution of the alphabet occasioned an age-long course of corruption. Some of these similarities were mentioned earlier in the present study. The confusion of the Hebrew letters corresponding to *d* and *r* was so common that the critic now is seldom moved to remark it. In this case the resemblances persisted through the several forms of the alphabet, but in general each stage of development entailed new similarities and the sloughing off of the old. It results that the range of possible confusion covers the entire alphabet. Thus it assumes considerable importance for the critic to know when any one book of the Old Testament came to be written in "Aramaic cursive," and when the fully developed "squared characters" were first employed. But our study of the history of the Hebrew text will have shown that on this matter our information is still very vague. The variants of the Septuagintal translation shed some light; some of them can be best explained as a confusion of the older letters. But unfortunately the total meaning is blurred, for some variants presuppose the squared alphabet. One gains the impression that the process of change was erratic, with much depending upon the preference of the individual scribe and on the book he chanced to be transcribing. Apparently there was a considerable period when manuscripts existed side by side in the two alphabets and were employed indiscriminately as exemplars by scribes and perhaps even by translators. However, concern with this special problem must not obscure the importance of paleography for a wide range of the text critic's work. Even in his conjectural emendation he will be obliged to take account of the alphabetic possibilities and probabilities of the reading which he is considering.

But it will be apparent that paleography can do no more than uncover the source of variant readings; it fails completely to reveal which of the two was original. In a given passage, for example, was the Septuagint *Vorlage* right in reading d where the Massoretic text has r? Or was the situation the reverse? In many cases the critic will perhaps reply that the answer is obvious. But in that very act he reveals his process of reasoning and demonstrates the close interrelation of paleographic and contextual considerations. An obvious superiority within the variants of a paleographic confusion arises only through a preponderant support of contextual considerations; one reading fits the context so much better than the other that decision between them is spontaneous and immediate. Indeed this situation is typical of the intimate interrelation of the two types of evidence, so that the critic employs both alike with little realization of his turning from one to the other.

The evidence of context is of various sorts. Simplest to apply is that of consistency with grammatical and syntactical usage. Then follow in uncertain order the author's preferences in vocabulary, his style, his thought, chronological and historical relevance, and a number of other matters that may be loosely described as logical consistency. It is reasonable to suppose that the writer made a statement which was rationally coherent and in some immediate way relevant to the context of his thought. Yet the critic must always be on guard against his own propensity to regard as logically dictated what he wants the passage to say; the course of text criticism has too often been distorted into one of rewriting the Bible in accordance with the critic's theories. The use of context as a critical resource is merely the complement of the process mentioned above as establishing the probability of corruption; briefly, to reverse the suspicious features there listed, and seek a reading which eliminates them. An emendation which notably elucidates a passage, removing its difficulties, and at the same time harmonizes with the author's usage and the immediate context of thought, has a probability of worth. But until it is corroborated by other lines of evidence it must remain no more than a clever guess.

The forms of Hebrew poetry happily provide textual evidence beyond that available in prose passages. First to consider is parallelism; it is apparent that the more usual expression of this device offers cogent indication of the content of corresponding part lines. Nevertheless, the feature partakes of the uncertainty inherent in all use of poetic criteria. For the Hebrew poets exercised considerable freedom and a sense of the artistry of variety. Even in parallelism the exceptional is by no means conclusive evidence of textual corruption. The structure of the line also demands attention from the critic. Most Hebrew poetry is in lines of two members—distich lines they are called, in the somewhat absurd way in which we invoke Greek terms for characteristically Hebraic features. But genuine tristich lines are not uncommon; further, they are often intruded into a poem which is mainly in distichs. Their presence creates a critical problem. Do they obviously declare the presence of foreign matter? Sometimes apparently so. It seems highly probable that sporadic lines of unusual form have suffered corruption. On the other hand, if tristichs occur together in unified groups of two or three, although their context is otherwise distich, their originality remains a reasonable possibility which must be tested by other considerations from the critic's repertoire.

The meter of these stichs, as the units of the Hebrew line are called, also provides an index of authenticity or corruption. Approached from traditional concepts of the scansion of English poetry, meter would appear to supply almost conclusive evidence of intrusion or omission. But it is well known that Hebrew meter is quite different, depending not upon the regular succession of a fixed number of stressed and unstressed syllables but upon a somewhat uniform pattern of major vocal stresses. The most common measure is that of three heavy beats in each stich, conventionally indicated as 3:3, or in case the line is a tristich, then 3:3:3. Yet, owing to the nature of Hebrew scansion, or else to our ignorance of its precise rules, it often occurs that one cannot be certain whether or not the presence (or absence) of a certain word actually disrupts the structure. Certainty is further discounted by the now well-recognized fact that for stylistic effects Hebrew poets not uncommonly altered their measure within a single poem. In a composition prevailingly of 3:3 scansion, lines of 3:2 and 2:3 are often interspersed under circumstances that give no sound basis for postulating corruption.

A passage which has received considerable attention in this regard will serve as an illustration. The first line of Isaiah 45:1 says:

> Thus says the Lord to his anointed,
> to Cyrus, whom I have grasped by his right hand.

The claim has been put forward that the word translated "to Cyrus" is excessive in the meter, hence is to be treated as a later intrusion. Now, what decision can we reach? The prevailing measure of the poem appears to be 3:3, though frequently altered to 3:2. This first line, however, contains eight words, neatly distributed four in each stich. One of these in the first stich is only a monosyllable, and one in the second is of a syllable and a half—to pass lightly over a Hebrew technicality. Both are connected with their immediately following word with a mark which we may call a hyphen, indicating, it would seem, that the Massoretes intended the combined words to be pronounced in each case as one. By this means the line falls into the 3:3 pattern. It appears then that the meter, instead of revealing corruption, actually supports the text. However, the combined unit in the second stich is heavy; it has four full and two half vowels, whereas the corresponding unit in the first stich has only three full vowels. Possibly the Massoretes were wrong; perhaps this combination in the second stich should be broken up into its constituent words and each of these given a metrical beat. In that case "to Cyrus" would clearly overload the stich and its spuriousness would be rendered highly probable. But even if the Massoretes were right, it remains entirely possible that this line was originally of 3:2 meter, as are the first lines of verses 2, 3, and 4 (to go no farther). Then once again "to Cyrus" would be excessive. And so what can we conclude? Only that argument from meter alone is highly tenuous; until other corroborative evidence can be adduced there is no sound basis for tampering with the traditional text.

Poetic structure offers yet one further criterion for the text critic. After more than a century of discussion it is now becoming clear that the Hebrew poets commonly grouped their lines in simple combinations which we would call verses, if that word had not already been pre-empted in Biblical usage, but for which the Greek term "strophe" has come to be generally adopted, notwithstanding its entirely false implications. These Hebrew strophes were groupings of two or three lines in a somewhat distinct unit of thought. In long poems a further organization can sometimes be detected, with strophes arranging themselves in larger groupings to which the name "stanza" has been applied. These consist generally of two or three strophes. Integral to all this structure is its regularity. Unless some established scheme of groupings of lines in thought units manifests itself in a poem, then it is a fallacy to speak of the presence of strophes or stanzas. Yet this is not to say that here at last the Hebrew poets arrived at an inflexible regularity. Neither can we say that they did not! We have not reached finality in this, more than in any other, aspect of our understanding of Hebrew poetic structure. It is deserving of note that certain longer Biblical poems, while manifesting a remarkable regularity in strophic structure, yet have occasionally an excessive line. Whether this is then to be declared spurious or whether it is but one more manifestation of the stylistic freedom of the Hebrew poets we simply do not know.

In the end, then, the work of the text critic may well seem to the non-professional observer just so much clever guessing. Yet fairness demands the confession that the survey now concluded has been deliberately and designedly conservative. It is well for all concerned to realize that critical results are devoid of the certainty commonly ascribed to those of the worker in the natural sciences. Text criticism is a department of text history; and all historical investigation is conditioned by the indeterminate character of human mental processes. The unpredictability of human volition and conduct in the original historic act or source, along with the limitations of the investigator's own thought and judgment such as to preclude better than an approximate precision, together combine to reduce the certainty of his conclusions. Added to this, in the case of the textual critic, is the fact that for many if not for most of his problems he is woefully poor in cogent evidence so that he must make the most of such mere traces as he can discover. It is then obvious that his results never are proven conclusions, but merely greater or less probabilities. Yet when it is recalled that this same human unpredictability and inaccuracy conditions all thought and knowledge, so that nothing can be considered proved, unless perhaps Descartes's famous axiom, the work of the textual critic is set in its proper perspective and seen to be much less erratic than the cynic may charge. Guessing—in more respectable terminology, conjecture!—has a rightful and valuable place in his work, as indeed we are told that it has even in mathematics. Yet this work is much more than conjecture. No reputable critic will fail to distinguish clearly, both in his own processes of thinking and in the results which he presents, between guesswork and demonstrated conclusions. He will be at pains also to confess when his evidence is inadequate for the conclusions he advocates, even though such as is available may all conduce thereto. He is a serious investigator who employs evidence in accord with its reputable rules and procedures in other departments of thought. For many of his problems the available facts do not suffice; he can only put out tentative answers and wait hopefully for new knowledge. But when a weight of objective and conjectural evidence unites in indicating one definite result, that result may be considered every whit as reliable as comparable conclusions in other scholarly or common circumstances where we assume the matter to be settled—and find that the assumption works!

CHAPTER X

The Apocrypha

THE so-called Apocryphal books cannot be overlooked in any discussion of the antecedents of the English Bible. They were included in the Wycliffe Bibles, as a translation of the Vulgate Latin, and have formed part of the contents of the English Bible from Coverdale's edition (1535) down through the issuance of the Authorized Version (1611); though omitted sporadically, they continued to be printed with this version until early in the nineteenth century. They are also a constituent part of the Rheims and Douai version of the Roman Catholic church. The completed edition of Luther's Bible (1534) likewise made use of the majority of the apocryphal books. We find them embodied in the edition of the Vulgate authorized and endorsed by the Council of Trent, and especially edited by papal authority in 1592. Still earlier, they were included, first of all, in the collection of sacred books in manuscripts of the Septuagint, and they have come down through the ages in close association with those now found as part of the Hebrew Bible. They are full of interest; most Bible students of today know too little about them. But trends of thought now operate which promise to restore them to their rightful place.

The name "Apocrypha" (in Greek, ἀπόκρυφος) means "hidden, concealed." Originally the word seems to have been entirely appropriate, for it was given to such works as were prepared for certain sects or companies of heretical believers, who carefully concealed them from the public. The evidence of this fact is seen in some of the titles of these sacred books; for example, a papyrus of the first century has as its title, "A Holy and Secret Book of Moses, called the Eighth or Holy." The term "apocryphal" in its original sense was thus honorable, but later it came to specify books that were rejected.

In the early lists of the sacred books of the church we find included all the books of the Septuagint. Hence the early significance of Apocrypha did not include what it was made to cover in later times. Its earlier meaning covered such works as the Book of Jubilees and the Book of Enoch. Jerome seems to have been the first to use it as applicable to all the books not found in the Jewish canon. He then classified as apocryphal all books found in the Septuagint which its translators did not find in the Hebrew Bible, from which they had prepared their version. In the time of the Reformation, Protestant churches adopted as their Old Testament Scriptures the books that had formed the Jewish canon, and thus came to disregard all other books found in the Vulgate and the Septuagint versions. The Roman Catholic church, on the other hand, declared the same books to be canonical as had the Alexandrian Jews, and applied the word "apocryphal" to books outside those of the Vulgate and Septuagint versions, which were often included in some versions. The Protestant churches called the latter, that is, those spurious books not contained in the list of the Apocrypha, Pseudepigrapha.

The books designated "apocryphal" by the Protestant churches are those usually found in the Greek and Latin but not in the Hebrew Bibles. That the reader may be able to locate them the following list presents them in their relations to the Protestant canonical books, remembering that our English order is practically that of the Greek and Latin versions. The books of Chronicles are followed immediately by I and II Esdras (Ezra-Nehemiah); Tobit; Judith; Additions to Esther, prefixed to, inserted in, and placed after the canonical portions of the book of Esther; after the Song of Solomon, Wisdom of Solomon; Wisdom of Jesus, Son of Sirach (or Ecclesiasticus); Baruch, with the Epistle of Jeremiah; Story of Susanna, prefixed to Daniel; Song of the Three Holy Children, inserted between verses 23 and 24 of Chapter 3, and Bel and the Dragon, appended to Chapter 12; I and II Maccabees following Malachi. In the Vulgate these books follow Revelation: Prayer of Manasses, III and IV Esdras. All the above except the last three are included among the canonical books of the Roman Catholic church.

The apocryphal books of the ancient church, now designated as the "Pseudepigrapha" by Protestant bodies, are very numerous. They cover a wide range of topics and reveal many literary peculiarities. Some of them are found in the best versions, and others are extant only as individual books. Search in European libraries and old monasteries of the East is frequently rewarded by the discovery of some new pseudepigraphical book or fragment. Direct references and hints in early ecclesiastical literature point to still others whose manuscripts have not yet come to light.

The books of the Apocrypha may be conveniently classified and described under the heads of (1) narrative (historical and legendary); (2) prophetic, and (3) didactic.

a. The historical books are: (1) I Maccabees, a part of the history of the Jews in the Maccabean period. The book is extant only in Greek and in translations therefrom, though it was originally written in Hebrew. (2) II Maccabees, an abridgment óf a large five-volume work by Jason of Cyrene. It is extant in Greek, and is inferior in historical value to I Maccabees. It is prefaced by two spurious letters to the Jews in Egypt. (3) III Maccabees, a fragmentary history of an attempt to massacre the Jews under Ptolemy Philopator (217 B.C.), and their deliverance. It is found in the Septuagint, but not in the Vulgate, or Roman Catholic canon. (4) IV Maccabees, which is extant in Greek, and is a philosophical document discussing by a concrete illustration the superiority of mind over matter. It is found in some manuscripts of the Septuagint, but was not part of its canon. (5) I Esdras (III Esdras in the Vulgate), which also is extant in Greek, and includes a recasting of Ezra-Nehemiah, along with a legend known to Josephus. The Vulgate embodies this book in an appendix, and hence it is not one of the canonical books of the Roman church.

b. The legendary are: (1) Additions to Esther; in the Septuagint there are several letters, prayers, and visions, inserted at intervals, to explain and amplify the story of Esther. In the Vulgate these are gathered together in an appendix, with an accompanying note, stating that they are not in the Hebrew canon. (2) Additions to Daniel found in Greek in the versions of the Septuagint and of Theodotion. A Hebrew original of the Song of the Three Children was found by Dr. M. Gaster in the Chronicle of Jerahmeel. (3) Tobit, a romance of the captivity, extant in Greek and Aramaic, written not later than the first century A.D. There are three Greek and three Old Latin versions, besides Jerome's version. (4) Judith, a romance in Greek, reciting how the city of Bethulia was delivered from the Assyrians by the shrewdness of Judith, a Jewish widow. It is also one of the books of the Greek and Latin canons.

c. The prophetic are: (1) Baruch, a book ascribed to Baruch, the amanuensis of Jeremiah, originally written in Greek probably after A.D. 70; it is found in Greek and Latin Bibles. To this is appended as Chapter 6 (2) The Epistle of Jeremiah, a letter ascribed to the prophet, claiming to have been sent to the Jews in Babylon. (3) The Prayer of Manasses, which purports to be the prayer of Manasseh while in prison (II Chron. 33); it is found in many Greek manuscripts appended to the Psalms; in the Vulgate it follows the New Testament, as do III and IV Esdras, and is not in the Roman Catholic canon. (4) IV Esdras, called II Esdras in the Authorized Version, but III Esdras when Ezra and Nehemiah are counted as one book, as in the Greek. It consists primarily of an alleged apocalypse of Salathiel, to which, however, some other material has been attached. The original Hebrew of this book is lost, as well as the Greek translation from which apparently the extant versions were made. It is now found only in Latin, Syriac, Arabic, Ethiopic, and Armenian, with a few traces of other translations as well. It was relegated by the Roman church to its appendix as not canonical.

d. The didactic are: (1) Wisdom of Jesus, Son of Sirach (commonly called Ecclesiasticus); it is one of the greater books of the Apocrypha. Much of its bulk consists of sage observations on life and conduct, in a style comparable with the Book of Proverbs; also it has discussions of "wisdom." Its praise of ancient worthies (Chaps. 44-49) is a famous passage. It was originally written in Hebrew by a Palestinian Jew, but the book as we know it is unique in that it contains the account of its translation into Greek by the author's grandson. For many centuries we were dependent on this Greek text and on the Syriac, likewise made from the Hebrew. But among the amazing treasures of the Cairo genizah were found considerable portions of this original Hebrew, although in late, and somewhat corrupt, manuscripts. (2) Wisdom of Solomon, which is found in the Greek Bible and was probably written by an Alexandrian Jew of the first century. It is a very able and altogether impressive book of ancient Jewish philosophy.

These apocryphal books are probably most familiar to many Protestants through their presence in older printings of the King James Version, notably in old family Bibles. Fortunately, however, this situation is being corrected through the revived interest in the Apocrypha manifest in recent years. The statements as to the origins of these books, in the brief introductions just given, must now be held in abeyance while we await detailed information about the notable find of ancient Hebrew manuscripts in a cave near the Dead Sea, as announced in April, 1948. It will be recalled that in a previous chapter the vague terms of the press account were cited to the effect that the group contained apocryphal books not hitherto known to have existed in Hebrew. We must await their publication before any conclusion may be drawn as to their bearing upon problems of the Apocrypha.

Leaving aside the Apocrypha, we turn to a large body of ancient Jewish literature known as the pseudepigraphical books. The title is an allusion to the fact that they claim an authorship which is clearly false; late as they are, they purport to be revelations given to one or another famous individual of far antiquity. One of them, the Book of Enoch, is quoted in the New Testament (Jude 14b), and others are quoted in some of the church fathers as if authentic and authoritative.

There are various classifications of these books, but it is convenient to treat them as, (1) legendary or Haggadic narrative; (2) apocalyptic; (3) poetical; (4) didactic.

1. The legendary: (1) The Testament of Adam, extant in Greek, Latin, Syriac, Arabic, and Ethiopic; (2) The Book of Jubilees (or Apocalypse of Moses), a commentary on Genesis, extant in Ethiopic; (3) Testaments of Abraham, Isaac, and Jacob, found in Greek, Slavonic, and Rumanian; (4) Apocalypse of Abraham, extant in Slavonic, from the Greek; (5) Testaments of the Twelve Patriarchs, extant in Greek and Latin; (6) Life of Asenath (wife of Joseph), extant in Greek, Syriac, and Latin; (7) Testament of Job, extant in Greek; (8) Testament of Solomon, extant in Greek; (9) Book of Noah, a fragment found in the Book of Enoch; (10) Penitence of Jannes and Jambres, extant only in Latin and Anglo-Saxon fragments.

2. Apocalyptic: (1) Book of Enoch, originally written in Hebrew or Aramaic, extant in Greek, Ethiopic, and Latin; (2) Secrets of Enoch, extant in Slavonic only; (3) Sibylline Oracles, extant in Greek

and Latin; (4) Assumption of Moses, extant in Latin, quoted in Jude; (5) four Apocalypses of Baruch, extant in Greek, Slavonic, Ethiopic, and Syriac; (6) The Rest of the Words of Baruch, or Paralipomena of Jeremiah, extant in Greek and Ethiopic; (7) Prophecy of Jeremiah, attached to the Epistle of Jeremiah in Ethiopic manuscripts; (8) Ascension of Isaiah, extant in its entirety only in Ethiopic, but fragments exist in Greek, Latin, and Slavonic; (9) Apocalypse of Elijah, extant in Coptic; (10) Apocalypse of Zephaniah, extant in Coptic; (11) A Revelation of Moses, extant in Hebrew; (12) An Apocalypse of Esdras, extant in Syriac; an Ethiopic manuscript of a book by the same name is in the British Museum; there are several other books of less note under this classification that are either quoted or referred to by various ancient authors.

3. Poetical: (1) Psalms of Solomon, eighteen Psalms in Greek that were once translated from Hebrew; (2) Additions to the Psalter: Psalm 151 in the Greek; three apocryphal Psalms in Syriac—all probably of Jewish origin.

4. Didactic: (1) Magical Books of Moses, extant in papyri found in Egypt; (2) The Story of Ahiḳar, the cupbearer, steward, signet keeper, and overseer of accounts to Esarhaddon (cf. Tobit 1:21 f.).

All the Apocrypha and Pseudepigrapha were produced between about 250 B.C. and some time in the early Christian centuries. They were written by devout and loyal persons who were deeply concerned for the welfare of their people, and anxious to serve their religious needs. The Pseudepigrapha, it is true, made spurious claims of authorship; how far the device misled the earliest readers it is difficult to say, but certainly we must beware of passing judgment upon the real authors on the basis of modern standards of literary ethics. Just as the expanders of the pentateuchal laws felt that they were working in the spirit of Moses, so these writers were doubtless innocent of any intent of fraud. Their integrity is in a way attested by their success among devout Jews of their time. And indeed it is a success that need not surprise the modern reader, for the religious earnestness of the authors and their elevation of thought are fully apparent, notwithstanding numerous ideas that have no power over our minds. We have seen how these books were carried into the numerous editions of the Septuagint, into the Vulgate, and into several other versions of later date. The church fathers now and then quoted from them, and the Roman church formally adopted many of them as part of their Biblical canon. But the spread of learning and the quickening of a spiritual life in Reformation times cut down the Biblical canon of the Protestant churches to the limits of the ancient Hebrew canon. This action led to increasing disregard of the Apocrypha and its consequent disappearance from most editions of the Bible.

In 1892, C. J. Ball issued the *Variorum Apocrypha,* being the King James Version with variant readings. The Revised Version of the Apocrypha appeared in 1895. A notable publication was R. H. Charles' two-volume *Apocrypha and Pseudepigrapha* (1913) with introductions and notes. But all these are now surpassed by the translation into modern speech published by Edgar J. Goodspeed in 1938, and incorporated into *The Complete Bible* in 1939. It is of unique significance as the only English translation made throughout direct from the Greek. The Revised Standard Version is preparing a new translation.

Why were the apocryphal books not received into the Biblical canon of the Old Testament? What constitutes the real difference between the two classes of literature? Who decided what should be Bible and what should not be Bible?

The answers to these questions are not simple, but the researches of scholars have provided us with the main clues to them. Since the formation of the New Testament is better known than that of the Old it throws much light upon the latter. The New Testament arose as a collection of smaller groups of Christian writings, namely, the letters of Paul, the Gospels, the general or Catholic letters (with which Acts came to circulate), and apocalypses. The primary motive for the collection and use of these and other writings was their value in the religious life of the churches. As a part of the movement to define more clearly the Christian faith which became necessary in the developing church, the attempt was naturally made to distinguish "authoritative" writings and writings which might be used along with the Jewish Scriptures in the public services of worship. The books which were eventually rejected are sometimes called New Testament Apocrypha, but they never achieved the same status as those of the Old Testament either singly or as a group. Yet among the early Christians a number of them at various times and places were regarded and used as Scripture. Included in actual manuscripts or cited as authoritative were the Shepherd of Hermas, the Letter of Barnabas, I and II Clement, the Revelation of Peter, the Gospel of the Hebrews, the Didache or Teaching of the Apostles, the Preaching of Peter, the Wisdom of Solomon, the Psalms of Solomon, III Corinthians, and the Apostolic Constitutions. Others appear in various lists of disputed or rejected books, e.g., the Acts of Paul, Book of James, Gospel of Thomas, etc. The chief of these writings or the main portions of them were published in a convenient English edition by M. R. James in 1924.

The first actual New Testament appears, however, to have been compiled by a heretic, the Gnostic Marcion, about A.D. 140, for the purpose of supplanting the Jewish with a Christian Scripture. His collection consisted of the Gospel of Luke and ten letters of Paul, i.e., exclusive of the Pastorals and Hebrews. By the end of the second century a New Testament Scripture as distinct from an Old had come into existence, but for over two centuries much geographical variation in its contents existed. By *ca.* A.D. 200 our four Gospels and thirteen letters of Paul were almost everywhere recognized. Opinion varied greatly on the rest, from the liberal view of Alexandria, where Clement used a canon of at least thirty-three and Origen of twenty-nine books, to the conservative East, where Acts and Hebrews were not admitted until the fourth century, the three major Catholics (I Peter, I John, James) not until the fifth, the remaining Catholics not until even later, and Revelation officially not at all. Rome seems to have taken that median view which finally prevailed, although Hebrews was slow to be accepted in the West. It is not until A.D. 367 in a festal letter of Athanasius, Bishop of Alexandria, that exactly our twenty-seven books appear in an extant official list. But its final determination is doubtless to be associated with the crisis in which Christianity under Constantine became the official religion of the Empire.

The Old Testament also arose in the form of separate collections, namely, the Pentateuch (Torah), the Prophets (Nebi'im), including the historical books, and the Writings (Kethubim). Much less is known of the exact dates of these and of the process of their formation. The Torah, whose nucleus was apparently the book of Deuteronomy discovered in 621 B.C., is thought to have been in use as Scripture by

400 B.C., the Prophets some time between 250 and 150 B.C. The group of books in the Writings is referred to as the "other books" in the preface to the Wisdom of Sirach, about 132 B.C., but its exact content at that time is unknown and in fact continued to be disputed for two centuries. Headed by the Psalter and the poetical books Job and Proverbs, it eventually came to consist of these plus the Five Rolls (Megilloth) associated with various festivals (Song of Songs, Ruth, Lamentations, Ecclesiastes, Esther) and a group of later writings, Daniel, Ezra-Nehemiah, and Chronicles. At the time of the discussions at Jamnia, about A.D. 90, Esther was still in dispute. The determination of the contents of each of these groups may probably be associated respectively with the crises of the exile and return, the persecutions under Antiochus Epiphanes, and the destruction of Jerusalem in A.D. 70.

Certain general conclusions may be drawn from the data. The religious life of the believing community quite evidently preceded the collection and use of its writings as authoritative and sacred Scripture. The latter process was stimulated and accelerated by various crises involving the need for defining the faith, for an authoritative statement and guide to be used in instruction and worship. The writings selected were such as had proved themselves of religious and inspirational value in actual usage. Authorship by certain great leaders, or association with the immediate circle of such leaders, helped to secure recognition for a book. Thus among the Jews the attempt was made to define a "prophetic" period (Moses to Ezra) and among the Christians, an "apostolic" circle or period. When differences of opinion on the authenticity or value of a writing existed, the pronouncements of outstanding churches and leaders were influential. Such judgments generally involved questions of authorship, antiquity, authenticity, language and place of origin (Old Testament), religious and ethical values, harmony with other books, and general accuracy and dignity of contents. It was manifestly impossible in a collection of books of such variety as is contained in the Bible to be consistent in all of these regards. Nor were the evaluators sufficiently informed on many points. Sometimes they sought to harmonize the books by allegorical and other methods. Sometimes in the early period, and again in early Reformation times, they distinguished books of greater and lesser value within the canon. The last step in the process of canonization was the decisions of church councils. But in reality these only officially confirmed the results of a development representing a growth over a long period of time and the eventual emergence of such books as by their intrinsic merits proved to be worthy of preservation, acceptance, and use.

PART TWO

The New Testament

CHAPTER XI

Writing and Manuscripts in General

THE New Testament differs widely from the Old in available resources for the study of its text. There is an abundance of manuscripts, several of them reaching to the third Christian century, that is, only about two hundred years from the original writing of the books and in some cases the interval is still shorter. Also the versions of the New Testament are several centuries nearer the original than are those of the Old Testament. This fact gives them much higher value than can be credited to those of the Old. On the other hand, the larger number of early and valuable manuscripts of the New Testament reduces the comparative value of the versions.

The books of the New Testament come down to us in Greek, most of them written in the first century. Most of the epistles of Paul, the earliest of the books, were written as letters to the churches which he had founded and fostered, and not one of them was intended by him to be preserved as a permanent part of a collection of sacred books. Indeed, Paul does not seem to have given any directions regarding his letters, except that occasionally he requested that they should be read before a church or interchanged with a letter sent to some other church (cf. Col. 4:16). They preserve the epistolary form even when, as in the case of Romans, the treatment is more elaborate and systematic than usual with him. The individuality of the writer stands out in greater boldness, and the familiar handling of themes in such direct address gives a certain personal touch and interest not found in formal literary documents.

These letters of Paul are our earliest records of the progress and expansion of Christianity. Paul's intimate relationship with the early churches and his daily burden of soul for them (cf. II Cor. 11:28) give them a special value. From hints and direct statements in these letters he must have carried on an extensive correspondence (II Thess. 3:17;

Col. 4:18). He received letters or messages from his churches (I Cor. 16:3; 7:1) and sent to them other letters (cf. II Cor. 10:10; I Cor. 5:9) besides those preserved to us in the New Testament. The so-called Catholic Epistles, James, I and II Peter, I, II, and III John, and Jude, have more of the form of literary epistles. Some of them were evidently intended, if not for general Christian reading, at least for large numbers of persons.

The Gospels are the written reports of the facts and interpretations known or gathered by their authors concerning the life of Jesus on earth. They used written records in their compilations, for direct discourse is introduced as if it were the identical words of the speakers. John's Gospel stands quite alone, and presents a view of the life of Jesus distinct from the first three—the Synoptics. Luke's narrative in the Acts is a setting forth in their order of events connected with the beginnings of the church and stretching to the arrival of Paul at Rome. Of all these the Gospels and the Acts seem to have been the only books of the New Testament that were obviously records intended to be of permanent and historical value. Yet even this interest appears to have been secondary to that of using the data in the preaching and teaching mission of the early churches.

After the books of the New Testament were written they were carried all over the Roman Empire. The Christians everywhere took care of them, and copied and multiplied them in the century immediately following their production. Marcion, who was a devout teacher during the reign of Antoninus Pius (A.D. 138-161), makes appeal to a rule of faith which consisted of "the Gospel" and "the Apostolicon." This latter is known to have contained ten epistles of Paul, which were recognized by Marcion as authoritative. Soon after this date other writers, especially of the church fathers, quote and refer to various books of the New Testament as if they constituted an authoritative collection of sacred documents.

But we do not possess one of the original manuscripts either of Paul's letters or of any other of the books of the New Testament. Scholars such as Origen, Eusebius, and Jerome greatly stimulated Biblical learning, and caused the multiplication and preservation of its sacred manuscripts. That sacred calling was later confined almost exclusively to monasteries, of which there were hundreds in the Orient.

In the period of the ninth to the fifteenth century cursive manuscripts were produced in great numbers in these monasteries, each of which had its scribe or scribes, whose chief business was the copying of the sacred Scriptures. The profession of scribe was so revered that a writer of the sacred books was exempted from working in the gardens of a monastery, lest the skill of his pen be marred by injury to his hands.

Since the original manuscripts have been lost, how shall we proceed to recover their contents? The process will be substantially that followed in restoring the text of the Old Testament (Chapter IX). In this case, however, we shall be obliged to employ a much greater quantity of highly significant data. We must examine the earliest extant manuscripts of the Greek, the versions which were translated directly from the Greek, and the quotations in the writings of the church fathers and others. The earliest extant Greek manuscript dates from the second century (not more than a hundred years after the writing of the New Testament books) and copies become increasingly frequent down to the invention of printing in the fifteenth century. In fact, many were copied after the printer began his work. The versions began to be made in the second century and continued to multiply until the tenth. Their evidence, however, in each case depends largely on the antiquity of the manuscripts still extant of such version and on the character of the version as a translation. The use of the New Testament made by the church fathers in quoting either from the original Greek or from one of the versions is valuable evidence for the reading of that text at the given date, and at a given place. On the other hand, the carelessness that some of the church fathers manifested in their quotations or references to current versions often diminishes their value for the textual critic. Both patristic evidence, as that of the church fathers is called, and versional evidence has been subject also to the same sources of corruption as the original Greek text. The diligent student of the text will, however, gradually discover the relative value of these ancient witnesses and accord them their due regard.

The known manuscripts of the New Testament produced prior to the invention of printing now number several thousands. They are found in public and private libraries and collections in almost every civilized country. Like the Septuagint manuscripts (see Chap. III), they are likewise divisible into uncial and cursive groups of similar chronological distribution. Besides the New Testament manuscripts properly so called, there are many lectionaries or service books which consist of selections from some parts of the New Testament arranged for use in church services.

The oldest uncials are written on papyrus or on the more expensive and durable vellum or parchment leaves about quarto or folio size, usually with two and occasionally three or four columns on each page, in imitation of the papyrus roll. Papyrus was used for centuries in the ancient world as a convenient and inexpensive medium for writing. It was made from a reed which grew in Egypt along the Nile, in Italy, and elsewhere, and strips of it were glued together to form a long roll upon which the writing was done, usually in narrow columns for easy reading as the document was unrolled. Vellum, or parchment, was made from the skins of animals, especially calves, sheep, goats, and gazelles; the term "vellum" was originally used of the calfskin only, and "parchment" of the rest. It was a more expensive material but came into early use. Not, however, until the second and third centuries A.D. did it begin widely to displace papyrus, at first especially for documents of literary or other importance. Although papyrus was occasionally used as late as the ninth century among the Arabs, vellum became the chief writing material, and so continued until replaced by paper. Arabic paper—its process of manufacture probably borrowed from the Chinese—appeared as early as the eighth century, but in the West paper did not replace parchment in general use until the four-teenth and fifteenth centuries. Even then vellum was sometimes em-ployed in Biblical manuscripts down into the seventeenth century. In printing, which began about the middle of the fifteenth century, paper was of course the usual medium. Another interesting transition oc-curred in the development of the codex or modern book form to re-place the roll. The old Roman wax tablet probably furnished the model for it. The change commenced at about the beginning of the Christian era, and was promoted, if not initiated, by Christian usage.

Manuscripts as a rule were written with no space between the words or sentences and, in the oldest uncials, with few pausal marks and no accentuation of words. Certain words, the so-called *nomina sacra*, were usually abbreviated and marked by a superlinear stroke. The actual appearance of such manuscripts may be seen in the Plates. In English letters an early uncial would thus look somewhat like the following passage (John 1:1-4):

```
INTHEBEGINNINGWASTHEWORDANDTHE
WORDWASWITHGDANDTHEWORDWASGD
THESAMEWASINTHEBEGINNINGWITH
GDALLTHINGSWEREMADETHROUGHHIM
ANDWITHOUTHIMWASNOTANYTHING
MADETHATHATHBEENMADEINHIMWAS
LIFEANDTHELIFEWASTHELIGHTOFMN
```

This method of writing gave to subsequent scribes and copyists considerable liberty as to the divisions of words and sentences. In this very quotation one such variant occurs. In the margin of the Revised Version we find: "Or, was not anything made. That which hath been made was life in him; and the life, etc." But the text puts the period after "hath been made." This shows how the copyist, as soon as he abandoned the endless-chain method of writing, could, by separating his words at different places, produce different meanings. Just this did occur in numerous places in the New Testament and gave rise to many of the variant readings collated from the different groups of manuscripts. Another class of variants consisted of expansions of the text in order to explain certain events mentioned; particularly is this frequent in the Gospels and the Acts.

Again it is evident that the same kinds of errors already enumerated in the Hebrew Old Testament were operative in producing variant readings for the Greek manuscripts. Of the involuntary sort of error caused by the carelessness of scribes probably nothing more needs to be said, except that the Greek did not suffer from the absence of written vowels as did the Hebrew. But the absence of written accents and breathings in the early manuscripts also caused mistakes; nor did the Greek have any division between words. An interesting confusion of one letter for another is found in I Corinthians 13:3 where the Beatty papyrus, P[46], came to the support of Vaticanus, Sinaiticus, and a few other witnesses in reading *kauchēsomai* ("boast") for *kauthēsomai* ("burn") (see Plate 29), a reading which had already been adopted by Goodspeed in his translation of the New Testament as the more probable original. The element of intention, however, may have entered, because to the scribe acquainted with the later custom of burning Christians at the stake the other reading doubtless seemed the more probable. An example of interpolation from the margin is probably to be found in the explanation of the troubling of the waters by an angel in John 5:3-4. Assimilation between the Gospels is frequent. Much of this is unintentional, but some, such as the addition of the incident of the spearing of Jesus' side in Matthew 27:49 from the Johannine account of the crucifixion, is deliberate harmonization.

Other types of intentional change are stylistic and grammatical, of which several may be seen in the Apocalypse; liturgical expressions, such as the addition of the doxology to the Lord's Prayer in Matthew 6:13 and, in a few manuscripts, also in Luke; corrections, such as the substitution of "prophets" for "Isaiah the prophet" in Mark 1:1 or the omission of "Jeremiah" in Matthew 27:9. The longer and shorter appendices found after Mark 16:8 are attempts to restore or supply the proper ending. Theologically motivated variants are also found now and then, reflecting sometimes the views of different schools of believers in various parts of the Christian world. The most famous is the trinitarian passage in I John 5:7 f., the omission of which in the Revised Version caused much excitement. The group of additions in the last chapters of Luke and elsewhere not found in the Western text are clearly doctrinal in origin and have been dropped to the margin of the new Revised Standard Version of the New Testament. The addition in Luke 22:43-44 is thought to be aimed at the Docetic heresy which claimed that Jesus did not actually suffer. In Luke 23:32 some manuscripts omit "other" in the phrase "two other malefactors" for obvious reasons. A variant like "God" for "who" in I Timothy 3:16 may be debatable, however, since it could at least have been suggested by a confusion of letters ($\overline{\Theta C}$ for OC).

These and other similar differences in the text began to exist very early, doubtless with the first copyist. In fact, the early period of transmission was productive of most variation, because the documents had not yet become sacred Scripture, and the scribes were often untrained. There was no compelling interest in always preserving the exact wording of the original. The situation was similar to that reflected in the Matthean and Lucan evangelists' use of the Gospel of Mark. Tatian's Diatessaron is also an example of the rather free treatment of the text in the early period. Origen and Jerome were greatly disturbed by the evident corruptions of the Biblical texts in their days, and, as we have seen, they made attempts to remedy the situation. Recensions of the text, such as those attributed to Hesychius of Egypt and Lucian of Antioch, were similar endeavors. When the New Testament literature became canonical and Christianity legalized, efforts to standardize the text received a special impetus as a part of the general movement toward fixation and definition of canon, creed, and ecclesiastical organization. We shall see how this resulted in standardized editions of the various versions and of the Greek text.

No Hebrew or Greek manuscripts earlier than the ninth century carry a date. The time of writing of any particular undated document is determined by one or more of several means. Some of these are (1) the material on which a document is written, (2) the form of the letters, (3) the style of writing, (4) the use or absence of the Ammonian sections of the Gospels, (5) the Eusebian canon and section numbers, (6) the system of Euthalius in the Acts and Epistles.

Apparently the earliest extant attempt in Greek manuscripts to break up the text into paragraphs is found in Codex Vaticanus. Tatian, however, in his Diatessaron seems to have divided the Gospels into larger section or "titles," to whose numerical designation was appended a summary of contents, either at the beginning of the Gospel or at the top or bottom of the pages or both.

Eusebius of Caesarea, who died A.D. 340, was probably stimulated by an idea of Ammonius of Alexandria (about A.D. 220) to work out a novel method of harmonizing the Gospels. Taking Matthew as his standard, he marked off in it 355 sections; in Mark, 233 (later carried out to 241 by the addition of 16:8-20); in Luke, 342; and in John, 232. These sections were marked by Greek letters with a fixed numerical value. To make practical his plan, ten lists or canon tables were made, in which all the parallel passages were classified by the section numbers. The first table contained all the passages common to the four Gospels; the second, those common to the first three; the third, those common to Matthew, Luke, and John; the fourth, those common to Matthew, Mark, and John; the fifth to the ninth tables, those common to different pairs of Gospels; and the tenth, those found in one only. Many manuscripts give these tables in a section preceding the text of the Gospels, often with a letter written by Eusebius to Carpianus explaining the system. In the text itself, also, the table and section number will usually be given in the margin and sometimes in addition at the bottom of the page together with the corresponding section numbers from the other Gospels. Nestle prints this data in his editions of the Greek New Testament.

In the latter part of the fourth century Euthalius of Alexandria introduced into Acts and the Pauline and General Epistles certain divisions called *stichoi*. These were indicated by a mark set at every fiftieth line. Though they were arbitrary divisions, they served as guides and checks for the copyist. The same term was later applied to another division, called *comma* or *colon*, which was made according to the sense. These devices, however, were not universally adopted, nor are they present in our modern Bibles. But their use sometimes supplies us with a key for ascertaining the date of the uncial manuscripts.

CHAPTER XII

The Greek Manuscripts of the New Testament

THERE are nearly 4,500 known Greek manuscripts of the New Testament. These include over 200 uncial documents, counting all fragments, which range in date from the second to the ninth century, about 100 papyri and ostraca, mainly uncial, approximately 2,500 cursive documents dating from the ninth to the fifteenth century, and nearly 1,700 lectionaries, some of which were written in uncials as late as the twelfth century.

Unfortunately, comparatively few of these witnesses contain the complete New Testament, and many are very fragmentary, especially those among the early uncials and papyri. Nevertheless, so far as the quality and quantity of the evidence go, the New Testament may be said to be by far the best-preserved ancient document in the world. It should be noted, too, that the manuscripts reflect in content an early grouping of the books which was partly the result of their canonical history and partly a matter of convenience in their circulation. Four such groups may be generally distinguished as follows: (1) the Gospels; (2) the Acts and Catholic (General) Epistles; (3) the Pauline Epistles; (4) the Apocalypse. The entire New Testament is substantially contained in only two uncials (Sinaiticus and Alexandrinus, most of Matthew being missing in the latter) and in about 50 cursives. Approximately 120 other manuscripts contain all but the Apocalypse, and about 50 all but the Gospels. The most numerous single group is naturally that of the Gospels, with some 1,500 documents, and the next in order would be combinations of (2), (3), and (4), with 250 representatives. Manuscripts containing each of the last three groups by itself number only about 30, 35, and 45 respectively. The remainder constitutes material too fragmentary to classify.

To designate these various manuscripts simply and conveniently, a system has been developed similar to that already indicated for the Old Testament. The uncials have been indicated mainly by capital letters, but officially they also carry an arabic numeral preceded by a capital "O." Several of the fragmentary documents, especially of recent discovery, have only this official identification (e.g., O124). Papyri, ostraca, and talismans are similarly indicated with a capital letter and superlinear number (e.g., P^{45}, O^{20}, T^{5} respectively). The cursives are simply designated by arabic numerals, in the case of lectionaries (uncial and cursive) preceded by an "l." Various abbreviations, indicating the contents of the manuscripts, are also in use, e.g.: Evan., Ev., E, e, for the Gospels; Act., A, a, AK, for Acts and the Catholic Epistles; Paul., P, p, for the Pauline Epistles; Apoc., Ap., R, r, for the Apocalypse; Evst. (Evangelistarion), lect., l, for a lectionary of the Gospels; Apost. (Apostolicon) for a lectionary of Acts and the Epistles.

Among the most fascinating stories in Biblical lore are those connected with the discovery, transmission, and preservation of early manuscripts. Their production was sometimes a matter of imperial edict, as when Constantine the Great ordered from Eusebius, the famed historian and Bible scholar of the fourth century, for the churches of Constantinople, the preparation of fifty manuscripts of the Bible, to be written "on artificially wrought skins by skilful calligraphists." The persecutions and wars of the Middle Ages destroyed such documents in large numbers. Fire, flood, and fanaticism combined to wipe out these perishable treasures of Christendom. But some were sheltered in out-of-the-way fastnesses, in monasteries upon the mountainside, in the sacred precincts of carefully guarded churches, and in the palaces of kings. They were given as presents, they were borrowed, bought, and stolen. Their intrinsic value was almost always underestimated, and they were subjected to inexcusable risks of being hopelessly lost.

Fortunately, however, there were some haunts unreached by the demons of destruction, wherein these treasures were preserved. Large-hearted benefactors and long-headed Christian statesmen secured many of these documents and deposited them where they are safe, and can be available for scholars through all time.

In the following account of New Testament materials some of the more important manuscripts for the study of the text will be described. Where the data regarding a document have already been given in connection with the Septuagint, only such additional information as pertains particularly to the New Testament will be presented.

Since it will also be desirable in describing a manuscript to say something about its textual characteristics, we must employ some terms which are not properly explained until Chapters XV and XVI are reached. A brief word of elucidation may therefore be helpful at this point. The work of textual criticism in the New Testament has resulted in rather wide agreement on the identification of certain general types of text, the nature and significance of which will be considered later. We shall refer to them here under the currently popular designations as follows: Alexandrian, Western, Caesarean, Eastern, and Byzantine. The unsatisfactory nature of most of these names has led Sir Frederick Kenyon recently to devise a Greek-letter nomenclature, calling them respectively the Beta, Delta, Gamma, Epsilon, and Alpha texts. All of these except the Byzantine represent forms which were probably extant in the second to fourth centuries; the Byzantine is a "standardized" edition which became current in various forms from the fifth century on. It should be kept constantly in mind that the basic text of all of these is substantially (perhaps 90 per cent) the same, and that much mixture of the so-called types exists. As we shall also see farther along, various subdivisions of them have been suggested and a few more intimately related groups have been identified within them, such as Family 1, Family 13, and others.

The oldest Greek manuscripts of the New Testament are papyri. We have already indicated their approximate numbers. They did not constitute a very extensive source of textual material, however, until the priceless discovery of the group of codices known as the Chester Beatty Papyri, some of which were described in connection with the Old Testament. Three of these manuscripts contain portions of fifteen New Testament books written in uncial hands ascribed to various parts of the third century. We have here, therefore, the oldest extensive text in existence, the Gospels and Acts being dated to within a century and a half of the autographs.

The codex of the Gospels and Acts (P^{45}) contains 30 of an original

110 leaves (Matthew—2, Mark—6, Luke—7, John—2, Acts—13), dating probably from the early third century. The text is written in one column of about 39 lines on leaves approximately 8 x 10 inches in size. The text of Mark is Caesarean in character; that of Luke and John, Alexandrian and Western. Matthew is too fragmentary for judgment. Acts agrees in general with the readings of the oldest uncial (‎ℵ [Aleph] A B C) against the Western text.

The codex of the Pauline letters (P^{46}) contains 86 of an original 104 leaves, 56 of which are in Mr. Beatty's collection and the remaining 30 in the possession of the University of Michigan. The date and format are similar to P^{45} but the leaves are smaller, averaging about 5½ x 8¾ inches. The document has been dated as early as A.D. 200. The letters occur in the following interesting order: Romans, Hebrews, I and II Corinthians, Ephesians, Galatians, Philippians, Colossians, I Thessalonians. The most serious gaps are Romans 1:1-5:17, I Thessalonians (only a few scraps remain), II Thessalonians, and Philemon. The Pastoral letters were apparently not originally present. The text is closer to that of the Alexandrian than of the Western type, supporting the oldest uncials in many interesting readings, such as "to boast" for "to be burned" in I Corinthians 13:3 and the omission of "in Ephesus" in Ephesians 1:1.

The third codex, that of the Apocalypse (P^{47}) has 10 of an original 32 leaves, containing Revelation 9:10-17:2 with some mutilations. The size and format resemble those of P^{45}, but the date is considered late third century. The text agrees in general with the group, ℵ A C P, especially ℵ C, representing the earliest known type. This manuscript remains in the Dublin collection of Mr. A. Chester Beatty. Although the Michigan papyri had been published separately by Professor H. A. Sanders in 1935, the whole collection was issued in an excellent fourteen-volume facsimile and text edition by Kenyon for the British Museum in 1933-41 (see Bibliography).

The other papyri are all quite fragmentary. Most of them date from the third or fourth century and are apparently from codices rather than rolls. A fragment of John 18 (P^{52}) in the John Rylands Library of Manchester, discovered by C. H. Roberts among the Grenfell papyri and published by him in 1935, (see p. 67) is dated by some scholars at the middle of the second century, and would thus be the oldest extant part of the New Testament. But in the same year of 1935 Bell and Skeat published three leaves of a codex which they believed to be of about the same date and "the earliest specifically Christian manuscript yet discovered in Egypt." This claim is open to question, as is also their view that the text represented a hitherto unknown Gospel. Its parallels to John and the Synoptics, especially Luke, seem rather to indicate that it is a free reproduction, perhaps from memory, of our present Gospel tradition. The papyri generally support an ℵ-B type of text with some Western attestation, and the evidence of a dozen of them in addition to the Beatty manuscripts has been incorporated into the text and apparatus of the recent editions of the Nestle Greek New Testament.

As indicated in our discussion of Septuagint manuscripts, some of the oldest uncial vellum codices are complete Bibles. Only a few words regarding their New Testament contents and characteristics need be added here. The fourth-century Codex Vaticanus (B, O3) contains 142 leaves in the New Testament, unfortunately breaking off at Hebrews 9:14. The Pastorals, Philemon, and the Apocalypse are therefore missing. This manuscript is the best representative of the Alexandrian type of text. It omits, for example, the following passages: Matthew 16:2-3, Mark 16:9-20, Luke 22:43-44, John 5:4, 7:53-8:11, Romans 16:24. The doxology of Romans occurs after 16:23. A peculiar chapter division is given in the Gospels and a double system is used in Acts.

Codex Sinaiticus (ℵ, O1), also of the fourth century, is one of our two complete uncial New Testaments; and it contains in addition to our twenty-seven books the Shepherd of Hermas and the Letter of Barnabas. Its canon is thus identical with that of Origen, who flourished in the first half of the third century. Tischendorf spent the night at the Mount Sinai convent where the manuscript was discovered in copying out the Shepherd, of which no complete Greek copy was then known. The text of Sinaiticus closely resembles that of Vaticanus. It has those same omissions noted above except the one in Luke; but the Lucan passage is marked as spurious by the first corrector. The two also agree in a number of notable readings, e.g., "only begotten God" in John 1:18 and "church of God" in Acts 20:28. Yet the differences are of such quantity and quality as to indicate that the codices are independent of each other. Even the order of books is different, Vaticanus having the AKP, Sinaiticus the PAK sequence. In Sinaiticus the Eusebian canon and section numbers have been added in red ink by what may have been a contemporary hand.

Codex Alexandrinus (A, O2), of the fifth century, has 143 leaves in the New Testament, in which it also is complete except for a few gaps. The most serious of these have already been indicated (p. 58). In addition it contains the epistles known as I and II Clement, the latter incomplete. These documents appear here for the first time, and were published by Patrick Young, librarian of the Royal Library, in 1633, soon after the acquisition of the manuscript by Charles I. A Table of Contents shows that the Psalms of Solomon also stood at the end of the codex, but it is now completely missing. Eusebian section and canon numbers, as well as chapter numbers and titles, are given. The text is Alexandrian in Paul, but Byzantine in the Gospels, representing here the earliest form of this recension. Of the passages cited above, for example, it omits only the Lucan and Roman. The Romans doxology occurs after both 14:23 and 16:23. Agreement with the Vulgate in several respects led Hort to infer that Jerome made considerable use of a related text.

Another fifth-century uncial of great importance, in spite of its fragmentary character, is Codex Ephraemi Rescriptus (C, O4), a palimpsest of 145 New Testament leaves, preserving parts of every book except II Thessalonians and II John (see Plate 23). Wetstein first completely collated the manuscript in 1716, and Tischendorf published it in 1843-45 as his first major contribution to textual studies. The codex gives section numbers, and in the Gospels it has chapter divisions. The text is in general Alexandrian but shows mixture with other and later readings. It has only the Lucan and Johannine omissions of the group noted above.

We turn now to the consideration of a few of the more important codices preserving only the New Testament text. From several viewpoints the most interesting is Codex Bezae or Cantabrigiensis (D, O5), a fifth- or sixth-century bilingual (Greek-Latin) manuscript of the Gospels and Acts (1:1-22:29). The Gospels occur in the Western order: Matthew, John, Luke, Mark. The Catholic letters were also originally present, but only a Latin fragment of III John (11-15) remains. The codex was perhaps written in Gaul, and Theodore Beza secured it in 1562 from the monastery of St. Irenaeus at Lyons. Beza, a friend and disciple of Calvin, made little use of it in his editions of the Greek and Latin texts of the New Testament because of its wide variation from other manuscripts. He finally presented it in 1581 to the University of Cambridge, where it is today. It is the oldest known bilingual manuscript. The Greek and Latin scripts are very similar in appearance, large uncials written in uneven sense lines (*cola*) in a single wide column on leaves (510 extant) measuring 8 x 10 inches, the Greek on the left-hand page and the Latin facing it on the right. Scholars are not yet agreed on the exact relationship between the two. Many correctors—nine according to Scrivener—operated upon the text between the sixth and twelfth centuries.

The most significant characteristic of Codex D is the quality of its text, for it is the most important Greek representative of the so-called Western type, a form marked by great variation from all others in what seem to be bold modifications and interpolations or additions. Most often in these it is in agreement with the Old Latin, frequently with the Old Syriac. Yet this type of text was an early and widespread form, as the writings of most of the church fathers of the second and third centuries testify. It is not surprising then that Bezae will also often be found reading with the Alexandrian codices against later witnesses. An interesting example of addition is the Sabbath saying attributed to Jesus by Luke 6:4-5: "On the same day, seeing someone working on the Sabbath, he said to him, 'Man, if you really know what you are doing, you are blessed, but if you do not know, you are cursed, and a transgressor of the law.'" (See Plate 36.) On the other hand, since interpolation seems to be so prevalent in the Bezan text, certain instances of shorter readings were accorded great weight by Westcott and Hort in their edition of the Greek text (see Chap. XV), the non-Western additions being double-bracketed as "Western non-interpolations." These instances, usually supported by D and a few Old Latin manuscripts, could generally be explained as theologically motivated accretions to the text (e. g., in Luke 22:20, 24:3, 6, 12, 36, 40, 51-52). John 5:4 is also among the omissions. "At all events," wrote Hort, "when every allowance has been made for possible individual license, the text of D presents a truer image of the form in which the

Gospels and Acts were most widely read in the third and probably a great part of the second century than any other extant Greek manuscript."

The codex was first published by Kipling at Cambridge in 1793 in two facsimile volumes. In 1864 Scrivener produced an edition in common type with full introduction and critical notes. The University of Cambridge in 1899 issued an excellent photographic reproduction.

In connection with Codex Bezae we should notice two other important Greco-Latin uncials which are of the same textual quality and are similarly written in sense lines. One of these is Codex Claromontanus (D$_2$ or D^p, O6), a sixth-century manuscript of the Pauline Epistles located in the Bibliothèque Nationale, Paris. It is written on 533 beautiful vellum leaves and, according to Beza, who was once the owner, it was discovered at Clermont, France. The Royal Library bought the codex in 1656, and in 1852 Tischendorf published an edition of the text at Leipzig. The other, Codex Laudianus (E$_2$, O8), is a sixth- or seventh-century manuscript of Acts, a prize possession of the Bodleian Library at Oxford, to which it was presented by Archbishop Laud in 1636. It had been brought to England in the seventh century and was known and used by Bede. The Western character of the text is modified by many Alexandrian readings. Tischendorf published it in 1870 in his *Monumenta Sacra Inedita*.

Among the significant discoveries of the twentieth century is the "Freer" or "Washington" Gospels (W, O32), a vellum codex of the fourth or fifth century purchased by Mr. Charles L. Freer of Detroit from a Cairo dealer in Egypt in 1906. It is now in the Freer Gallery of Art, Washington, D.C. The manuscript contains the Gospels in the Western order written in a single, thirty-line column on 187 leaves about 5½ x 8¼ inches in dimension in a small, sloping uncial script. Professor H. A. Sanders of the University of Michigan, who first announced the find at a Chicago meeting of archaeologists in December of 1907, published an edition and photographic facsimile of the manuscript in 1912. Professor Goodspeed of the University of Chicago published a description and collation in 1914. The text of the document is curiously mixed, being Byzantine in Matthew and Luke 8:13-24:53, Alexandrian with some Western elements in Luke 1:1-8:12 and most of John, Western in Mark 1:1-5:30, and Caesarean in Mark 5:31-16:20.

A peculiar addition, not found elsewhere, though partly quoted by Jerome, occurs after Mark 16:14. (See Plate 30.) The passages previously cited from Luke and John are omitted, as is also the Lucan genealogy.

In the collection bought by Mr. Freer was also a vellum codex of eighty-four very fragmentary leaves of the Pauline letters written perhaps in the fifth or sixth century. Known as the Washington Manuscript of the Pauline Epistles (I, O16), it is also in the Freer Gallery. Portions of all of the (fourteen) letters except Romans are preserved, and the textual character is Alexandrian. Professor Sanders published the pertinent data about it in 1918 as Part II of his volume on the New Testament manuscripts in the Freer collection.

Another important find of about the same time was the Koridethi Gospels (Θ, O38), so named from the monastery in the Caucasus area near the east end of the Black Sea to which it had once belonged. Although known since 1853, the codex had been moved to St. Petersburg in 1869 and later returned to a convent near Kutais, where it was "lost" for about thirty years until rediscovered in 1901 by Bishop Kirion. Eventually it was brought to its present location in the Library of Tiflis. Von Soden drew attention to it in 1906 in his edition of the Greek New Testament, and it was published by G. Beerman and C. R. Gregory in 1913. The manuscript is a vellum codex of the four Gospels of 249 leaves written, or, more accurately, drawn, in two columns in a rough uncial hand by a scribe who was not fully at home in Greek but seems to have known Coptic. The unorthodox script makes dating difficult, but opinion favors the ninth century over suggestions for an earlier (seventh or eighth century) period. R. P. Blake thought that the scribe may have been a member of a Georgian colony which was resident at Mount Sinai in the ninth century. The manuscript is not only an important witness to the Caesarean text but, as we shall see, played a significant part in the identification of this textual family. Of the passages which we have been noting, only the *pericope adulterae* (John 7:53-8:11) is absent.

A few other uncials of special value deserve brief notice. Of important witnesses to the Alexandrian text, Codex Regius (L, O19) is a nearly complete Gospels manuscript of 257 leaves dating from the eighth or ninth century and now in the Bibliothèque Nationale, Paris.

It omits the *pericope adulterae*, leaving a blank space for it as many manuscripts do, and it has both the longer and shorter endings of Mark. Codex Sangallensis (Δ, O37), a ninth- or tenth-century uncial of the Gospels, also nearly complete, is Alexandrian in Mark only, the remainder being Byzantine. This manuscript, now containing 195 leaves, was written by an Irish scribe in the monastery of St. Gall, Switzerland, where it now remains; and it is provided with an inter-linear Latin translation. It once belonged with Codex Boernerianus (G3, O12) a ninth-century Greco-Latin codex (Western character) of the Pauline Epistles, now in Dresden. The following are some other documents of Alexandrian character: Coislinianus (H3, O15), a sixth-century fragmentary manuscript of Paul (including Hebrews), twenty-two of whose leaves are at Paris and sixteen scattered in four or five other localities; Porphyrianus (P2, O25), a ninth-century palimpsest New Testament (except Gospels) in Leningrad (in Acts Byzantine with some Western readings); Borgianus (T, O29), a fifth- or sixth-century Greek-Sahidic manuscript of Luke and John (fragmentary) in Rome; Monacensis (X, O33) a ninth- or tenth-century Gospels frag-ment in Munich; Codex Z (O35), a Dublin fragment of Matthew from the fifth or sixth century; Zacynthius (Ξ), a somewhat frag-mentary Gospel of Luke of the eighth century in London; Laurensis (Ψ, O44), a Mount Athos manuscript of the New Testament (except Revelation) from the eighth or ninth century, but with Matthew and much of Mark (1-8) missing, and the text in Luke and John mainly Byzantine. Laurensis also has both endings of Mark.

Three other codices of Western character should also be mentioned: Augiensis (F2, O10), a ninth-century manuscript of Paul (including Hebrews in Latin only) in Trinity College, Cambridge; Mosquensis (K^{ap}, O18), a ninth- or tenth-century manuscript of Acts, Paul (includ-ing Hebrews) and the Catholic letters, in Moscow; Nitrius (R, O27), a sixth-century palimpsest fragment of Luke in the British Museum. Some Caesarean characteristics are displayed by an unusual group of four sixth-century codices of the Gospels written on purple parch-ment, two of them in silver and gold letters. The manuscripts are Purpureus Petropolitanus (N, O22) of Leningrad, Sinopensis (O, O23) of the Bibliothèque Nationale (fragment of Matthew), Rossanensis (Σ, O42) of Rossano, Calabria (Matthew and Mark), and Beratinus

(Φ, O43) of Berat, Albania (Matthew and Mark). Rossanensis and Sinopensis contain respectively eight and five miniatures of great interest because of their age and character. These codices seem to represent an early form of the Byzantine text.

The remaining uncials are chiefly representative of the Byzantine text and date mostly from the eighth to the tenth centuries. Special mention may be made of the Gospels codices Basiliensis (E, O7), an eighth-century manuscript in Basle, Cyprius (K, O17), a ninth-century Paris codex, Campianus (M, O21) of the same date and location, V (O31, Gospels, Moscow, 9 cen.), Λ (O39, Luke and John, Oxford, 9 cen.), Π (O41, Gospels, Leningrad, 9 cen.), and Ω (O45, Gospels, Mount Athos, 8/9 cen.).

The cursive manuscripts, like the later uncials, mainly reflect the Byzantine form of the text and therefore occupy a smaller place in the considerations of the textual critic. Several of them, however, also preserve an early text or one which contains early readings. Otherwise they are chiefly of value where the weightier authorities disagree and when the history of the text is to be reconstructed for what light it may shed upon the origins of variant readings. The latter discipline is really a minor branch of church history. Some manuscripts are also of interest and significance for their text illustrations and other decorative illumination illustrative of Byzantine art and bookmaking. We can mention only a few outstanding cursives representative of these various values.

Codex 33, the "Queen of the Cursives," as Eichhorn called it, is a ninth- or tenth-century Paris manuscript of the New Testament (except Apocalypse) and of the Prophets in fragmentary condition. From its Alexandrian character it was also judged by Hort to be the best of the cursives. A valuable copy of Acts, of the same type of text, is represented by Codex 81, a British Museum document of the New Testament (EAKP) written in A.D. 1044 and brought from Egypt by Tischendorf in 1853. Other cursives frequently Alexandrian in their readings are the following: 424 in Paul (KP, Grottaferrata, 11/12 cen.); 517 (N.T., Oxford, 11/12 cen.); 579 (Gospels, Paris, 13 cen.); 892 (Gospels, London, 9/10 cen.); 1241 (EAKP, Sinai, 12 cen.); 1342 (Gospels, Jerusalem, 12/13 cen.), very mixed in Mark; 1739 (AKP, Athos, 10 cen.), the best of the cursives in Paul; 1852 in Romans

(AKPAp, Uppsala, 13 cen.); 1908 (Paul, Oxford, 11 cen.); 2427 (Mark, Chicago, 14 cen. ?). The last, discovered about 1938 in Athens, is an unusual manuscript in every way. It appears to have a text more Alexandrian than Codex Vaticanus itself, with which it agrees more than any other known document. It also contains sixteen excellently executed text illustrations of an antique Byzantine character. These and the text are in process of study and publication at the University of Chicago, where the manuscript is located.

Caesarean readings are often found in the Gospels manuscripts 28 (Paris, 11 cen.), a beautiful gold-on-purple-vellum document sometimes called the Empress Theodora's, 565 (Leningrad, 9/10 cen.), 700 (British Museum, 11/12 cen.), and the New Testament Codex 1424 (Maywood, Ill., 9/10 cen.). The last, from the collection of the late President Franklin L. Gruber of the Maywood Lutheran Seminary, represents a family of related codices (see Chapter XVI). The groups known as Family 1 and Family 13 (or the "Ferrar" manuscripts) are also Caesarean in character. They are named respectively from Codex 1, a Basle manuscript variously dated in the tenth to the twelfth century, which was slightly used by Erasmus in the preparation of his 1516 edition of the Greek New Testament, and from Codex 13, a Paris manuscript, written in southern Italy in the twelfth or thirteenth century, as were two other members (124 and 346) of the original four in the group. The fourth, Codex 69, now at Leicester, was written in England in the fifteenth century. The most outstanding variation which these have in common is the reading of the *pericope adulterae* after Luke 21:38 instead of in John, and Luke 22:43-44 after Matthew 26:39.

A number of Western readings are found in a group of related manuscripts of Acts, the best representative of which would now seem to be Codex 2412, a twelfth-century Praxapostolos (AKP) given to the University of Chicago in 1933 by the late Professor Ira Maurice Price. Previous study had regarded Codex 614 as the head of this group, e.g., in J. H. Ropes's text of Acts (1926) and the work of Valentine-Richards, interrupted by death and posthumously published in 1934. Other manuscripts of this allied tradition are Codices 58, 383, 431, 876, 1518, and 2401. (See Bibliography: Kenneth Clark, *Six Praxapostoloi*

F.C.B. del.

2. The Nash Papyrus. Exodus 20:2-17.

1. Page of a Biblical fragment from the genizah. I Samuel 26:20-27:5.
(By permission of the Oriental Institute.)

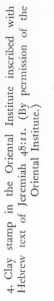

4. Clay stamp in the Oriental Institute inscribed with Hebrew text of Jeremiah 48:11. (By permission of the Oriental Institute.)

2. A Hebrew letter, sixth century B.C., found on the site

6. Complutensian Polyglot, 1514-17; Hebrew, Vulgate, Septuagint with interlinear Latin translation, Targum with Latin translation. Genesis 1:1-12.

5. Leningrad Hebrew Codex. A.D. 916. Isaiah 14:31-16:3.

7. First American edition of the Hebrew Bible. Philadelphia, 1814.

8. From Erfurt Manuscript of the Hebrew Bible (Joshua 1:1-2:5), showing Targum in alt verses. Formerly property of Johann Reuchlin.

9. Genesis 1:1 in the Jacob ben Chayim Bible, with Targum of Onkelos accompanying the Hebrew text.

11. Jacob ben Aaron, notable high priest of the Samaritans

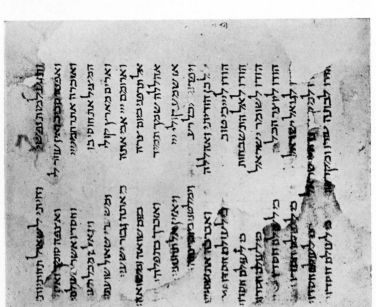

10. Hebrew fragment of Ecclesiasticus. Taylor-Schechter collection of the University Library, Cambridge, England. Ecclesiasticus 51:6c-12.

13. Codex of the Old Syriac Gospels over which was written in A.D. 778 a narrative of the Holy Women. Found at Convent of St. Catharine in 1892. Matthew 1:1-17a.

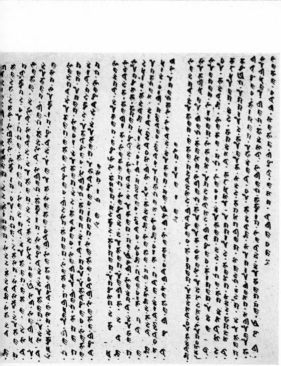

12. The Samaritan Pentateuch: the beginning of Genesis 1.

14. Syriac Peshitta text. Deuteronomy 19:2-5.

15. Gregory Armenian Manuscript of Gospel (Matthew and Mark) at University of Chicago. Mark 4:14-21.

ወታሰብሶሙ፡እልባ
ሲሆሙ፡ወታቀነጾሙ
ቅኔታቲሆሙ፡ወትወ
ዴ፡ዴቤሆሙ፡መዐፈር

11 ቶሙ፡ወይክወናሆሙ
መዋዕት፡ሲትለዓለ
ም፡ወትፈጸም፡እደዊሆ፡
ለእርን፡ወእደወውለዱ

10 ወታቀርብ፡ለሀው፡ንበ
ኖዓት፡ደብደራ፡ዘመር
ጡር፡ወየነብሩ፡እርን፡
ወደቂቁ፡እጀዊሆሙ፡ዴ
ቡ፡ርእስ፡በሀሙበቅደ
ም፡እግዚእ፡ብሔር፡በ
ኀቡ፡ናዓት፡ደብተራ፡

12 ዘመርጡር፡ወተሐርዪ፡
ለሀዋ፡በቅደ፡ሙእግዚ
እ፡ብሔር፡በኀበ፡ኖዓት፡
ደብተራ፡ዘመርጡር፡ወ

13 ንሣእ፡እምውእተ፡ደ
ለሀሙ፡ወትወዴ፡ውስ
ተ፡አቅርንቱ፡ቤተመ
ቅደክ፡በእጻበዕትክ፡
ወዘተርፈ፡ኩሉ፡ደሙ፡
ክዐው፡ጠቃ፡ቤቱለመቅ

14 ደክ፡ወትንሣእ፡ኩሉስ
ብሕ፡እርሁ፡ወእክብደ
ወክልኤ፡ኩላየ፡ችውታ
ዕ፡ወሥጋ፡ለሀሙ፡ወው
እሱ፡ወፀፈደ፡ታውሒ
እውዴአክ፡እፍእ፡እም
ዴብት፡ራ፡እክለ፡ለነጢ

15 ረእት፡ወእንቱ፡ወትንሣእ፡
እሕዴ፡በግዑ፡ወየነብሩ፡
እርን፡ወደቂቁ፡እዴዊሆ
ሙ፡ሳዕስ፡ርእስ፡በግዑ፡

16 ወተሐርደ፡ለውእተ፡

በግዑ፡ወትነሥእእደሙ፡
ወትክዑ፡ውክተ፡ቤተ

17 መቅደክ፡ወክተ፡ዙሱ
እውዴ፡ትነሣንህ፡ወት
ጠብኛ፡በበ፡መሌሲቱ፡
ወተኀፅብ፡ንዓዪ፡ወእኅ
ጡ፡ወእንሬሁ፡ወተነብ
ር፡ርእስ፡ወክተ፡ዘሌ

18 ሌክ፡ወታዕርግ፡ኩሉ፡
በግዑ፡ውክተ፡መሠዋ
ዕት፡ቁርበን፡ለእግዚ
እ፡ብሔር፡

19 ወንሣእ፡በግዑ፡ካልአ፡
ወየነብሩ፡እርን፡ወደቂ
ቁ፡እዴዊሆሙ፡ሳዕስ፡ር

20 እስ፡ወሕርደ፡ወንሣእ፡
እምደሙ፡ወእንብር፡ወ
ክተ፡ክተማ፡እዝ፡ን፡ለ
እርን፡እንተ፡የማን፡ወ
ውክተ፡ክተማ፡አጽባዕ
ተ፡እዴሁ፡ዘየማን፡ወው
ክተ፡ክተማ፡እዝሌሆሙበ
ደቂቁ፡እርን፡ዘየማን፡
ወውክተ፡ክተማ፡አጽባ
ዕተ፡እዴዊሆሙ፡ዘየማ
ን፡ወውክተ፡ክተማ፡እጻ
ባዕቲ፡እንሬሆሙ፡ዘየ

21 ማን፡ወንሣእ፡እምው
ክተ፡ደም፡ዘመሠዋዕ
ት፡ወእምውክተ፡ቅብ
እ፡ቡሩክ፡ወትነሥንሥ፡
ሳዕሰ፡እርን፡ወባዕሉ
እልባሲሁ፡ወአጸደ
ሬሁ፡ሳዕሉ፡ደቂ፡ወሳዕ
ሉ፡እልባሲሆሙ፡ይት
ቀደክ፡ውእጹ፡ወዕሩ

16. Ethiopic text. Exodus 29:9-21.

17. Gothic Gospels. Codex Argenteus (Uppsala). Fifth or sixth century. *Mark 5:3-5*.

18. The Coptic Bible: a page from the Book of Proverbs (1074 a.d.).

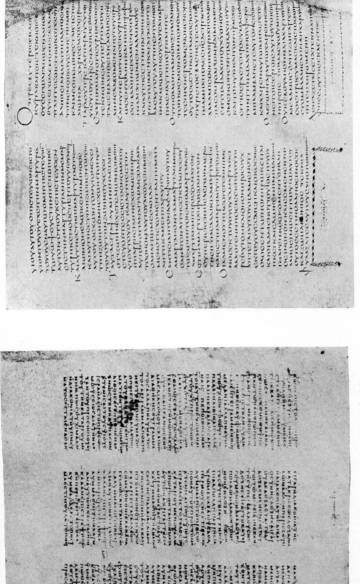

20. Codex Alexandrinus (A). Fifth century. I John 5:9 to II John 13.

19. Codex Vaticanus (B). Fourth century. II Corinthians 3:1–4:6.

21. Codex Sinaiticus (S). Fourth century. Esther 1:15-2:14.

22. Convent of St. Catharine, Mount Sinai. Where Tischendorf found Codex Sinaiticus.

23. Greek Bible. Codex Ephraem. Fifth century. A palimpsest—Greek written over the Greek in the twelfth century. Matthew 20:16-23.

24. Aquila's version of Greek Bible. A palimpsest with Hebrew written over the Greek. II Kings 23:15-19.

25. Codex Marchalianus (Q). Sixth century. Ezekiel 5:12-17.

26. A page from the John H. Scheide Biblical Papyri: Ezekiel (edited by Johnson, Gehman, and Kase). Ezekiel 36:22-23; 38:1-10. (By permission of Princeton University Press.)

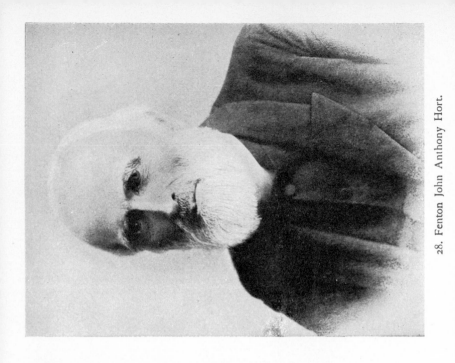

28. Fenton John Anthony Hort.

27. Bishop B. F. Westcott.

ΚΑΝΕΧΩΠΡΟΦΗΤΕΙΑΝΚΑΙΕΙΔΩ
ΤΑΜΥϹΤΗΡΙΑΠΑΝΤΑΚΑΙΠΑϹΑΝ
ΤΗΝΓΝΩϹΙΝΚΑΝΕΧΩΠΑϹΑΝΤΗ
ΠΙϹΤΙΝΩϹΤΕΟΡΗΜΕΘΙϹΤΑΝΑΙ
ΑΓΑΠΗΝΔΕΜΗΕΧΩΟΥΘΕΝΕΙΜΙ
ΚΑΝΨΩΜΙϹΩΤΙΑΝΤΑΤΑΥΠΑΡΧΟΝ
ΤΑΜΟΥ ΚΑΙΠΑΡΑΔΩΤΟϹΩΜΑΜΟΥ
ΙΝΑΚΑΥΧΗϹΩΜΑΙ ΑΓΑΠΗΝΔΕ
ΜΗΕΧΩ ΟΥΘΕΝΩΦΕΛΟΥΜΑΙ ΗΑΓΑ
ΠΗ ΜΑΚΡΟΘΥΜΕΙ ΧΡΗϹΤΕΥΕΤΑΙ
ΗΑΓΑΠΗ ΟΥΖΗΛΟΙ ΟΥΠΕΡΠΕΡΕΥ
ΕΤΑΙ ΗΑΓΑΠΗ ΟΥΦΥϹΙΟΥΤΑΙ ΟΥ
ΚΕϹΧΗΜΟΝΕΙ ΟΥΖΗΤΕΙ ΤΑΕΑΥ
ΤΗϹ ΟΥΠΑΡΟΞΥΝΕΤΑΙ ΟΥΛΟΓΙΖΕΤΑΙ
ΤΟΚΑΚΟΝ ΟΥΧΑΙΡΕΙΕΠΙΤΗΑΔΙΚΙΑ
ϹΥΝΧΑΙΡΕΙΔΕΤΗΑΛΗΘΕΙΑΠΑΝΤΑ
ϹΤΕΓΕΙΠΑΝΤΑΠΙϹΤΕΥΕΙΠΑΝΤΑΕΛΠΙ
ΖΕΙΠΑΝΤΑΥΠΟΜΕΝΕΙ ΗΑΓΑΠΗ
ΟΥΔΕΠΟΤΕΠΙΠΤΕΙ ΕΙΤΕΠΡΟΦΗΤΕΙΑΙ
ΚΑΤΑΡΓΗΘΗϹΟΝΤΑΙ ΕΙΤΕΓΛΩϹϹΑΙ
ΠΑΥϹΟΝΤΑΙ ΕΙΤΕΓΝΩϹΙϹ ΚΑΤΑΡ
ΓΗΘΗϹΕΤΑΙ ΕΚΜΕΡΟΥϹΓΑΡ ΓΙΝΩϹ
ΚΑΙ ΕΚΜΕΡΟΥϹΠΡΟΦΗΤΕΥ
ΟΜΕΝ ΟΤΑΝΔΕΕΛΘΗ ΤΟ
ΤΕΛΕΙΟΝ ΤΟ ΕΚΜΕΡΟΥϹ

29. From the Chester Beatty Biblical Papyri: Pauline Epistles. I Corinthians 13:2-11. (By permission of Mr. A. Chester Beatty.)

30. Facsimile of the Washington Manuscript of the Four Gospels in the
Freer Collection. Fourth or fifth century. Mark 16:12-17. (By permission
of the University of Michigan Press.)

31. Koridethi Gospels (θ). Ninth century. Mark 1:1-6.

32. From "Price Praxapostolos." Twelfth century. Codex 2412 (University of Chicago). Romans 10:1-18a.

33. Codex 2400 (Rockefeller-McCormick New Testament [University of Chicago]). Mark 8:27b-9:1.

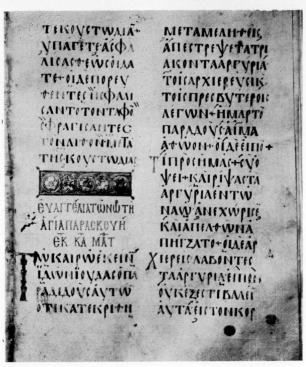

34. The Argos Lectionary, a tenth-century Gospel lesson
book in uncials discovered in Chicago. (Gregory-von
Dobshütz 1599.)

Greek

Latin

35. Codex Claromontanus (D₂, d). Fourth or fifth century. Romans 7:4-7.

Greek · Latin

36. Codex Bezae (D). Fifth or sixth century. Luke 6.1-9.

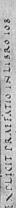

37. Jerome's version, the Latin Vulgate. About A.D. 840. Job 1:1-8a.

38. Codex Amiatinus. Seventh century. Leading manuscript of the Vulgate. Luke 4:32b-5:6.

INCIPITLIBER
ISAIAE·PRO
PHETAE ▾

Cap. i.

ISIOISA
IAEFILII
AMOS·
QUAMUI
DITSUP
IUDAM·
ETHIERU
SALEM·IN
DIEBUS·O
ZIAEIOATHA

achaz ezechiae regum iuda· Audite caeli
et auribus percipite terra qnm dns locutus
est· filios enutriui et exaltaui· Ipsi autem
spreuerunt me· Cognouit bos possessore
suum et asinus praesepe domini sui· Israhel
non cognouit me· populus meus non intelle
xit· Uae genti peccatrici populo graui· Ini
quitate semini nequam filiis sceleratis·

39. Alcuin's revision of Vulgate, A.D. 801. Isaiah 1:1-4a.

41. Vulgate manuscript formerly in Earl of Ashburnham's library. Seventh century. Numbers 1:22b-38a.

40. Old Latin Gospels. Codex Vercellensis. Late fourth century. John 16:23-30.

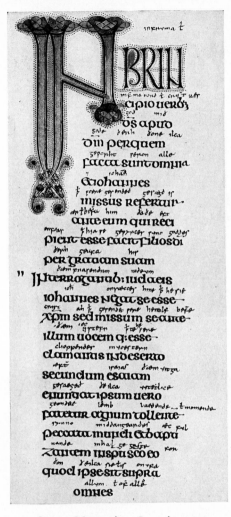

42. Cotton Manuscript. Seventh century, and interlinear Anglo-Saxon paraphrase of about A.D. 950. A summary prefixed to the Gospel of John.

44. Wycliffe's Bible, before 1397. Introduction to Isaiah and part of Chapter 1:1.

43. John Wycliffe.

45. William Tyndale.

crates/ which shall fall from their masters table. Then Jesus answered and sayde vnto her. O woman greate is thy fayth/ be it to the/ even as thou desyrest. And her doughter was made whole at that same tyme.

Then Jesus went awaye from thence/ and cam nye vnto the see of galyle/ and went vppe in to a mountayne/ and sat doune there. And moche people cam vnto hym havynge with them/ halt/ blynde/ dom/ maymed/ and other many: and cast them doune at Jesus fete. And he healed them/ in so moche that the people wondred/ to se the dom speake/ the maymed whole/ and the halt to go/ the blynde se/ and glorifyed the god of israhel.

Mar. viij.

Jesus called his disciples to him and sayde: I have compassion on the people/ because they have continued with me now iij. dayes/ and have nothinge to eate: and I wyll not let them departe fastinge lest they perysshe in the waye. And his disciples said vnto him: whence shuld we gett so moche breed in the wyldernes as shuld suffise so greate a multitude? And Jesus said vnto them: howe many loves have ye? and they sayde/ seven and a fewe fysshes. And he commaunded the people to syt doune on the grounde. and toke the seven loves/ and the fysshes and gave thankes/ and brake them/ and gave to his disciples/ and his disciples gave them to the people. And they all ate/ and were suffysed. And they toke vppe of the broke meate that was lefte vij. baskettes full. They that ate were iiij. M. men/ besyde wemen and chyldren. And he sent awaye the people/ and toke shyppe and cam in to the partes of magdala:

The xvi. Chapter.

Then cam to him the pharises

Mar. viij.
Luc. ix.

with the saduces also / and dyd tempte him / desiringe that he wolde shewe the some sygne fro heven. He answered and saide vnto them: At even ye saye/ we shall have fayre wedder/ and that because the skye is redd. And in the morninge ye saye/ it shalbe troubelous weddre to daye/ and that because the skye is troubelous and redd. O ye ypocryttes/ ye

Mar. xi.
Luc. xii.

46. Tyndale's New Testament. A.D. 1525. Matthew 15:27-16:3.

47. Myles Coverdale.

The XI. Chapter.

Sende thy vytayles ouer the waters, and so shalt thou fynde them after many yeares. Geue it awaye amonge seuen or eight, for thou knowest nor what myserye shal come vpon earth. Whan the cloudes are full, they poure out rayne vpon the earth. And whan ye tre falleth, (whether it be towarde the south or north) in what place so euer it fall, there it lyeth. He that regardeth ye wynde, shal not sowe: and he that hath respecte vnto the cloudes, shal not reape. Now like as thou knowest not the waye of the wynde, ner how ye bones are fylled in a mothers wombe: Euen so thou knowest not the workes of God, which is the workemaster of all.

Cease not thou therfore with thy handes to sowe thy sede, whether it be in ye mornynge or in the euenynge: for thou knowest not whether this or that shall prospere, z yf they both take, it is the better. The light is swete, z a pleasaunt thinge is it for the eyes to loke vpon the Sonne. If a man lyue many yeares, and be glad in them all, let him remembre the dayes of darcknesse, which shal be many: z when they come, all thinges shal be but vanite. Be glad then (O thou yonge man) in thy youth, and let thine hert be mery in thy yonge dayes: folowe the wayes of thine owne hert, and the lust of thine eyes: but be thou sure, that God shal brynge the in to iudgment for all these thinges.

48. Coverdale's Bible. A.D. 1535. Ecclesiastes 11:1-9.

The xx. Chapter.

Hezekia is sicke, & receaued the signe of his health, He recouereth [...] of Isaij because he shewed vnto the treasure &c vnto [...] and Manasseh his sonne targueth in his trade.

Boute that tyme was Hezekia sicke vnto the death. And the prophete Isay the sonne of Amoz came to him, and sayde vnto hi: Thus sayth the Lorde: put thyne householde in an ordre, for thou shalt die, and not lyue. And Hezekia turned his face to y wall, & prayed vnto the Lorde, sayeng: I beseche the now, O Lorde, remembre how I haue walked before the in trueth and with a perfecte herte, & haue done that which is good in thy syght, and Hezekia wepte sore.

And it fortuned that ↠ afore Isay was gone out into y myddle of y courte, y worde of y Lorde came to hi, sayeng: turne agayne, and tell Hezekia the capytayne of my people: Thus sayth the Lorde God of Dauid thy father: I haue herde thy prayer, & sene thy teares. And beholde, I wyll heale the, so that on the thyrd daye y shalt go vp into the house of y Lorde. And I wyll adde vnto thy dayes yet fyftene yeare, and will delyuer the & this cytie out of the hand of the kynge of Assyria, & wyll defende this citie for myne awne sake, & for Dauid my seruauntes sake. And

---

Aul *an Apostle (not of men, nether by b ma, but by IESVS CHRIST, and God the Father w hathe raised him from the dead)

And all the brethren w are with me, vnto y Churches of Galatia:

3 Grace be with you and peace from God the Father, & from our Lord Iesus Christ,

4 Which gaue him self for our sinnes, that he might deliuer vs *from this c present euil worlde according to the wil of God euen our Father,

5 To whome be glorie for euer and euer, Amen.

6 I marueile that ye are so sone remoued away vnto another "Gospel, from him that had called you in the d grace of Christ,

7 Which is not another Gospel, saue y there be some which trouble you, and intend to e peruerte the Gospel of Christ.

8 But thogh that we, or an f Angel from heauen preache vnto you otherwise, the that which we haue preached vnto you, let him be accursed.

9 As we said before, so say I now againe, If anie man preache vnto you otherwise, the y ye haue receiued, let him be accursed.

---

3 *A voyce cryeth in wildernesse: Prepare the way of the Lorde, make strayght the path of our God in the desert.

4 All valleys shalbe exalted, and euery mountayne and hyll layde lowe: what is croked shalbe made strayght, and the rough shalbe made playne.

5 *For the glorie of the Lorde shall appeare, for all fleshe shall at once see that the mouth of the Lorde hath spoken it.

6 The same voyce spake: Nowe crye. And the prophete aunswered, what shall I crye? That all fleshe is grasse, and that all the goodlinesse therof is as the floure of the field.

7 The grasse is withered, the floure falleth away, for the breath of the Lord bloweth vpon them: of a trueth the people are grasse.

8 The grasse withereth, and the floure fadeth away: *yet the worde of our God endureth for euer.

9 Go vp vnto the hye hyll O Sion thou that bryngest good tidinges, lyft vp thy voyce with power O thou preacher Hierusalem, lyft vp without feare, & say vnto the cities of Iuda: Beholde your God.

ND there vvere in the Church vvhich
vvas at Antioche, Prophets and Doctors,
among vvhom vvas Barnabas, & Simon
that vvas called Niger, and Lucius of Cy-
réne, and Manahen vvho vvas the foster-
brother of Herod the Tetrarch, and Saul.

2 † And ᶜ as they vvere ″ miniſtring to our
Lord, and faſting, the holy Ghoſt ſaid : ″Separate me Saul and
Barnabas vnto the vvorke, vvhereto I haue taken them.

3 † Then they ″ faſting and praying, and ″ impoſing hands vpó
them, dimiſſed them.

4 † And they being ″ ſent of the holy Ghoſt, vvent to Se-
5 leuciá, and thence ſailed to Cypres. † And vvhen they vvere
come to Salamîna, they preached the vvord of God in the
ſynagogs of the Ievves. And they had Iohn alſo in their mi-
6 niſterie. † And vvhen they had vvalked through out the

ｃλ ᴧᴏᴠｒ
ｒꙩꙍⲗⲱⲛ
ᾳᴰⲗⲱⲛ

52. The Rheims New Testament. ᴀ.ᴅ. 1582. Acts 13:1-6.

ND I ſawe when the
Lambe opened one of the
ſeales, and I heard as it
were the noiſe of thunder,
one of the foure beaſtes,
ſaying,   Come and ſee.

2 And I ſaw, and behold, a white
hoꝛſe, and hee that ſate on him had a
bowe, and a crowne was giuen bnto
him, and hee went fooꝛth conquering,
and to conquere.

3 And when hee had opened the ſecond ſeale, I heard the ſecond beaſt ſay,
Come and ſee.

4 And there went out another
hoꝛſe that was red : and power was
giuen to him that ſate thereon to take
peace from the earth, and that they
ſhould kill one another : and there was
giuen bnto him a great ſwoꝛd.

5 And when hee had opened the
third ſeale, I heard the third beaſt ſay,
Come and ſee. And I beheld, and loe,
a blacke hoꝛſe : and hee that ſate on him
had a paire of balances in his hand.

53. King James, or the Authorized Version. ᴀ.ᴅ. 1611. Revelation 6:1-5.

etc.) A special relationship also seems to exist with the marginal readings of the Harclean Syriac and with the African Old Latin.

Lectionaries, both uncial and cursive, generally have been neglected in attempts to reconstruct the history of the text or critical editions of it. This was at first a part of the neglect of the later minuscule manuscripts and due to the belief that the lectionary text was of late Byzantine character and of little value. Slight changes made at the beginnings of lections to make them liturgically usable probably also created the erroneous impression of general inaccuracy. While, therefore, a few scholars appreciated their worth, e.g., Scrivener and Gregory, the beginning of their adequate evaluation and study really dates within the last two decades, especially with the publication at Chicago of *Prolegomena to the Study of the Lectionary Text of the Gospels,* edited by Professors Riddle and Colwell in 1933. These and subsequent studies indicated among other things that the texts of lectionaries varied by lections and must be so studied, and that an early text was often preserved in them. The text of the individual lection is the basic unit for comparison rather than a total manuscript, except as the earlier uncials may not have suffered as much assimilation to the current Byzantine readings as the later copies. On the other hand, lectionary readings often influenced the text of non-lectionary manuscripts, an outstanding example being the location of the passage John 7:53-8:11 after Luke 21:38 in the Ferrar group. In lieu of a critical text of the lectionaries, the Patriarchate edition of the Eastern Orthodox church, based upon some sixty documents, is only a fair representative. It is often corrected to the Byzantine standard, and where church lessons are not found, as especially in Acts and Revelation, it gives the Byzantine text.

Finally, some attention should be given to the interesting form of semi-symbolic Byzantine illumination which occurs often in Greek manuscripts. Ornamentation and embellishment of the codices consisted of stamped and decorated covers, of decorative headpieces, canon tables and initial letters, of author portraits and text illustrations. These arts flourished especially in the later or minuscule period, and evangelist portraits were of the most common occurrence. The illumination was multicolored, the most vivid hues being found in the period of the eleventh to thirteenth centuries. Of the uncial period we have already mentioned the earliest (sixth-century) important New Testament example in the purple parchments, Codices Rossanensis and Sinopensis.

The most extensively illustrated Greek manuscripts known are the Gospel Codices 187 (Laurentian VI. 23) and 269 (Paris 74), both of the eleventh or twelfth century. The latter, in the Bibliothèque Nationale, has 375 miniatures besides Evangelist portraits, and the Laurenziana Library manuscript of Florence has 288. The most highly illustrated Greek New Testament (lacking only Revelation) is the Rockefeller-McCormick New Testament (Codex 2400), named after the late Mrs. Edith Rockefeller McCormick, who purchased it from a Paris dealer after its discovery there by Professor Goodspeed in the summer of 1927. Written probably in Constantinople in the scriptorium of the Byzantine Emperor Michael Paleologus (A.D. 1261-82), it preserves 98 of an original 124 miniatures, 15 of which are without parallel in known East Christian art. The profuse illumination, the silver-plated covers, and the general sumptuousness of the volume lead to the belief that it was made for the court of the Emperor himself. Richly illuminated manuscripts were apparently thus prepared for royalty. Codex 38 (Paris, B.N., Coilin 200), written by the same scribe as Codex 2400 and in its 14 miniatures iconographically related to it, was prepared as a gift for Louis IX of the Western Empire. The present covers of Paris 74, dated 1603, have upon them the arms of France and Navarre and the figure of King Henry V.

Mrs. McCormick kindly loaned her manuscript to the University of Chicago where it was studied in the Department of New Testament and Early Christian Literature and published with detailed attention to its text and iconography by Professors Goodspeed, Riddle, and Willoughby. The miniatures were all beautifully reproduced in full color. The text of the codex was not found to be of unusual significance, except in Paul, where from Romans 10 and on it had many Alexandrian and Western readings and was closely related in Professor Riddle's judgment to a twelfth-century manuscript, Codex 330. In the Gospels it also preserved several early non-Byzantine variants, in Mark often of Caesarean quality.

Two other iconographically significant manuscripts were studied and published at Chicago by Professors Willoughby and Colwell soon after this. One of these, published in 1937, was the "Karahissar Gospels," a Leningrad codex (No. 105; Gregory 574) of the thirteenth century containing 65 miniatures related to those of Codex 2400 and to a group of similarly illuminated codices. The other, published in 1940, was the "Elizabeth Day-McCormick Apocalypse," a seventeenth-century manuscript purchased by Miss McCormick in Paris in 1932 and donated to the University of Chicago. It contains the text of Revelation in modern Greek, with the Commentary of Maximos the Peloponnesian and a unique cycle of 69 text illustrations.

We cannot, of course, even list here the many significant publications and iconographic studies of the Greek documents, not to mention those of the versions or the related materials to be found in the murals, frescoes, and mosaics of catacombs and cathedrals. In this area the Princeton Index of Christian Art, under the general direction of Professor A. M. Friend, is one of the most inclusive and effective instruments of humanistic research. Two important, related projects are the Princeton Corpus of Septuagint Illustrations and, under the direction of Professor H. R. Willoughby, the Chicago Corpus of New Testament Illustrations.

We have called attention to the publications of several important individual manuscripts. There are also various published collections of facsimile leaves for manuscript and paleographic study. Professor W. H. P. Hatch, for example, published in this manner the Greek manuscripts at Mount Sinai (1932) and Jerusalem (1934), as well as a collection representing the principal uncial manuscripts of the New Testament (1939); and in 1951 he also brought out a volume illustrative of the minuscules. F. G. Kenyon published facsimiles of the manuscripts in the British Museum (1900), H. Omont of those in the Bibliothèque Nationale, Paris (1887-92). The Paleographical Society and New Paleographical Society of London made available much material of this sort. Professor and Mrs. Lake undertook to publish such facsimile leaves of all dated Greek manuscripts before 1200, and between 1934 and 1939 ten large folio volumes were issued by the American Academy of Arts and Sciences in Boston. Catalogues of various museums, libraries, and monasteries often include facsimiles of their important documents. The modern methods of microfilming now have also brought many relatively inaccessible manuscripts as well as rare printed editions within the reach of scholars everywhere. The great bulk of manuscripts at Mt. Sinai and Jerusalem have been microfilmed, largely through the efforts of the Library of Congress, where the negative film is deposited. The extensive collection of the Vatican Library is likewise being reproduced, and will be housed in a specially constructed building at St. Louis University. The Beuron Latin material, consisting of some 500,000 items, has been microfilmed through Catholic-Protestant collaboration. The negative of this is at Notre Dame University, with copies at a few other Catholic institutions and in the files of the International New Testament Text Project (see page 220). A small beginning has been made with the rich treasures of Mt. Athos, and only the unfortunate lack of financial resources prevents its completion. Never have the materials for the study of the text of the New Testament been so numerous or so available.

CHAPTER XIII

The Old Latin and the Vulgate

THE two preceding chapters have treated the subject of the Greek manuscripts of the New Testament as the principal bases of our present-day Greek Testament. These do not exhaust our sources, as we have already seen in the various references to the church fathers. Very early in the history of the Christian church the New Testament was translated into the tongues of the peoples who inhabited and bordered on the Greek-speaking world. As rapidly as Christianity pushed into these outer regions, the Gospel had to be presented in the language of its converts. To do this most effectively it was translated from the Greek into the languages of several of the most influential peoples.

These several versions or translations furnish us only indirect evidence as to the readings of the original text. But the fact that some of them were made in the second century, almost two centuries back of the oldest complete Greek texts, gives them added value. They therefore stood nearly two hundred years closer to the autographs than Codex Vaticanus and were made, in fact, no more than a century, perhaps only a generation, after the penning of the latest New Testament books. They are thus an invaluable aid for the recovery of the earliest text of the New Testament. In order, then, to make proper use of them in textual work, one must retranslate them into Greek to see what the basis of their translation was.

But difficulty faces the scholar who attempts this kind of work. He must remember that these versions have been subject to the same kind of scribal errors and corruptions as those found in Greek and all other manuscripts. If now we had the first translation of each separate version from the Greek we should have a prize for determining the original Greek from which the translation was made. But we have neither this nor any manuscript of any of the versions reaching back of the fourth century. Of several of the versions there is not as yet any reliable critical edition. Scholars must either make scant use of what we have, or at great pains produce a text that gives us a consensus of the best readings of all the best manuscripts.

The most valuable of the versions of the New Testament are the Latin, the Syriac, the Coptic, the Ethiopic, the Gothic, the Armenian, and the Georgian.

The Latin Bibles of the Old Testament were discussed somewhat in detail in Chapter V. We observed there that the Old Latin was a translation, for the Old Testament, from the Septuagint, while for the New it was made directly from the original Greek. Of the Old Testament, the Old Latin text exists only in fragments, but in the New Testament the text is substantially complete. The Vulgate of the New Testament is a revision of the Old Latin that was made by Jerome, one of the greatest Biblical scholars of the early church, who did his work near the close of the fourth century (see p. 86).

From quotations in the writings of the Latin church fathers, such as Tertullian, Cyprian, Lucifer of Cagliari, Hilary of Poitiers, Ambrose, Jerome, Rufinus, Augustine, and Pelagius, the Old Latin New Testament can be almost entirely recovered. The prevalence of this version in the second century is unquestioned. It is one of the chief witnesses to the so-called Western type of text, but was often modified and corrected to bring it into harmony with some of the variant readings of the Greek manuscripts found in different provinces and dependencies of the Roman Empire. The resulting wide divergencies led to the revision of the Old Latin by Jerome in the latter part of the fourth century. As in the Old Testament, scholars have recognized three groups of texts: (1) African, (2) European, (3) Italian. But the distinction of the last two is often questioned. Jülicher, for instance, preferred the two categories "Afra" and "Itala" (see below). The history of the origin and growth of these different families of texts is but imperfectly known. They are classified and arranged largely on the basis of the quotations of the fathers. Classification of some copies, however, is difficult or impossible because of mixture, especially with the Vulgate.

As the Vulgate superseded the Old Latin version, the latter lost its authority in the church. As a consequence the manuscripts of the version fell into disuse, and in course of time largely vanished from sight. Yet there are about fifty manuscripts and parts of manuscripts extant today. Some of them are so fragmentary as to be almost negligible. Of the Gospels there are listed about thirty, fragments and all; of the Acts nine, Catholic Epistles five, Pauline Epistles ten, and Apocalypse three. But since some of these different groups are contained within the same manuscript, the entire number of substantial documents and fragments totals only about forty. Manuscripts of the Old Latin are indicated by small italic letters of the Roman alphabet: *a, b, c,* etc. But the Benedictine edition uses arabic numerals.

The following are some of the most notable of these documents. Codex Vercellensis (*a*), which contains the Gospels, with lacunae, in the Western order (Matthew, John, Luke, Mark). It is of the European type, and is written in silver uncials two columns to a page on fine purple vellum. It was supposedly written by Eusebius, Bishop of Vercelli, about A.D. 365, and is thus equal in age to such Greek manuscripts as Sinaiticus and Vaticanus. It is now in the Cathedral of Vercelli, Italy.

Codex Veronensis (*b*), which contains, with some lacunae, the Gospels, and is a fourth- or fifth-century manuscript similar in text and appearance to Vercellensis, and likewise of great value. It is preserved in Verona, Italy.

Codex Colbertinus (*c*), which contains the Gospels in Old Latin of the European type, and the rest of the New Testament in the Vulgate. It was written in the eleventh or twelfth century in Languedoc, where the Old Latin was used down to a comparatively late period. It is preserved in Paris.

Codex Bezae (*d*), the Latin column of D. Compare page 164.

Codex Palatinus (*e*), of Vienna, a fourth- or fifth-century fragmentary Gospels manuscript of the African type, written in gold and silver letters on purple parchment.

Codex Brixianus (*f*), which contains the Gospels, with a few gaps. It seems to be an Italian text, dating from the sixth century, and is now at Brescia.

Codex Bobiensis (*k*), a fifth- or sixth-century form of the African text of the first half of Matthew and Mark, very close to the text of Cyprian. It is now preserved in Turin, and, like Codex *e*, is of outstanding value.

The Acts is represented by Codex Bezae (*d*) and by the sixth-century bilingual Codex Laudianus (E₂, *e*) in their Latin columns. The latter has the Latin on the left and the Greek on the right-hand page, the reverse of Bezae. It is written in large uncials in lines of uneven length, most of them containing no more than one or two words. Together with Codex E₂ (see p. 168) it was presented by Archbishop Laud in 1636 to Oxford University, where it is now one of the most valuable possessions of the Bodleian Library. Codex Gigas Holmiensis (*gig*), preserved in Stockholm and said to be the largest manuscript in the world, contains the Acts and Apocalypse in the Old Latin, the rest of the New Testament in the Vulgate. It is a complete Bible (including Apocrypha, Josephus, and a Bohemian Chronicle) of the thirteenth century, but includes some fragments of a palimpsest of the fifth or sixth century.

The Pauline Epistles are represented by Codex Claromontanus (*d*), a bilingual sixth-century text after the style of D, which holds an important place in the estimation of textual critics. It may belong to Codex Bezae, and was once in the possession of Beza, who obtained it from the Monastery of Clermont in Beauvais. Today it is in Paris in the Bibliothèque Nationale. The ninth-century Dresden manuscript, Codex Boernerianus (G, *g*), is an important witness in the Latin column of its bilingual text. Both of these codices are classified as European.

The seven Catholic Epistles, which usually follow Acts in the Greek manuscripts, were not all incorporated into the Latin canon until the fourth century. I Peter, I John, and Jude were the only ones previously recognized and received, although Jude was also much in doubt. One of the best representatives of this division of the New Testament is Codex Corbeiensis of James (*ff*), a manuscript of about the tenth century now in Leningrad. This translation is thought to be as old as the early part of the fourth century, but the questionable status of the books is indicated by the fact that this manuscript also included three extra-canonical treatises, the Latin text of the Letter of Barnabas being of special interest. Cyprian supplies numerous quotations from what appears to be the African text of these epistles.

The Apocalypse formed part of the Old Latin New Testament as far back as we can trace it. The African text of the Apocalypse does not seem to have been revised in the fourth century as were other parts of the New Testament except Acts. Hence the text found in Primasius' commentary of the sixth century differs only slightly from the text quoted in Cyprian. The quotations from the Apocalypse in the writings of the church fathers are so numerous as almost to determine with certainty the character of the text from which they quoted.

The edition of the Old Latin by Sabbathier has been mentioned in Chapter V. Important study and publication has also been made by scholars such as Burkitt, De Bruyne, Jülicher, Belsheim, Buchanan, and Vogels, and several of the more important manuscripts have been published in facsimile. The beginnings of an excellent modern edition appeared with the publication of Adolph Jülicher's text of Matthew and Mark in 1938 and 1940 respectively. This work makes the version available in two forms, the "Afra" and the "Itala," together with all of the variant readings found in the manuscripts. Unfortunately it does not cite the patristic evidence. (See also Bibliography.)

The extant manuscripts of the Old Latin were doubtless written just as this form of the text was gradually receding from a position of influence and power in its competition with the revised New Testament of Jerome. The fact that the two versions existed side by side for a couple of centuries—the fourth to the sixth—contributed toward their intermixture. Scholars and scribes who either studied the two translations or copied them were not always careful to refrain from inserting in margin or text familiar expressions from one or the other. Such simultaneous use of two similar Latin versions led to a larger mixture of the two versions in the New Testament than in the Old. We have noted that the superiority of Jerome's translation led scholars eventually to regard it with high favor. In the New Testament not only the faithfulness of its revision on the basis of the Greek but its harmonistic character—an attempted union of the different Old Latin texts—also gave it a larger place in the thoughts of leaders in the church. The seventh century saw its almost universal adoption in the church, except in Africa. As we have seen, however, the Old Latin text held its own for several centuries. In the New Testament it was generally quoted in Gaul in the sixth century. One old manuscript from the ninth century (St. Germain) retains the Old Latin text of Judith, Tobit, and Matthew. Codex Colbertinus (*c*), already noticed, of the twelfth or thirteenth century, has the Gospels in Old Latin and the rest of the New Testament in the Vulgate. The Perpignan manuscript (*p*) of Paris, of the thirteenth century, has Acts 1:1 to 13:7, and 28:15-31 in Old Latin but the Gospels in the Vulgate.

Christianity's conquest of Great Britain and Ireland took place while the Old Latin still held sway. Augustine's mission to England introduced there the Vulgate. The scholars of Northumbria soon adopted this improved text and later secured the great Codex Amiatinus, already mentioned, originally written in northern England and one of the best manuscripts of the entire Vulgate now extant. The Lindisfarne Gospels of about A.D. 690 (see Chapter XVII), the Stonyhurst Gospels, also of the seventh century, and Codex Fuldensis of the sixth represent the same type of text. The last was apparently made from an Old Latin form of Tatian's Diatessaron.

The Irish, too, until after Columba's time, used the Old Latin; a single almost pure Old Latin text of the Gospels is extant in Codex Usserianus (*r*). After the year 700 the Vulgate text gained an increasingly strong foothold among the Irish, with the result that the Latin Bibles of Ireland and North Britain partook of a mixed type of manuscripts of which the famous Book of Armagh of the eighth or ninth century is an example. A discussion of the early texts in England is reserved for Chapter XVII.

There were early attempts to arrest the corruptions of the Vulgate— to purge from it the arbitrary interpolations of scribes and scholars. Within about 150 years after Jerome's day Cassiodorus made a serious attempt to revise the current text of Jerome. The bulk of our information regarding his work is found in his own instruction to the younger brethren in the monastery at Vivarium, about 544. He desires that they study their Bibles in the "emended codices," and says that his nine codices, covering the whole Bible, were revised by him "with the collation of early codices," and that he left them a Greek pandect, or whole Bible, by which, as Jerome had done, they could correct the errors in their Latin version. We have no list of the corrections of Cassiodorus, nor have we any fragment of his work, unless it be part of the great Codex Amiatinus (of the eighth century), already described.

The divisions of this codex and its introductory matter accord with Cassiodorus' own account of his work.

The Vulgate was carried to England, and thence also into Ireland, in Augustine's day and immediately thereafter, becoming somewhat modified by the Old Latin. Later this English text was carried back to the continent, to France, Switzerland, and Germany. It was copied and multiplied by Irish and British monks in continental monasteries, and further changed to accord with other texts found in these several countries. To this condition of things we are indebted for the prolific crop of manuscripts from the ninth century.

The Moors practically shut up northwestern Spain to itself. Closed in their mountain fastnesses the Spanish monks perpetuated their own Old Latin Bible, which they interpolated and expanded to suit their fancy until their text became exceedingly corrupt. Outstanding examples of this Spanish text are contained in codices Cavensis of the ninth century and Toletanus of the eighth. The Irish manuscripts that had been brought to Europe and the Spanish documents met in Gaul or France, and created a double confusion.

Charlemagne was fully aware of the situation and set about to find a remedy, that the church might have a unified or uniform standard Bible. The records tell us that in 797 he put the task into the hands of an Englishman, Alcuin, Abbot of St. Martin at Tours and the leading scholar of the day. Having at hand both Spanish and Irish manuscripts, he sent to his native place, Northumbria, for additional documents and documents of a less corrupt character. On the basis of these manuscripts, regardless of the Greek, Alcuin revised the current Latin Bible. On Christmas, 801, he presented to Charlemagne his revised edition. This is most nearly represented today in the fine Codex Vallicellianus at Rome.

Others besides Charlemagne became conscious of the need of a revision of the Bible. Theodulf, Bishop of Orleans (787-821), through his acquaintance with southern France and northern Spain put himself in possession of both Irish and Spanish manuscripts. By an industrious study of all these texts he produced a revised text of the Vulgate. But his revision is not of much critical value because of its unevenness, and because of his method of putting in the margin the variants which he had collected, thus giving a permanent place to many corruptions of the Spanish texts. This revision is best represented by a Latin Bible in the National Library at Paris, numbered Lat. 9380. Theodulf's privately undertaken revision exercised little influence on the history of the text.

The monastery of St. Gall, near Lake Constance in Switzerland, was the home of a particularly zealous and active school of Bible students in the ninth century. Irish monks flocked to its retreat and took with them their own style of writing. Under the great scholar Hartmut, in the ninth century, this school produced many Biblical manuscripts written by Irish scribes, and by native scribes in imitation of the Irish style. This peculiar style seems to have prevailed in the upper Rhine Valley. The text, however, perpetuated at this place came from Italy and Spain. The St. Gall fragments of about A.D. 500, edited by C. H. Turner and posthumously published by his colleague Alexander Souter in 1931, are considered to comprise the oldest extant Vulgate manuscript of the Gospels. Another non-Cassiodorian Italian text of the same type is represented by the Harleian Gospels, a sixth- or seventh-century British Museum manuscript. These are generally inferior to the Amiatinus or Cassiodorian group. According to Wordsworth and White's classification into six varieties, there is also another type midway between them and the Irish group, represented by a sixth- or seventh-century manuscript in the Bodleian Library at Oxford.

But the close of the ninth century saw the decline of Charlemagne's influence, the deterioration of the Biblical texts copied in the monasteries, and the decadence of the power of Christianity in France. The invasion of the Normans crushed the school at Tours, and the Danes broke up the famous schools at Wearmouth and Jarrow in England. In these calamities, Biblical scholarship of every kind received almost a death blow. Lanfranc, the Archbishop of Canterbury (1069-89) is said to have done some correcting of all the books of the Bible and to have taught his pupils the same. But unfortunately nothing of these labors remains. Stephen Harding, Abbot of Citeaux, about the middle of the twelfth century collated good Latin and Greek manuscripts and made a revision of some considerable value that is now preserved in four volumes in the library at Dijon, France. Cardinal Nicolaus Maniacoria likewise issued a revision, now extant in a manuscript at Venice.

The thirteenth century was marked by an astounding spirit of revision in France, due in the main to the influence of the king, St. Louis, and to the vigorous scholarship generated by the new University of Paris. There was most extraordinary activity in the production of new Latin Bibles. Roger Bacon tells us that theologians and booksellers combined to produce a fixed type of text, which he calls Exemplar Parisiense. The fame of the University created a large demand for these books, and they went far and wide. But the Exemplar Parisiense was a corrupt text which Bacon deplored. This defect scholars attempted to remedy by uniting their researches in the production of a list of corrections based mainly on Latin and Greek manuscripts and called *Correctoria Bibliorum*. Four separate bodies of men or individuals prepared as many lists of corrections to be employed by the Bible students and copyists in Paris and in Rome. These counters to the multiplication of degenerate texts of the Vulgate furnished a partial remedy. The most important contribution to the form of our Bible that sprang out of the Paris activity was the formal division of the Bible into chapters. Paragraph and section divisions had already existed for centuries. But Stephen Langton, a doctor in the University of Paris, and later Archbishop of Canterbury, probably made the divisions of our Bible known as chapters, about A.D. 1228.

The masses of corrections that had been collected were profitably employed before the Vulgate was put into permanent form by the printing press. When the literary revival of the fifteenth century struck the various national coteries of Biblical students, strenuous effort was made to find the best possible text of each version. At the invention of printing steps were taken to put the Latin Bible into permanent form. As we have already noted, the first complete book to be issued from the printing press was a Latin Bible—the Vulgate—printed in two volumes by Gutenberg and Fust, at Mayence (Mainz), about 1455. It is commonly known as the "Mazarin Bible," for it was first found in recent times in the library of Cardinal Mazarin. It was made, however, from some inferior manuscripts, and, with all its beauty as a piece of mechanism, it is full of errors. Thenceforth Latin Bibles poured forth in profusion from the press. It is said that during the first half-century of printing 124 editions were published. In 1514-22 the Complutensian Polyglot presented as one of its texts the Vulgate revised with the aid of several ancient manuscripts. In 1528, Stephanus' Vulgate Bible, a critical text based on three manuscripts, was issued at Paris; later (1538-40) a larger edition appeared which had been prepared on the basis of seventeen manuscripts. This is in reality the foundation of the official Roman Vulgate, adopted at the Council of Trent, April 8, 1546. The first Latin Bible to contain the modern verse divisions was a small octavo edition of Stephanus, dated 1555.

The authority granted by the Council of Trent for the publication of an official Vulgate was not immediately put to use. Professor John Hentenius, of the University of Louvain, by the use of thirty-one manuscripts and two printed copies, prepared a private edition (1547) that was often reprinted. Several of the popes bestirred themselves to prepare an official edition that would answer the requirements of the church. After the Council of Trent in 1546 decreed the Vulgate to be the official text and called for an emended edition of it, the oldest and best manuscripts were collected and a commission was appointed to undertake the project. The work lagged, however, until Sixtus V came to the pontificate, 1585-90. With great zeal and diligence he pushed forward the work. Manuscripts, printed editions, and the original Hebrew and Greek were taken into consideration, the readings which agreed with the Hebrew and Greek receiving the preference where there was disagreement between authorities.

The edition produced by the commission was printed and published by the Vatican press in three volumes in 1590, and was designated the "Sixtine edition." It was intended to be that authorized by the Council of Trent; and by the bull recited in the Preface it was to be used in all the churches in the Christian world. No other edition should be published without the permission of the Apostolic See, nor should it be reprinted in any other place than the Vatican for the next ten years. Such other editions as might appear subsequently should be carefully collated with the Sixtine edition, should be accompanied with an official attestation, and should have "no variant readings, scholia or glosses printed in the margin." Violation of these orders was to be punished by the greater excommunication.

But this first official Vulgate did not meet with an enthusiastic reception. Its requirements and its new translations were unpopular, and after the death of Pope Sixtus V in the year of publication the College of Cardinals almost immediately stopped its sale. In 1592, Clement VIII called in the edition and published another official one, claiming as a pretext that Sixtus V had intended both to recall the 1590 edition because of its many typographical errors and to issue another in its place, but death had prevented it. In reality, the Sixtine edition had been carefully printed and published. The real reason for the publication of the Clementine text of 1592 is thought to have been either hostility to the author of the 1590 edition or a desire to produce a more faithful text as authorized by the Council of Trent and recommended by the translation commission, whose authority Clement had apparently somewhat presumed. The text of this new edition contains about three thousand variations from that of 1590, and leans toward the text issued privately by Hentenius in 1547. Except for the correction of indisputable errors, however, it represented no considerable improvement over the Sixtine text. Pope Clement VIII avoided the penalties of the Sixtine edition Preface by inserting on the title page the name of Sixtus V, thus in reality issuing it as a new Sixtine edition. After 1604 Clement's name appears on the title page conjointly with that of Sixtus V. This Clementine Vulgate of 1592 is today the standard edition of the Roman Catholic church. The few modern editions that have been issued vary only slightly from it. Hetzenauer has published an edition of the New Testament Vulgate (1899) that correctly represents its great predecessor, the Clementine text.

New translations from the Greek were produced by scholars in the Reformation period (Erasmus, Beza, Pagninus, and others), several of which exerted a great influence upon some of the early English translations. But the place of the Vulgate was never seriously questioned. The first complete English Bible—the Wycliffite Bible—was translated from it, and the quality of its text (largely Alexandrian and Western) was often superior to the late Greek text. Certain of its readings occurring here reappeared only in modern English revisions and retranslations based on the critically established Greek text. Examples of such are the translation in Luke 2:14, "Peace on earth among men of good will," and the omission of the doxology at the end of the Lord's Prayer in Matthew 6:13.

While important recent work has been done on the Vulgate by Roman Catholic scholars, such as Vogels, De Bruyne, Chapman, Denk, Ayuso, and others, the publications of the Benedictine Commission referred to in Chapter V have not yet reached the New Testament. Meanwhile Protestant scholars have also expended long years in an attempt to construct a critical text of Jerome's Latin, carefully studying and collating thousands of manuscripts and many printed editions in the process. Among the most active pioneers in this research were Richard Bentley, Bishop Wordsworth, and H. J. White of England, Samuel Berger in France, and P. Corssen in Germany. More recently valuable contributions have come from Souter, Von Soden, Milne, Von Dobschütz, and many others. This work has added much to our knowledge of the original version. The labors of Wordsworth and White eventuated in the publication of a critical text, of which at last the Apocalypse has now been issued. The Gospels were published in 1889-98 and Acts in 1905. In 1911 Wordsworth died. The Epistles through Ephesians were issued in 1934, and in the same year White died. The remaining Pauline Epistles and Hebrews were brought out in 1937-41 under the direction of H. F. D. Sparks and Claude Jenkins. The Catholic Epistles were edited (1949) by Sparks and A. W. Adams, the Apocalypse (1954) by Sparks. The edition is based largely upon the Northumbrian-Cassiodorian group of manuscripts. In the meantime pocket editions of the complete Vulgate text were published by White (1911) and Nestle (1906). The latter, representing the Clementine text, has been periodically revised, a twelfth edition appearing in 1937.

CHAPTER XIV

The Syriac and
Other Eastern Versions

THE Syriac Old Testament occupied our attention in Chapter VI. One of the first requirements of the Syrian converts to Christianity was an edition of the New Testament in their native tongue. Just how early it was made is not known. Indeed, there are many questions regarding the origin of the Syriac New Testament which still remain unanswered. This chapter can give only in outline some of the most interesting points in the discussion.

The earliest editions of the Gospels in Syriac that are now known to Biblical scholars are (1) the Diatessaron of Tatian; (2) the Old Syriac Version or Gospel of the Separated; and (3) the Peshitta. Just when, where, how, and why these versions came to be are puzzling questions. The existence of some of them was not known in Europe until the sixteenth century and some have even come to light within the last century.

1. The earliest Syriac translation was apparently a version of the Gospels current in the early centuries of Christianity, the so-called Diatessaron of Tatian, a pupil of Justin Martyr, whose death occurred about A.D. 165. This Diatessaron, as the Greek name indicates, was a composite or interweaving of our four Gospels. Produced about A.D. 170, it became so popular in the Syrian church in general that the bishops in the fifth century had to take vigorous steps to replace it with the "separated" Gospels. They were apparently entirely successful, for there is no known copy of the Syriac Diatessaron in existence today. Our chief information regarding the text comes from several translations of it in whole or part. (a) An Arabic form is extant in two manuscripts, now at Rome, and some fragments. Editions of this text were published by A. Ciasca in 1888 and Marmardji (with a

French translation) in 1935. The best modern translation is probably the German of Preuschen and Pott (Heidelberg, 1926). (b) Quotation in Armenian is found in a translation of the commentary of Ephraem Syrus (died 373). It was discovered by Ezra Abbot in 1880 from a Latin version of the Armenian published by Mösinger in 1876. (c) A fourteen-line fragment in Greek from the early third century was discovered at Dura Europa in 1933 and published in 1935 by Professor Carl H. Kraeling, then of Yale. A few quotations are also found in some Syriac commentaries on the Gospels, and something of its composition and contents may be judged from the Latin form in Codex Fuldensis (see p. 182) and four or five readings from Holy Week preserved in Syriac lectionaries. Traces of its influence are also found in early vernacular versions of western Europe, especially the Dutch, as Professor Plooij has indicated in his studies (1923-33).

Scholars have, in fact, been divided on the original language of the Diatessaron. Several factors, such as the Greek title, the Latin translation, and now the Greek fragment found in Syria, have led to much support for the view that it was first made in Greek and then translated into Syriac. The textual quality is definitely Western in type. Some scholars, notably Von Soden, thought that it had exerted a very corrupting influence on the Greek text, but this has doubtless been overstated.

2. The second version of the Syriac Gospels used in the early church was the "Gospel according to the Separated (Evangelists?)." This is known today in two forms: (a) The "Curetonian Syriac," represented by a manuscript of eighty leaves found at the Convent of St. Mary Deipara in the Nitrian Desert west of Cairo in 1842, is now in the British Museum. It was named after Dr. W. Cureton, who privately published the text in 1858. (b) The "Sinaitic Syriac" is represented by a palimpsest discovered at the Convent of St. Catherine at Mount Sinai in 1892 by the Cambridge sisters, Mrs. A. S. Lewis and Mrs. A. D. Gibson. It was published in transcription in 1894 by Messrs. Bensly, Harris, and Burkitt, with an introduction by Mrs. Lewis. Subsequent studies of this important manuscript have been numerous. In 1904 F. C. Burkitt published an edition of the Curetonian Syriac (*Evangelion da-Mepharreshe*) in which the readings of the Sinaitic manu-

script were given in the margin. This subordination did not satisfy Mrs. Lewis, who proceeded in 1910 to issue an edition in which the positions of the manuscripts were reversed. She also listed and discussed here some 300 passages in which she and Professor Burkitt differed in their transcriptions. But an excellent photographic facsimile of the Sinaitic Syriac was published in 1930 by Arthur Hjelt, so that competent scholars may now judge for themselves in disputed passages. The manuscript itself remains at Mount Sinai.

The Cureton manuscript is assigned to the middle of the fifth century and contains the Gospels, with many omissions, in the Western order. The Sinai palimpsest is thought to be a half-century older. It gives about three-quarters of the Gospels, supplementing the Curetonian in such a manner as to provide us with a reasonably complete text of the Old Syriac. This version itself probably originated in the late second or early third century and is therefore a highly significant witness to the primitive text of the Gospels. Although the two forms differ considerably in those passages where they parallel each other, the readings in general are of the Western, Alexandrian, and, especially in the Sinaitic Syriac, a form of the Caesarean type. The Curetonian seems to represent a text somewhat more modified by later developments. For example, it reads Luke 22:43-44, which the Sinaitic omits, and has the longer ending of Mark. One of the most famous variants of the latter manuscript is the reading in Matthew 1:16: "Joseph . . . begat Jesus, who is called the Christ." Mrs. Lewis published a volume in which she discussed this and many other interesting readings of the codex.

3. The Peshitta, the "simple" or "common" version of the Syriac New Testament, has been in continuous use in the Syrian church from the fifth century. While the name is not traceable beyond the ninth century, it may have arisen in order to distinguish the Syriac version proper and that translated from Origen's Hexapla by Paul of Tella in the early seventh century (see p. 77). The version is now generally credited to the work or direction of Rabbula, Bishop of Edessa in A.D. 411-435, since to him is attributed a translation of the New Testament into Syriac which he ordered to be put in place of the popular Diatessaron in all of the churches of his diocese, and since there is no conclusive evidence that the Peshitta was in existence before this time.

Thus the Peshitta became the "Syriac Vulgate," the supreme version of the Syriac churches, in particular, since the schism of about A.D. 431, of the Nestorian branch of the church. While, therefore, the Diatessaron and Old Syriac have nearly perished, the Peshitta has survived in some 250 manuscripts, about 15 of which are as early as the fifth and sixth centuries.

The text of the Peshitta represents a further revision in the direction of the later Byzantine form, of which it may be said to be an early example. Yet it retains an ancient element, especially of Western character. Its style is both less free and more idiomatic than that of the Old Syriac, so that the version is comparable in this respect, as well as in general excellence, to the Latin Vulgate. In fact, it is thought that the latter may have served as a model for the revision.

A few words should be added here to our brief notice regarding the contents of the Syriac canon (see p. 95). The Syriac New Testament of the fifth century was still lacking several of the books of the full canon, namely, the four minor Catholic letters (II Peter, II and III John, Jude) and Revelation. We have seen that the Gospels, Acts, and the Pauline Epistles formed the entire New Testament of the early Syriac church. Although up to the present time there is no known manuscript or text of the Old Syriac of Acts and Paul, there doubtless was such a version, for it is distinctly confirmed in the quotations of Aphraates and the commentaries of Ephraem of the fourth century. The latter are extant only in an Armenian translation, for the supremacy of the Peshitta forced out of use all rival Syriac texts. But the Catholic Epistles and the Apocalypse were evidently not found in the Old Syriac, nor were any of them a part of the Syriac canon until the Peshitta included three of the Catholic letters. The Syriac "Doctrine of Addai" of the second half of the fourth century offers the following instructions: "The Law and the Prophets . . . and the Gospel . . . and the Epistles of Paul . . . and the Acts of the Twelve Apostles . . . these books read in the church of God, and with these read not any other, as there is not any other in which the truth that you hold is written."

Though there is scarcely a Syriac manuscript that contains the twenty-seven books of the present New Testament, there are some documents which contain books not found in our Greek texts. Codex

1700 in Cambridge University contains "The Epistles of St. Clement to the Corinthians" in Syriac. These Epistles stand between the Catholic and Pauline letters and have the same notations for use in church services. Other manuscripts contain Clement's *De Virginibus,* or *De Virginitate.* These instances, as well as what we have said about the Eastern canon, indicate the unique development of the Syriac church and its scholarship.

The first printed edition of the Peshitta was issued in Vienna in 1555 at the expense of the Emperor, Ferdinand I, by Albert Widmanstadt. It was based on only two manuscripts. A better text was edited by C. Schaff in 1717. This was used by Tischendorf in his editions of the Greek text. A critical text of the Gospels with a Latin translation and critical apparatus appeared at Oxford in 1901, edited by Pusey and Gwilliam on the basis of forty-one manuscripts. As yet we do not have a complete critical text of the version, although Gwilliam was at work upon the remainder of the Peshitta New Testament when death unfortunately interrupted his labors in 1913. The Pusey and Gwilliam Gospels and much of Gwilliam's work in the other books were incorporated in a two-volume edition of the New Testament by the British and Foreign Bible Society in 1905-20.

4. The Jacobite branch of the Syrian church was not satisfied with the current authoritative Peshitta revision. At least two attempts seem to have been made to provide a new translation and to carry over into the Syriac canon the full list of books found in the Greek New Testament. The first of these was apparently produced in 508 by Philoxenus, or Mar Xenaia, Bishop of Mabug (485-519) in eastern Syria, with the assistance of his "Rural Bishop," Polycarp. The endeavor was made to translate the whole Bible into Syriac. Authorities disagree as to whether any of this version is still extant, though the translations of II Peter, II and III John, and Jude, that are now bound up with the Peshitta, are thought to owe their origin to Philoxenus. Edward Pococke first edited these books in 1630 at Leyden from a manuscript of the Acts and Catholic letters in the Bodleian Library, and they were included in the Paris Polyglot of 1645 along with a text of the Apocalypse (first printed by Louis de Dieu in 1627) in what was the first complete New Testament printed in Syriac. The relationship between these Catholic Epistles and the somewhat different form

edited and published by John Gwynn in 1909 is obscure, though Gwynn himself argued that the former represented the Philoxenian and the latter the Harclean version, and a recent study by Gunther Zuntz seeks to support this view. Gwynn also discovered a better manuscript of the Apocalypse in the John Rylands Library and published it in 1897. Incidentally, too, he considered these five books to be the work of the Maronite church of Lebanon rather than of the Jacobites. The books were included in the British and Foreign Bible Society edition mentioned above.

5. If the Philoxenian version has survived elsewhere, it is in the form of the "revision" purported to have been made in 616 by Thomas of Harkel (Heraclea) in Mesopotamia at the same time that the Old Testament was translated by Paul of Tella (compare p. 77). This revision or version was based upon some Greek manuscripts from the Monastery of Enaton near Alexandria, apparently of the Western type, and the Syriac manuscripts record in their margins important variant readings found in Greek and Syriac codices. In addition, the version in comparison to the other Syriac versions, including perhaps the Philoxenian, is extremely literal and hence of considerable interest and value to textual critics.

An edition of the Harclean (called "Philoxenian" by the editor) was published by H. J. White in 1778-1803 and has never been superseded. Yet it was based mainly on two manuscripts (J. G. C. Adler added the evidence of two others in 1789), whereas there are now some fifty or more codices of this version known, some of them very old. The earliest dated copy is a Florence manuscript of A.D. 757, but there are seventh- and eighth-century copies in Rome. Many Syriac lectionaries also contain this version. A new critical edition based on all of the available data is clearly needed, and such an edition is currently in preparation by a British scholar, William Duff McHardy.

6. A fragmentary version of the Syriac also exists in a peculiar Palestinian dialect which has much in common with the Western Aramaic such as is found in the Targums to the Hebrew Old Testament. Some scholars claim that it is to be closely identified with the form of Aramaic spoken in Palestine in the time of Christ. The Aramaic language is divided into the classical Edessene, or Eastern Aramaic, and the Western Aramaic, including Jewish Aramaic and Samaritan.

The Palestinian Syriac is thought to have originated in the sixth century, perhaps in connection with an attempt by Justinian to root out the Samaritan beliefs. The version is found in a number of fragments, mostly lectionaries, dating from the sixth to the twelfth centuries. Besides the Gospels there are portions of the letters of Paul, Acts, James, and Hebrews.

This version was discovered in a Vatican lectionary dated A.D. 1030 near the end of the eighteenth century by Adler, described by Adler and Assemani in 1789, and published by Count F. M. Erizzo (2 volumes, 1861-64) and by Professor Paul Lagarde (1892). The Cambridge sisters, Mrs. Lewis and Mrs. Gibson, republished the text in 1899 on the basis of Lagarde's edition and the evidence of two new manuscripts discovered on Mount Sinai. The text of this Syriac is mixed in type, but generally supports Western, Caesarean, and Alexandrian readings. While it has been subject to the influence of the Peshitta, it appears to have been quite independent of this and all other Syriac versions in origin. Some scholars have considered it to be related to the text from which the Georgian and "old Armenian" versions were made (see below).

The Egyptian or Coptic versions of the Old Testament were noticed in Chapter VIII. The three branches of the Egyptian version of the New Testament are likewise (1) the Sahidic, or dialect of upper Egypt; (2) the dialects of middle Egypt; (3) the dialect of Alexandria and the delta region, the Bohairic.

The Sahidic was the dialect of the Christian community whose headquarters was at Thebes. Hence it was formerly called "Thebaic." The version may have originated in the early third century, and it definitely reflects a text of the Alexandrian type, with a considerable mixture of Western readings especially in Mark and Luke. At the end of the eighteenth century (1799) Woide published the known fragments of the Sahidic New Testament. Since then, and especially within recent decades in connection with the extensive finds of Egyptian papyri, large numbers of other fragments have been discovered, almost enough to complete the New Testament. Some of these reach back to the fifth and even to the fourth century.

While editions of the Sahidic were published by Gousseau in 1895 and Balestri in 1904, the most valuable text was that produced by

George Horner in 1911-24 at Oxford in seven volumes. The edition was based on about 750 fragments and contained an English translation of the Coptic and a critical apparatus of variant readings. But even this excellent and painstaking work is now somewhat antiquated by new material, e.g., in the valuable J. P. Morgan Library collection and in the University of Michigan. The former, comprising about fifty codices, contains several New Testament manuscripts and has been privately published in a facsimile edition. An important text of the Acts and Pauline Epistles was published by Sir Herbert Thompson in 1932 from three Beatty papyri of about A.D. 600, two of which are in the Michigan collection and one in Mr. Beatty's own collection.

The second main Coptic dialect is the Bohairic, the primitive Christian language of lower Egypt after the decline and disappearance of the Greek in the early Christian centuries. Its central city and home was at first Alexandria, and afterwards Memphis; hence this dialect has been called, though improperly, "Memphitic." Bohairic was the literary language of Alexandria, and in spite of certain restrictions of Coptic idiom and rigidities of word order it was capable of remarkably precise translation of ideas from the Greek. More developed and artistically complete than the other dialects, it soon became supreme throughout all Egypt, so that "Coptic" today means the Bohairic form of the language.

Of the Coptic dialects the Bohairic alone preserves a complete New Testament. Over a hundred manuscripts are known, the oldest that can be certainly dated belonging to the twelfth century, though there are fragments reaching back to the ninth and a leaf of Ephesians supposedly of the fifth. Coptic manuscripts in general are difficult to date from their script alone. The Bohairic is thought to be a little later than the Sahidic in origin. It is a very good and careful rendering of the Greek, and represents a definitely Alexandrian type of text. The best manuscripts have the shorter ending of Mark and omit John 7:53-8:11. Both Sahidic and Bohairic versions seem to have regarded the Apocalypse as uncanonical.

The *editio princeps* of the Bohairic was produced by Wilkins at Oxford in 1716. The best and most complete edition is that of George Horner, published in four volumes in 1898-1905 with a critical apparatus and literal English translation. He notes readings of forty-six manuscripts in the Gospels and about thirty-four in the other books.

Other Egyptian versions, also, occupying a place midway between the Sahidic and Bohairic, seem to have been current in the Fayum, just west and southwest of Memphis and south of the Delta. Scholars now distinguish three or more of such dialects: the Memphitic (not to be confused with the older name for the Bohairic), Fayumic, and Akhmimic. Many fragmentary manuscripts of these versions have been coming to light in recent decades. Notices of them were published serially until about 1933 in *Revue Biblique* by Hyvernat and Vaschalde (see also bibliography); a few fragments have been edited and published; and an important papyrus of the Gospel of John in "sub-Akhmimic" was published by Sir Herbert Thompson in 1924. This manuscript, assigned to the last quarter of the fourth century, differs often from both the Sahidic and Bohairic while still showing close affinities with B and W. No complete edition, critical or otherwise, of any of the middle Egyptian versions has yet been completed. When the evidence has all been made available for study it may prove of importance to an understanding of the relationship between the Western and Alexandrian texts and, perhaps, of the origins of the so-called Caesarean text.

The Armenian version of the New Testament originated about A.D. 400, according to an old tradition, the work of St. Mesrop. Owing to the flexible character of the language and the classical form of the Armenian used, the translation is probably the most accurate and beautiful of the versions. For a long time it was generally held—also in accordance with an Armenian tradition—that the first translation was made from the Syriac and later so thoroughly revised to Greek copies that scarcely any evidence remains of the Syriac base. According to recent scholars who still hold this view the translation was made from a text of Caesarean type such as may partly survive in the Palestinian Syriac. This is to explain the Caesarean characteristics of the present Armenian version, as well as of the old Georgian (see below), which was supposedly made from its unrevised form. Streeter's view that the revision was made to Greek manuscripts of Caesarean type does not seem to be supported by the evidence. Of the Caesarean element found in the Armenian there is, however, no doubt. Study by such scholars as Streeter, Macler, Lyonnet, Blake, Lake, Colwell, and others have shown it to be an important witness to a form of this textual type, agreeing especially with the group: Georgian Θ 565 700.

There is also the old Armenian tradition, however, that the version was made directly from the Greek, and recent scholarship is divided in its opinion, with a growing tendency to doubt the Syriac theory. This may be seen, for example, in the significant work done in the area recently by Lyonnet, Peters, C. S. C. Williams, Essabalian and, somewhat earlier, by Conybeare. What Syriacisms may occur in the Armenian can be explained, it is felt, through the use of the Syriac Bible in the Armenian church up through the fourth century, or through the influence of Tatian in the form of a primitive Armenian Diatessaron, or both. The present Armenian text also has so great a homogeneity that it is difficult to identify clear traces of a revision.

Armenian manuscripts are very numerous, probably more numerous than those of any other version except the Latin Vulgate. The Armenians were zealous translators and copyists, so that several important works of antiquity have been preserved to us in their language alone. All lists of Biblical manuscripts are inadequate. The oldest dated document is a Gospels codex of A.D. 887 at Moscow, which has been published in photographic facsimile, but there are several others from the ninth and tenth centuries. Lagrange recently described thirty-one early codices. In one manuscript, dated A.D. 989, an interesting colophon occurs ascribing the doubtful ending of Mark (16:9-20) to the presbyter "Ariston." It is also the oldest extant Armenian manuscript to include the pericope, John 8:1-11. Armenian manuscripts, especially the older ones, otherwise frequently omit both of these sections or mark them as doubtful. The Johannine story often is given at the end of the Gospel. The Apocalypse, though probably translated in the fifth century, was apparently not included in the Armenian canon until the twelfth. Philemon seems also to have been missing, but an apocryphal letter, "III Corinthians," is found.

The first printed edition of the Armenian Bible was that of Oskan published at Amsterdam, the New Testament in 1666 and the complete Bible in 1668. A better text was issued by John Zohrab (New Testament, 1789; Bible, 1805), based in the New Testament on eight manuscripts of the Bible, thirty Gospels, fourteen AKP, and four lectionaries. Actually Zohrab mainly transcribed one manuscript of A.D. 1319 containing an excellent text. His edition, although therefore very good, is not really critical, and his brief critical apparatus is inadequate. The official Armenian Bible published by the Mechitarists of Venice (1864) is based on Zohrab and carries no *apparatus criticus*. The American Bible Society also publishes an inexact reprint of the Zohrab text. A good edition of the Apocalypse was published by F. C. Conybeare in 1907.

The traditions about the origin of the Georgian version are similar to those regarding the Armenian, except that the Georgian was made from the latter. As we have already briefly noted, some scholars believe that this was an older form of the Armenian than we now possess. Research by Lake, Blake, and New (Mrs. Silva Lake) identified the Georgian as an important witness to the Caesarean type of text. Professor Blake distinguished three groups of manuscripts, representing two types of text which he called G^1 and G^2 respectively, and a third form somewhat more revised in the direction of the Byzantine text which became the Vulgate of the Georgian church.

There are many important and relatively ancient manuscripts of the Georgian version, but apart from some early study and publication in Acts and Paul by Conybeare and recent research by a few scholars like Baumstark, Zorell and Peradze, little critical study has been undertaken except in the Gospels of Matthew and Mark. Blake published the text of the important "Adysh Gospels" (A.D. 897) in Mark (1928), Matthew (1933) and John (1950) with a Latin translation. Maurice Brière, his collaborator in the Johannine volume, is carrying on the work in Luke, following Professor Blake's lamented death in 1950. The entire Georgian text was printed in Moscow in 1723 and subsequently, but the only critical text is that of Matthew and Mark published by Professor V. N. Beneševič at Leningrad in 1909-11. It was based on two tenth-century uncials, the Opiza Manuscript (A.D. 913) and Tbet' Manuscript (A.D. 995). These codices differ considerably from each other, the Opiza Manuscript, for example, alone omitting Mark 16:9-20; and they are thought to represent two different recensions of the text, since other manuscripts of each type exist. Blake cites their readings in his editions. Together, however, they constitute the G^2 form of text, while the Adysh codex, which Blake thought may represent a text current in Georgia about A.D. 600 or earlier, has been designated as G^1. The canon of the Georgian, like the Armenian, did not originally include the Apocalypse.

The beginnings of Christianity in Abyssinia have been recounted in Chapter VIII. While Christianity secured a foothold in this country as early as the fourth century, the Ethiopic or Ge'ez version probably does not reach back beyond the fifth. There are traces of an older translation allegedly made from the Old Syriac, but the version now current was made from the Greek and often agrees with the Coptic versions. It is therefore frequently of Alexandrian quality, colored also by Western elements. There are many manuscripts, of a late date, representing revisions to the medieval Arabic text current in Alexandria. The Ethiopic New Testament also included a collection of "Clementine" literature, which was discovered to contain the Revelation of Peter, a book which had been used as canonical by Clement of Alexandria, about A.D. 180-200, and which has also come to light in an Akhmimic version. The Ethiopic New Testament was first printed in Rome in 1548-49 and reprinted at the same time in Walton's Polyglot. The British and Foreign Bible Society issued (1830) an edition prepared by T. P. Platt, which long remained standard. A similar text was published by F. da Bassano at Asmara in 1920-26. None of these editions, however, are truly critical.

The Gothic version, prepared by Ulfilas, Bishop of the Goths about A.D. 350, has also been referred to in Chapter VIII. The New Testament fragments of this translation show that it was made directly and very accurately from the Greek. The remnants that we possess seem to have belonged to northern Italy, about the time of the Lombard conquest in the sixth century. The largest fragments are portions of over half of the Gospels preserved in Codex Argenteus, a manuscript of Bohemian origin now at Uppsala, Sweden, written upon purple vellum in letters of silver and gold, and dating from the fifth or sixth century. Except for some portions of the Pauline Epistles found on a few palimpsests at Milan and a Gothic-Latin leaf of Luke at Giessen, the remainder of the New Testament is lost. The Greek text from which Ulfilas made his translation was mainly of the Byzantine type, but with a considerable mixture of other, especially Western, readings. Several editions of the text have been published, beginning with that of Gabelentz and Loebe (1836-43). The best is the two-volume work of W. Streitberg (1908; second edition, 1919). A photographic facsimile was published by the University of Uppsala in 1927. Significant studies of the language and text of the version were published by C. W. S. Friedrichsen (Gospels, 1926; Epistles, 1939). Representing as they do the only extant Gothic literature, the Biblical remains of this translation are of special philological as well as textual interest.

The other versions are of comparatively little value for the textual criticism of the Greek New Testament. The Arabic were made, some from Syriac, some from the Greek, and some from Coptic, in the seventh to ninth centuries. The current form is mainly from the Bohairic, with corrections and additions from the Greek and Syriac. The salient facts about the origins of the Slavonic and Persian, which are even later, have been given in connection with the Old Testament discussion. There are many manuscripts of the Slavonic, the best text of which was based on the Greek, but they are apparently not earlier than the eleventh century and are of minor critical value. Some preliminary study and publication has been made by Professors G. N. Vospresenski at Moscow and Josef Vajs at Prague. The late Professor Ropes suggested that the old Bohemian might be worthy of study in Acts for its Western elements, and traces of a Caesarean element have been claimed for the Persian. Minor as well as major versions may thus have a contribution to make to the restoration of the earliest Greek text and to a knowledge of the history of the text.

CHAPTER XV

Textual Criticism
and the Printed Text

IN THE preceding chapters we have described scores of manuscripts, versions, and quotations. We have also noted that the text of the New Testament became corrupted in the process of transmission, and that the corrupt text became dominant as time went on. By the judicious use of the textual materials, however, Biblical scholars can now detect and remove scribal and other errors and give us a form of the text closely approaching the very writings of the apostles and evangelists.

Unfortunately this process of textual criticism in the New Testament was seriously retarded by the circumstances surrounding the first printings of its text. For, although the new method of reproducing documents did away with the fallible work of the copyist, the earliest printed editions of the Greek New Testament reproduced a form of the late medieval text. This is, of course, not strange, since these printings preceded both the discovery and use of the oldest and best documents and the real work of textual criticism. Such work, when it got under way, consisted first of showing the inadequacy of the late text and then of efforts to displace it with an earlier one. By that time, regrettably, the late form had been firmly established by many reprintings and by translations made from it into Latin, English, and other languages, so that its displacement was no easy task.

It will help to an understanding of the process, however, if we sketch briefly the developments of this early period, when the late or "received text," as it came to be called, had its rise and supremacy in printed form. This period lasted roughly from the time of the Erasmus edition of 1516 to the time of Lachmann (1831), or actually over three hundred years.

The earliest printed edition of the Greek New Testament was that incorporated in the Complutensian Polyglot, printed in 1514-17 and published in 1522 under the supervision of Cardinal Ximenes. Its text was based on many manuscripts whose identities are now uncertain, but it was late in form and exerted comparatively little influence. Erasmus, the Dutch scholar, was the editor of the first published Greek New Testament (1516). Although one of his half-dozen manuscripts was the important minuscule 1, his text was based chiefly on two inferior documents preserved in Basle, one of the Gospels and one of the Acts and Epistles, and only one manuscript of the Apocalypse. The latter was incomplete, particularly in the last six verses, so that Erasmus translated from Latin into Greek to fill up the lacunae. The first edition, which like the Complutensian Polyglot also included the Latin Vulgate in a parallel column, contained many errors, partly due to hasty preparation in order to anticipate the Ximenes edition. These were largely corrected in four later editions published between 1519 and 1535, but Erasmus never seems to have had more than eight or nine manuscripts at his disposal, and the text remained late Byzantine in form. The third edition (1522) is noted for its introduction of the "three witnesses" passage in I John 5:7, read by the Vulgate and therefore also by the Complutensian Polyglot. But it has never been found in any Greek manuscript since Erasmus' day, when he was persuaded to include it on the basis of an inferior Greek document. He omitted the passage in his later editions, but because the third edition became the basis for the later standardized text it came into the English Bible and remained there until the time of the Revised Version.

The famous scholar and printer, Robert Stephanus (Estienne), of Paris, also published several editions of the Greek New Testament, beginning in 1546. His text was based on Erasmus (1535), the Complutensian Polyglot, and eventually fifteen manuscripts in the Paris Library. The third edition (1550), the superb Paris folio known as the "*editio regia,*" became the standard text of Britain. The fourth (1551) is notable for the first appearance of the verse divisions in the New Testament. These were prepared by Stephanus during a horseback journey from Paris to Lyons, the poor divisions in spots suggesting that some of the work was done on the horse.

The next great editor of the text was Theodore Beza, whom we
have already had occasion to mention in connection with the codex
which bears his name. Beza produced ten editions, four folio and six
octavo, beginning in 1565. The folios contained a Greek text almost
identical with that of Stephanus, together with the Latin Vulgate and
Beza's own Latin translation in parallel columns and an extensive
commentary of notes. The last folios of 1588-98 exerted a great influence upon the King James Version, especially through the Geneva
Bible, and Beza's authority helped fix the current Greek text. On the
Continent, however, the form of text which became standard, and
from which the name "Textus Receptus" or "received text" itself de-
rives, was an edition by the two Dutch printers, the Elzevir brothers.
They published seven editions based on Stephanus and Beza between
1624 and 1678. The second (1633) edition contained in its Preface the
claim that this was the text received by all and free from change or
error (*"Textum ergo habes, nunc ab omnibus receptum: in quo nihil
immutatum aut corruptum damus"*). This text differed from the
Stephanus 1550 edition in only 287 instances according to Scrivener's
estimate.

It is plainly evident that such a text, based on a few comparatively
late manuscripts, was not likely to be a very exact reproduction of
the original documents of the New Testament. As the years went by,
manuscripts of earlier dates were discovered on every hand. Documents reaching back as far as the fourth century were brought to
light, which stood several centuries nearer the autographs than any
of those that formed the basis of the "Textus Receptus." The gift of
Codex Alexandrinus to Charles I in 1628 stimulated much interest in
the study of the text. Bishop Walton's Polyglot of 1657 (also known
as the London Polyglot), though printing the text of Stephanus 1550,
gave readings of Codex Alexandrinus, sixteen other manuscripts, and
several of the versions. Scholars began to compile collections of variant
readings. The text of John Fell (1675) had a large critical apparatus
for its day. By the time that John Mill published his edition of the
Stephanus text in 1707, he was able to cite over 30,000 variants. Mill
himself added evidence from 78 new manuscripts, the greatest single
contribution to the time of Tischendorf over 150 years later. He also
made the first extensive use of patristic quotations.

Other scholars who in the eighteenth century added significantly to the materials available were Richard Bentley, J. A. Bengel, J. J. Wetstein, J. S. Semler, J. J. Griesbach, C. F. Matthaei, and Andrew Birch. Wetstein issued a two-volume text in 1751-52, largely Elzevir, in which he gave the largest and best critical apparatus to date and introduced the present form of manuscript nomenclature. Griesbach's editions of 1774-77 and 1796-1806 also contained a rich apparatus. Matthaei (1782-88) added about 75 Moscow and other manuscripts, and Birch, whose valuable work was subsidized by the King of Denmark, collated many important Italian documents and first published the readings of Codex Vaticanus. F. C. Alter at about the same time contributed the evidence of Vienna sources. The Roman Catholic John A. Scholz a little later (1830-36) added evidence from about 600 codices, but only a dozen or so were complete and the work unfortunately was inaccurate. On the other hand, the English scholar S. P. Tregelles contributed many descriptions and collations which were notable for their excellence. Although Sinaiticus was not available to him, and he was unable to recollate Vaticanus, his edition of 1857-72 had the fullest and best apparatus to that time and exerted a great influence against the Textus Receptus in England. In this period, also, F. H. A. Scrivener and J. W. Burgon collated a number of manuscripts, and the latter compiled an amazing collection of several manuscript volumes of patristic citations, now in the British Museum.

But the greatest discoverer, collator, and publisher of manuscripts was L. F. Constantin von Tischendorf, a professor at Leipzig and, as we have noted, the finder of the great Codex Sinaiticus. A tireless traveler and worker, he discovered over twenty uncials, published editions of most of them for the first time (including $\aleph$ B₂ C D₂ E₂ L), and published many editions of the Greek New Testament. The most important of these for its extensive and still indispensable critical apparatus was the eighth major critical edition (1869-72). The patristic evidence was of special value. Tischendorf died in 1874 and Professor C. R. Gregory of Leipzig, a disciple of his as well as of Hort, prepared the prolegomena to the edition with assistance from Ezra Abbot. Originally appearing in a three-volume Latin form (1884-90-94), it was translated into German and expanded into a complete introduction to the subject and the most extensive catalogue of the known materials (manuscripts, versions, and church fathers) compiled to the time of publication in 1900-09 (see Bibliography). Nearly two thousand manuscripts were listed, and the nomenclature introduced by Wetstein was adopted and improved. This monumental contribution remains an indispensable tool for the student of New Testament text. Gregory had also planned a ninth edition of Tischendorf to bring it up to date, but death intervened to prevent this.

Tischendorf's text in his last editions was strongly influenced by Codex Sinaiticus and the work of Lachmann, which represented a radical departure from the Textus Receptus of the preceding period. We must touch here briefly upon this development and upon the rise of critical method in the use of the materials now available.

Up to this time all editions of the Greek New Testament had reproduced forms of the received text. But several important contributions besides the collection of variant readings were made to the development of a methodology which was eventually to overthrow it. Richard Simon, a French scholar, made valuable observations in several historical treatises (1689, 1695). Edward Wells (1709-19), William Mace (1729) and E. Harwood (1776) first printed texts which often departed from the Textus Receptus in the adoption of earlier readings. In 1720 Bentley, a great classical scholar, issued certain important "Proposals" for publishing a text of the fourth century, but caustic criticism, other work, and finally death prevented him from carrying out his purpose. Bengel (about 1734) introduced into his apparatus five classes of readings, three of which were considered to be better than or as good as were to be found in his text. Following a suggestion of Bentley's, he first proposed a classification of manuscripts into families ("Asiatic" and "African") and first enunciated certain important principles of criticism, such as that manuscripts should be "weighed" and not merely counted, and that a harder reading is generally to be preferred to an easier one. Semler carried on Bengel's work and eventually (about 1767) prepared a threefold classification of authorities ("Oriental," "Western," and "Alexandrian"), which he first called "recensions."

But the real work of textual criticism begins with Griesbach, a pupil of Semler's. In his editions (1774-76, 1805) he preferred to call the late text "Constantinopolitan" or "Byzantine," and proposed that its source was the other two. He also proposed five canons of criticism, which added to previous ones the principles that no reading without the support of some ancient witness should be adopted—though conjecture was eventually not entirely excluded—, that families rather than individual manuscripts primarily should determine readings, and that the shorter reading and the reading which at first appears to convey a false sense should generally be preferred. The chief weakness in his work seems to have been failure to take adequate account of mixture in texts, although he first clearly called attention to it in individual manuscripts. His views were followed by J. L. Hug, who suggested that a primitive text had been variously corrupted into the forms of the "Western" text, which in turn was subjected to recensions by Origen (Palestine), Hesychius (Egypt), and Lucian (Syria), corresponding to those of the Septuagint. His views oversimplified the problem, but he anticipated certain modern developments in the more prominent place given to the Western text and in his characterization of the text of B as a recension. Aside from his work, however, Griesbach's views were generally disregarded, and little progress was consequently made for the next fifty years.

With Carolus Lachmann, Professor of Classical Philology at Berlin and editor of a number of classical texts, begins what may be called the recession and rejection of the Textus Receptus. In his small edition of 1831 and larger edition of 1842-50 he first entirely disregarded it and the manuscript support upon which it rested. With the purpose of establishing a fourth-century text, he was interested in only the two families of documents which he called "Oriental" (A B C etc., Origen) and "Occidental" (D D_2 E_2 F G_3 H_3, etc., Old Latin, Vulgate, Western Fathers). In the six rules of criticism which he proposed he placed an emphasis on consideration of regional support for a reading. More weight was to be given to a reading whose support came from different geographical areas. The weakness of Lachmann's work lay in a neglect of documentary groups and in his almost entire disregard of the minuscule evidence, as well as in an inadequate use of patristic and—aside from Latin—of versional testimony. Nonetheless, his influence was heavy against the Textus Receptus on the Continent.

As we have noted, a similar effect was produced in England by Tregelles, who followed up the achievements of Lachmann with the more ambitious aim of producing the oldest possible text. His use of the evidence was more accurate, comprehensive, and judicious, and he is credited with the first clear enunciation of the important principle of the comparative criticism of documents, i.e., the identification of early readings by the combined testimony of manuscript, versional and patristic evidence. He also gave special regard to matters of internal or intrinsic evidence, that is, due consideration to what the author of the document may originally have written, as judged by his general purpose, interest, prejudices, style, etc. Tischendorf included this emphasis among his "rules," and also enunciated the principles of preference for readings which might explain the rise of all other variants in a given passage and for readings in the Synoptic Gospels which showed differences in parallel passages.

In spite of the excellent work of Lachmann, Tregelles, and Tischendorf, proponents of the traditional text continued active in the nineteenth century. It was championed by the learned and belligerent Burgon and the scholarly Scrivener. The latter reissued the Textus Receptus at Cambridge in 1860 and subsequently, the edition of 1877 containing variations of Beza (1565), Elzevir (1624), Lachmann, Tischendorf, and Tregelles. Henry Alford, Dean of Canterbury, who published six editions between 1849 and 1861, inclined at first toward the Textus Receptus, but later came over to the Tregelles-Tischendorf type of text.

The final blow was administered to the Textus Receptus by the work of the British scholars, Dr. F. J. A. Hort and Bishop B. F. Westcott. The two collaborated in the production of a text and in the elaboration of a theory of criticism which has had an enormous influence from their day to this. Building upon the achievements of the scholars whom we have noticed, they brought out in 1881-82 a two-volume edition of text (without critical apparatus) and method which was some thirty years in preparation and has become a sort of watershed in the history of the textual criticism of the New Testament.

In their classification of authorities for the text Westcott and Hort used the terms "Western" and "Syrian" (or "Antiochian") for two of the groups previously identified, and divided the third into "Alexandrian" and "Neutral." In our discussion of materials we have already referred to these designations and have indicated certain of the chief witnesses to each, anticipating also the later definition of the so-called "Caesarean" type of text. But for an understanding of the Westcott-Hort theory and method, as well as of developments subsequent to their time, it will be well at this point to add a few words about the reasons for the classification and about the characteristics of each group.

The "Neutral" text, as the name implies, was considered by Hort to be the purest extant form. It was thought to be entirely free from corruption and mixture with other texts and to represent the nearest approach to the New Testament autographs. Its best representative was Codex Vaticanus, and its second best, Sinaiticus. These two codices were thought to be derived independently from a common original, at no great distance from the autographs. When their readings agreed, the evidence for Westcott and Hort was generally conclusive against overwhelming numerical evidence of later witnesses, unless internal testimony contradicted. An outstanding example of the latter is found in the "Western non-interpolations" to which we have previously alluded. In general, readings unknown to the Neutral, Alexandrian, or Western texts were to be rejected as "Syrian," and no reading from the Western or Alexandrian was to be admitted without some support from the Neutral. The other chief witnesses to the Neutral text have been mentioned in the preceding chapter. We may add that among the church fathers such "Neutral" elements were considered to be most numerous in Origen, Didymus, Cyril of Alexandria, and Eusebius; and, among the versions, in the Coptic.

The "Alexandrian" text supposedly represented Greek scholarship such as might be expected to emanate from Alexandria, a center of Greek learning, operating upon the text to give it smoothness and linguistic correctness. Such a text was therefore to be found predominantly in the quotations of the church fathers of Alexandria, such as Clement, Origen, Dionysius and, Cyril, to some extent in Eusebius of Caesarea, and in the Coptic version, particularly in its Bohairic form. There was a notable absence of the extraneous additions found in texts like those of the Western group in both Neutral and Alexandrian, but the latter was thought to be distinguishable as less primitive than the former.

The "Western" text, so-called, was to be most readily recognized in the Old Latin version and the bilingual uncials written in the west (cf. the previous chapter). But traces of it were to be found in the other versions, especially the Old Syriac; and the Greek text used by the ante-Nicene fathers, where they did not come into contact with Egypt, was in general Western in character. This type of text seems, therefore, to have had its origin very early, before the copying of manuscripts was done with adequate care, and before it was regarded as wrong to interpolate, expand, contract, or omit at will such passages as to a scribe seemed in need of alteration. For these appear to be the outstanding characteristics of the Western text. Many old and important readings are to be found in it, and it is therefore often in agreement with the "Neutral" text; but its peculiar readings must be weighed carefully before being adopted.

The "Syrian" text was produced in Hort's opinion by the Greek and Syrian church fathers as a revision of existing texts in the vicinity of Antioch in the late fourth century. Being later in origin than the other groups, it was consequently not of equal authority with them. In fact it was simply considered to be the result of combining non-Syrian readings. As such it was a full text, characterized by conflation and attempts to smooth out difficulties. The uncial codex, Alexandrinus, in the Gospels, and the Peshitta Syriac are good early representatives of this text, and Chrysostom, Archbishop of Constantinople (died 407), made use of it in his extensive homiletical works. The later Greek fathers, including the great Biblical scholar, Theodore of Mopsuestia (died 429), also employed it. And most of the later uncials as well as the large mass of cursive Greek manuscripts belong to this group. The Textus Receptus is a late and corrupt form of it.

The most signal contribution of Westcott and Hort, however, was in the area of method, as set forth by Hort in their second volume in a comprehensive theoretical statement and a discussion of disputed passages. In brief summary, they indicated that from a study of the sources of corruption of the text in the manuscripts (involuntary or intentional) it becomes clear that some manuscripts are better than others because their readings possess a higher presumption of primitiveness when judged according to the "observed proclivities of average copyists" ("transcriptional probability") and according to the context judged most suitable to the characteristics of the original author's thought and style ("intrinsic probability"). Such witnesses were to be preferred in a given reading either individually ("evidence of documents") or, especially, in groups ("evidence of groups"), unless there were weighty reason to the contrary. Emphasis was thus again placed upon the quality rather than quantity of the evidence, and upon the age of the text of a manuscript rather than the age of the manuscript itself. In this connection great stress was also laid upon the study of the interrelationships of the witnesses on the assumption that their ancestries could be thus established, the relative age and value of their texts determined, and the primitive text discovered by the reconstruction of a family tree of the documents ("genealogical evidence"). Recognition was also made of the difficulties involved here due to conflation and mixture of readings. When the better manuscripts were found to be ranged on different sides, the personal judgment of the critic would be the final arbiter. He would be guided by certain principles of probability such as we have already noted. In addition, Hort, like Tischendorf, emphasized preference for a reading which would explain the origin of other variants but could not itself be so explained. Also, a variant which combined the appearance of improvement with the absence of its reality was to be suspected ("coincidence of intrinsic and transcriptional probability"), because a scribe was unlikely actually to improve the text even though he thought he was doing so.

While the theory and text of Westcott and Hort were currently and subsequently subjected to certain valid criticisms and modifications (see next chapter), the influence of their work was tremendous and it was widely received with favor and approbation. As members of the British Revision Committee they made their text available to the English revisers, and their personal influence was effective in helping to establish as the basis of the Revised Version a much more accurate and primitive text than had ever previously been used for such an undertaking. Students and translators made much use of it, and several modern speech versions were made from it. Although a number of major and minor editions of the Greek New Testament appeared later, and Scrivener republished the Textus Receptus in 1882 and subsequently, the Westcott-Hort text soon became a standard for general usage, and other critical texts have not varied greatly from it. It marked, therefore, the final rejection of the "received text," and itself became a sort of textus receptus in Britain and America.

CHAPTER XVI

Textual Criticism
Since Westcott and Hort

THE supremacy and popularity of the Westcott-Hort text continued for many years. The research of Bernhard Weiss and the propagation of the Nestle text (see below) especially helped to establish its wide usage. At the same time questions were inevitably raised about it owing to the discovery of new materials and to the critical study of the textual theory upon which it was based.

Our review of materials in a previous chapter has indicated something of recent discovery. Unknown to Westcott and Hort—to mention only a few items—were the Beatty papyri, the Washington Gospels, Koridethi, the Washington Manuscript of Paul (I), the four purple parchment codices of the sixth century, Laurensis (Ψ), the Sinaitic Syriac, several important Coptic and Old Latin texts, and the more reliable editions of the patristic writings which have appeared both in the two great series of publications, the Berlin Corpus of the Greek and the Vienna Corpus of the Latin fathers, and in a variety of monographs and studies.

In addition much progress has been made in textual theory. The Westcott-Hort "Neutral" text was found to be practically without support in the earliest fathers, and appeared itself to be a recension virtually indistinguishable from their so-called "Alexandrian" form. The growing realization of uncontrolled variation in the transmission of the text in the first two or three centuries and of extreme mixture in its later history led to considerable doubt of Hort's emphasis on the possibility of traveling back nearly to the autograph by the reconstruction of a family or genealogical tree. There were—to change the figure a bit—too many missing links. The method actually worked out in very limited areas and Hort himself made very little use of it, neglecting the history of the text in favor of an extreme reliance upon Vaticanus and Sinaiticus. A restatement of the method in terms of a statistical "rule of iron" was made by Dom Quentin in connection with the Benedictine Vulgate project; but this was severely criticized, among others by M. J. Bédier, who also showed that the genealogical method applied to classical authors generally resulted in a two-branched family tree which conveniently allowed the editor a final choice of readings. Indictment of the Westcott-Hort theory and method was climaxed by H. C. Hoskier's detailed treatment in his two-volume work, *Codex B and Its Allies* (1914). It became increasingly clear that the term "Neutral," not to mention the title, *The New Testament in the Original Greek,* was at least presumptive, if not erroneous.

The attachment of more significance to the evidence of versions and fathers marked one of the main paths of divergence from the Westcott-Hort position. Growth of interest in the Western text was one important result. This was stimulated by the discovery of the Sinaitic Syriac, by study of the Old Latin, by studies of Codex Bezae (R. Harris, B. Weiss, and, later, H. J. Vogels), and by Rendel Harris' significant *Four Lectures on the Western Text* (1894), in which he warned against canonizing the Westcott-Hort edition. Such studies of patristic writings as P. M. Barnard's work on Clement of Alexandria and Sanday's on Irenaeus showed the extreme antiquity and widespread usage of the Western form. Various theories were proposed to explain it. Hort had thought of it as a revision, perhaps made at Antioch about A.D. 125-140, which quickly became the official New Testament text in widely scattered areas. Harris and Vogels claimed that Codex Bezae represented a Latinized Greek text. F. H. Chase thought that it was influenced by the Syriac. F. Blass revived and gave some currency to an older view that Luke had himself produced two editions of Luke-Acts, represented respectively by the Western and Alexandrian forms. The problem of these strikingly divergent texts, especially in Acts, has continued to be agitated now for well over half a century without complete settlement. A. C. Clark in his treatment of the Gospels and Acts (see Bibliography) defended the Western form, regarding the shorter readings of the great uncials first (1914) as accidental and later (1933) as purposeful excisions of the supposedly more primitive and longer text. But in his valuable volume on the text of Acts in *The Beginnings of Christianity* (1926), J. H. Ropes took the view that the Western text was in general an inferior rewriting, perhaps expressly created for the earliest canon. This estimate of general inferiority has prevailed, but it is modified by the conviction that Western readings cannot be dismissed without careful consideration, and that a number of them bear the marks of authenticity. This was well demonstrated by Professor G. D. Kilpatrick in articles published in 1943 in the *Journal of Theological Studies*.

The use of the term "Western" has also become subject to some criticism and modification. Hort had used it of almost anything which did not fall into his other textual categories. But it is now generally felt that the name should be limited at least to those witnesses which are geographically western, i.e., the bilingual codices, the Old Latin, and certain of the fathers such as Cyprian. The Old Syriac and comparable texts would better be designated separately as "Eastern" or "Syrian" (not to be confused with Hort's "Syrian"). This separation of the Old Syriac is justifiable on at least two counts. It is not geographically western, and its readings almost as often support Alexandrian or Caesarean texts as they do Western. Even so, considerable divergence exists within the remaining Western group, for example between the European and African forms of the Old Latin.

It thus became evident that a number of different and somewhat localized texts appeared in the second and third centuries. In his important study, *The Four Gospels,* published in 1924, Canon Streeter proposed a theory of such "local texts," in which he classified the early witnesses in five groups and connected each with one of the principal ancient sees of Christianity, namely, Alexandria (BℵL sa bo), Antioch (Old Syriac), Caesarea (Θ fam 1 and 13 28 565 700), Italy-Gaul (D b a), Carthage (k W^{Mk} e). Besides the primary and secondary evidence, which we have reproduced here, he identified two other groups of subordinate value, plus patristic witnesses. While this reconstruction has not entirely held up, it conveys much truth. Differences of opinion especially concern details of definition and the significant question whether most of the so-called texts should not be considered as processes of growth rather than definite, editorial recensions made at a particular time and place. Strangely enough, therefore, while there has come to be widespread agreement that the Alexandrian text represents a geographically and chronologically localized treatment, the same interpretation of the other supposed "recensions" is being seriously questioned.

The total picture has been further complicated by the discovery of the so-called "Caesarean" text, of whose character, support, and significance we have already given some intimation. This interesting and significant development deserves a further word of explanation. Professor W. H. Ferrar of Dublin discovered, in about 1875, that four manuscripts (13, 69, 124, 346) were textually related. To these, collectively known as Family 13 or the Ferrar group, other scholars added new witnesses from time to time, until now there are about a dozen altogether. In 1941 the Lakes attempted a genealogical reconstruction of the family relationships and printed the "archetype" in Mark. Their investigation also led them to conclude that the ancestor of the group was a document written before the eleventh century in Palestine or on Mount Sinai.

Meanwhile Kirsopp Lake identified another related group of manuscripts (1, 118, 131, 209, to which 1582 was later added), which he called Family 1, and of which he published a description and evaluation in 1902. Here he demonstrated the relationship of this group to Family 13, as well as to certain other codices, viz., 22, 28, 565, 700. In 1923, after the discovery of Codex Theta, he and Professor R. P. Blake showed the connection of this manuscript to the total group, which then became known as Family Theta. Subsequently Codex W in Mark (5-16), some early papyri, and the Beatty papyrus, P^{45}, were added to the related documents. Some other weaker representatives were also found in von Soden's groups (see below), especially in I^{ϕ}.

Canon Streeter in 1924 followed up the suggestions regarding the Koridethi text and showed that its characteristics were to be found in the other Gospels as well as in Mark. He also christened it "Caesarean" because he found that Origen had employed a form of this text in certain of his writings composed in Caesarea after A.D. 231, although earlier in Alexandria he had used an "Alexandrian" text. Eusebius, too, was a partial witness to its existence there. But while it is conceded that such a text was localized at Caesarea—and, indeed, Lake had suggested back in 1900 that certain minuscules of the Theta group might be connected with that locality—yet the designation "Caesarean" proved to be unfortunate as a general name for the whole aggregation. This was indicated by the fact that Origen also used such a text in Alexandria and that Codex W and certain papyri reflected its presence in Egypt. It was most dramatically demonstrated by the discovery of the Beatty papyri, which in the Gospels proved to be of this textual type. On the other hand, the work of various scholars (e.g., Macler, the Lakes, Blake, Colwell) had confirmed Streeter's citation of the Georgian as a witness and had also identified the Armenian as of equal or superior value in this regard. Caesarean readings were also detected, as we have noted, in other versions, especially the Sinaitic and Palestinian Syriac; and traces of Caesarean influence have supposedly been found in the Harclean Syriac, Persian, and Arabic, as well as in the Greek lectionaries. Certain of these suggestions need study and reconsideration. It has nevertheless been shown that this type of reading had an early and widespread existence.

More definite conclusions concerning a Caesarean text and its as yet uncertain relationship to the Alexandrian and Western types of text must await more investigation. Research in this area has so far been almost entirely limited to a few chapters in Mark. But current study has definitely called in question the unity of such a text and has shown the need of distinguishing at least a Caesarean form proper and an earlier Egyptian form, which for lack of a better name has been called "pre-Caesarean." The Lakes had made such a distinction between a "better" form (θ 565 700 Geo) and a "less good" text (W fam 1 and 13 28 P^{45}). The latter was considered "pre-Caesarean" because P^{45} was older than Origen. Similar distinctions have since been advocated by Ayuso and others, but they need further study, particularly in relation to Origen. It thus appears increasingly probable that the Caesarean text may also be more accurately designated as a textual process than as a definite recension.

Likewise, significant studies of the Syrian or Byzantine text have led to similar suggestions about its character. Hort had thought of it as a recension originating in Antioch in the fourth century, and it has often been attributed to Lucian on the probably mistaken interpretation of a statement by Jerome. But recent demonstration of the extremely mixed character of the text of the mass of witnesses (e.g., by the

Lakes and E. C. Colwell) and attempts to reconstruct its complex history have raised serious doubts about attributing it to any specific time and place.

A most valuable contribution to the reconstruction of its history was made by Herman von Soden in a publication (1902-13) of a new Greek text and apparatus. In this he made an elaborate attempt to create a new classification of witnesses and an extensive apparatus which would include a large number of the late manuscripts. The result has been both the hope and the despair of scholars ever since. Von Soden's often confusing theory was complicated by the introduction of a new nomenclature both for the witnesses to the text and for his group classifications. Thus he distinguished three main types of text: H (Eta), attributed to Hesychius; I (Iota), of supposed Jerusalemic origin; and K (Kappa or *Koine*, i.e., "common"). The first of these is roughly equivalent to the Alexandrian text and needs no special comment. The Kappa form is approximately the same as the Byzantine but somewhat more inclusive. The Iota text is represented as a new group, which actually, by virtue of its inclusion of a variety of incongruous elements, corresponds mainly to a combination of Western and Caesarean types of text. Von Soden broke it down into a dozen bewildering subdivisions, one of which is even a Kappa sub-group (K^a). Codex Bezae is allocated to I^a, a mixture of I and K^1. Von Soden thought that this text was used by Cyril of Jerusalem, and that it may have been created by Eusebius. But his theories and classifications have here been considered especially unsatisfactory.

The chief contribution of the work was in the area of the Kappa text. Here some sixteen sub-groups were identified, the earliest one being K^1, itself the ancestor of two chief later revisions, K^r and K^x. The latter became dominant from the tenth-eleventh century on, but the most popular early form was K^a, a revision of I by K^1. Codex Alexandrinus, Theodoret, and Chrysostom were considered witnesses to the K^a text in certain areas. Subsequent investigations have substantiated with modifications these main Kappa groupings, and von Soden's apparatus does give us the fullest presentation of the evidence of the late, minuscule manuscripts. Unfortunately the work is marred by many errors in the citation of readings, so that it must constantly be checked. The use made of the versions and patristic evidence was also rather limited and eclectic. This was largely owing to von Soden's rather eccentric theory of the corruption of the early text by Tatian's Diatessaron. On this account, for example, the Old Syriac, Old Latin, and early fathers were depreciated; and Tatianic influence was seen in the great amount of variation which characterized that early text (*ca.* A.D. 200), which ought otherwise to be recoverable as the ancestor or archetype of I-H-K by a majority vote. The rejection of what were considered to be Tatian-supported readings actually led, however, to the adoption of a text by von Soden which did not differ radically from that of Westcott and Hort.

Along with the otherwise general rejection of his theory and method, von Soden's new scheme of nomenclature was also by-passed. This renumbering of manuscripts had definite merit in that it indicated at a glance the date and content of a document, but under the leadership of C. R. Gregory the Tischendorf system was continued and improved, a revised list of manuscripts being published in 1908. Upon Gregory's death in 1917 the official listing of new materials was carried on by Professor von Dobschütz in the *Zeitschrift für die Neuetestamentliche Wissenschaft* until his death. Professor Kurt Aland of Berlin has now assumed this task for the Greek witnesses.

Efforts to reconstruct the history of the Byzantine text have continued. The Lakes contributed much work in this direction, and Silva Lake in 1937 published a study of Family *Pi* and the Codex Alexandrinus, and a reconstruction of the text of Family *Pi* in Mark. This family was identified as a group of twenty-one manuscripts headed by Codex Π and roughly equivalent to von Soden's K^a (later I^k) group, but related to Codex A by a common ancestry and prior to it. A similar early Byzantine text for the other Gospels is reported to be ready for publication by the same author.

Besides the editions of text by von Soden, Scrivener, and others previously mentioned, several additional publications of the Greek New Testament deserve brief notice. These have generally taken into account the new evidence and the results of study in the field. However, they are more or less of the same type of text as Westcott and Hort, with here and there a certain amount of variation, usually in the direction of the Textus Receptus readings. Bernhard Weiss published a study and edition (1894-1900) in which he gave much attention to intrinsic evidence and largely supported the Beta text. Beginning in 1898 Eberhard Nestle published an inexpensive edition for the Stuttgart Bible Society, the text of which was at first based on the majority reading of Westcott-Hort, Tischendorf, and Weymouth, Weiss being substituted for Weymouth in the third edition. The British and Foreign Bible Society in 1904 replaced its Textus Receptus with the Nestle text. On the death of Nestle in 1913 the work of editing was carried on by his son, Erwin Nestle, who added a brief apparatus of the most important evidence. This text has had a very wide usage, and a twentieth edition was published in Germany in 1950. The apparatus is continually revised to include new evidence of importance. A manual edition of Tischendorf was issued by Gebhardt in 1902. In 1910 Alexander Souter published the revisers' Greek text with a brief critical apparatus. A second edition of it was issued in 1947 by the Clarendon Press, with a revised apparatus.

Some significant Roman Catholic contributions have also appeared recently. H. J. Vogels in 1920 (third edition, 1949) issued a text similar to Nestle's in character and format, but with somewhat more Latin and Syriac evidence in the apparatus. In 1933 A. Merk published a comparable edition for the Papal Biblical Institute which has had a wide usage by Roman Catholic scholars. The apparatus was unfortunately marred by many errors, but later editions (seventh, 1951) have corrected many of these. The text is more Byzantine than Westcott-Hort. The Spanish scholar, Joseph M. Bover, brought out a Greco-Latin text in 1943 (second edition, 1950) whose apparatus cites a good many minuscule manuscripts. The evidence is cited by groups, and again the text departs frequently from the Westcott-Hort type, sometimes in the direction of other non-Byzantine texts. Of the Vulgate Bover writes that *eam tamen mutare non audebamus* ("yet we did not dare to change it").

Recognition of the need for a new, full, and up-to-date critical apparatus—a need not adequately filled by the von Soden edition—led in the early twenties to the initiation of a British-German project for the publication of a "new Tischendorf." Because of differences of opinion, especially with regard to what text to print, the British proceeded independently. Under the editorship of S. C. E. Legg a committee of scholars prepared and published the Gospels of Mark (1935) and Matthew (1940). The text of Westcott-Hort was printed, and with some exceptions the edition presented the fullest critical apparatus to date. However, it was still found to be unsatisfactory in completeness, consistency, and accuracy of presentation. No attempt is made, except in limited instances, to give or symbolize related witnesses by groups. In 1948 the resignation of Professor Legg as editor led to a reconsideration of the scope and execution of the work and to overtures for co-operation with scholars who had meanwhile initiated similar undertakings in America. The result has been expansion of the project to one of international scope with two main centers of work, Oxford and Chicago. Publication of Luke is the first objective.

Among publications of individual books of the New Testament mention should be made of the huge two-volume edition of the Apocalypse by H. C. Hoskier issued in 1929 after ten years of preparation. This gives the most complete extant apparatus to the book, consisting of about 230 manuscripts divided into ten groups. But the designation of the manuscripts by Scrivener's instead of Gregory's numbers is a drawback to its ready use. Weiss, Bousset, von Soden, R. H. Charles, and Josef Schmid have also contributed studies bearing upon the text of Revelation. In his Commentary on Romans (fourth edition, 1933) H. Lietzmann gives a brief but valuable introduction to the textual criticism of the Pauline Epistles, a relatively neglected area. Important work on Acts was previously mentioned (pp. 213-14). Albert Huck's Synoptic Gospels Harmony (revised edition by Lietzmann and Opitz) provides a good apparatus of readings by classes and groups of witnesses. The continuing collation of manuscripts is exemplified by the work of the Lakes, Goodspeed, K. Clark, and others and will receive a new impetus from the "new Tischendorf" project. General introductions of merit have come from Gregory, Nestle, Jacquier, Kenyon, Lake, Souter, Vogels, Vaganay, and Lagrange. The reader is referred to these and to the Bibliography for information on the many other contributions which have been made in every area of the subject. In such a brief survey as this a large number of workers must remain unhonored and unsung.

In conclusion something should be said of current theory and practice. We have briefly reviewed the development of various "rules" of procedure in textual criticism in connection with our sketch of its history. Certain of these have proved of undoubted value, and some, indeed, have become axioms. A summary of those of most importance would run somewhat as follows:

1. The age of the text of a manuscript is more significant than the age of the manuscript itself.
2. Readings supported by ancient witnesses, however, especially from different groups, are generally preferable.
3. The reconstruction of the history of a variant is basic to judgment about it.
4. The quality rather than quantity of witnesses is more important in determining a reading.
5. Identity of readings, particularly in errors, implies identity of origin.
6. The shorter reading is generally preferable.
7. The more difficult reading is generally preferable.
8. Readings which bear the earmarks of stylistic or other improvements are suspect.
9. Readings which bear the earmarks of doctrinal controversy are suspect.
10. Variants combining the appearance of improvement with the absence of its reality are suspect.
11. The reading is preferred which best suits the author's characteristic tendencies.
12. The reading is preferred which best explains the origin of all other variants in a given passage.
13. In parallel texts differing readings are preferred.

These "rules," however, must naturally be employed together, and, in fact, it will be seen that several of them overlap. Always to adopt the shorter reading, for example, would make no allowance for accidental omission and might eventually result in no text at all! Always to adopt the harder reading would result in an unintelligible text. There is a current tendency, therefore, to reduce all such "rules" to a minimum summary statement along the line of what we have given in numbers 11 and 12: The reading is preferred which best suits the context and which best explains the origin of all other variants. This kind of statement also makes clear that a subjective element is inevitably present in judgments upon a reading. And while efforts to study and reconstruct the external evidence will continue as a basic necessity, it has also become apparent that any attempt to determine the text which existed anterior to that of our third- and fourth-century witnesses will involve an increased measure of rational criticism.

Over two centuries ago William Mace observed that "There is no manuscript so old as common sense"; and, more recently, in their study of the Caesarean text, Lake, Blake, and New declared that "Ultimately all intelligent criticism is subjective." What this means is that the critic who would restore the most ancient text must needs be a philologian, historian, and theologian. He must be equipped not only with a knowledge of the sources of the text, including the language and idiom of it and its authors and of the important early versions, but also with the knowledge and comprehension of the events, institutions, and doctrines of the period, both pagan and Christian. The line, in other words, between "lower" and "higher" criticism has become very thin or has often ceased to exist. The student of the text has to deal with documents whose variant readings are like hundreds of facets reflecting the interests and thoughts of the Christian churches and their members, from exalted leaders to humble scribes.

Aside from this rather disconcerting situation, the mere existence of such an enormous number of variations in the text of the New Testament has continued to startle many Christians. They fear that the whole question of the discovery of the true text is thrown into hopeless confusion. In one sense they may be right; the exact autograph text may never be recovered in every detail. On the other hand, the multiplication of witnesses and variants attests the tremendous importance of the New Testament in the early centuries and really guarantees the general integrity of its text. Only 400 or so of the 150,000 variants materially affect the sense, and of these perhaps 50 are of real significance. But no essential teaching of the New Testament is greatly affected by them. Modern study of the text has contributed, it is true, to the undermining of certain theories of verbal inspiration which once existed. For it has helped to show that the spirit rather than the letter was of primary importance in the early transmission of the text, even as the apostle Paul long ago pointed out. But the work of textual criticism will go on so long as it appears possible to recover an older text than we now possess for the basic document of the Christian faith, the Greek New Testament.

PART THREE

The English Bible

CHAPTER XVII

Early English Manuscripts

CHRISTIANITY was introduced into Great Britain as early as the second century. Its progress was comparatively slow before the sixth century, but in Ireland it had taken deep root. This Irish acorn grew to immense proportions, until in the sixth century it extended to Scotland and northern England, where the invasions of the Teutons had largely crushed out earlier gains. The landing of Augustine at Kent, in A.D. 597, gave a new lease of life to the struggles of the few remaining Christians. The vigorous efforts of that giant saint soon pushed the gospel to the front. In spite of his rather irascible temper and occasional unwise movements, Christianity made notable advance, particularly in southern England. And by the loyalty of one of his own converts special favors were granted to missionaries in Northumbria.

Almost the entire progress of Christianity throughout Great Britain came about through the active preaching of the gospel. Few could read, and there were fewer copies of the Bible to be read. Therefore the most effective and rapid method of spreading the good news of the Kingdom was through the heralding of the truth by the missionaries of the Christian church. The mingling and commingling of languages on the isles of Britain placed a barrier to the early translation of the Bible into anything that could be popularly recognized as the one language of the country. The version of the Bible in use was, of course, the Latin; and the preachers who traveled everywhere declared the truth in the tongues of their listeners. These preachers were usually the educated monks, or their pupils, who were able to interpret the Latin Bible to their auditors.

The earliest beginnings of the English Bible are apparently to be dated about the middle of the seventh century. The great Anglo-Saxon scholar, Bede, has preserved for us a story of a certain Caedmon with a gift for poetical paraphrase, who about that time composed verses on a variety of Biblical subjects from the creation of the world to the spread of the early church. Colorful legends are related about him but dependable information is meager. Even the few samples of his verse that have survived are admitted to have been worked over by later hands. While his poetry is in no sense a translation, it merits attention as the first known attempt to render Biblical materials into Anglo-Saxon; it is one of the forerunners of our Bible of today.

South England at about the same time was receiving religious instruction through popular poetry attuned to the harp of Aldhelm, Abbot of Malmesbury. This shrewd official observed that the usual sermon had little attraction for the ordinary run of Englishmen. Being a skillful musician, he put on the garb of a minstrel and took up a position on a bridge over which many people were obliged to pass. His artistic playing soon attracted a group of listeners. As soon as he had thus collected an audience he gave his music and words a religious turn, and by the strains of his splendid instrument and the persuasive form of his attractive language won many to Christianity.

This same Aldhelm, later Bishop of Sherborne, who died in 709, was the first known translator of the Psalms into Anglo-Saxon English. There is a manuscript in Paris which is thought by some scholars to be the Psalter of Aldhelm; but this document was written in the eleventh century, and bears marks of a later time. About the same time, it is thought, and at Aldhelm's request, Egbert, Bishop of Holy Island, produced a translation of the Gospels. Of this work there is a copy in the British Museum.

The most renowned Christian and scholar of this period was Bede, born about 673, died 735. He is called the brightest light in western Europe in the eighth century. He stands at the head of the long procession of translators of the Bible stretching from the eighth to the twentieth century. One of his followers, Cuthbert, has left us the story of the death of this good old monk of Jarrow. All through the day before Ascension Day, A.D. 735, he had been dictating his translation of the Gospel of John. For he said, "I do not want my boys (monks) to read a lie, or to work to no purpose after I am gone." By evening only one chapter remained untranslated. The great scholar seemed very near to death. All day, although in mortal weakness and interrupted by farewells to brethren of the monastery, he had painfully translated on.

As evening approached, his sobbing scribe leaned over and whispered, "Master, there is just one sentence more." and he said, "Write quickly." The scribe wrote on, and then said, "See, dear master, it is done now." "Yes, you speak truly; it is finished now." Then, by his request, they laid him down on the pavement of his cell, and he departed with the "Gloria" on his lips, to be with the dear Master whom he had so faithfully served during a long and devoted life. Of this translation, however, there is no trace left. It is supposed that it perished, with many other treasures of Northumbria, when the country was laid waste by the Danes. The source of the translation remains uncertain. One naturally thinks of the Latin Vulgate, which was then the Bible of all western Europe. But Bede had some knowledge of Greek; if he actually worked from the original, his translation takes on still greater historic significance. Further, his profound influence upon the Christianity of England in its formative period may not be overlooked. It is a reasonable inference that all four Gospels had now been translated.

One of the greatest patrons of religion and Biblical learning in these centuries was King Alfred (848-901). His name stands with the best of England's kings, as one who planned and promoted the intellectual and moral well-being of his subjects. Christianity was on the wane, but he quickly instilled new life into it and gave the use of the Bible a new impulse. He was so convinced of its genuine value that he translated, or caused to be translated, and placed at the head of the laws of his country, a copy of the Ten Commandments; to these he added other laws from the Pentateuch. His activity did not cease here, for he seems to have regarded himself as one in the succession of Aldhelm and Bede. He is said to have been instrumental in the production of a translation of the Psalter. There is no known copy of this work in existence, though a manuscript in the British Museum carries the name, King Alfred's Psalter. It contains the Latin text with an interlinear English translation but is now generally conceded to belong to the eleventh century. There is, however, another Latin Psalter in the British Museum, thought to have been written about A.D. 700, which was supplied with a word-for-word translation in the dialect of Kent about the close of the ninth century.

This same period is thought to have produced our earliest surviving translation of the Gospels into English. One would suppose that the

Gospels would have been first to be translated, but, apart from that of Bede, no known version is older than the Psalter just mentioned. One of the Cotton manuscripts in the British Museum is a Latin version of the Gospels copied toward the end of the seventh century by Eadfrith, Bishop of Lindisfarne, from a text which Adrian, friend of Archbishop Theodore, had brought to England in 669. About 950 Aldred, a priest, prepared and wrote between the lines of this Latin text his Anglo-Saxon paraphrase. This is the earliest known version of the Gospels in the English language; but its dialect is that of Northumbria. This text is now known by the names of "The Lindisfarne Gospels," "The Book of Durham," and "The Gospels of St. Cuthbert." The manuscript is famous for its magnificent illuminations of the text.

The Bodleian Library at Oxford possesses another interlineated copy known as "The Rushworth Gospels," which had its origin a little later. The translation was done in Yorkshire, although the manuscript in which it is preserved is supposed by some to have been written in Ireland. The translation through Mark, Luke, and John is believed to have been derived from the Lindisfarne version, but that of Matthew is in a different dialect. The manuscript takes its name from Mr. John Rushworth, in whose possession it was for many years. He served as Deputy Clerk of the House of Commons during the Long Parliament.

The Latin text used in all these interlinear versions was not that of the Vulgate but of the Old Latin, already described in Chapter V.

The earliest copies of translation of the Gospels, with no accompanying Latin text, are of the tenth century. Six such copies are known varying slightly the one from the other. Of these, two are found in each of the libraries of Oxford, Cambridge, and the British Museum. The oldest of them, at Cambridge, was written at Bath about A.D. 1000. The variants of these manuscripts are so slight as to indicate a common original from which they were all copied; that is, the evidence indicates a single Anglo-Saxon translation of the Gospels. Some of these copies, however, carry glosses in the Northumbrian dialect.

In this same latter part of the tenth century, which was notable for its revival of learning in England, the Abbot Aelfric wrote many homilies and translations. His style was clear, as fitted work for general readers. In the homilies he summarized, or rendered freely, the contents of considerable portions of the Books of Judges, Kings, Job, Esther, Judith, and the Maccabees, but also translated the greater part of the Hexateuch, omitting only material that would not be of general interest, such as details of the ritual legislation and lists of names. Judith and Maccabees seem to have been included to fire the patriotic spirit of his countrymen against the invading Danes. One of the interesting phases of Aelfric's work is that he made use in his translation, so he says, of older versions. Thus far, however, no such works have been discovered. The lack of any such versions today may be due to the terrific destruction which the Danes visited upon the country, and to the devastations of the Normans. Of Aelfric's work there is one manuscript in Oxford and one in the British Museum.

In 1066 the Normans conquered England. Their invasion meant the dethronement of the Anglo-Saxon language and the substitution therefor of the Anglo-Norman. The former was ostracized from the court, from books, and from schools. It was turned out of doors by royal decree, to find a refuge only with the cloistered monk, the priest, and the peasant. But its flavor could not be entirely destroyed. The new language, brought in by the conquerors and authorized by royal edict, slowly but gradually percolated the conquered realm. The resultant confusion of tongues prevented the production of anything that could claim the name of literature until the thirteenth century. All activity, too, in the production of Bible translations became nearly extinct during this period.

But we have one notable piece of Scriptures from the early part of the thirteenth century (1215). An Augustinian monk by the name of Orm made a metrical version of parts of the Gospels and the Acts for use in church services, which is known today as "The Ormulum." This version is not a translation but a paraphrase, accompanied with brief explanatory notes, designed for use in that day. The language is a peculiar compound. The vocabulary is Teutonic, but its cadence and syntax are colored by Norman characteristics. The Ormulum is preserved in a fine manuscript of 20,000 lines in the Bodleian Library at Oxford. It seems to have been easier to make a paraphrase than a translation in the early thirteenth century. Following the Ormulum someone put Genesis and Exodus into verse for general use.

A little later, an unknown author produced a version of the Psalter, metrical in form and almost a translation in its faithfulness to the original. It is curious, and yet explicable, that there was no real translation-version of any book of the Bible after the Norman conquest until about the middle of the fourteenth century, except of the Psalter. Of it there were two prose translations that require special notice in any discussion of this period. So general was the use of the Psalter, and so universal its appeal, that for more than a century it seems to have almost monopolized the attention of leading Christian scholars and evangelical authorities. One notable translation sprang up in southern England, and the other in the north. The translation attributed to southern England is credited to the skill and scholarship of William of Shoreham, in Kent, and located in time about 1320. This man Shoreham was a poet of no mean proportions. His poems are in the Kentish dialect, while his Psalter is in the dialect of the West Midlands. The northern England translation was produced about the same period by Richard Rolle, the so-called "Hermit of Hampole," near Doncaster, in Yorkshire. In Rolle's translation each verse is followed by a commentary in order thereby to make it of the utmost value to the common preacher of his day, who might not completely understand the significance of the translation. The original from which they translated was the Latin Vulgate, and their work furnishes us today admirable specimens of the English language of that time.

The time of the work of these two Biblical scholars falls before the middle of the fourteenth century. Some students say 1320 for William of Shoreham and 1340 for Richard Rolle. In other words, their translations were completed, distributed, and in full use about the time of the birth and youth of Wycliffe, about 1320-40. These translations of the Psalter, widely known in England, created a thirst for larger portions of God's Word and thus prepared the soil for the great service of Wycliffe, whose work will engage us in the next chapter.

The spread of the Shoreham-Rolle versions of the Psalter was the beginning of the triumph of the English language proper. The old Anglo-Saxon gradually faded out before the newcomer, which was given grace and favor through the Psalms that were so well beloved by the people at large. Political concessions to the common people had opened up before them the beauties of a liberty and independence that filled life with a new impetus and new inspiration. The production of such English literature as that of Langland, Gower, and Chaucer presented a new side to the life of the awakening Englishmen of the fourteenth century. These productions, together with the Psalters already noted, stirred up the appetitie of the English nation intellectually and religiously, so that Wycliffe, by his mental and religious instinct, could rightly divine the moment when a new translation of the Bible would satisfy the intellectual and spiritual hunger of a people.

CHAPTER XVIII

Wycliffe's Version of the Bible

JOHN WYCLIFFE stands out as one of the most illustrious figures of the fourteenth century. He was born in Yorkshire about 1320, and completed his education at Oxford. He is said to have become Master of Balliol College, and to have won a high place among the scholars of his day. In 1361 he resigned the arduous post of Master, and settled on a living at Fillingham, Lincolnshire. This mode of life gave him more leisure for the production of pamphlets and addresses on the stirring questions of those troublous days. With Oxford and its attractive circle of scholars close at hand, Wycliffe became deeply interested in the great ecclesiastical controversies of the times. His own personal knowledge of the conditions and needs of the common people, as seen among his parishioners, and his thorough acquaintance with the intellectual life of Oxford, prepared him for doing a large service for the people of his day. Wycliffe's public life may be divided for convenience into three periods: (1) his education and training at Oxford, and the beginning of his ecclesiastical activity (1336-66); (2) his semi-political and anti-papal, as well as purely ecclesiastical, work (1366-78); and (3) his open war against Rome, and his preparation from the Latin Vulgate of a translation of the Bible for the common people (1378-84).

The fourteenth century was a period of transition. It was neither the Middle Ages nor the Reformation. It was a kind of middle ground between the two. Politics, society, and the church were struggling to hold on to the old order, and at the same time to make friends with new thoughts, ideals, and progress. The Hundred Years' War with France was in progress and brought on the country all the countless fruits of such bloody struggles. The papal quarrels at Rome, and lavish expenditures, had so depleted that central ecclesiastical treasury that the Pope made demands on England for funds. Parliament refused to accede to such orders, and Wycliffe stood by the government. The immense wealth of the great dignitaries of the church and the organized corporations through which they constantly added to their accumulations were the objects of some of Wycliffe's most determined assaults.

The power of his attacks lay not so much in his enthusiasm as in the purity, spirituality, and unselfishness of his character, in his determination to crush the wrong and enthrone the right, and in his broad views on the questions of the day and the best method of solving them in the interests of the common people as over against the oppressions of church and state.

Wycliffe had reached middle life before he struck the keynote to his great lifework. In 1366, when he was forty-six years old, he publicly justified and approved Parliament's action in refusing to hand over money at the demand of the Pope. This act soon drew him into the center of the fight against Rome. In 1371 he was the most prominent reformer of the religious and social forces in England. Papal encroachments, and abuses of wealth in church quarters were vigorously exposed and resisted. As an inspiration to him, Wycliffe had the University of Oxford at his back, except when he promulgated some doctrine distinctively heretical. Since Oxford had become, or was popularly regarded as, the center of liberalism in thought for all Europe, Wycliffe could cut a wide swath without losing its moral support. With keen, logical argumentation he met and defeated his papal opponents. He had no peer in the lecture hall or the pulpit, and was the terror of the corruptionists and the promoters of the papal church. But Wycliffe's logic and metaphysics, his scholasticism and political views, are not the outstanding characteristics for which he is most remembered and honored in the church today. These were only elements of his symmetrical mind that helped him to divine the crying need of his times. He perceived that there was a gulf between the common people and the church authorities, and that it should be bridged; that they should be brought together on the Word of God. He saw, too, that the surest method of defeating Rome would be to put the Bible into the hands of the people. The version current in that day, except a few scattered fragments from earlier centuries, was the Latin Bible. Only the learned could use it, and those responsible for teaching the common folk were recreant to their task.

Wycliffe "came to the kingdom for such a time as this." He saw that the true emancipation of the soul of man lay in his opportunity to read the Bible in his own tongue, in his own home, that such a reversal of the prevalent condition of the people would mean the loss of Rome's power. This realization led Wycliffe to turn his whole attention to the work of putting the Bible into the language of the everyday man and woman—the common people who had looked for their spiritual nourishment to a careless, indolent, and haughty priesthood. Wycliffe had already shown himself to be an open antagonist of the methods and officials of the church; and this new undertaking made him still more unpopular; he became an object of attack by the influential ecclesiastics of England. Though a schoolman, Wycliffe laid supreme emphasis on the Scriptures as a basis for religious life, and thus had no hesitation in throwing the weight of his energies into the production of a version of the Bible that could be read by the simplest peasant.

Wycliffe's objective was a translation of the Latin Bible, or Vulgate, into the English of his time. Just when and where work began is not known. But the New Testament was finished about 1380; and within two years (in 1382) the whole Bible appeared in English dress. Wycliffe, of course, did not do all the work himself. Indeed, his personal share in the actual work of translation is uncertain, but the impulse of his leadership, at least, was of vital importance. As rector of Lutterworth, in Leicestershire, he sustained close relations with the great centers of intellectual and spiritual thought, particularly at Oxford and London. He called into service other scholars whose sympathies and abilities were in accord with his own. Ample evidence is at hand to show that most of the Old Testament work was done by one of his devoted disciples and fellow workers, Nicholas of Hereford. There is a manuscript now in the Bodleian Library, at Oxford, which was doubtless written under the direction of Hereford; it breaks off in the middle of Baruch 3:20, which point some suppose to indicate the time when Hereford was suddenly summoned to London to answer the charge of heresy. In any case, the rest of the translation was done by another scholar, some believe by Wycliffe himself, but this is doubted on the grounds of his frail health in these later years and his activity in other matters.

As a practical part of his efforts for reform, Wycliffe organized a sort of religious order of poor, though not mendicant, preachers, whom he sent abroad through England teaching his doctrines. The completion of the translation of the Bible provided them with new and most valuable equipment for their evangelism; and the combination of the preaching of these Lollards, as they were called, and their spread of this the first English Bible, exerted a profound influence on English life through the fifteenth century. They were voluntary workers, not church clergy, but co-operated, when possible, with the clergy. If the church authorities opposed them, they carried on their work independently, and with all the vigor of their consecrated leader, Wycliffe. The movement spread so rapidly that one of his sharpest opponents said, "You cannot travel anywhere in England but of every two men you meet one will be a Lollard." This illustrates the immense popularity that soon greeted Wycliffe, and made him the chief advocate of personal religion and of loyalty to the Scriptures. This fact, too, gave him great influence with the church authorities, and made him the most successful reformer on English soil. The success of his translation marked the first serious defeat for the church's complete control of the people of England; it marked, too, a notable achievement in the long story of English literature.

Wycliffe did not live to see the best fruits of his translation. Two years after its completion in 1382, he died of a stroke of paralysis brought on by continuous and heavy work. But he had planted a tree whose fruits, spiritual and literary, were to be the joy and the exaltation of the common people down through the centuries.

This first edition of the Wycliffe Bible was far from satisfactory. Hereford's style was stilted, his translation mechanical, and his language a Midland dialect not representative of the central strand of development in English. The version called for revision; and not long after Wycliffe's death, it seems, the work was undertaken. Apparently it continued through many years. Manuscripts of parts of the revised translations are ascribed to the years just before or just after 1400. But the oldest manuscript of the complete work bears the date 1408. It is not known definitely who did the work, but it has been attributed, in part at least, to John Purvey, Wycliffe's former curate at Lutterworth. The prologue tells us on what principles the revision was made, but omits all names of revisers, except to say that the writer was "a simple creature." A few lines out of this prologue in modern spelling read:

> Though covetous Clerks are mad through simony, heresy and many other sins, and despise and impede Holy Writ as much as they can, yet the unlearned cry after Holy Writ to know it, with great cost and peril of their lives. For these reasons, and others, a simple creature hath translated the Bible out of Latin into English. First, this simple creature had much labor, with divers companions and helpers, to gather many old Bibles, and other doctors and common glosses, and to make a Latin Bible somewhat true, and then to study it anew, the text with the gloss, and other doctors, especially Lire [Nicholaus de Lyra] on the Old Testament, who gave him great help in this work.

This prologue shows that the "simple creature" attempted to establish a Latin text on the basis of all the Latin versions and authorities that he could consult, and then to translate his corrected text—a good case of textual criticism in operation.

The revision soon took the place of the first translation. Within less than a century it became the regular edition of Wycliffe's Bible. Its popularity grew rapidly. It was eagerly sought for, and large sums were paid for it by the rich. Multiplied by transcription only, a copy was worth a great deal of money. Early in the fifteenth century a complete copy would have brought, in our money, about one hundred and fifty dollars. Foxe records, 'Some gaue a lode of hay for a few chapters of S. James or of S. Paule in English.' Wycliffe's Bible was proscribed by Archbishop Arundel in 1408, when he made it a penal offense to read any of Wycliffe's writings or translations within the province of Canterbury. In 1414 a law was enacted that all persons who should read the Scriptures in the mother tongue should "forfeit land, catel, lif, and goods from their heyres for ever." Such prohibition could not smother the fire. There are now about one hundred and seventy known manuscript copies of Wycliffe's Bible. Of these less than thirty contain the original translation of 1382, while the remainder are copies of Purvey's version—all written before 1430. Many of these copies were written in a small hand without ornamentation, and were used by private individuals or in families. Some of the finest copies known have been traced to the possession of such royal personages as

Henry VI, Henry VII, Richard, Duke of Gloucester, Humphrey, Duke of Gloucester, Edward VI, and Queen Elizabeth.

Notwithstanding its great popularity in the fifteenth century, the Wycliffe Bible existed until recent times in manuscript only. The reasons for this become evident on brief consideration. Printing was unknown in Wycliffe's day; it will be recalled that Gutenberg's revolutionary achievement occurred after the middle of the following century, and more than eighty years after Wycliffe's death. And by the time printing had become somewhat common, the newer English translations, which we are to consider in our next chapter, were attracting general attention, with the result that Wycliffe's Bible gradually passed out of use, although as late as 1520 it was adapted for use in Scotland. It had served wonderfully its day; it had made a profound contribution to English life. But its day was short. Yet doubtless Wycliffe himself would have been the one most gratified in the outcome, for after his Bible had prepared the way, it gave place to the better versions of the sixteenth and seventeenth centuries. Yet we must beware of concluding that thus Wycliffe's work was superseded. On the contrary, his rich achievement was poured into English life, and manifested itself in growing enlightenment and in the struggle for human freedom in which England so remarkably gave leadership to the Western world; it lives to this day in the truth to which Wycliffe gave himself without stint. He merits fully the epithet commonly given him, "the morning star of the Reformation." Nor may we overlook the importance of his translation in the history and evolution of the English language. The various dialects of his time found in his Bible a common expression and, in its dissemination and the preaching of the Lollards, a unifying medium that crystallized the long evolution and intermixture of Norman and Anglo-Saxon into English: early English, it is true, but still the direct antecedent of our speech of today.

After an interval of centuries, Wycliffe's Bible was at length printed. His New Testament, in the Purvey version, was published by Lewis in 1731, again by Baber in 1810, and a third time in Bagster's English Hexapla in 1841. Of the Old Testament the only part printed prior to the middle of the nineteenth century was the Song of Songs published by Adam Clark in his *Commentary* in 1808. The original Wycliffe version of the New Testament was published by Lea Wilson in 1848, but at length in 1850 the entire Bible, in both the Wycliffe and the Purvey versions, was published in the now-famous edition of two English scholars, Forshall and Madden. They spent twenty years on the task, making use of 170 manuscripts, and published their results in four large quarto volumes that bear the title *The Holy Bible, containing the Old and New Testaments, with the Apocryphal Books, in the earliest English Versions made from the Latin Vulgate by John Wycliffe and his followers, edited by the Rev. J. Forshall and Sir F. Madden.*

The production of the first translation of the whole Bible into English for the use of the common folk of England thus came about through the foresight, insight, and energy of John Wycliffe. Dr. (subsequently Cardinal) Gasquet, an English Roman Catholic scholar, in 1894 challenged the authenticity of the Bible attributed to Wycliffe; but the evidence in favor of the great reformer's having originated and carried through this work is too specific and convincing to admit of such doubt. His translation was made, it is true, not from the original languages of the Bible, but from the Latin Vulgate current in England in his day. Nevertheless, it opened the secrets of the divine Word to all who could read; and it gave preachers and teachers an unfailing source of divine truth to set before those who could not read it for themselves. Wycliffe's work, and that of his co-laborers, has indelibly stamped itself on our present-day Bible. Some of the permanent words and expressions that are first found in his version are: "strait gate," "make whole," "compass land and sea," "son of perdition," "enter thou into the joy of thy Lord." Some compact methods of expression also have remained with us: "I wente, and waisehid, and sai" (John 9:11); "all things ben nedeful to me, but not alle thingis been spedeful" (1 Cor. 6:12).

It will doubtless be of interest to compare the language of King Alfred's day (870-901) and of Wycliffe's time (1382), with our own —three periods roughly five hundred years apart. Three versions of the Lord's Prayer provide a convenient means of such comparison; they are given here, line by line, in first the Anglo-Saxon translation of Alfred's time, then Wycliffe's version, and last the American Standard Version:

Uren Fader dhic art in heofnas
Our Fadir that art in heuenes
Our Father who art in heaven

Sic gehalyed dhin noma
Halewid be thi name
Hallowed be thy name

To cymedh dhin ric
Thi Kingdom comme to
Thy Kingdom come

Sic dhin willa sue is in heofnas and in eardhs
Be thi wille done as in heuen so in erthe
Thy will be done, as in heaven, so on earth

Vren hlaf ofer wirthe sel us to daeg
Gyve to us this dai oure breed ouer other substance
Give us this day our daily bread

And forgef us scylda urna
And forgive to us oure dettis
And forgive us our debts

Sue we forgefan sculdgun vrum
As we forgyven to oure dettouris
As we also have forgiven our debtors

And no inleadh vridk in costung
And leede us not in to temptacioun
And bring us not into temptation

Als gefrig vrich fro ifle
But delyvere us fro yvel
But deliver us from the evil one.

CHAPTER XIX

Tyndale's Version of the Bible

THE fifteenth century was one of the great epochs of human history. Profound forces were stirring into a vigorous life that was soon to transform the culture of Europe and lead the way for the wonders of our own times. Feudal society was breaking down; new cities were arising and all were growing in population. Their enterprise and their spreading commerce were bringing about conditions for which older social forms were insufficient, and previous structures of thought gave little direction. The Roman Church, which had been the guide, and too often the despotic ruler, of all western Europe was showing itself inadequate to meet the problems of the time. Its rigid thought forms and established system of dogmas could not adapt themselves to the intellectual forces which from the thirteenth century onward had been growing in vigor. The activity of Wycliffe, discussed previously, while of far-reaching influence was yet but a symbol of the uneasy stirring of men's minds in many lands under the tyranny of the church.

This awakening, commonly known as the Renaissance, manifested itself first in Italy under the leadership of certain thinkers and writers of that country. Its progress was greatly enhanced by a series of notable events that occurred from about the middle of the fifteenth century onward and made of this "new birth" the primary fact of the thinking of western Europe. Far-reaching changes came about which in the course of a few decades created nothing less than a new world of the mind, a revolution comparable alone with that effected by scientific advance during the nineteenth century.

In part, progress was won at the price of human agony. In 1453 the Turks captured Constantinople. The victory was accompanied by much brutality, as was inevitable in those days—and war has not become gentle even yet! Numbers of scholars fled westward to find refuge in the various countries of Europe. They were in themselves a sort of physical link with the culture of the ancient world. But, too, their familiarity with the classical literature, as well as the westward movement of classical manuscripts which their migration stimulated, became of the highest significance for the reviving culture of Europe. A similar exodus at the end of the century had comparable influence. In the very year from which the Western Hemisphere dates its history, in A.D. 1492, Ferdinand, King of Spain, who with his Queen, Isabella, is honored for support of the epochal venture of Christopher Columbus, expelled from his dominions the entire Jewish community of some 300,000 persons. And five years later the same tragedy overtook the Jews of Portugal, except only for a few timorous souls who went through a form of submission to an alleged Christianity. These homeless wanderers, selling their knowledge, since they had no other resource between them and destitution, became teachers of numerous famous men and stimulated a widespread interest in Hebraic studies. Indeed, the beginning of Hebraic scholarship among Christians in the modern world dates from this time, notwithstanding some prior desultory interest chiefly in the thirteenth century. The stimulating effect upon the intellectual life, first of Italy and then of Germany, France, and England, was scarcely less than that of the revival of classical scholarship a half-century earlier.

The "new birth" was not, however, restricted to the humanities; an intellectual awakening so profound must inevitably affect all aspects of life. The springs of modern science lie within this pregnant time. The names of Leonardo da Vinci and Copernicus will suffice to suggest what was taking place. Both lived through the latter part of this century. Later came Galileo, Francis Bacon, and Kepler. But this is only part of the story, for we must bear in mind that geographic discovery also is science, and it was a scientific theory that impelled the venture of Columbus, which must certainly take a high place among the amazing events of this remarkable time. Can we by an exercise of imagination sense the revolutionary nature of the voyages he initiated? The tight little world of medieval times, centered on the Mediterranean Sea almost as completely as the civilizations of antiquity, and only half-aroused by the travels of Marco Polo to the vast expanses of Asia and the civilizations of the Far East, suddenly discovered itself to be a mere accident, as it were, on a world of immensity and of untold mysteries and riches—on a globe, moreover, which men could and did sail right around and return to their original haven without ever retracing their course! What a ferment of excitement, what stirrings of adventure, what sense of enlargement in a new age of unimagined possibilities, as one bold navigator after another set forth in his absurd cockleshell of a ship to toss for months in its confined quarters on the might and mystery of uncharted seas. Across the Atlantic they went, feeling out the contours of the American coasts, round the Cape of Good Hope to the fabled "wealth of Ormus and of Ind," through the Straits of Magellan and into the immensity of the Pacific, and on and on! They brought back with them, it is true, gold of the Spanish Main and "ivory and apes and peacocks" of the Far East, but a far more precious cargo as well. Those little ships carried home a new world of man's mind! Medievalism was dead, except as its ghost walks in every age with dire menace to human liberty. The modern world had begun.

But this was not the total of this amazing period's bequest of treasure. In 1453-56 Gutenberg printed the Bible, a Latin Bible, it is true. But however fitting it was for him to issue first an edition of this great version which had profoundly influenced the culture of western Europe for a thousand years, the essential fact is that he printed a book. He could not have realized—even the most thoughtful of his contemporaries could not have realized—the significance of his achievement. There have been few inventions in all the ages since the evolution of systems of writing that have so profoundly affected human culture. One thinks of the place of the printing press in our days, perhaps with some sense of the evil as well as the good it accomplishes. But of vastly more meaning than the newspapers and magazines of varying worth that pour without cessation their torrent of words upon us, and a whole world away from the tawdry "best sellers" baited with salacious episodes to lure away the public's dollars, is the fact that the art of printing has made possible a vast increase in knowledge and has actually expanded the scope and accuracy of human thinking.

The fifteenth century quickly awakened to the advantages of Gutenberg's invention. Within a few decades printing became widely practiced. We have already noted the enthusiasm with which Jewish leaders accepted it, as well as their steadily growing use of it from 1477 onward, when apparently the first printed Hebrew books appeared: the Psalter, and the commentary of Gersonides on Job. A listing of Hebrew incunabula runs to more than eighty items published prior to the close of the century, with, indeed, ten of them vaguely said to date before 1480. The practice of printing spread rapidly. Gutenberg himself, even before the publication of his first Bible, came into acute difficulties through a creditor who seized his press and set up a rival publishing house. But soon famous printing firms were established in many of the countries of Europe, from Spain and Portugal to Turkey. Most famous of them were the presses of Venice, which enjoyed the patronage of the Doge. English printing began with William Caxton in 1470. Before 1500 a total of ninety-two editions of the Latin Bible alone had been issued by these various firms. But impulse was given, also, to translating and printing of the Bible in many of the chief languages of continental Europe. A German Bible was printed in 1466. The Waldensian Bible in manuscript was already old, and it exerted an influence upon the Bohemian and the Italian translations. The Spanish version was notable, for in the Old Testament it was made direct from the Hebrew, not from the Vulgate as were the others.

The period was to witness yet one further remarkable development in matters of the human spirit. Heir as this was of all that had gone before, it yet transcended all in its far-reaching significance. This was the Protestant Reformation. It may be surveyed as just one more of the great movements which were so effectively changing the entire aspect of the world. But we fail to grasp its deepest meanings unless we see it in perspective of age-long human aspirations. One of the threads running through history has been what we may call the struggle for the freedom of the human soul. Since remote prehistory individual man has been oppressed by vested interests having social, economic, or political power. But strange to relate, organized religion has all along provided similar opportunity for conscienceless exploitation, the more ruinous in that to a combination of the other forces it has added a superstitious overpowering of men's minds. Here then is the historic significance of the Reformation. It is the latest and greatest affirmation that man as man has the right to a freedom where, subject to

God alone, he may work out his own destiny unhampered by prince, priest, or tyrant. Protestantism and the democratic ideal are but different aspects of the same aspiration. Its greatness is that it but reaffirms "for freedom did Christ set us free."

Such was the vibrant atmosphere of a new age and a new world in which the modern English Bible had its beginnings, itself in turn to become one of the potent forces in the making of the succeeding centuries. Just about one hundred years after Wycliffe's death William Tyndale was born (1484). A native of Gloucestershire, "about the borders of Wales," Foxe says he was "brought up from a child" in the University of Oxford, and was "singularly addicted to the study of the Scriptures." He studied in Magdalen Hall under the famous classical teachers, Grocyn, Latimer, and Linacre. Somewhere about 1510 he left Oxford and went to Cambridge, probably to study under Erasmus, the renowned Greek New Testament scholar. His university career seems to have covered some ten years, for about 1520 he returned to his native countryside and for two years was a tutor in the family of Sir John Walsh. The inspiration that he had received at Oxford and Cambridge fired his soul to action, for during these years he carried on vigorous thinking and discussion with the conservative and unthinking clergy regarding the work of the church. In one of these controversies with a churchman, according to Foxe, Tyndale said, "if God spare my life, ere many years I will cause a boy that driveth a plough shall know more of the Scriptures than thou doest." Tyndale's thorough preparation for handling the Greek of the New Testament—for Erasmus' Greek New Testament appeared in 1516, while he was still studying at Cambridge—and his familiarity with the needs and requirements of the times furnished him the stimulus and inspiration to produce an English Bible translated directly out of its original languages.

When his opponents became too numerous, and even began to endanger his life, Tyndale went to London. Here he sought out Tunstall, Bishop of London, of whose love of learned pursuits he had heard through Erasmus; he hoped to secure his approval, and also to win his support for the plan he had conceived of translating the Bible into English. But the Bishop made excuses and did not receive him. Tyndale, however, soon found a friend and helper in Humphrey Monmouth, an alderman of London, who for his favor to Tyndale was afterward incarcerated in the Tower of London. This Monmouth gives a description of Tyndale in which he says: "I took him into my house half a year; and there he lived like a good priest as methought. He studied most part of the day and of the night at his book; and he would eat but sodden meat by his good will, nor drink but small single beer. I never saw him wear linen about him in the space he was with me. I did promise him ten pounds sterling, to pray for my father and mother, their souls and all Christian souls. I did pay it him when he made his exchange to Hamburg." His life of almost a year in London was an eye opener to Tyndale. Brought up in the country, he soon was impressed by the cosmopolitan character of the city. Here he met tradesmen and merchants from many countries, and through them secured much valuable information regarding the progress of religious and political thought. Doubtless he learned the possibilities, too, of finding a place where he could put into print the translation that he was making. His experiences with churchmen and politicians in London for almost a year seem to have driven him to the following conclusion: "I . . . vnderstode at the laste not only that there was no rowme in my lorde of londons palace to translate the new testament, but also that there was no place to do it in all englonde."

Though he left London practically as an exile, he was given assurance that means would be provided to print his translation, and that it would be secretly imported into England and distributed where it would serve its high and noble purpose. In the springtime of 1524 he went to the free city of Hamburg. Evidence goes to show that most of the following year was spent in Wittenberg, in close relations with Luther, the giant reformer of Germany. Early in the spring of 1525 he returned to Hamburg to receive a remittance of funds from his London friend, Monmouth.

In April, 1525, he went to Cologne to put into print his completed translation of the New Testament. Here he found Quentel, an expert printer, who undertook the work. But the enemies and spies of the anti-reformation party were busy, especially in Germany. Cochlaeus, a vigorous enemy of Luther and the reform movement, was now in Cologne, carrying a book through the press where Tyndale's translation was being printed. By some accident he heard the printers boasting of the new successes about to be won for Lutheranism in England. To be certain of his ground, he invited to his home and dined and wined these same printers until they talked freely, and gave away the secret that they were printing three thousand copies of the New Testament in English for Tyndale, to be secretly distributed throughout England. Cochlaeus immediately informed the authorities at Cologne, who put a stop to the work. Tyndale, however, with Roye, his amanuensis, took their printed sheets and escaped by boat on the Rhine up to the city of Worms, already famed for its Lutheran strength.

Tyndale found a welcome refuge in this hospitable city, and put his work into the hands of the printer Schoeffer. Cochlaeus had already sent to England a description of the work done in Cologne, so Tyndale laid it aside temporarily and first issued an octavo edition of three thousand copies, without either introduction or notes. But this was soon followed by the edition begun in Cologne, which was in quarto, with marginal notes. Both editions were shipped into England hidden away in cases of merchandise. Being completed late in 1525, it is probable that they were in England early in 1526; for Edward Lee, later (1531) Archbishop of York, who was then on the continent, wrote Henry VIII, under date of December 2, 1525, "that an Englishman, at the solicitation and instance of Luther, with whom he is, hath translated the New Testament into English, and within four days intendeth to return with the same imprinted into England." It is of interest here to note an entry in the diary of a German scholar by the name of Spalatinus, in August, 1526. Among other things he says that Tyndale "was so skilled in seven languages, Hebrew, Greek, Latin, Italian, Spanish, English, French, that whichever he spoke you would suppose it his native tongue." He further adds "that the English, in spite of the active opposition of the king, were so eager for the Gospel as to affirm that they would buy a New Testament even if they had to give a hundred thousand pieces of money for it."

As soon as Tyndale's English New Testament reached England there was a great demand for it: by the common people, that they might read it, and by the ecclesiastical authorities, that they might burn it! Archbishop Warham issued a decree for its destruction. Bishop Tunstall added fuel to the fire by saying that he could find two thousand errors in it. Decrees and denunciations, however, were of little avail to stay its popularity. By order of the ecclesiastical authorities the books were bought up and burned in London, Oxford, and Antwerp, but without avail. An effective organization of distributers in England was supplied by numerous clandestine shippers from the Continent. The fight was desperate, on one side to disseminate Tyndale's New Testament as widely as possible, on the other to annihilate it. The bishops liberally contributed to buy up whole editions to consign to the flames. An English merchant at Antwerp by the name of Packington was a friend both of Bishop Tunstall and of Tyndale. The Bishop made a contract with Packington to buy all the books he could, at any cost, and send them to him so that he might burn them at St. Paul's Cross. Hall, the chronicler, describes the case as follows; "So Packington came to William Tyndale, and said, 'William, I know thou art a poor man, and I have gotten thee a merchant.' 'Who?' said Tyndale. 'The Bishop of London.' 'He will burn them,' said Tyndale. 'Yea, marry,' quoth Packington. And so forward went the bargain. The Bishop had the books, Packington the thanks, and Tyndale the money."

Thus the enemies of Tyndale's translation tried with persistent energy to obliterate it. All the machinations of the court seem to have been employed to stamp out so dangerous a heresy. Even King Henry, who had paid no heed to Tyndale's appeals, described the works as "imagened and onely fayned to enfecte the peopull." The success of their campaign of destruction may be partially inferred from the scant remnants now extant of Tyndale's translation. Of the quarto edition begun at Cologne and completed at Worms, there is known to be in existence just one fragment, now in the Grenville Library in the British Museum. It consists of thirty-one leaves and contains a prologue, a list of New Testament books, a woodcut of an angel holding up an inkstand into which Matthew is dipping his pen, and Matthew 1:1 to 22:12. Eight of these sheets were printed by Quentel in Cologne in 1525 and carried by Tyndale to Worms. Of the octavo edition one copy, perfect except for a missing title page, is now preserved in the Baptist College at Bristol, England; another copy, very imperfect, is in the library of St. Paul's, London. The fierceness and destructiveness of the opponents of Tyndale's translation systematically followed up and destroyed the thousands of copies that had been widely sold through England and Scotland. Of the estimated eighteen thousand copies printed between 1525 and 1528 the two just mentioned are the only known fragments.

Tyndale's English New Testament began a new epoch in the history of the English Bible. It was not a translation of a translation, as was Wycliffe's, but was rendered out of the original Greek text of the New Testament, probably as published by Erasmus in 1516 and revised in 1522. Tyndale made use of such helps as the Vulgate, Erasmus' Latin translation of his own Greek text, and Luther's German translation. Many of the errors charged against his English New Testament are due to the differences between Erasmus' Greek text and the Latin Vulgate. The violent opposition of the church authorities was due to causes other than the mere putting of the Bible into the hands of the common people. Tyndale had followed the custom common in the issuance of the Vulgate, and had incorporated marginal notes in his earlier editions. These were sometimes controversial, and so fired the wrath of his adversaries. In later editions, however, they were modified or omitted. Also, Tyndale was not careful to retain in his translation the long-cherished words of the Vulgate and of the church, but freely translated the Greek into words that seemed to him best to convey the thought of the original. Such freedom meant the abandonment of many long-cherished phrases, for which there were substituted words that seemed strange in a book so beloved as the Bible. Then, too, the determination and persistence of Tyndale's friends in their clandestine importing of his New Testaments into England, and their success in giving it wide distribution, only inflamed the church authorities to more desperate methods of suppression. But its real value, despite all opposition, was so great as to make it a really dangerous weapon against many of the hollow claims of the church. Its faithfulness to the Greek established its importance as the best translation of the New Testament for all classes.

As soon as Tyndale's New Testament had been well launched upon the English reading public, he took up the work of translating the Old Testament out of the Hebrew text. In 1530 he published a translation of the Pentateuch, accompanied by marginal notes that were severely controversial. Their form would indicate that they were printed separately, for Genesis and Numbers appear in blackface type, as over against the other three, which are plain roman. In 1531 the book of Jonah appeared in translation—the Pentateuch and Jonah being the only portions of the Old Testament published during Tyndale's life-time. He spent the next three years busily engaged in a revision of his earlier work. In 1534 he published a revision of his Pentateuch, 1530 edition, and of the New Testament of the 1525 edition. The motives that led him to revise his translation of the New Testament rather than to complete that of the Old Testament were (1) to meet the sharp criticism that had been hurled at his first edition, and (2) to checkmate a revision, wholly unauthorized, by his old amanuensis, George Joye, which appeared the same year. Joye had corrected some of the earlier printers' errors and made changes that more closely harmonized with the Vulgate and his own theological opinions. Tyndale made several important improvements upon his earlier editions. He supplied brief introductions to each of the New Testament books, except Acts and Revelation, took the sting out of many of his marginal notes, and at the end of the volume added the "Sarum" epistles, extracts from the Old Testament to be used in the church services "upon certain days of the year." He also included several passages from the Apocrypha.

The persistent and continued efforts of Tyndale and his friends had made a distinct gain in the distribution of the New Testament. Though the opposition to his work had somewhat abated he dared not return to England. In fact, his work had already so impressed Crom-well and Cranmer that they began to agitate for a translation of the Bible into English under royal patronage. Tyndale, however, took up his residence at the "English House," an English merchants' club, in Antwerp. Here he worked, apparently safe, amid a number of his merchant friends. But the bitterness of the opposition now showed itself by its sending or employing of an Englishman, Henry Philips, a Romanist, to do a treacherous deed. After pretending to great friend-ship for Tyndale, he stealthily and murderously betrayed him, in May, 1535, into the hands of officers of Emperor Charles V, who seized him, carried him off, and thrust him into a dungeon in Vilvorde Castle, near Brussels. While confined in this place he was permitted, it is thought, in response to an appeal to the governor of the castle, to use his Hebrew Bible, grammar, and dictionary, and possibly his Greek New Testament. For during his imprisonment he is credited with having once more revised his New Testament, adding headings to the chapters of the Gospels and the Acts. While here he is also thought to have translated Joshua to II Chronicles, though its publication was left in the hands of his friend, John Rogers. There is no evidence that Henry VIII or Cromwell had anything to do with his arrest or imprisonment; but on the other hand, their efforts, if any, for his release were halfhearted. On October 6, 1536, Tyndale was brought to trial

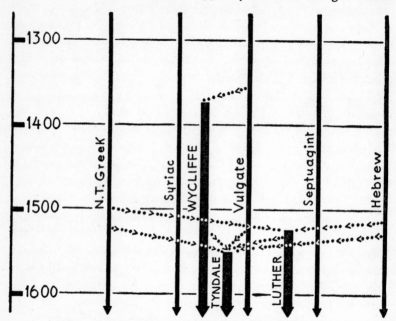

**DIAGRAM SHOWING THE BEGINNINGS OF ENGLISH VERSIONS,
EARLY IN THE SIXTEENTH CENTURY**

and, being proved a heretic, was condemned to death. He was tied to a stake, praying, according to Foxe, in these, his last words: "Lord, open the King of England's eyes," and then was strangled and burned.

But Tyndale won his battle. In the face of fierce opposition from the church authorities, he had determined to give the Bible to the common people in their native tongue. Though the books were bought up and burned in quantities, they contributed greatly to the creation of an appetite for the Bible in English that could not be extinguished. Popular demands soon reached the throne and, in spite of earlier adverse action toward Tyndale's work, made an impression. The court and the government wisely recognized the necessity of providing an edition of the English Bible for popular use. Even in 1534, before Tyndale's death, a convocation under the presidency of Cranmer petitioned the King that he would "think fit to decree that the holy scriptures shall be translated into the vulgar tongue by certain upright and learned men to be named by the said most illustrious King and to be meted out and delivered to the people for their instruction."

Tyndale's victory had far-reaching results. He was a master of a simple and forceful literary style. This, combined with exactness and breadth of scholarship, led him so to translate the Greek New Testament into English as largely to determine the character, form, and style of the Authorized Version. There have been some painstaking calculations to determine just how large a part Tyndale may have had in the production of the version of 1611. A comparison of Tyndale's version of I John and that of the Authorized Version shows that nine-tenths of the latter is retained from the martyred translator's work. Paul's Epistle to the Ephesians retains five-sixths of Tyndale's translation. These proportions are maintained throughout the entire New Testament. Such an influence as that upon the English Bible cannot be attributed to any other man in all the past.

More than that, Tyndale set a standard for the English language that molded in part the character and style of that tongue during the great Elizabethan era and all subsequent time. He gave the language fixity, volubleness, grace, beauty, simplicity, and directness. His influence as a man of letters was permanent on the style and literary taste of the English people, and of all who admire the superiority and epochal character of the literature of the sixteenth century.

CHAPTER XX

Versions Close to Tyndale's

TYNDALE'S last words and prayer, "Lord, open the King of England's eyes," were even at that moment being fulfilled. The one upon whom was laid the burden of carrying out the spirit of the petition of the convocation of 1534 was Myles Coverdale. As early as 1527 he was an intimate friend of Cromwell and More, and it may be that under their encouragement he began to prepare for his translation of the Bible. If Foxe is to be believed, Coverdale met Tyndale in Hamburg and helped him on his translation of the Pentateuch. However this may be, one thing seems certain, viz., that he was busily engaged in preparing a translation of the Bible into English, though it is positively asserted that he was neither a Hebrew nor a Greek scholar. King Henry's antipathy to Tyndale and his work, on the one hand, and the growing popular demand for the Bible in English, on the other, may have led the monarch to approve of the plan of his friend Coverdale, thus encouraging him to complete his translation. Besides, Cromwell, Secretary of State, gave him his active support in getting his work before the public.

The moral and financial support of high officials immediately brought Coverdale's work into the public eye. While Tyndale was incarcerated in Vilvorde Castle, in Belgium (1535) an English Bible suddenly appeared in England. It had evidently crept in from the Continent. It was printed in black letter, small folio size, and dated, "fynished the fourth daye of October." Either Coverdale's relation to the authorities or his desire to court their approval is seen in an effusive dedication to Henry VIII, signed if we may judge from the edition of 1537, by his "humble subjecte and dayle oratour, Myles Coverdale." It gave neither printer's name nor place of printing. The title page of the original edition stated that this Bible had been "translated out of Douche [German] and Latyn in to Englishe." The first imprint of this edition left out "Douche and Latyn." It has been ascertained that the printed sheets reached London in the winter of 1535-36, and that they were bound and supplied with a new title page by Nycolson, which carried on it "faythfully translated in Englysh and newly oversene and corrected." The cutting out of "Douche and Latyn" from the title page, as in the second issue mentioned above, probably avoided the current antagonism in the church to Lutheranism, and also may have led the reader to suppose that the book was translated out of the original Greek and Hebrew. At any rate, it seems not to have been arrested in its circulation, though there does not appear to have been either any royal prohibition or sanction for the earlier editions.

Myles Coverdale must be credited with having published the first complete Bible in the English language. In contrast with the work of Tyndale, it was not translated from the original Hebrew and Greek texts but was based on (1) the Zürich Bible of Zwingli and Leo Juda, completed in 1529; (2) Luther's German; (3) the Vulgate; (4) the Latin text of Pagninus (1528); and (5) probably Tyndale's work in the Pentateuch. In the New Testament Coverdale's main sources of help were Tyndale's latest (1534-35) revision and Luther's German (1522). In that part of the Old Testament of which Tyndale had published no translation, viz., the historical books, Joshua to II Chronicles, the poetical and prophetical books, Coverdale made the most familiar use of Zwingli's Zürich Bible. It is apparent then that Coverdale was essentially an editor, who gathered together the best materials within reach, and so selected and so modified them as to construct a Bible that would meet both the demands of the public and those of the ecclesiastical authorities. His great good sense, as shown in the use of language to secure beauty, harmony, and melody, made him a wise editor. His essentially peaceful nature led him to restore many beloved ecclesiastical terms that Tyndale had thrown out for new and more exact translations of the original Greek and Hebrew texts. Indeed, so happy are some of the translations of Coverdale that they were perpetuated in the King James Version.

Coverdale's Bible so met the requirements of all parties that it immediately achieved popularity. In 1537—one year after the martyrdom of Tyndale—two revised editions appeared, carrying this statement, "set forth with the king's most gracious license." In 1538, Coverdale published a revised New Testament with the Latin in parallel columns. Thus within twelve years from the issuance of Tyndale's New Testament, which had to be printed abroad and clandestinely carried into England, and less than one year after Tyndale's death, we find the entire Bible translated, printed, and distributed apparently with royal approval.

The character and position of the men who fostered the enterprise doubtless aided in the reception accorded Coverdale's work. Tyndale was a genius, self-poised, original and creative. He was every whit a scholar and stood absolutely on his convictions, regardless of consequences. Coverdale was an imitator, a follower in the tracks of others, harmonistic, sympathetic, and gentle. He was modest, dependent, and regarded, always and everywhere, the interests of others in his decisions. Tyndale was convinced that he had a great mission in this world and he bent everything to accomplish that end. Coverdale worked quietly, with no apparent expression of a burning zeal. Tyndale's tremendous energy and love of the right led him to translate into English the best Biblical texts that he could find. Coverdale's marvelous capacity for harmony, in spite of his lack of scholarship, led him to compile and to publish the first complete Bible in the English language. Each man was a kind of complement to the other, and together they were able to set forth the English Bible in such form and character as to command the English Bible-reading public.

Bible translation and revision were now in the air. Popular demands and royal favor joined hands to aid such work. John Rogers, an Oxford graduate of 1525, went to Antwerp some years afterwards as chaplain to the "English House," in which Tyndale was making his home. Here he soon became a close friend of the translator and, as some think, of Coverdale. When Tyndale was spending his last days in Vilvorde Castle, he turned over to John Rogers his unpublished work, his translation of Joshua to II Chronicles inclusive. Rogers doubtless was acquainted with the version that Coverdale published in 1535. But now, being in possession of all that Tyndale had translated, both published and unpublished, he seems to have desired to give it to the public in a complete edition. Accordingly he prepared a Bible with Tyndale's work from Genesis to II Chronicles inclusive,

Coverdale's version for the rest of the Old Testament and the Apocrypha, and Tyndale's New Testament of his last revision in 1535. This mass of material was revised with few changes, furnished with introductions, summaries of chapters, illustrations, and some controversial marginal notes.

That the name "William Tyndale" should not appear on the title page seemed essential to the public sale of the work; therefore it bears the name "Thomas Matthew," supposed to be either a pseudonym for John Rogers or the name of some merchant who backed up the enterprise in a financial way. At any rate, the book began to be printed, it seems, in Antwerp, where Rogers had for several years held the somewhat leisurely office of chaplain. When the printing reached Isaiah there was a stoppage for lack of funds. Two London merchants came to the rescue and carried the work through to completion in 1537.

This Matthew Bible was 12 by 8 inches in size and printed in black letter. Its boldest stroke is its dedication to "The moost noble and gracyous Prynce Kyng Henry the Eyght and Queen Jane," and signed "Thomas Matthew." The "Prayer of Manasses," omitted from Coverdale, was taken from the French Bible of Olivetan. The dedication may have been advised by such men as Cranmer and Cromwell, who seem to have welcomed its appearance. Cranmer in a letter to Cromwell says, "You shall receive by the bringer hereof a Bible in English, both of a new translation and of a new print. . . . So far as I have read thereof, I like it better than any other translation heretofore made. . . . I pray you, my Lord, that you will exhibit the book unto the king's highness, and to obtain of his Grace, if you can, a license that the same may be sold and read of every person, without danger of any act, proclamation, or ordinance, heretofore granted to the contrary, until such time that we the Bishops shall set forth a better translation, which I think will not be till a day after doomsday." Within a week Cromwell replies that he had "obtained of his grace that the same shall be allowed by his authority to be bought and read within this realm."

Thus Henry VIII, who had proscribed Tyndale's New Testament in 1525, who apparently made no effort to save the life of its translator in 1536, within one year after his martyrdom authorized the sale and use of Tyndale's work, though under another name. Hence, by the

influence of Cranmer, the co-operation of Cromwell, and the authorization of Henry VIII the Matthew Bible was given free course on
English soil. Being a compilation, as it were, of Tyndale and Coverdale, it was the best English Bible in print.

There were now two English Bibles, Coverdale's and Matthew's,
which were sold on authorization of the King. But the decree had
gone no further. Cromwell was a shrewd politician and a farsighted
churchman. He doubtless saw the deficiencies of the two English revisions that were so freely circulated by royal decree. Coverdale's Bible
had been compiled from various sources, and not translated from the
original Hebrew and Greek. Matthew's Bible was a compilation of
translations of varying values, whose marginal notes carried here
and there a sting of controversial character. Besides, royal discovery
of the Tyndale translations under the mask of "Matthew" might pre-
cipitate a storm in the court. Consequently Cromwell secured the
services of Coverdale to prepare a revised Bible that should be free
from the objections to the two already authorized. Coverdale was
to make the translation, as far as possible, more faithfully to represent
the Hebrew and Latin texts of the Complutensian Polyglot. His deficiency in Hebrew and Greek learning seems to have been supplemented by his employment of scholars efficient in these languages.
His editorial sagacity, his popular grasp of the needs of the times, his
power to use others, and his favor at court seem to have combined in
him just those elements of character that could produce a Bible that
would be acceptable to all parties.

The editorial work having been done, Coverdale could find no
facilities in London for executing the work on the scale that he had
marked out for it. With Richard Grafton, the London publisher, he
went to Paris in the spring of 1538. With Regnault, the French printer,
and under royal license, the printing began. But the Inquisition uttered
its voice, and ordered the work to be confiscated. By shrewd management and trickery equal to that of the inquisitors, Coverdale safely
transferred printed sheets, printers, presses, type and other outfit to
London. In April, 1539, the new revision was completed. Because of
its splendid proportions and magnificent form it was called "The
Great Bible." It was in large folio, black letter, and carried neither
notes nor dedication. Its unique title page reads: "The Byble in

Englyshe, that is to saye the content of all the holy scrypture bothe of ye old and new testament, truly translated after the veryte of the Hebrue and Greke textes, by ye dylygent studye of dyverse excellent learned men, expert in the forsayde tonges. Prynted by Rychard Grafton and Edward Whitchurch. Cum privilegio ad imprimendum solum, 1539. . . . Fynisshed in Apryll, Anno MCCCCCXXXIX. A Dño factū est istud."

One of the remarkable features of this book is its artistic frontispiece. It consists of a design often erroneously attributed to Hans Holbein, 9 by 14 inches, in which the King's authority is strikingly set forth, apparently as a method for securing royal patronage and favor in the distribution and use of this new work. For Henry VIII is depicted handing down the Bible to Cranmer and Cromwell, who in turn distribute it to the people amid their shouts of *"Vivat Rex!"* and "God save the King!"

What now were the Biblical contents of this Great Bible? The title page specifies that Coverdale had made use of Hebrew and Greek experts in its preparation. But the short space of time between the appearance of his own revision and that of the Great Bible would scarcely permit much expert work to be done. The Old Testament is Matthew's (Rogers-Tyndale-Coverdale) edition, revised on the basis of Sebastian Münster's Latin translation of 1535. In the New Testament, Tyndale's translation was the basis, revised by making comparison with the Latin translation of Erasmus, and also of the Vulgate. So the result of Coverdale's careful editorial supervision, "The Great Bible," was only a revised edition of John Rogers' "Matthew" Bible, which was the most complete presentation of the translation work of William Tyndale, whose martyrdom had occurred only three years earlier (in October, 1536).

The hand of Cromwell had been supporting Coverdale in his great work, so that without fear of interference he could prosecute his plans on a large scale. In fact, "the King's most honourable Council" had taken enough active interest in the enterprise to cut out all marginal notes. The publication of the so-called extra volume of annotations was postponed indefinitely. Furthermore Cromwell, as the King's right-hand officer, showed his interest in the work by promulgating in 1536, but not issuing until September, 1538, an order to the clergy throughout the kingdom to provide before a specified day "one boke of the whole Bible, of the largest volume, in Englyshe, and the same sett up in summe convenyent place within the said churche that ye have cure of, whereat your parishners may most commodiouslye resort to the same and rede yt." What a revolution! In 1525-26, Tyndale's New Testament was publicly burned at St. Paul's. In 1538 the same book, under another cover and name, was ordered by sanction of royal authority, if not decree, to be placed in public places, where all could read it. Tyndale had been martyred, but his battle had been won. The Bible in English was commanded to be put in every parish church in the land. The church historian Collier says that a paper dating from 1539 declares: "Englishmen have now in hand, in every church and place, the Holy Bible in their mother tongue, instead of the old fabulous and fantastical books of the 'Table Round,' 'Lancelot du Lake,' 'Bevis of Hampton,' 'Guy of Warwick,' etc., and such other, whose impure filth and vain fabulosity the light of God has abolished utterly" (Hoare, p. 194).

Although Archbishop Cranmer was not actively engaged in the production of the Great Bible, he soon championed its cause. King Henry VIII gave to Cromwell the absolute right of licensing the publication of the Bible for five years. Archbishop Cranmer prepared a Preface for the second edition, which appeared in April, 1540. From the Preface the version was often called "Cranmer's Bible." In July and November two other editions (third and fourth) followed. In 1541 three editions (May, November, and December) were issued from the London presses. Six of them carry Cranmer's Preface; and the third and fifth have on their title pages the names of Tunstall and Heath, who had "overseen and perused" the book "at the commandment of the King's Highness." So Bishop Tunstall, who had so vigorously condemned, bought up, and burned Tyndale's New Testament, now formally on the title pages indorses its publication and use. Suspicion had been attached to Cromwell's acts and name, for he was sent to the executioner's block in July, 1540. But the Bible had free course for a time. The seven editions of the Great Bible within two years testified to its immense popularity and the public demand for it. Indeed, so firm a hold did it take upon the church authorities that it formed the basis of the English Prayer Book, and was secure in its authority as the Bible of the English people for thirty years.

Its presence in the churches where everyone could approach and read it became an actual menace to the preacher and the public services. For readers would crowd about it, read and discuss it, while the preacher was trying to deliver his sermon. These events became so irritating to the clergy that Henry VIII issued a warning or injunction that every preacher charge his congregation to use this Bible "most humbly and reverently," not "having thereof any open reasoning in your open taverns or alehouses," using it "quietly and charitably every [one] of you to the edifying of himself, his wife and family."

Whatever else may be said of the open Bible, it is perfectly plain that the authorization of Cromwell, in putting it within the reach of everyone, aroused the English nation to a new conception of the meaning of Biblical teachings and furnished new incentive to a more liberal, personal type of religion than was generally represented by the ecclesiastical establishment.

During the same year that Coverdale was completing the printing of his Great Bible, an Oxford scholar, a layman and lawyer, Richard Taverner, was printing another revision, apparently at the instigation of the King's printer, Thomas Barthlet, or perhaps even of Cromwell. Taverner was a good Greek scholar, but apparently was unacquainted with Hebrew. He dedicated the revision to King Henry in dignified, courteous, and straightforward language. The Old Testament followed the Matthew revision with only slight changes, occasioned by comparison with the Vulgate. The New Testament revision bears some marks of Taverner's Greek scholarship and contributes several readings to the later King James text.

Taverner's Bible appeared in 1539, in two editions, a folio and a quarto; his New Testament appeared the same year, separately in two editions, a quarto and an octavo. It was the first English Bible to be completely printed in England. The whole Bible was but once reprinted; the Old Testament was adopted in a Bible of 1551. Otherwise the revision was entirely superseded by the Great Bible, now circulated and used by royal authority.

CHAPTER XXI

The Genevan, Bishops',
and Douai Versions

CROMWELL'S political and religious policy had caused his downfall and execution. His wholesale confiscation and destruction of shrines, images, and other religious symbols; his forcible plundering of abbots, monks, and monasteries; his wrecking of even the buildings connected with worship stirred up a revolution among the Roman Catholic subjects throughout the kingdom. Cromwell's head was only one of their demands. The exalted place that he had given the English Bible and the Reformation movement could not long be maintained. A most determined reaction set in against everything that looked like Lutheranism or the Reformation that had made such astounding progress on the Continent, particularly in Germany. King Henry VIII was in danger. He was forced not simply to modify but almost to reverse the policy inaugurated by Cromwell. In 1543 Parliament proscribed all translations bearing the name of Tyndale. It also "required that the notes in all other" versions should be expunged. Furthermore, it was enacted that no "laboring men or women should read to themselves or to others, publicly or privately, any part of the Bible, under pain of imprisonment." In 1546 King Henry proscribed every Bible and every separate New Testament, except the Great Bible. The reading and use of this was restricted to the upper classes—to the people of leisure, as it were. At this time Bibles and Testaments were burned by the hundreds to satisfy the anti-reform movement, which had taken off the head of Cromwell. Tunstall and Heath, who had caused their names to be printed on the title pages of the Great Bible in approval thereof, now said "they never meddled therewith." At the climax of this reaction against the Reformation King Henry died (January 28,

1547). It looked as if Bible translation work had received its death blow.

With the accession of Edward VI, the sun temporarily rose on the Reformation. This young king, even at his coronation, affirmed his devotion to the Bible, commanding that it be carried before him. His religious and political policy was that of the reform party. During his reign of six and one-half years (1547-53) the English Bible was reprinted many times and in many editions. Thirty-five editions of the New Testament and thirteen of the Old were issued from the press. The king's attitude and policy were set forth in certain injunctions issued at his coronation. Among these we find that every beneficed person shall provide "one book of the whole Bible of the largest volume in English, . . . the Paraphrasis of Erasmus also in English upon the Gospels," and shall set up the same "in some convenient place within the . . . Church, . . ." where "their parishioners may most commodiously resort unto the same and read the same." What a reversal of the last policy of King Henry! Reformers, too, who had fled to the Continent to escape the wrath of King Henry, now came back to meet the welcome of the new ruler, and of Archbishop Cranmer. These warm friends of the new king formed a choice group for promoting the reform. Calvinism and Lutheranism were flourishing, although the extreme measures of the protectorate which was the real power behind the throne helped make possible a new period of Catholic ascendancy.

At the close of Edward's all too short reign, Mary Tudor came to the throne (1553). England again fell back into the hands and power of Roman Catholicism. Mary quickly turned the tables upon Protestantism, and inaugurated a reign of terror by lighting the fires of Smithfield. Archbishop Cranmer and John Rogers, with hundreds of others, were burned at the stake. Myles Coverdale, now Bishop of Exeter, escaped with difficulty to the Continent. Scores of reformers took the same road to safety. But the fierceness of Mary's persecution defeated its own purpose. The burning of such men as Archbishop Cranmer caused a revolt in the hearts even of his opponents. The use of the English Bible in public was prohibited, and the copies placed in churches by the order of Edward VI were removed and burned. But there was no searching or spying out hidden copies in order to destroy them. The horrors of Smithfield and the suppression of the English Bible had driven into voluntary exile some of the best Biblical scholars of England. These men drifted to Germany and Switzerland, and naturally took up the cause they loved so dearly. After five years (1553-58) of bloody persecution and terror, in which some of the best men of England had suffered martyrdom, Mary went to her place.

One of the direct results of the persecution of Mary was the flight of some of the reformers to Geneva, Switzerland, the home of Beza, the most noted Biblical scholar of the time, and of Calvin, the theologian. The city of Geneva was the home of free thought, hampered by no political or religious restrictions. It was a home of Biblical scholars of more than one nationality. Beza's critical and exegetical work had done much to clear up some of the difficulties of translation and interpretation. The company of English scholars now improved their long-desired opportunity to revise the Great Bible and bring it up to the new standards of scholarship. William Whittingham, a brother-in-law of Calvin and an able scholar, is credited with the preparation and printing of the Genevan New Testament of 1557, with an introduction by Calvin. The reviser's Preface contains some instructive information. He says, "I have divided the text into verses [first marked on the margins of Stephanus' Greek Testament of 1551] and sections, according to the best editions in other languages." He provided marginal notes wherever he could thereby explain obscure Hebrew or Greek phrases. This often amounted virtually to a running commentary, and was strongly Protestant in nature. He also introduced in italics words required to complete the sense but lacking in the original tongues, a practice continued down through the Revised Version.

This was the most completely annotated, and also the most accurate English New Testament that had yet appeared. Its merits soon won for it a hearty welcome, even in England. Its notable reception led its promoter to engage in a larger work for the cause of the Reformation and of Biblical learning.

Whittingham, with the aid of a group of scholars, whose names we know only in part, although Coverdale was probably one of them, assiduously worked on a revision of the Great Bible. This work continued "for the space of two years and more day and night." It is reported that "Whittingham, with one or two more, being resolved to go through with the work, did tarry at Geneva an year and an half after Q. Elizabeth came to the Crown" (November, 1558). Thus it is evident that not all the group of scholars worked during the entire time of revision. The work was completed and the new Bible published in 1560, dedicated to Queen Elizabeth in simple, dignified language. The cost of the printing was defrayed by the congregation at Geneva, among whose members we find John Bodley, the father of the founder of the Bodleian Library, at Oxford. He secured from Queen Elizabeth the exclusive right to print the Bible in England for seven years. In 1561 he printed a folio edition in Geneva.

The size of the Genevan version was a quarto—small in comparison with the folios of Coverdale, Matthew, and the Great Bible. Another innovation, both in the edition of the New Testament and in that of the complete Bible, was the abandonment of black letter for the plain, simple roman type. As in the New Testament of 1557, the chapters were divided into verses, and the margins carried explanatory notes that smacked somewhat of Calvinism and were in places, e.g., the Revelation of John, polemically anti-Catholic.

The Geneva Bible immediately sprang into popularity. Its superiority to every other preceding version, and the silent assent of Queen Elizabeth to its distribution and use, gave it a tremendous impetus as an instrument of popular religious reform. In the Old Testament the learned revisers took as their basis the Great Bible, and thoroughly revised the translation on the evidence of the best texts. The most sweeping changes were made in the prophetical and hagiographical books—books unrevised by Tyndale. The New Testament work, based on Tyndale's last revision, was largely affected by Beza's Latin translation and commentary.

The Geneva Bible, however, did not displace the Great Bible for ecclesiastical use, but it became the most popular Bible among English-speaking Protestants, and its presence everywhere soon instituted comparisons that were detrimental to this long-established Bible of the parish church. Thus the two books were used side by side from the beginning of Queen Elizabeth's reign, until the appearance of the Bishops' Bible in 1568. Thenceforth the Geneva Bible was nevertheless demanded in increasing ratio, so that by 1644 not less than one hundred and forty editions had appeared. The most important revision to appear was a New Testament of Lawrence Tomson, in 1576, which was strangely influenced by Beza, whose Greek, in fact, he claimed to be translating. This New Testament was substituted in many later editions of the Geneva Bible.

The popularity and patent superiority of the Geneva Bible was not pleasing to the authorities, and a movement was begun to produce an officially acceptable version which could compete with it. Archbishop Parker, therefore, who was a devoted and learned Biblical scholar, took steps in 1563-64 for a revision of the Great Bible. His plan involved the dividing of the whole Bible into parts, and the assigning of one part to each of a large number of scholars. He assigned to himself the offices of general editor and overseer of the printing of the text. At least nine of the revisers were bishops, hence the resultant Bible came to be called "The Bishops' Bible." The directions given the revisers included specifications that they were to follow the Great Bible, except where "it varieth manifestly" from the Hebrew and Greek. They were to regard especially the Latin versions of Münster and Pagninus. "Bitter notes" and controversial matter were to be omitted. "Genealogies" and other non-edifying passages were to be so indicated as to be passed over by the reader. Language that gave offense to good taste was to be "expressed with more convenient terms and phrases." Several of the bishops engaged on the work carried on a frank correspondence with Archbishop Parker. The work was evidently done without conference or consultation among the revisers, so that the result was a considerable degree of unevenness. On the completion of the revision, the editorial work, and the printing (in 1568), Parker made an effort to secure for the new Bible the recognition of the Queen. But so far as evidence goes, it was not granted. Convocation, however, decided (1571) that "every archbishop and bishop should have at his house a copy of the Holy Bible of the largest volume as lately printed at London . . . and that it should be placed in the hall or the large dining room, that it might be useful to their servants or to strangers." Every cathedral was to have a copy, and so were all other churches, "as far as it could be conveniently done."

The Bishops' Bible was a large folio, in type and format similar to the Great Bible except for the introduction of verse division. The title page bore the words, "The holie Bible conteyning the olde Testament and the newe," and a portrait of Queen Elizabeth. As a frontispiece of the book of Joshua there was a portrait of Lord Leicester, and of the Psalms, one of Cecil, Lord Burleigh. The division into verses followed that of the Geneva Bible, although the Preface ascribes it to the Pagninus Bible. Then the book was provided with marginal notes, almanacs, calendars, tables, pictures, and maps. Besides the Preface of Archbishop Parker, the Bible contained that of the martyr Cranmer, which was found in the Great Bible.

The internal character of the work is about what would be expected. The contents were of unequal merit. In the Old Testament the readings of the Great Bible are quite faithfully followed, while the Apocrypha is almost identical with it, though the Great Bible was based largely on a Latin text. The New Testament, on the other hand, exhibited marks of real scholarship in its revision. Even the Geneva version exerted a considerable influence, and many of its marginal notes were actually adopted. In the second edition in 1572, the New Testament was notably revised and improved, while the Old remained as it had been.

But the authorization of the bishops was enough to displace the Great Bible at once from public use. For its last edition appears to have been printed in 1569, only one year after the publication of the Bishops' Bible. The Psalter of the Great Bible was retained, however, as we have indicated. The second edition printed both in parallel columns but all later editions except one contained the earlier form. This new Bible was far from satisfactory to the increasingly large number of able scholars. Its ponderousness and its ecclesiastical sanction were not enough to popularize it. Its illustrations were such as to make it an object of reproach—the second edition being called the "Leda" Bible, from its objectionable picture of "Leda and the Swan" in the initial letter of the Epistle to the Hebrews. It was held in high ecclesiastical regard for about forty years, and passed through twenty editions, six in quarto, one in octavo, and thirteen in folio—the last bearing the date of 1606.

Protestant refugees from the persecutions of Queen Mary produced the Geneva Bible. On the other hand, upon the accession of Queen Elizabeth some of the Romanist party, now forced to the background, migrated to the Continent. The popular demand for the English Bible, and the answer to this demand by the Protestant revisions now freely circulated, led the Romanists to see the necessity of providing a version for their own adherents. In 1568, the year of the issuance of the Bishops' Bible, some of the Romanist refugees to the Continent established an English college at Douai, in Flanders. This city was the seat of a university founded by Philip II of Spain in 1562, and was an important Continental center of English Roman Catholicism. The founder of this English college, William Allen, was an Oxford man and a canon under Queen Mary. He projected the plan of producing an English Bible for English Roman Catholics. The translation of the work, however, was prosecuted under the oversight of Gregory Martin, another Oxford graduate. During the progress of the work political upheavals compelled the removal of the college from Douai to Rheims in 1578. By 1582 the entire work of translation had been completed, and the New Testament section published. The next year after its appearance William Fulke printed a sharp rejoinder to Martin's controversial marginal notes in the New Testament. In 1589 he issued in parallel columns the Rheims New Testament and that of the second edition (1572) of the Bishops' Bible together with his comments. This was very popular for a time. In 1593 the college, being compelled to leave Rheims, returned to Douai. Here the translation of the Old Testament, hitherto unprinted for lack of funds, was published in 1609-10. Hence this is called the Douai Version. The New Testament was reprinted three times between its first appearance in 1582 and 1750, and the Old Testament once—thus there was a receding demand for them.

The Douai Version (1609-10) carries this on its title page: "The Holie Bible, Faithfully Translated into English out of the Authentical Latin." A comparatively long Preface apologizes to the reader for the production and publication of such a version, assigning as a reason the prevalence and widespread use of various heretical and false versions. To counteract these menaces to the church of Rome, and to vindicate the good name of Roman Catholic scholarship, this particular version, well fortified with controversial notes, was issued.

As stated on the title page, the Douai Version is a translation "from the authentical Latin," the Vulgate, because "it is the same which St.

Augustine so commendeth . . ." and was declared by "the holy Councel of Trent . . . to be authentical, . . . because "the Adversaries them selves, namely Beza, preferre it before al the rest." These, among ten reasons, are assigned by the New Testament translators for the use of the Vulgate as the original, or basis, of their work. No acknowledgment whatever is made to the various English versions that had appeared, though the resemblance to the Genevan is often striking. Some use is said to have been made of the Hebrew and Greek originals, but it was slight and the result of small value.

The translation itself is extremely literal; even where the Latin is obscure, its confusion is faithfully carried over into English. The translators say: "We presume not in hard places to mollify the speeches or phrases, but religiously keep them word for word, and point for point, for fear of missing, or restraining the sense of the Holy Ghost to our fantasy." The adoption of such a policy carried over into English words and phrases that are stiff, formal, wooden, and often meaningless. The Psalter is the most defective part of their Bible, for its translation was made not from Jerome's Latin translation, but from his second revision of the Old Latin, that is found incorporated in the Latin Bible adopted by the Council of Trent.

The Rhemish New Testament, however, mainly through Fulke's publication, exercised some influence in the preparation of the King James Version of 1611, in which many of its Latinisms were adopted.

CHAPTER XXII

The King James Version of 1611

THE reign of Queen Elizabeth (1558-1603) was replete with great events. In the religious sphere we have (1) the appearance (1560) of the Geneva Bible that soon attained large popularity and use; (2) the publication (1568) of the Bishops' Bible that immediately displaced the Great Bible as the ecclesiastical version in use in the churches; (3) the Rhemish New Testament (1582) as the product of the English Catholic college at Rheims, Flanders, and its completion, the Douai Old Testament (1609-10) at Douai; (4) the tolerance enjoyed by the reform party in England, securing for it practically unrestricted growth. The two events in the political sphere that contributed to the success and liberties already achieved were the execution of Mary Stuart (1587) and the overwhelming defeat of the Spanish Armada in 1588. In the literary world there arose a galaxy of scholars and writers which has made the period unique in England's history and given the language a purity, style, and beauty that have never been surpassed by any subsequent age. Among these worthies may be mentioned Shakespeare, Spenser, Bacon, Hooker, Jonson, and Richard Hakluyt. The religious and intellectual forces set to work stirred up and molded the desires, aspirations, and endeavors of the Englishmen of the close of the sixteenth century. Scholarship had achieved a high standard of excellence and was not satisfied with anything small or less than the best.

James I came to the throne in 1603. His early life and training had made him a student of the Bible. He had even tried his hand at authorship, having written a paraphrase of the book of Revelation and translated some of the Psalms. The beginnings of the movement that ended in the translation of the so-called "Authorized Version" were apparently unpremeditated. King James had summoned a conference to meet at Hampton Court in January, 1604, to consider complaints by the Puritans. The circumstances are thus described in the Preface of the Authorized Version:

> . . . the very historical truth is that upon the importunate petitions of the Puritans, at his Majesty's coming to this crown, the conference at Hampton Court having been appointed for hearing their complaints: when by force of reason they were put from all other grounds, they had recourse at the last, to this shift, that they could not with good conscience subscribe to the Communion [Prayer] book, since it maintained the Bible as it was there translated [in the Great Bible], which was, as they said, a most corrupted translation. And although this was judged to be but a very poor and empty shift, yet even hereupon did his Majesty begin to bethink himself of the good that might ensue by a new translation, and presently after gave order for this translation which is now presented unto thee.

The recommendation for a new revision was made to the conference by Dr. John Reynolds, president of Corpus Christi College, Oxford. His examples of "a most corrupted translation" were cited from the Great Bible and the Bishops' Bible, for from the translation of the former of these the Prayer Book had been constructed.

So far as is known the conference adjourned without taking any definite steps toward meeting the issue of the Puritans. But the strong words of the Oxford president had been sown in fruitful soil.

The charge of the Puritans that mistranslations of the Scriptures were found in the Prayer Book was the first definite step toward a revision. As the statement from the Preface indicated, James I was thoroughly in accord with the idea of a new revision of the Bible. Although he had been brought up on the Geneva Bible and had used it in his Biblical studies, he had now come to adopt the viewpoint of the bishops, and his attitude is reflected in his words recorded by William Barlow, Dean of Chester, "but the worst of all [the translations] his Maiestie thought the Geneva to bee." James therefore entered heartily into the preparation and execution of a plan to provide a uniform translation "by the best learned in both the Universities; after them to be reviewed by the bishops and the chief learned of the church"; to be ratified by the Privy Council, and by royal authority.

James seemed to regard this as the opportunity of his life to do a popular and permanent piece of work on the Bible. His own Bible-trained spirit and his theological turn of mind made the whole enterprise congenial to him. The extemporized suggestion of Dr.

Reynolds soon sprang forth into full fruition. It is not known with whom James made all the plans and arranged all the details. But about six months later, not only the general plan of procedure but the list of scholars who were to do the work had been fully prepared. By July 22, 1604, James wrote to Bishop Bancroft that he had "appointed certain learned men to the number of four and fifty for the translating of the Bible." The only prerequisite for the position of translator seems

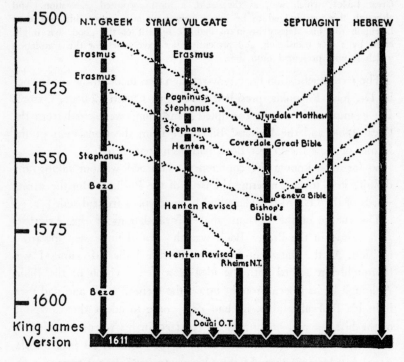

THE PRINCIPAL SOURCES EMPLOYED BY THE TRANSLATORS
OF KING JAMES VERSION OF 1611

to have been proved efficiency as Biblical scholars. The list included Anglican churchmen, Puritans, and laymen. Though James's letter mentions fifty-four, the list that has been preserved contains only forty-seven. The discrepancy between the original number and the actual workers is supposed to be accounted for by resignations and deaths between the time of appointment and the time when the real work began.

The revisers were organized into six groups—two at Westminster, two at Oxford, and two at Cambridge. Each of the six groups worked on a specified portion of Scripture, separately at first. The Westminster group revised Genesis to II Kings inclusive, and Romans to Jude inclusive; the Oxford group took Isaiah to Malachi inclusive, and the Gospels, the Acts, and the Apocalypse; the Cambridge group revised I Chronicles to Ecclesiastes inclusive, and the Apocrypha.

The competency of the revisers was undoubted. Nevertheless, such an array of scholarship could not do the work harmoniously without stringent rules. To guide them fifteen specific rules were provided by the scheme for work. Some of the most important things required were that (1) the Bishops' Bible should "be followed, and as little altered as the truth of the original will permit"; (2) the old ecclesiastical words should be retained; (3) there were to be no marginal notes except for the citation of parallel passages, of "suitable" alternative translations, of different readings found in "good copies," and of "the more difficult Hebraisms and Graecisms"; (4) whenever Tyndale's, Matthew's, Coverdale's Whitchurch's (the Great Bible, here named after one of its printers) or the Geneva translation, agreed better with the original text than the Bishops' Bible, it was to be used. It was provided, too, that a comparison of translations of each individual translator with every other one in each company should be made, and when any book was completed by any group it was to be sent to all the other groups for review and suggestion. Translators, too, were authorized to call on any other scholars outside of the regular list, if they deemed it wise so to do. Thus every man of the entire company of forty-seven passed upon the work of every other man in the company.

Very little is known as to the strictness with which the fifteen specifications were followed. It seems evident that there must have been practical harmony in their methods of procedure, for the work sped on at a commendable rate until completed.

The group work having been finished, two members of each of the three companies were chosen to pass upon the final revision for the press in London. It is said that a copy of the whole Bible was sent to London by each of the three companies. The six final revisers thus chosen put the finishing touches upon the work submitted by the three companies, and made the final preparations for the press. This part of the process does not seem to have been carried out too well.

The entire time for carrying out the great enterprise is sometimes divided into two periods. (1) The first three years (1604-07) were occupied in perfecting the preliminary arrangements and, on the part of some of the translators, in carefully working over in private study the material soon to be handled by the entire body of revisers. (2) The next two to three years were consumed in the individual and co-operative labor of the six groups of revisers, during which the revision work was finished. Then the following nine months were occupied upon the final revision in London.

In 1611 the version appeared from the press of Robert Barker, in a large folio volume that in appearance, both external and internal, was very like the Bishops' Bible. The type, chapter and verse divisions, chants and tables, running titles, and chapter summaries were similar. An effusive dedication to King James was, of course, included; and a long and learned Preface was contributed by Miles Smith, one of the translators. It explained the purpose of the translation and reviewed the controversy with the Roman Catholic church regarding the desirability of an English Bible. Unfortunately this Preface is now generally omitted by publishers, to the serious detriment of understanding and appreciation of the version. Professor Edgar J. Goodspeed sought for years to have this practice corrected, but failed. Accordingly he republished the Preface in a monograph under its original title, *The Translators to the Reader*; he presented the text in facsimile and transcription, and provided with a suitable introduction. Some brief excerpts will illustrate its temper and, perhaps, induce the reader to explore farther the motivations and principles of the great seventeenth-century translators.

But now what piety without truth? what truth (what saving truth) without the word of God? What word of God (whereof we may be sure) without the Scripture? The Scriptures we are commanded to search. John 5:39. Isa. 8:20. They are commended that searched and studied them. Acts 17:11 and 8:28, 29. . . . If we be ignorant, they will instruct us; if out of the way, they will bring us home; if out of order, they will reform us; if in heaviness, comfort us; if dull, quicken us; if cold, inflame us. *Tolle, lege; Tolle, lege,* Take up and read, take up and read the Scriptures, (for unto them was the direction) it was said unto S. Augustine by a supernatural voice. . . .

Many men's mouths have been open a good while (and yet are not stopped) with speeches about the Translation so long in hand, or rather perusals of Translations made before: and ask what may be the reason, what the necessity of the employment: Hath the Church been deceived, say they, all this while? Hath the sweet bread been mingled with leaven, her silver with dross, her wine with water, her milk with lime? (*Lacte gypsum male miscetur* saith S. Ireny.) We hoped that we had been in the right way, that we had the Oracles of God delivered unto us, and that though all the world had cause to be offended and to complain, yet we had none. . . . Thus certain brethren. Also the adversaries of Judah and Jerusalem, like Sanballat in Nehemiah, mock, as we hear, both at the work and the workmen, saying: . . . Was their Translation good before? Why do they now mend it? Was it not good? Why then was it obtruded to the people? . . . We will answer them both briefly: and the former, being brethren, thus with S. Jerome, . . . *Do we condemn the ancient? In no case: but after the endeavors of them that were before us we take the best pains we can in the house of God.* . . . And to the same effect say we, that we are so far off from condemning any of their labors that travailed before us in this kind either in this land or beyond sea . . . that we recognize them to have been raised up of God, for the building and furnishing of his Church, and that they deserve to be had of us and of posterity in everlasting remembrance. . . .

Now to the latter we answer; that we do not deny, nay we affirm and avow, that the very meanest translation of the Bible in English, set forth by men of our profession . . . containeth the word of God, nay, is the word of God. . . .

Yet before we end, we must answer a third cavil and objection of theirs against us, for altering and amending our Translations so oft; wherein truly they deal hardly, and strangely with us. For to whomever was it imputed for a fault (by such as were wise) to go over that which he had done, and to amend it where he saw cause? . . .

But it is high time to leave them, and to show in brief what we proposed to ourselves, and what course we held in this our perusal and survey of the Bible. Truly (good Christian Reader) we never thought from the beginning, that we should need to make a new Translation, nor yet to make of a bad one a good one, . . . but to make a good one better, or out of many good ones, one principal good one, not justly to be excepted against; that hath been our endeavor, that our mark. To that purpose there were many chosen. . . . If you ask what they had before them, truly it was the Hebrew text of the Old Testament, the Greek of the New. These are the two golden pipes, or rather conduits where-through the olive branches empty themselves into the gold. Saint Augustine calleth them precedent, or original tongues. . . .

The original title page of the version read: "The Holy Bible, Contayning the Old Testament and the New: Newly Translated out of the Originall tongues; & with the former Translations diligently compared and revised by his Maiesties speciall Commandment. Appointed to be read in Churches."

However, the new "translation," as has already been mentioned, was really a revision based on the Bishops' Bible, with free use made of the Genevan, the Rheims New Testament, and the material of Tremellius (1579), Beza (1556, 1565, and 1598), and other Latin versions. When we consider that the Bishops' Bible was a slightly revised edition of Tyndale's translation we can appreciate better his far-reaching contribution to the history of the English Bible and also the basic unity that links together all our great versions since the Reformation. King James's translators had no standard, or "received" Hebrew text, hence they were compelled to use the four current Hebrew Bibles and the Complutensian and Antwerp Polyglots. For the Greek New Testament they had Beza's improvements on Erasmus and on Stephanus. The Old Testament far surpassed any English translation in its faithful representation of the Hebrew text, and did it in a simplicity of language admirably representative of the Elizabethan age. The New Testament is so expressive in language and form that it is even said to surpass the original Greek as literature.

From the activity of King James in connection with the production of the revision it became widely known as the "King James Version" or the "King's Bible." But eventually it came to be designated as the "Authorized Version." It is true, as we have seen, that the title page read "Appointed to be read in Churches" and that the version was prepared under the direct order of the King and his advisers, but there is no record of any order, act, or decree, by Parliament, convocation, privy council, or King, authorizing or sanctioning its use as implied by the title page, or the title in general use. But the King in 1604 had specified that "a translation be made of the whole Bible, and only to be used in all Churches of England in time of Divine Service."

Notwithstanding its royal and scholarly paternity, its birth occurred without any blast of trumpets, any royal edict or public proclamation. It seems that the mere fact of its national character was regarded as a sufficient guarantee of its rapid adoption and use in the churches and in private reading. Some claim is made that an act of formal authorization occurred and that the record was destroyed by fire. At any rate, the King's name, and the eminence of the many great scholars who brought about its production, gave it an immediate hearing. It met opposition, of course, as does any new revision, even in these days. But it soon outran in popularity the Bishops' Bible, that had not been reprinted since 1606. With the Genevan Version it waged a running fight for a full half-century. But character and merit won the contest, and the "Authorized Version" completely took the field.

The first edition appeared in 1611. In 1613 another edition was printed which contained more than four hundred variations from the first, and differed in several other features. A second issue partly printed in 1611 and partly in 1613 containing a few variations and using some leaves printed for the first issue has caused considerable controversy as to which came first. The two are sometimes called the "He" and "She" Bibles from their respective translation of the pronoun in Ruth 3:15. The former is generally considered to be the first published edition. The sharp criticisms that were hurled at the new version, largely by Hugh Broughton, whose irascible disposition had deprived him of a place, as his scholarship deserved, on the translation committee, forced a revision in 1629. Another, on a minor scale, was made in 1638. Then in 1653 the Long Parliament submitted a bill calling for revision. The reasons that lay back of the bill were in part the errors, mainly printers' but some in translation, and also the so-called prelatical language of the version. The matter went so far as to be put into the hands of a committee appointed especially to take charge of the scheme. Some preliminary work was begun, but the dissolution of Parliament put an end to the project. Some of the most noted men of the century were on the committee. Among these may be named Brian Walton, Bishop of Chester, who, with the active support of Oliver Cromwell, edited the colossal Polyglot Bible, and also through his arduous textual studies pointed out the variations existent between manuscripts, particularly of the New Testament. Cudworth, the eminent theologian and philosopher, was another; his work has given him a permanent place in history. Private attempts at either betterment or radical revision were not infrequent, but they remained private and rarely exercised any large influence.

The most important changes occurred in the eighteenth century. In 1762 Dr. Thomas Paris published an extensive revision at Cambridge, and in 1769 Dr. Benjamin Blayney, after about four years of work, brought out another at Oxford. The latter work included much modernization of spelling, punctuation, and expression, and apart from minor changes such as correction of printing errors (of which there were many) it represents the generally current form of the King James Version.

The Cambridge Paragraph Bible of 1873 gave a list of variations from the text of the King James Version as it first appeared in 1611 that covered sixteen closely printed pages. The Oxford Parallel Bible of 1885 made a selection from these variants and put them in the margin.

The original instructions to the revisers regarding marginal notations were not entirely observed. The first edition contained about nine thousand cross references and some eight thousand other marginalia, about two-thirds of which would qualify as more literal representations of the original text and most of the remainder as alternative translations together with a few, perhaps 250, textual variants. But five or six hundred other notes were used, mostly explanations of names, weights, coinage, and the like, together with a few attempted harmonizations of the text and miscellaneous information (especially in the Apocrypha). Notes of an exegetical nature were, however, rigorously excluded. There was, in fact, more such interpretation in the implications of the running titles and chapter summaries. In later editions the notes were gradually and greatly increased in number, beginning especially with an edition of 1649; by the time of the Blayney revision they totaled some 65,000, about half of which were cross references.

Bishop Lloyd's Bible in 1701 was the first to incorporate in it the Biblical chronology that had been worked out by Archbishop Ussher and published in 1650-54. This system, which fixed the creation at 4004 B.C., was generally followed by Biblical scholars until recent times, when discoveries have shown conclusively that it is worthless in all of its earlier calculations, and erroneous in most of its later dates before the fall of Samaria (722 B.C.).

For almost three centuries the Authorized, or King James, Version has been the Bible of the English-speaking world. Its simple, majestic Anglo-Saxon tongue, its clear, sparkling style, its directness and force of utterance have made it the model in language, style, and dignity of some of the choicest writers of the last two centuries. Its phrasing is woven into much of our noblest literature; and its style, which to an astonishing degree is merely the style of the original authors of the

Bible, has exerted very great influence in molding that ideal of simplicity, directness, and clarity which now dominates the writing of English. It has endeared itself to the hearts and lives of millions of Christians and has molded the characters of leaders in every walk of life. During all these centuries the King James Version has become a vital part of the English-speaking world, socially, morally, religiously, and politically.

CHAPTER XXIII

The Revised Version

THE Authorized Version held undisputed sway in the English-speaking world for more than two centuries. There were only occasional efforts to improve it, and they were personal and unauthorized. In fact, after the abortive effort of the Long Parliament to secure a new translation, the main ecclesiastical and national interests pursued other lines of action. The early half of the eighteenth century was submerged religiously in controversies that dealt with theological questions more from a dogmatic and philosophical point of view than from that of the Scriptures. The second half of the century was largely occupied by the English in political and economic questions. The ecclesiastical life of the nation was at a low ebb, awaiting some thunderbolt of discovery or invention to arouse it to new energy and action. The nineteenth century saw new movements in every line of activity. Discovery, invention, scholarship, politics, religion—all arose to new life as the century advanced, promising not only larger action but a wider horizon for the future.

Biblical scholarship, though confined to comparatively few men, had in the interval made progress. On the textual and philological side, with which we at the moment are most concerned, the most valuable contributions were made by Kennicott, De Rossi, and Davidson, who collated and published critical materials bearing upon the Massoretic text of the Old Testament. The work of Mill, Bengel, Wetstein, Griesbach, and others in the collection of thousands of variant New Testament readings has been discussed in Chapter XV along with the contribution of Lachmann, Tischendorf, Tregelles and Hort in attempts to reconstruct the early text. The first critical use of some of the oldest manuscripts, like Vaticanus, Alexandrinus, and Beza, opened the eyes of scholars to the immense possibilities of improvements in translations of the Bible. The number of scholars at work on the Biblical text was increasing, and the material which they could use, particularly of the New Testament, was multiplying rapidly as ancient manuscripts were dug out of the old libraries of Europe and the monasteries of the East. These finds, and especially the dramatic discovery of Codex Sinaiticus in 1844-59, revealed and emphasized some of the most glaring defects of the Authorized Version and initiated efforts to produce new revisions or translations of parts or of the whole Bible. Professor Goodspeed has estimated that close to a hundred such productions, mostly New Testaments, were published in the two and a half centuries between the King James and the Revised versions, the majority of them in the nineteenth century. In 1857-61 five English clergymen published translations of the Gospel of John and Paul's Epistles. Of these translators, Dean Alford and Bishop Ellicott were afterwards chosen to be members of the Committee of Revisers. Four English scholars, Drs. Gotch, Davies, Jacob, and S. G. Green, prepared a Revised English Bible. G. R. Noyes, of Harvard University, published a translation in 1869, with some notes by Ezra Abbot in 1870. The American Bible Union, too, gathered together a choice Biblical exegetical library at large expense, and prosecuted a new translation of the Bible. The New Testament and part of the Old were published in 1860-71 by T. J. Conant, a leader in American Biblical scholarship. All these efforts on both sides of the sea were indicative of the drift of scholarly opinion and movement in the last half of the nineteenth century. The sentiment for a new revision of the Bible was steadily advancing.

The first official move in this direction was made February 10, 1870, in the Upper House of the Convocation of Canterbury. Bishop Wilberforce (of Winchester) presented a resolution that a committee of both Houses be appointed to report on the desirability, on the basis of certain principles named in the document, of a revision of the Authorized Version of the New Testament. By an amendment the Old Testament was included. This important resolution was seconded by Bishop Ellicott (of Gloucester and Bristol), and it was adopted. Two such names at the head of such a proposal were sure to give it a strong impetus. The committee provided for in the resolution was appointed to report in the following May. After due consideration it almost unanimously recommended, and both Houses of Convocation adopted, a resolution that a revision should be undertaken. It also provided that a body of its own members should be nominated to undertake the work of revision, who should "be at liberty to invite the co-operation of any, eminent for scholarship, to whatever nation or religious body they may

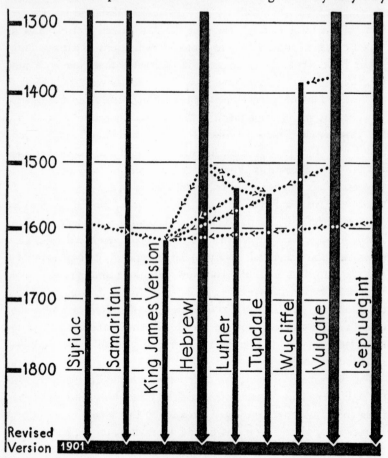

MAIN SOURCES OF OLD TESTAMENT OF THE REVISED VERSION, 1901

belong." The Church of England took the lead in the management of the movement, and a committee of sixteen men was appointed to carry out the letter and spirit of the resolution. This committee decided to invite about forty Biblical scholars to become members of the Revision Committee. With Episcopalians in the lead, the committee was

representative of nearly all evangelical bodies, Baptist, Congregation-
alist, Methodist, Presbyterian, and Unitarian. But no Roman Catholics
accepted. The full number of this committee, for both Testaments, was
fifty-four, the same as that originally named on King James's Revision
Committee.

According to the Preface of the Revised Version, some of the general principles which were agreed to on May 25, 1870, by the Revision
Committee of Convocation for their guidance were: "(1) To introduce
as few alterations as possible into the Text of the Authorized Version
consistently with faithfulness; (2) to limit as far as possible, the expression of such alterations to the language of the Authorized and
earlier English Versions; (4) that the Text to be adopted be that for
which the evidence is decidedly preponderating; and that when the
text so adopted differs from that from which the Authorised Version
was made, the alteration be indicated in the margin; . . . (7) to revise
the headings of chapters and pages, paragraphs, italics, and punctuation." A discussion of the method of carrying out these instructions
follows likewise in the same Preface.

The general committee was organized into two companies, the Old
Testament and the New Testament, of twenty-seven members each.
The New Testament Company was formally organized and began
work in the famous Jerusalem Chamber of Westminster Deanery,
London, June 22, 1870, and on the thirtieth the Old Testament Company began its long and arduous toil. Each company was required to
work through its portion of the Bible twice. The companies met together in sessions at stated intervals, generally for six hours a day; the
Old Testament Company usually met in ten-day sessions five times in
the year, but the New held meetings for four days every month except
August and September. The procedure in the meetings has been officially related thus:

In the first Revision it was the practice for the Secretary to read over each
verse, first in the original and then in the Authorised version: the proposals for
change were then taken. . . . Each proposal was moved, and if seconded was
discussed and voted upon; the decision in the first Revision being by a majority
only. . . . In the second Revision, the Secretary read out in order the changes
which had been made at the first Revision; if these were unchallenged they were
allowed to remain, otherwise they were put to the vote and affirmed or rejected
according as they were or were not supported by the requisite majority of

two-thirds. In the second Revision new propositions could only be made by special permission of the Company, and discussion was limited, as far as possible, to exceptional cases. In the final review, which was in reality the completion of the second Revision, the Company employed themselves in making a general survey of what they had done, deciding upon reserved points, harmonizing inconsistencies, smoothing down roughnesses, removing unnecessary changes, and generally giving finish and completeness to their work. Everything in this final survey was decided by the vote of a majority of two-thirds.

In 1870 Dr. Angus visited America and, at the request of Bishop Ellicott, held a conference with some American scholars on the possibility of co-operation with the British Revision Committee. A plan of such co-operation was framed, and a list of American Biblical scholars representative of the leading religious bodies and denominations of the country was drawn up. The British Revision Committee approved the plan and list of names. Accordingly a body of thirty men was organized December 7, 1871, which first began active service October 4, 1872, as Old and New Testament companies, after the pattern of the British organizations. These two American companies, after beginning their service, met for committee work one session every month, except July and August, in the Bible House in New York. Of the New Testament Company, ex-President Woolsey of New Haven was chairman; and Professor William Henry Green, of Princeton, occupied the same position for the Old Testament Company. The details of the plan of co-operation with the British Revision Committee were not easily arranged or adjusted. It was not until 1875 that a mutually agreeable and workable scheme was concluded. Dr. Philip Schaff, leader in the formation of the American group, gives a clear statement of the substance of that agreement in his valuable *Companion to Greek Testament and Revised Version* (pp. 400-401):

The English Revisers promise to send confidentially their Revision in its various stages to the American Revisers, to take all the American suggestions into special consideration before the conclusion of their labors, to furnish them before publication with copies of the Revision in its final form, and to allow them to present, in an Appendix to the Revised Scriptures, all the remaining differences of reading and rendering of importance, which the English Committee should decline to adopt; while, on the other hand, the American Revisers pledge themselves to give their moral support to the authorized editions of the University Presses, with a view to their freest circulation within the United States, and not to issue an edition of their own, for a term of fourteen years.

The New Testament companies were naturally the first to complete their task. The whole time devoted to the work by the British Company was ten and one-half years. The first revision was completed at the end of six years. The second by the end of two and one-half more. The remainder of the time was occupied in the consideration of the suggestions from America on the second revision, and of many details, and of special questions that had arisen. The average attendance for the whole time was sixteen each day, out of a total original membership of twenty-seven, which however was actually reduced by death or resignation to twenty-four.

Thus after about four hundred days of sittings on their work the British New Testament Company affixed their names to the Preface to their version November 11, 1880. On May 17, 1881, Bishop Ellicott, one of the two original movers of the resolution in 1870 to undertake the work of revision, laid the first copy of the Revised New Testament before the Convocation of Canterbury, and then gave in a brief address an account of the production of the volume. On that Tuesday, May 17, the Revised New Testament was published and put on sale in England, and on Friday, May 20, in the United States.

The reception accorded the work was unprecedented in the history of the Bible. One million copies were ordered in advance from the Oxford University Press, and nearly as many from that of Cambridge. Dr. Schaff states that a telegram from London, May 21, 1881, reported the sale of two million copies of the Revised New Testament in that one city. The pressure for copies in New York and Philadelphia began before daybreak of May 20. The agent of the Clarendon Press in New York alone sold 365,000 before the end of the year, largely, however, during the first few days. Other agents in Philadelphia sold about 110,000 copies. Within a few days after its appearance more than a score of reprints of different kinds were thrown on the market. Two firms sold during the summer of 1881 about 165,000. It is estimated that almost three million copies of the Revised New Testament were sold in England and America in all editions within less than one year after its publication. In addition to these recorded sales there were various periodicals and papers that did large service, by the publication of either a part or the whole of the new volume. The Chicago *Tribune* and the Chicago *Times* published the book entire in their issues of May 22, 1881. The Gospels, Acts, and Romans, containing about 118,000 words, were telegraphed from New York, and the remainder of the book was set up from copies received in Chicago on the evening of May 21.

Thus the Revised New Testament sprang at once into a full-fledged popularity and was widely and, for a time, eagerly read by the religious and literary elements of the English-speaking world.

The work of revising the Old Testament was greater. It was not concluded until 1884, fourteen years after the beginning of the task. This space of time wrought many changes in the personnel of the British Old Testament Company. Only fifteen of the original twenty-seven lived to see the completion of their work; ten had died and two had resigned, their places being filled by others until 1875, after which no one was added to the company. The revision was completed in eighty-five sessions, ending June 20, 1884; it occupied 792 days, or more than two and one-half years of working days.

The British Company had gone twice through the Pentateuch before co-operation with the American Company had been arranged. The first revision of the British Company was submitted to the American, and in every case except that of the Pentateuch the British had the benefit of their criticisms and suggestions before taking up their second revision. The second revision was also submitted to the Americans, whose latest thoughts were in the hands of the British Company at their final review. As in the case of the New Testament, the Revised Old Testament carries an Appendix that contains many of the American preferences which were not adopted by the British Company. The Preface of the completed Old Testament was signed by the British Old Testament Company in Jerusalem Chamber July 10, 1884; and the entire Revised Version appeared bound in one volume May 19, 1885. Its reception was general, cordial, and thoughtful. There was no such phenomenal, popular demand for the entire Revised Bible as there had been just four years before for the Revised New Testament. But there was a healthy and encouraging market for this result of long years of toil by eminent Biblical scholars.

The Old Testament text was the Massoretic Hebrew, substantially the same as that used by the company that produced the Authorized

Version. The revisers profited by collations of Hebrew manuscripts and by readings of the ancient versions. But it was a cautious revision, and no one need feel surprise that there are so few striking changes from the text of the Old Testament of the King James Version. But the Greek text of the New Testament used by the revisers was much better than that used by King James's revisers. Since 1611 all the great New Testament manuscripts (Chapter XII) had come into scholarly use. As members of the British New Testament Company were Drs. Scrivener and Hort, two of the most able textual critics of the New Testament. The text used by the revisers was the result of a critical examination and estimate of all the known Greek New Testament manuscripts. The differences of the Greek text used by the revisers from that used for the King James Version, according to Dr. Scrivener's notes (as cited by Dr. Schaff, *Companion,* p. 419, note) are apparent in 5,788 readings. Only about one in four of these makes any material difference in the substance of the text. Another estimate placed the number of changes in the English text at 36,191, or an average of four and one-half changes in each of the 7,960 verses. In other words, the Revised Version of the New Testament differs in more than 36,000 places from the Authorized Version.

A comparison of the two Testaments in the King James and the Revised versions reveals important features. In 1611 the Hebrew language was not perfectly understood, while the Greek had been well mastered. Consequently the Hebrew Old Testament was often inaccurately rendered into English, beautiful English though it was, while the New Testament was a fairly good and accurate translation of the Greek text. But the Old Testament of the Revised Version, although based on practically the same Hebrew text as that used for the 1611 version, is a much clearer translation of the Hebrew, making sense out of many passages that were obscure in the King James. This improvement is very marked in the prophetical and poetical books, where obscurities, as we all know, were frequent.

While the greatest gain in the New Testament was, as we have indicated, in the employment of a superior Greek text, yet it was also true that a more discriminating recognition of the principles of the grammar and syntax of New Testament Greek introduced valuable improvements, particularly in certain difficult passages of the Pauline letters.

The Authorized Version has been in use over three hundred years and, of course, contains scores, even hundreds of words and expressions whose meanings have become greatly modified, or entirely changed. One of the urgent tasks of the revisers was to weed out these obsolete words, archaisms, and expressions that do not now mean what they did originally, or what the original text is now seen to mean; certain terms, too, which in the course of time had become offensive to good taste, especially for public reading, needed modification.

The revisers were required to translate the originals into modern, modest, and yet forcible language that would properly represent the original texts and at the same time give no needless offense to any thoughtful reader. In addition they strove for consistency; they undertook to translate, as far as possible, the same original by the same English word. Under the first principle they made changes such as "Holy Spirit" for "Holy Ghost," "Sheol" or "Hades" for "hell," "strange" for "outlandish," "smooth" for "peeled," "inwards" for "purtenance," "condemnation" for "damnation," "falsehood" for "leasing." The second principle had not been followed by the 1611 revisers; instead, they often used synonyms for the same Greek or Hebrew word, and thus gave variety and beauty to their translation.

The Revised Version possesses other commendable qualities. The old separation of chapters and verses has been abandoned in favor of divisions according to sense, and thus the text reads continuously like any other book. Some of the poetical sections in the Old Testament are printed in separate lines corresponding to the original form. Unfortunately the practice is not followed in the prophets, although these books contain a very large bulk of poetry. The version also omitted chapter headings and chronological material, which had come to occupy a prominent place in the Authorized Version and had occasioned much misunderstanding and misinterpretation. Marginal notes constituted a special problem. Early in its work the British Committee appointed a group of its members to consider the advisability of a series of marginal references; they decided, however, that until the version should prove itself, the labor entailed would be premature. Consequently the first edition was devoid of them, although it contained a large number of notes of alternate translations or of variants in the originals. But by 1895 it was felt by the University Presses of Oxford and Cambridge, the publishers of the version, that "an increasing demand, both at home and in America, for an edition of the complete Revised Version with marginal references" warranted the undertaking. A committee was appointed, and in 1898 the annotated edition was published. In it the notes of the former edition became footnotes, while an extensive series of references was placed in the margins. According to the statement of the committee, these were of five classes: "(1) Quotations, of exact verbal parallels. (2) Passages referred to for similarity of idea or of expression. (3) Passages referred to by way of explanation or illustration. (4) Historical and Geographic references . . . names of persons, places, etc., which recur. (5) Passages referred to as illustrating differences of rendering between the Authorized and Revised Versions." *In toto,* the marginal material was greatly reduced from that of the Authorized Version, notwithstanding that some of these classes marked a considerable increase.

The Revised Version was produced through the co-operation of about seventy-five of the leading Biblical scholars of Great Britain and America, who represented the most prominent religious bodies of the two greater English-speaking democracies. The age of the King James Version, its antiquated language, and its recognized defects of several kinds were some of the reasons for revision. These conditions insured for the Revised Version a hearty welcome from most of the better-trained and more intelligent Bible students of the day. Such readers quickly recognized its merits as more truly representing the original texts and welcomed its clear diction and language according more nearly with the simple, direct speech of today. Nonetheless the version did not meet with immediate approval, nor has it in the sequel won for itself a place of undisputed supremacy. There were critics with sharp pens who found many defects in it; and in much of their criticism, we must admit, they were right. Then too, tender and sacred associations clinging about the King James Version led some readers to regard any change as almost sacrilegious and to combat the abandonment of so precious a Bible for a new and untried rendering. Yet, as in the history of earlier versions, all these considerations did not suffice to outweigh for more thoughtful minds the indisputable superiority of the Revised Version. Inevitably the King James Version will be put on the shelf as the most venerable and influential among all older English Bibles. The Revised Version, too, will follow it in time, as will every other version that may ever be produced. For the growth of a living language, to say nothing of advance in Biblical scholarship, entails that no translation of the Bible can ever be final. It suffices that each serves worthily its day and generation.

The production and merits of the American Standard Revised Version of 1901 deserve also some notice. It will be remembered that an American Revision Committee was not organized until 1871, and that its work did not begin until October 4, 1872, more than two years later than the British Committee. Its task was to pass in review the revisions of the British Committee and to make any suggestions or emendations that seemed to be required from the viewpoint of American scholarship, or of the needs of the American churches. But the actual terms on which the two committees worked together were not formulated until 1875. They agreed that the suggestions of the American Committee should be duly considered by the British Committee before the conclusion of their labors, and that they (the British Committee) should allow the American Committee to present in an Appendix to the Revised Scriptures all the remaining important differences of reading and rendering which the British Committee should decline to adopt. This Appendix was to be published in every copy of the Revised Bible during a term of fourteen years. "The American Committee on their part pledged themselves to give, for the same limited period, no sanction to the publication of any other editions of the Revised Version than those issued by the University Presses of England."

The British Committee disbanded soon after the conclusion of its work, but the American Committee continued, for it saw the possibility that an "American recension" of the Revised Version might be desired. And this would require much more serious work than a mere introduction of the readings of the Appendix into the text, for these had been prepared under conditions that precluded an expression of the real position of the American Committee.

A pressing need for an American revision is seen in the use in the 1885 edition of a large number of words and phrases whose meanings or spellings are wholly antiquated. Some of these are: "bewray," "grisled," "holpen," "hough," "marish," "pourtray," "sith," "strowed." Then there are many words that are English but not American in meaning. "Corn" means grain of all kinds in England, but only maize or Indian corn in America. "Chargers" are not "platters," but "horses" here. "Traders" are not "chapmen" with us, nor are "merchants" "occupiers." "Fat" is not "vat" here, nor is the "capital" of a column called a "chapiter." Our soldiers are not arrayed in "harness," nor do we take our shoes "to be clouted." What is "go to"? To retain such words in our Bible would necessarily require a glossary to explain them.

Yet the American revision was less drastic than the British edition in its treatment of features external to the text. It restored running headlines in revised form, and included a new set of scriptural cross references. The marginal notes were about the same in nature and quantity as the British, except that the citation of Old Testament variant readings based upon versional evidence was reduced to about one-sixth of its former quantity and such citations as remained specifically named the supporting version. The text was also reparagraphed, and the use of punctuation and italics was improved and systematized.

Adequate time was provided the American Committee by its agreement with the British Committee to refrain from publication for fourteen years. Consequently the work was well in hand as this period drew to a close; and on August 26, 1901, the version was issued to the public by Thomas Nelson and Sons of New York City. Its title page was that of the Revised Version, with the significant additional note, "Newly Edited by the American Revision Committee. A.D. 1901. Standard Edition"; thus it has come to be known as "The American Standard Version." It embodied the ripest scholarship of Great Britain and America. The claim made shortly after its publication that "it is the most perfect English Bible in existence" was probably justified. It represented the best scholarship and Biblical learning of its time and was a fitting climax to the great advance in knowledge of the Bible made during the latter half of the nineteenth century. The hearty reception given it and the readiness with which it was adopted by all classes of the Bible-reading public were a tribute to its excellence and to its rich promise for the religious life of our times.

But it was not final; no translation of the Bible ever can be! Even within the relatively brief period since its publication great progress has been made in knowledge of Bible life and times, and specifically of the Biblical languages. In part this has come through the remarkable archaeological activity that was a notable feature of scholarly interest in "Bible lands" through the decades between the two world wars. But for whatever reason, the American Standard Version already lags behind the scholarship of the present. Then too, certain of the methods of the translators which at the time were thought to mark the superiority of the version have come in perspective of the years to be recognized as serious defects. The use of the word "Jehovah" as the name of God is a barbaric touch from which better taste has recoiled. The name represents no ancient original but roots entirely in ignorance of a feature of Hebrew manuscripts. The only adequate term is "the Lord," dignified as it is by ages of Jewish and Christian use. The consistency of the translators also became a vice; it is a mechanical procedure, and not true translation, to follow rigidly chosen word equivalents. Words take on meaning from their context, so that an elasticity of rendering is demanded if the true sense is to be served.

Then, strange as it may sound, the American Standard Version was far too conservative; or more strictly, it was uneven in its attitude to the King James, changing when often the old was better, and yet conforming its rendering as a whole to the form of seventeenth-century scholarship. A single illustration will suffice. Modern knowledge of the existence and nature of poetry in the Old Testament dates from the publication in 1753 of Bishop Lowth's *De Sacra Poesi Hebraeorum*. The matter had been set forth by Rabbi Azariah de Rossi two centuries earlier, but had attracted little attention. From the time of Lowth, however, it has been common scholarly knowledge. King James's translators, then, were nearly a century and a half too early to profit by this important discovery. Their rendering of the Psalms and other poetry, notably of the prophetic books, is thus set up uniform with the certainly prose parts of the Old Testament. The vivid imagery of Hebrew poetry and its characteristic form are such that, in spite of the translators, a poetic quality attaches to considerable of their rendering. Nonetheless, it was essentially a prose translation of Hebrew poetry. The American translators effected a great improvement when they printed the Psalms in lines corresponding to the original form; yet beyond considerable revision of the wording, their actual rendering is just as prosaic as is that of the Authorized Version. Their responsibility demanded a completely new translation created in full recognition of the poetic nature of the original and dominated by a feeling for its forms and imagery. Such a course was too radical for half a century ago; the translators gave only a verbal modification of the seventeenth-century prose.

Reviving interest today in Jewish literature outside the canon impels mention that the British Revision Committee did not limit its work to the Old and New Testaments but went on to revise the translation of the Apocrypha, and published its version in 1894.

CHAPTER XXIV

Recent and Modern-Speech Translations

ABOUT the time when the work of the American Committee of Revision was drawing to a conclusion, astonishing discoveries of ancient Greek papyri were made in Egypt, especially in the Fayum. They have had a revolutionary influence upon the study of the Greek of the New Testament. For centuries this dialect had presented a vexing problem, since it was neither classical Greek nor the Greek of the Septuagint. But now it was shown to be the vernacular Greek of the papyri—the colloquial language of common people in Egypt and perhaps in Palestine in the first and second centuries. For these papyri contain letters, contracts, leases, decrees, diaries, and many such private and public documents, written in the everyday Greek language of the people. Obviously they have profoundly altered the study of New Testament grammar and syntax. In addition they have toned down and clarified the formerly rather stilted classical interpretation of New Testament language. In other words, interpreters, finding that they were handling colloquial words and idioms, have been led to rethink the New Testament in the everyday speech of the common man.

These developments conduced strongly to fresh translation of the Bible. It will be recalled that the past fifty years have witnessed also an unparalleled series of discoveries of ancient Biblical manuscripts, some of them of high importance, which have created a keen interest and have focused attention upon the Biblical text. When, further, one recognizes the sense of inadequacy of the revision of 1901 which has become steadily more manifest with the passage of time, it does not seem at all strange that ours has been one of the notable periods of activity in translation both of the New Testament and of the Bible as a whole. Several of these translations have undertaken to exploit the colloquialism revealed by the papyri and so to produce "modern-speech" versions; but others have been of a more traditional character.

Out of the total a few that for various reasons have attracted most attention may be mentioned here.

The Spurrell Translation of the Old Testament was an independent translation made by Mrs. Helen Spurrell, of London; it appeared in 1885. She was a talented woman, competent in music, painting, and sculpture. She learned Hebrew after she had passed fifty years of age, and translated the whole Old Testament from the unpointed Hebrew text. But she did not hesitate to correct the text when the reading of the Samaritan Pentateuch or of the Septuagint seemed to her to warrant change. Her style does not vary greatly from that of the King James Version. She adopts "Jehovah" where the King James Version has "LORD." She has caption headings printed in italics at the top of the page. Hebrew textual and explanatory notes are found at the bottom of the page. Poetry is put in verse form. The verse numbers, sometimes combined, as ¾, are found in the text. Some other peculiarities of printing will be apparent to those who understand the Hebrew text.

The Bible in Modern English by Ferrar Fenton was published in London, New Testament 1895, Old 1905. It was "translated into English direct from the original Hebrew, Chaldee and Greek languages." The order of books of the Old Testament is that of the Hebrew Bible. The text is broken up by the insertion of subject headings, but the chapter and verse numbers are printed on the margins. The translation is the modern English of Great Britain. It has some peculiarities of translation and spelling. The word rendered "Jehovah" in the American Standard Version is almost everywhere the EVER-LIVING. Micah is spelled "Mikah," and Zechariah is "Zakariah." The poetical portions are printed in verse form. The New Testament of this Bible is Fenton's second edition, "newly translated direct from the accurate Greek text of Drs. Westcott and Hort." Quotations from the Old Testament are printed in capitals. The translation is accompanied by occasional introductory textual and explanatory notes, useful to the reader. Though quite popular for a time, its erroneous and inaccurate renderings have rather damaged its earlier favor.

Toward the middle of the past century an agitation arose in this country for an "immersion" version, to be used among the several immersionist denominations. In 1850 the American Bible Union was

organized for this purpose and initiated plans for a revision of the
whole Bible. Job was published in 1856. In the years 1862, 1863, and
1864 the New Testament was issued in three successive volumes that
then were united in a single edition in 1865. It used the word "immerse" throughout where the Authorized Version had "baptize." The
publication of the Old Testament began with Genesis in 1868 and
dragged along variously until lack of funds brought the project to a
halt after 1879. But by 1891 it was revived, when a revision of the New
Testament was published. Then in 1912 the complete work appeared
under the title, *The Holy Bible—An Improved Edition.* In sixty years
the original impulse had so far moderated that this final edition
employs the double rendering, "baptize (immerse)" wherever this
rite is mentioned. Poetry in the Old Testament appears in verse form.
There are no subject headings. The text is run in solid except for
occasional paragraphing. The verse number in very small unobtrusive
type is set in the text just at the first word of the verse. Occasional
textual and explanatory but not expository notes appear at the bottom of the page.

The Hebrew text has remained authentic Scripture for the Jews.
Yet presently the same forces and needs that had impelled the great
ancient versions operated in the modern lands of the Jewish dispersion.
In English-speaking countries the King James Version of the Old
Testament was first adapted to Jewish use, but in 1851 a translation
into English made by Abraham Benisch was published in England.
In 1853 Isaac Leeser, an enthusiastic and aggressive American scholar,
published in Philadelphia a translation of the Hebrew Bible; then
thirty years later *A Jewish Family Bible,* in English and Hebrew,
edited by Michael Friedlander, was published in England. But
Leeser's translation remained the commonly approved version in all the
synagogues in the United States, and was even reprinted in England.

All these were, it will be observed, private translations, produced
by the devotion and enterprise of single scholars. Whatever their excellence, the advance of scholarship in course of time dictated an
improvement upon even the popular version of Leeser, and, as indicative of the growing importance of Judaism on this continent which has
continued to the present, it fell to an American group of Jewish scholars
to produce the version which, transcending the others in its merit,

has become a *de facto* authorized Bible of English-speaking Jews. It was in 1888 that the Jewish Publication Society of America was organized; and only four years later it initiated steps toward a new translation. The plan as developed was to secure translations of the several books of the Bible (that is, of the Old Testament) by individual allotment to Jewish scholars in Great Britain and the United States, these translations then to be submitted to the critical revision of an Editorial Committee which would carry on discussion with the translators by means of correspondence. However, by 1901 it became apparent that the process was far too slow. Nonetheless, it was not until 1908 that the entire scheme was revised and the project taken up with energy. A Board of Editors was created, consisting of six scholars representative of the Jewish Theological Seminary of America at New York, Hebrew Union College at Cincinnati, and the Dropsie College at Philadelphia, and with Professor Max Margolis, a seventh member, appointed editor in chief and secretary to the board. It devolved upon Margolis to prepare the translations; these were submitted to each member of the board and later discussed in its meetings. Thus by discussion and constant criticism and recriticism, making use of all the relevant ancient and modern translations and literature, the work moved on through seven years. Sixteen meetings of the board were held, totaling 160 working days. At length at the final meeting in November, 1915, a prayer of thanks was offered "that the great task was completed and that the group which during seven years had toiled together was intact."

The first important modern-speech translation was Weymouth's New Testament, published in London, 1903. The text used was his own *Resultant Greek Testament*, embodying the readings of the majority of textual critics. The version, so the Preface says, "is a bona fide translation made directly from the Greek, and is in no sense a revision." And indeed it has so little in common with the King James Version that often they cannot be compared. Weymouth is more free than either Moffatt or Goodspeed. Some peculiarities of the work are: (1) there are subject headings in black-faced type indented at the beginning of a given theme; (2) quotations from the Old Testament are printed in capital letters; (3) chapter and verse numbers are put on the margin; (4) extensive notes in justification of the translation or in comparison with other readings are found in fine print at the bottom of the page; (5) direct discourse is marked by single quotation marks. The fourth edition of 1924 is provided with introductions to the several literary divisions of the New Testament.

The Twentieth Century New Testament is said to have had its origin in the desire of a mother to translate the New Testament into language that her children could understand. She finally succeeded in enlisting the help of about twenty competent scholars, who by means of committees carried the work through to completion. No names were given out, and no one received compensation. The basic Greek text was Westcott and Hort. A "tentative edition" was issued in three parts 1898-1900. On the basis of elaborate criticisms the permanent edition was published anonymously in 1904, in London and New York. In this New Testament translation the books are arranged in the chronological order determined by the authors under three heads, Historical Books, Letters, and the Apocalypse. The letters have been grouped under the names of the writers to whom they are usually assigned, and in each such division in their chronological order. Chapter and verse notations are on the margin. Subject headings are in black-faced type indented at the appropriate places. Direct discourse is in quotation marks. Quotations or borrowed phrases from the Old Testament are printed in smaller type enclosed by single quotation marks. References to parallel passages and sources of quotations are printed in small type at the bottom of the page.

James Moffatt, who in 1901 had issued in Edinburgh a *Historical New Testament*, published a translation of the New Testament in New York in 1913. It is a strikingly independent modern-speech translation, based on von Soden's recently published Greek text; where Moffatt adopts a different reading, he mentions it in a footnote. No subject headings are given. Chapter and verse numbers are printed on the margins. Direct discourse is put in quotation marks. Quotations or direct reminiscences of the Old Testament are given in italics.

Yet Moffatt's contribution to Biblical translation did not cease here. In 1924 he astonished the Bible-reading public with a translation of the Old Testament also. It was a notable achievement. There have been few scholars who have possessed the competence to produce single-handed a great translation of the entire Bible. Indeed, in the history of the English Bible Moffatt's accomplishment stands, in this regard, without a rival.

A primary problem of any translator is the finality of the text on which he works. Moffatt made free to modify the Massoretic readings in accord with his best judgment as to their original form. Although neither in the King James nor the Revised Version had the traditional text been slavishly followed (instead the translators had occasionally followed variants in the early versions), yet such changes were always made with notable conservatism. But Moffatt states, "The traditional or 'Massoretic' text is often desperately corrupt." It is sometimes "broken or defective" though the English versions do not reveal it. And so he has made bold to correct errors in the Hebrew which he considered plainly evident. In this he consulted, obviously, the ancient versions as well as requirements of Oriental idioms and literary common sense. His policy has occasionally led to a transfer of phrases, of verses and sometimes of entire sections. Whatever justification this course may have as exposition of the Bible, it cannot but be considered to exceed the proper function of a translator, which is to render faithfully and worthily the text as attested by the best ancient authorities.

The translation is pre-eminently original. Moffatt himself says that it "is a fresh translation of the original, not a revision of any English version." Its language may be described, not unjustly, as modern colloquial British English. The poetry he has printed in verse form; a doubtful feature is the occasional use of rhyme (e.g., II Sam. 23:1). For "Jehovah" of the American Standard Version he has followed the French in using "The Eternal." By a system of italics and brackets he attempts to disentangle the alleged sources of the J and E narratives in the Pentateuch. There are no subject headings. Chapter and verse numbers are all on the margins. Moffatt had an acute feeling for the power of English words and the beauties of English style. Not infrequently his phrases are of an impressive appeal and his insights brilliant. Nonetheless, it must be admitted that too often his rendering is paraphrase rather than translation.

In 1926 Moffatt completed his work by publishing his Old and New Testament translations in a single volume. The Moffatt Bible is a distinctive and conspicuous contribution to modern-speech translations. It is Moffatt's running commentary on the whole Bible.

The *Riverside New Testament* by W. G. Ballantine was published in Boston in 1923. It was "made directly from the original Greek, Nestle's text (of 1901) being generally followed." In the English phrasing, the translator says, he made use of modern-speech translations, as well as of the Revised and the Authorized versions. He sought to reproduce as nearly as possible in English the exact sense of the original Greek. The book is printed like any other book, the number of the chapters, but not of the verses, being indicated. There are no subject headings at all. Quotations from the Old Testament are printed in the same type as the rest of the page but are enclosed in quotation marks. There are no references or footnotes. A clean beautiful page attracts the reader. A revised edition was published in 1934.

Goodspeed's New Testament is the work of Professor Edgar J. Goodspeed of the University of Chicago. It is based on Westcott and Hort's text and was published in Chicago in 1923. Its language is a distinctly American English, in contrast with the modern-speech translations of Weymouth, the Twentieth Century, and Moffatt, which are in the English of Great Britain. Excepting a special pocket form of the first edition, chapter and verse numbers were printed at the bottom of the page. Otherwise and in most later editions they were placed on the margins. Subject captions are not given, and quotations are enclosed in proper marks. The solemn "thou," "thee," and "thy" are not used even in prayers. The book is printed like any other book, and in the language of the common man. Among modern-speech translations of the New Testament this work has no peer.

The Centenary Translation of the New Testament was made by Mrs. Helen Barrett Montgomery of Rochester, New York, who thus attained the distinction of being the only woman to produce a modern-speech translation of the New Testament. It was published in Philadelphia in 1924, in two 12mo volumes, with an approximate total of 724 pages. Its publication celebrated the close of the first hundred years of service of the American Baptist Publication Society. Each book of the New Testament is introduced by about a half-page of introduction, which gives date, author, key verse, characteristics, symbol, method, and the like. Modern-speech translations minimize the breaks of chapter and verse divisions, but Mrs. Montgomery emphasizes chapters by assigning to each a title, which is printed in capital letters.

In addition she breaks up the chapters into paragraphs, each carrying a theme printed in dark-faced type. This policy offers wide scope to the author's ingenuity, as seen in these colloquial topics: "A 'Close-up' of Sin" (p. 401); "Paul's Swan Song" (p. 578); "Orchestrate Your Virtues" (p. 647). Direct discourse is put in quotation marks. Quotations from the Old Testament are printed in italics. The sources of these, and a few textual notes, are found at the bottom of the pages.

An interest in the bearing which a knowledge of Semitic backgrounds may have upon the understanding and the translation of the New Testament has led also to some versions which have sought to exploit these resources. In 1933 two such translations appeared, a New Testament translated by George Lamsa and *The Four Gospels—A New Translation* by Professor Charles C. Torrey of Yale University. The former was nothing more than a rendering of the late (Peshitta) Syriac, itself a translation of the Greek. The latter sought to reconstruct and translate hypothetical Semitic documents of which supposedly the Greek Gospels were translations. While Torrey's work, along with similar but less comprehensive efforts by scholars such as Dalman, Montgomery, Burney, and Burrows, has thrown valuable light, in places, upon the Greek text, New Testament scholarship in general hesitates to accept the view that our present documents are translations. The possibility of Semitic sources back of our Gospels is not excluded; yet it is felt that the linguistic phenomena can be explained by the supposition of translation during a period of oral transmission of the material in Aramaic and Greek, or by the native idiom of the authors and editors of the Greek documents, or by the influence of the style of the Greek Old Testament. In addition, the historical situation reflected by the contents of the Gospels, as well as their use of already extant Greek documentary sources, would seem to render the hypothesis untenable.

The Old Testament, an American Translation appeared in Chicago in 1927. It was the joint work of Alexander R. Gordon of Montreal, Theophile J. Meek of Toronto, Leroy Waterman of Ann Arbor, Michigan, and J. M. Powis Smith, who was editor of the whole volume. Gordon translated Proverbs, Isaiah, Jeremiah, Ezekiel, and Daniel; Meek rendered the Pentateuch, Joshua, Judges, Ruth, Song of Songs, and Lamentations; Waterman's work was Samuel, Kings,

Chronicles, Ezra, Nehemiah, and Esther; Smith's translations were Job, Psalms, Ecclesiastes, and the minor prophets. The translation seemed to be required by "the great advance in Hebrew scholarship within the past forty years, resulting in a better knowledge of Hebrew, a fuller understanding of the fundamental textual problems involved and a clearer recognition of poetic structure" (Preface).

The Massoretic text was the basis of the translations, but with such textual changes as the evidence of the versions or critical conjecture seemed to justify. The extent to which such changes were adopted is indicated by the immense bulk of the notes in which they are listed; they constitute an Appendix of ninety-one small-type, closely printed pages. Such free treatment of the text, in particular the large use of conjectural emendation, is a feature in which this translation has gone beyond all others. But otherwise, the actual phrasing deviates less from the King James Version than, for example, Moffatt's version. A commendable feature is that the divine name is rendered the LORD, not "Jehovah" as in the American Standard. The page exhibits good typography, is well spaced and paragraphed. Subject headings, printed in capital letters, are inserted where the text seems to require them. Poetry is printed in verse form. "Thee," "thou," "thy," and the archaic verb forms are used only in addressing the Deity.

In 1931 the Smith Old Testament and the Goodspeed New Testament were published together as *The Bible—An American Translation*. A few changes were made in the former separate volumes. In the Old Testament the Appendix of textual notes was dropped out. In the New Testament both chapter and verse numbers were transferred to the margins. Also, running heads give "New Testament" on the left-hand page and the name of the book on the right-hand page. There were no subject captions either over the chapters or in the text, and no footnotes. But the volume was still paged as two separate books, with 1,619 pages in the Old Testament and 418 in the New. With minor changes the translations remained as when issued in two separate volumes. The Old Testament translation was given a hurried revision by Professor Meek in 1935. An exhaustive revision was initiated in 1950, together with a project of annotating both Testaments.

A selection of passages from this translation was issued in 1933 in a volume of only 545 pages, entitled *The Short Bible—An American Translation*. J. M. P. Smith had died, September 26, 1932, and the editing of the entire work was carried through by Edgar J. Goodspeed. In a selection so restricted it is apparent that less important books were of necessity passed over; and thus, of the Old Testament, Chronicles, Song of Songs, Lamentations, Obadiah, and Malachi are completely missing, as likewise II Peter, II and III John, and Jude from the New Testament. The books are arranged in chronological order. The Old Testament selections begin with Amos and end with Ecclesiastes; those from the New open with Thessalonians and close with Titus. A valuable feature is the brief introduction, of one-half to two pages, printed in italics, which the editor has prefixed to each book. Another novel element is the inclusion of a fragment from Ecclesiasticus, only verses 1-15 of Chapter 44, which follows the selections from Ecclesiastes. This action was in a sense a promise on the part of Professor Goodspeed, for through the following years he made a completely new translation of the entire Apocrypha, which then was published, also by the University of Chicago Press, in 1938. And then this course of translation and publication reached its logical culmination in the appearance in 1939 of *The Complete Bible: An American Translation*; it was "complete" in that it contained, as already mentioned, the Apocrypha as well as the Old and New Testaments.

Roman Catholic scholarship has not remained negligent of the need for an acceptable English translation of the Bible. The Rheims-Douai Version was subjected to notable revision in the eighteenth century by Bishop Challoner of London and Archbishop Troy of Dublin. This and subsequent work was so far-reaching that it has been at times remarked with exaggeration that scarcely a word of the original translation remains. Yet all this has been surpassed by the activity of recent years among Catholic scholars in translation of the Bible, a stirring comparable to that among Protestant translators which we have been surveying. An early expression of this activity was the work on *The Westminster Version of the Sacred Scriptures*, which began to appear in 1913. However, publication was slow, but then a "small edition" was published in 1948. The latter is a volume of 479 pages, printed in modern paragraphing, with verse and chapter numbers removed to the outer margin, but having numerous divisional and sectional headings interspersed in the text. The pages carry no titles except those of the successive books; at the foot of the pages is a series of explanatory and doctrinal notes. Much more striking, however, is the fact that the translation is made from the original Greek. The editors state that their "first aim" was to "stimulate the study of the Scriptures, first by providing as faithful a rendering as possible from the best available Greek text, and then by presenting it with all the aids to intelligibility and readability which a rational typographical arrangement, plentiful notes and the removal of all arbitrary interruptions of the sense could supply." The Old Testament is now nearly complete.

Another important version was that published in 1941 by St. Anthony's Guild Press, of Paterson, New Jersey, bearing the title, *The New Testament of Our Lord and Savior Jesus Christ Translated from the Latin Vulgate; a Revision of the Challoner-Rheims Version Edited by Catholic Scholars Under the Patronage of The Episcopal Committee of the Confraternity of Christian Doctrine.* It is a volume of 762 pages, equipped with maps, glossary, and numerous footnotes. Of these latter, one series consists merely of parallel references, but the other is in a broad way explanatory. Textual features come in for not-infrequent comment, including divergences from the original Greek. Many of the explanations are doctrinal. Peter's confession (Matt. 16:16-19), for example, gives occasion for a half-page discussion which asserts, *inter alia*, that "the rock was Peter." In addition each book is prefaced with an introduction, of one-half to one and one-half pages, where again the official Roman position is set forth. The text is printed in a single column to the page; paragraphing is frequent; poetic passages are set in appropriate form. The format is attractive; the excellence of the translation, though based on the Vulgate, approximates the quality of versions made direct from the Greek.

Yet this did not exhaust the industry of Catholic translators. It was to be expected that they would push on to a version of the Old Testament as well. But the actuality merits remark, for the Old Testament is being translated direct from the Hebrew and Aramaic originals "by Catholic Biblical scholars under the patronage of the Bishops of the U.S." The Book of Genesis was published in 1948, then later included in volume one of the Old Testament in 1952. Also Fathers Kleist and Lilly in 1954 published *The New Testament Rendered from the*

Original Greek, with explanatory notes, a volume of 688 pages inspired by the wish "to render the Greek into such modern English as . . . would approve itself to American Catholics." These signalize developments in Catholic Biblical scholarship unrivaled since Jerome.

About the time when the "Confraternity" version was being produced, a similar undertaking was in process among the Roman Catholics of England and Wales. In 1944 there appeared *The New Testament of Our Lord and Saviour Jesus Christ newly translated from the Vulgate Latin at the Request of Their Lordships, the Archbishops and Bishops of England and Wales.* It was the work of Ronald Knox, who explains in his Preface that the hierarchical request was made in 1939. Like its American counterpart, the version abandons verse divisions in favor of paragraphing, relegates verse numbers to the margin, and prints one column to the page. Glossary and introductions are omitted; footnotes are much less frequent and, in general, less doctrinal. But this must not be attributed to superior principles, for the note on Matthew 1:25, for example, attempts to defend the dogma of the perpetual virginity of Mary, and that on Mark 8:27-39 claims that omission of "the promise to Peter" was perhaps due to his humility! Another similarity to the Confraternity version is the retention of archaic pronouns and verbal forms.

Father Knox continued his labors. His translation of the Book of Psalms was published in 1947. It is a modest little volume of 239 pages, with no preface or introduction, and bears the simple title, *The Psalms, a New Translation, by Ronald Knox.* In addition to the canonical Psalms it contains sixteen "canticles from the Song of Moses to that of Simeon." The jacket flap tells that the translation was made from "the new Latin version of the Psalms, with reference to the Hebrew." Poetic form is ignored; there are no page headings, and no titles other than the ancient Psalm introductions. The entire task progressed rapidly; the first volume of the complete Old Testament translation, containing the books Genesis to Esther, came on the market late in 1948, and the second and concluding one in 1950.

A very important translation project was initiated in Great Britain in the summer of 1947. After some preliminary conferences, a joint interdenominational committee was set up by the Church of England, the Church of Scotland, and the Free Churches of Great Britain, with representation from Ireland and Wales, to undertake a new translation of the entire Bible, including the Apocrypha, "into modern English." Subsequently representatives of the British and Foreign Bible Society and of the National Bible Society of Scotland were added. Meeting in the historic Jerusalem Chamber in Wesminster Abbey in January, 1948, the committee organized into four panels, one each for the Old Testament, the New Testament, and the Apocrypha, and a panel of literary advisers. The late Bishop of Truro was originally chairman of the Joint Committee, with Reverend G. S. Hendry as secretary. These have now been succeeded by C. H. Dodd and J. K. S. Reid respectively. In harmony with British usage, publication has been entrusted to the University Presses of Oxford and Cambridge.

Yet all this impressive activity, serving to make the present the most remarkable age of English Bible translation, does not exhaust the subject. Mention must also be made of *The Bible in Basic English,* 1950, prepared in England by a committee under the direction of Professor S. H. Hooke, which accomplished the astonishing task of presenting the Bible in acceptable form with a total vocabulary of nine hundred words. E. V. Rieu published *The Four Gospels* in 1953; as a "Penguin" book it is of more than passing interest. *The New Testament Letters, prefaced and paraphrased* by J. W. C. Wand, appeared in Australia in 1944. In the following year Gerrit Verkuyl published his *Berkeley Version of the New Testament from the Original Greek, with brief footnotes.* His aim was to escape Biblical English and render the scriptures in the idiom of today. Similar was the purpose of J. B. Phillips' *The Gospels translated into Modern English,* 1952; and *Letters to Young Churches, a translation of the New Testament Epistles,* 1947. Comparable is *The New Testament in the Language of the People* by Charles B. Williams (copyright 1936); yet his straining after accurate representation of Greek inflection reveals a failure to appreciate the rich resources of the English tenses. *The New World Translation,* 1950, 1953, carried this mood farther, awkwardly rendering the Hebrew "waw conversive" by "proceeded to."

CHAPTER XXV

The Revised Standard Version

THE defects of the American Standard Version became increasingly apparent with the passage of the years. The King James Version, notwithstanding the worthy scholarship that had gone into its making and the resonant majesty of its wording, was quite out of date. The modern-speech translations, with all their excellence, stood apart from the great tradition which had flowed on from Tyndale and Coverdale and the great versions of the sixteenth century. Thus it came about that the English-speaking world found itself devoid of a Bible translation that could without reserve be set forward as *the* English Bible. And so, when in 1929 Thomas Nelson and Sons offered their expiring copyright on the American Standard Version to the International Council of Religious Education, one of the great unitive movements of American Protestantism, it was accepted promptly. Renewal of copyright was secured on April 3, in that year, and proceedings were at once set in motion for a revision. The American Standard Bible Committee was constituted; it was to be composed of leading Biblical scholars of the country, instructed to consider the advisability of revision, and to make recommendations as to its character and basic principles in case their decision should be affirmative. It was hoped that then the revision could be completed by 1941.

In February, 1930, the composition of the committee was announced. It consisted of thirteen members: William P. Armstrong, Princeton Theological Seminary; H. J. Cadbury, Bryn Mawr College; F. C. Eiselen, Garrett Biblical Institute; E. J. Goodspeed, University of Chicago; A. R. Gordon, United Theological College; James Moffatt, Union Theological Seminary; J. A. Montgomery, Philadelphia Divinity School; A. T. Robertson, Southern Baptist Theological Seminary; J. H. Ropes, Harvard University; John R. Sampey, Southern Baptist

Theological Seminary; Andrew Sledd, Emory University; C. C. Torrey, Yale University; and Luther A. Weigle, Yale University.

On April 15 the committee convened in New York City for organization and planning of its work. Dean Weigle was made chairman, a post he has subsequently held without interruption throughout the entire history of the committee. It was a happy choice, since apart from his high qualifications for leadership of a scholarly venture, his recognized place in the International Council provided at once a ready means of communication and understanding with that body. W. P. Armstrong was elected vice-chairman, and Hugh S. Magill of the International Council, secretary. Old and New Testament sections were also organized. Of the former John R. Sampey became chairman and F. C. Eiselen secretary; in the New Testament section the officers were J. H. Ropes and H. J. Cadbury.

The fundamental issue was debated long and earnestly; for vigorous opinion was expressed that the King James Version was still adequate and any change from it would be a mistake. Only after two years of wrestle with this and consequent problems did the committee reach a near unanimity in favor of revision. It is obvious that important questions would arise also in these discussions about the general character of the revision, if undertaken, and about many details of procedure. What should be the position relative to the King James, on one side, and to the modern-speech translations, on the other? How should the committee render the divine name in the Old Testament which the American Standard had called Jehovah and Moffatt had given as The Eternal? What about the archaic forms of pronouns and verbs which contribute to the King James not a little of its distinctive flavor? Seemingly less acute were questions as to continuance of older forms such as "whosoever," "lest haply," "if perchance," "was come," and the like. Had the English subjunctive been so far sloughed off that it might be ignored in good usage? Should "the children of Israel" continue to give the impression that the wanderings in the Wilderness were a sort of ancient prototype of the Babes in the Wood? The minutes of the early meetings of the Committee contain records of extended discussions of such problems.

A second meeting was held in New York City in 1930, and two more in 1931, and then another January 21-23, 1932. With that the work lapsed. The country was then in the depths of the great financial depression, and money could not be found to proceed. In the meantime the death of Professor Gordon had occurred March 5, 1931; his place was taken by W. R. Taylor of the University of Toronto. The committee was enlarged also by the addition of J. A. Bewer of Union Theological Seminary, and J. M. P. Smith of the University of Chicago. Considerable progress was made on actual revision. At the meeting in the Prince George Hotel in New York in September of 1931 an evening's session was devoted to the reading of extended passages from the Book of Genesis and the Gospel of Matthew. The solid impressiveness of the results remained long in the memory of those present. Plans were also completed for the revision of the rest of Matthew, and of Genesis and all of Exodus, by the designation of different sections to various members of the committee working in pairs. Much of this revision had not, however, been passed through the committee by the time it was obliged to discontinue its work.

Notwithstanding the prevailing financial stringency, efforts were put forth through the following years to secure funds with which to resume the task. But it was not until 1936 that the skies had so far cleared for American business that Dr. Roy G. Ross, General Secretary of the International Council, was able to negotiate an agreement for the advance of working capital against prospective royalties. Perhaps it should be explained that the money was needed for obvious expenses, which through the years required for the revision would total a considerable sum. But these expenses never included stipends or honoraria for the members of the committee. They have been reimbursed for their expenses, notably for travel to the place of meeting, but apart from the executive secretary, whose duties make a major demand on his working time, no member of the committee has ever expected or received payment for his work. The immense toil required has been given without stint, the one reward being participation in an undertaking of such importance.

On the basis of Dr. Ross's success, the International Council at its meeting in February, 1937, took up once more its consideration of the revision, and action was formalized in a motion which has become a sort of charter of the entire project. The Council decided:

That we record the conviction that there is need for a version which embodies the best results of modern scholarship as to the meaning of the Scriptures, and expresses this meaning in English diction which is designed for use in public and private worship and preserves those qualities which have given to the King James a supreme place in English literature. We, therefore, define the task of the American Standard Bible Committee to be that of revision of the present American Standard Edition of the Bible in the light of the results of modern scholarship, this revision to be designed for use in public and private worship, and to be in the direction of the simple, classic English style of the King James Version.

Further action related to the composition of the committee; it was to "be understood that not less than three and not more than five of the fifteen members of the Committee be chosen with a view to their competence in English literature, or their experience in the conduct of public worship or in religious education." The others were to be chosen "for their competence in Biblical scholarship."

In the intervening years death had taken other members of the original Committee. Professor Smith died in 1932, Professor Ropes in 1933, Professor Robertson in 1934, and Professor Eiselen in May of 1937. Then too, Professors Montgomery and Torrey, Armstrong and Sledd requested to be relieved of a task which was expected to continue through five to seven years. Through the summer of 1937 the committee canvassed names of scholars to fill these vacancies. Invitations were extended to, and presently accepted by, George Dahl of Yale University, Frederick C. Grant of Seabury Western Theological Seminary (later of Union Theological Seminary), W. A. Irwin of the University of Chicago, and Leroy Waterman of the University of Michigan. Professor James Moffatt was appointed executive secretary, to assume his duties in the summer of 1938, after his retirement from the faculty of Union Theological Seminary.

To implement the resolution of the International Council relative to men competent in English style and experienced in public and private worship there were appointed Reverend W. R. Bowie, Rector of Grace Church, New York (later Professor in Union Theological Seminary), and Dean W. L. Sperry of Harvard Divinity School; along with Dean Weigle these made up the required total of three. The committee was still incomplete when it convened in December, but shortly afterwards C. T. Craig of Oberlin (later of Yale) and Millar Burrows of Yale became members. After the first meeting

President Sampey found it inexpedient to continue, and Kyle Yates of Southern Baptist Seminary took his place. In 1939 A. R. Wentz of the Lutheran Theological Seminary, Gettysburg, was appointed, and in 1945 W. F. Albright of Johns Hopkins University, J. P. Hyatt of Vanderbilt University, H. G. May of Oberlin Graduate School of Theology, James Muilenburg of Union Theological Seminary, and Harry Orlinsky of the Jewish Institute of Religion. A severe loss was sustained in the death of Professor Moffat on June 27, 1944. His gracious qualities had endeared him to all his colleagues through the intimacy of detailed committee discussion across six years; his rare facility in English style had been a rich resource and guide when, as commonly, the problem turned upon the best phrasing of a meaning upon which agreement had been reached. A large part of the secretarial work for the New Testament version had been completed by the time of his passing, but responsibility in the heavy tasks incident to seeing the volume through the press fell primarily upon Dean Weigle. The office of executive secretary remained vacant for more than two years. Then early in 1947 Fleming James, dean emeritus of the School of Theology, the University of the South, Sewanee, Tennessee, accepted its responsibilities.

The committee, reconstituted and revived, convened for its first meeting of this second period of activity in the Directors' Room of Union Theological Seminary at 9 A.M., December 3, 1937. With portraits of notable figures from the history of Union Seminary looking down upon it and with memories of Edward Robinson, Francis Brown, and C. A. Briggs still vital, it was an impressive atmosphere in which to set about a task of such far-reaching promise for the place of the Bible in the modern world. The meeting, which continued through three sessions on that day and two on the next, was obviously concerned primarily with the reorganization and planning of its work, although one session was actually given to corporate work on sample passages in separate Old and New Testament sections.

Once again general matters of procedure came up for serious consideration. It was agreed that the task was one of revision of the American Standard Version in the light of the King James; the objective was not a new translation. In other words, the new version should stand in the direct course of the great English Bibles which reach back by direct dependence to Tyndale and Coverdale. Changes from the American Standard were to be made only for good and sufficient reason. They should be decided by majority vote as the work proceeded in each of the Old and New Testament sections into which the committee would obviously divide itself; in case of a tie the older reading must remain. But final action on any and all changes must be on the basis of a two-thirds vote. Authoritative original texts to be employed were the consonantal Hebrew text of the Old Testament (or Aramaic in the case of the well-known Aramaic sections) and Westcott and Hort's Greek text of the New Testament. It was laid down as a guiding principle that textual emendation on the basis of the ancient versions was admissible, but conjectural emendation might be practiced only very rarely and with great caution.

Lengthy debate was given to certain matters of English style. In particular the problem of the retention or disuse of archaic pronominal and verbal forms consumed much time. It was finally agreed, although not without dissent, that the older forms should be reserved for passages of divine utterance or of address to God. Later the usage was narrowed to the latter class. There was, however, no uncertainty as to the treatment of the divine name in the Old Testament; the committee agreed immediately and unanimously to "return unto the Lord"! It abandoned the novelty introduced by the American Standard Version in its use of the name "Jehovah" and reverted to the dignified title hallowed by centuries of devout use. To distinguish the Old Testament "Lord" from the title for Christ in the New Testament the former was to be printed in small capitals, as also the word God when it stood for the divine name in the original. Many other matters were discussed: paragraphing, the form of poetic passages, the use of quotation marks, and the like. Also a long list of minor details worked out by the committee in its first period of activity was endorsed and adopted as comprising rules of procedure.

Then setting itself to the labors that were to engross it through many years, the committee allotted groups of chapters to its several members for revision. While recognizing fully the accomplishment of its earlier activity, the committee considered it expedient for the Old Testament section to begin once more with Genesis, Chapter 1, and the New Testament section with the opening of Matthew's

Gospel, each section then in its work to make such use of the former results as it should see fit. As a method of procedure, the sections were further subdivided into pairs, three in each of Old and New Testament. The intention was that in each case these two men should exchange and criticize and reconsider their revisions before sending them on to other members in agreed rotation. These in turn were to send detailed comments back to the original reviser. By this method of double reconsideration it was hoped that relative finality could be attained before the assembling of the committee. In course of time this refined scheme fell into disuse; it was found most expeditious for each reviser, after seeking such assistance as he desired, to have his individual results mimeographed and circulated among his colleagues; but it remained the duty of these to study the revision in detail, send their notes to the reviser, and come to the meetings of the committee prepared to discuss in detail the passages under consideration.

At this organization meeting the Old Testament section allotted to each of its members a block of fifteen chapters—for the six of them, then, ninety chapters, which by coincidence was the total of the Books of Genesis and Exodus. It was a brave beginning, and offered high promise of an expeditious consummation of the entire task. But a cold awakening was in store. The section reconvened, in its first working meeting, at the University of Michigan in July, 1938. It worked eight hours a day from July 11 to 15 in the relatively easy narrative chapters of Genesis and Exodus, and covered approximately twenty-seven chapters! A similar result emerged from the meeting the following December, held at the Divinity School, Yale University; through the days 27-31 inclusive, again, as by coincidence, the total was twenty-seven chapters, although on this occasion much of the subject matter was in the legal sections.

The perplexing fact became clear that the meetings were the bottleneck of the committee's accomplishment. It was relatively easy to secure large blocks of individual revision, but the differences revealed among the members when they came together resulted in lengthy debate and slow progress. Various expedients were adopted to overcome this delay. An effective one was the holding of sectional meetings to treat assigned bodies of text. The Book of Ezra was thus done by the men on the Atlantic coast, and Daniel by those in the Middle

West; when these were subsequently reviewed by the full member-ship of the section, final action consumed relatively brief time. How-ever, the most consistent and effective device has been merely the efficient conduct of the meetings under constant effort to hold the discussions rigidly to the matter in hand and, while avoiding any limitation of effective debate, yet to seek to determine argument as soon as possible and bring the matter to a vote. When this policy had been efficiently administered, the committee came to recognize that, how-ever slow progress might be, no other course was practicable in the interests of the revision but to take the time necessary for adequate consideration of every contribution that each member could make toward an understanding and proper translation of the Biblical text.

The New Testament section met for two weeks in June, 1938, and again in the summer of 1939, as guests of Professor and Mrs. Good-speed at their summer home in Wisconsin. But subsequent meet-ings of both sections were held in the East, a few in Northfield, Massachusetts, but more in New York or New Haven. Frequently the Old Testament section worked through Christmas week in Union Theological Seminary and convened in June or early July in the Divinity School of Yale University for its summer meeting. But this oscillation never attained the fixity of a rule; in the better sense of the word, the program was opportunist. As the work advanced, the New Testament section hastened its progress with more frequent meetings, and presently the Old Testament section did likewise.

The procedure of the meetings became a routine dictated by the character of their work. The members of the Old or New Testament section, as the case might be, chose seats around a long central table at one end of which the presiding officer, normally Dean Weigle, took his place. On other tables close at hand were accumulated a mass of commentaries, dictionaries, and other relevant material. The central table had a number of copies of Biblical translations, ancient and modern, in addition to the materials which the individual mem-bers brought. The meeting opened with prayer. Commonly a few minutes were consumed with business; and then the work of the meet-ing began. The Biblical passages to be considered were already known; commonly the agendum was agreed upon at the previous meeting. And so, with his copy of the revision to be studied lying open before each member, and his ancient texts close at hand, discussion began, verse by verse, or indeed phrase by phrase. There were few verses of the revision that did not provoke question. In some cases it was felt that the proposed rendering was unnecessarily drastic in its departure from the American Standard, which it will be recalled was the basic text of the revision. Not infrequently decision reverted to the wording of the King James Version. No matter was too trifling for attention. On occasion there was lengthy debate over a preposition; sometimes even a comma provoked discussion. In some cases proposals carried with little comment; at other times a seemingly innocent passage uncovered a wide divergence of opinion. Argument frequently became earnest, sometimes heated; but it was recognized that there was no place for personal recriminations. Members who had opposed one another with intensity on the meaning of a Hebrew phrase or its most accurate and graceful rendering in English would be found, a few moments later, when the session had terminated, walking together in cordial conversation that manifested their genuine friendship. Cliques and partyism were non-existent. True, some of the men had been personal friends for years; also the course of the work revealed unexpected affinities of point of view. Yet the issues as they arose were faced on their merits as each member saw them. In a given proposal no one knew in advance who would support or oppose him. Old friends found themselves frequently arguing in strenuous opposition. In the voting new alignments were constantly appearing; the men who had stood together on this issue split asunder on that. The totals of votes showed a similar vacillation: all the way from unanimity—which was rare—to a minority of one, which often emerged. Of course that individual might comfort himself with the thought that one man *with God* was a majority. But the others had a contrary view of God's vote in the matter!

The sessions were long and tiring. The regular schedule was of eight or nine hours a day. After sitting through such days, constantly on the alert to follow or participate in the discussion, and this sometimes in the intense heat of midsummer for one or even two weeks, it is little wonder that most participants in the meetings came to find that they required some days of relative rest to recover normal vigor. However, the tedium was lightened with considerable good-natured banter—does a group of men, however serious their purpose, ever work together for long without finding some fun in their comradeship? Perhaps this suggests an answer to the question laughingly raised on one occasion, whether King James's translators had so much fun.

It was inevitable that the work on the New Testament should be completed first. When the members of this section had carried their revision through committee discussion, they began at the beginning once more and went through it all again. The advantage, indeed the necessity, of this course will be apparent. The next step was to distribute mimeographed copies of their results to the members of the Old Testament section for study, criticism, and final approval or dissent. When these reports had been received, the New Testament scholars gave a final meeting to consideration of results. Through August 15-29, 1943, in Northfield, Massachusetts, the entire New Testament was thus reviewed. The votes of the Old Testament scholars were counted along with those of the New Testament section, and by this process the opinions of the entire committee were registered. Only by a two-thirds majority of the entire committee was any revised reading finally adopted. This concluding meeting of the New Testament section was its thirty-first; in total it had spent 145 days in session. There remained still the details of editing the manuscript for publication and of overseeing its progress through the press. This responsibility was committed to a selected smaller group from the committee.

On February 11, 1946, the *Revised Standard Version of the New Testament* was published. Bound in blue cloth, and issued in a jacket that boldly announced "the most important publication of 1946," the volume was a credit to the printer's art and one of the most satisfying editions of Scripture to have appeared. The type was clear and attractive; the text was presented in full-page format; and the volume's 553 pages imparted to the reader a sense of ease and breadth. On each page the name of the New Testament book and the chapter number were printed at the outside of the top margin, and a factual heading descriptive of the subject matter stood at the corresponding inside corner. Page numbers were set in the center of the lower margin. Chapter numbers were indented, verse numbers were large at the beginning of a section, but elsewhere were in small, inconspicuous figures at the beginnings of successive verses. At the foot of the page there were commonly two series of notes. The first, in small print, gave literal meanings, variant readings, or, quite rarely, brief explanations; the second cited parallel passages, with blackface type for the original passage and lighter type for the parallels. Only four pages were given to a Preface, since the large number of introductory matters relevant to the version were dealt with in a paper-bound brochure, *Introduction to the Revised Standard Version*, consisting of essays by the members of the New Testament section.

The publication was celebrated in a service of thanksgiving and dedication conducted by the International Council of Religious Education, then in session in Columbus, Ohio. What could have been more fitting for the occasion than the singing of "How Firm a Foundation," as the processional hymn, and as recessional "O Word of God Incarnate"? For the Scripture lesson, Hebrews 11:1-3 was read by chosen representatives in the original Greek, then in the Latin, the Tyndale, the King James, the American Standard, and the Revised Standard versions. Dean Weigle delivered the address on "The Bible and Religious Education," in the course of which he outlined the initiation of the new revision, traced its history and its relationship to previous English Bibles, and gave a sampling of its readings. Symbolizing the actual publication, copies were formally presented to the International Council, to its president, and to five other representative persons.

A few days later, in the course of its annual meeting, the International Council adopted a resolution expressing "To the members of the Standard Bible Committee its deep appreciation for the monumental work . . . already accomplished through their preparation of the Revised Standard Version of the New Testament and for the work already done on the Old Testament. . . ." It expressed too its belief "that this version is a worthy successor to the works of earlier translators which served well their own days, . . ." and that it would "be an effective instrument in making known God's will for men through Jesus Christ." The resolution voiced deep regret that Dr. Moffatt had not survived to see this "proud moment," and concluded with the devout prayer that the translation might "lead many to serious New Testament study and to fuller fellowship with Him of whom its pages speak."

It was not expected that the publication would be greeted with such tumultuous welcome as had been accorded the Revised Version of 1881. Nonetheless, interest was deep and widespread. Available supplies quickly sold out; not for several months could the printers overtake the demand. A year after the original publication the International Council, at its meeting, presented the millionth copy of the edition to Reverend Martin Niemöller, then on a visit to the American churches. The steady demand was indicative of general satisfaction. More and more, as time went on, expressions of approval were heard from individual readers, from teachers in colleges or seminaries, and from leaders in religious work who found that in the test of actual use in a variety of circumstances it was proving a source of enlightenment. Formal reviews were in general favorable; one or two were of the "freak" type that evidenced more the reviewer's ignorance than any deficiency in the translation. Biblical scholars read papers on the version at their meetings which, while finding much to call in question—as was inevitable, for no translation can ever be perfect—yet conceded a general, if cautious, approval.

Work on the Old Testament continued. In its session in the summer of 1949 the committee reached the end: all had been revised. Then, just as was done in the case of the New Testament, it started once more at the beginning and went through it all again. This was necessary, and was eagerly undertaken; for much of the work lay ten years in the past, years that had been very fruitful in clarification of the character and methods of the revision. Comments and criticisms were sought and gratefully received from a wide representation of the life of the church; individuals on their own initiative contributed suggestions, all of which were accepted seriously and debated; the New Testament members took up their responsibility and submitted their views in lengthy series of notes. On these documents, as well as the detailed written comments of the Old Testament group, the committee worked for two years. At length in June, 1951, just short of thirteen years after its first meeting in working session, the task was finished. It had been a time of high scholarly adventure, of rich and rewarding comradeship, of toil, not infrequently arduous, but sustained by faith and hope for the worth of the common endeavor. There had come moments of sadness also; for in addition to the losses already recorded, the committee had been shocked by news of the sudden death on February 24, 1951, of Principal W. R. Taylor of University College, Toronto. His participation in the work had been second to none. Most of all he will be remembered for his revision of the Psalms. Fortunately, the committee's second study of his rendering was almost complete when he went from us, so that he saw the translation in practically the form in which it was later published.

An editorial group appointed from the committee had yet a year's work before it; copy began to go to the printers in April, 1951; but August had come and run its full course when at last they completed their tedious and meticulous care of minor details. There followed months of waiting, as it seemed, but in reality months of intense activity on the part of the publishers. Thomas Nelson & Sons, who had recognized the importance of the undertaking when it was as yet little more than a pious hope, and had given it generously of their moral and tangible support, now took the bold course of preparing a first edition of a million copies. It is said to have been the largest single printing enterprise ever undertaken, and some interested themselves in calculating the physical bulk of so many volumes and the mass of paper and other commodities required. Work went forward concurrently in New York and Edinburgh, and publication was simultaneous in America and Britain. The edition was in two forms, a two-volume Old Testament uniform with the New Testament published in 1946, and a single volume containing both Old and New Testaments, of which eighty thousand copies were bound in leather. Both were beautiful examples of the printer's art, presenting a page that was clear and attractive. Prose was set in paragraphs, poetry in its original lines. Chapter numbers, in Roman numerals, were incorporated in the text by indentation of two lines; verse numbers were similarly included, though in small size where they occurred in the body of the paragraph. Captions of a strictly factual sort stood at the top of the page on its inner side; in the lower margin were textual notes and a limited number of cross references.

Long before completion of the revision, publication date was set for September 30, 1952. More than a year in advance plans were well afoot for adequate recognition of an event to which most of the Protestant churches of this continent had given their approval, and in which they had participated in varying measure. A vigorous campaign of publicity was put in the hands of a prominent advertising firm. Popular magazines carried accounts of the revision and its place in the history of the English Bible. All headed up in a great series of religious meetings throughout the United States and Canada on the evening of publication day. Plans called for three thousand of them; actually there were 3418. Since programmes were prepared in the central offices, it is probable that the meetings were of uniform character. They were religious services, with singing, prayer, liturgy, and an address, then concluding most appropriately with the great hymn, "How Firm a Foundation." In the course of the meeting copies of the new version were presented to a few appropriate persons chosen from the community. Then at the conclusion, the version was on sale in the foyer of the building. And publication had come about.

The edition was quickly exhausted. Within a few days stocks were sold out, and only with extreme difficulty could an urgent copy be secured. Never before, it is safe to say, were a million copies of a volume so quickly absorbed by the reading public. Yet interest was not abated. Communities which for one reason or another could not hold their celebration on the appointed day, followed as they might; so that in the end it was uncertain where the final total stood. Notable among these was the seventh annual Festival of Faith of the Council of Churches of Greater Cincinnati on October 26, 1952. Eight members of the committee accepted the invitation to attend; the participation of press, radio, and television was enlisted; the Sunday services, with the guests assisting, gave prominence to the version. But the climax came in a great public gathering in the afternoon where more than fourteen thousand persons were in attendance. An appropriate religious service was conducted; then an impressive pageant of episodes of the history of the Bible was enacted in brief tableaux spotlighted in the immense auditorium, otherwise in complete darkness. As the culmination of the ceremony, Dean Weigle, chairman of the revisers and on their behalf, formally presented a copy of the version to the president of the Council of Churches, symbolic of the contribution which it was hoped the translation might make to the ongoing life of the church.

As time went on, the version was subjected, just as the New Testament six years before, to examination by scholars. It was not expected that their reaction would be devoid of adverse comment, for no translation can ever be perfect. Yet as on the previous occasion, the major opinion was one of cordial, if qualified, endorsation. Not so, however, that of extreme, conservative religious groups. Almost coincident with the publication, they began to voice objections, which presently became vociferous. Central in their complaints was the baseless charge that the committee had intruded its theology into the translation; apparently the concern of such critics was not primarily with what the Bible says, but with having *their* theology written into it. Yet these also served an end far beyond their quibbles. The words of St. Paul were relevant: "Some indeed preach Christ from envy and rivalry, but others from good will. . . . What then? Only that in every way, whether in pretence or in truth, Christ is proclaimed." It is doubtful that there was ever a time since the great impulse of Reformation days, when the Bible was, through whatever motivation, brought into such prominence with the general public. The occasion was a symbol of the deep stirrings of our time toward new apprehensions of the realities that are of the essence of the Biblical revelation, and was also, it is hoped, a promise of greater things to come.

Soon after the publication, members of the committee, friends, and Bible readers in general began sending suggestions for correction or reconsideration. Typographical errors were dealt with at once, but questions of translation were retained in a growing file for action by the committee. For the distinctive feature of this version is that it is in a constant process of revision that will take account of growing knowledge as well as of seasoned reconsideration. Every worthy criticism, from whatever source, receives serious attention, for the committee desires only a translation of the Bible as near perfect as is possible. Unfortunately, the most vociferous objectors contributed nothing to this end, due not so much to their animosity as to their obvious unfamiliarity with the facts of the history of the Bible and the principles and problems of translation. For just as in the case of the King James, abuse that not infrequently sank to scurrility was heaped on the version and its translators and auspices. Since all this will soon become small in the perspective of the years, it is of worth to record some of it for the encouragement of future Bible translators. For a time there were public burnings, in church services, of the version or of pages from it. It was called a "blasphemous unholy Bible," "an odious and contemptible crime," perpetrated by a "master strategy" using "fraudulent and under-hand means." It was a "corrupted version, produced by religious infidels" from "centers of socialism and modernism." More ingenious was the juxtaposition, "The old Devil and his new Bible." Evidently much of this arose out of the presupposition that the King James was the original Bible; hence lists of divergences were published, commonly with a citation of Rev. 22:19. Slightly different was the affirmation, "The TEXTUS RECEPTUS, original Greek text . . . copies of it substantially exist today without corruption"!

Final appraisal must await the perspective that comes only with the slow lapse of the years. Opinions of scholars, however important, are not conclusive; oratory and polemic are of little worth; argument signifies nothing. The real test of the version's worth lies in its usefulness, day after day, for the varied hosts of Bible readers. The devout, simple soul who knows little of the meaning of Bible translation, the college or seminary teacher who looks for a source of illumination for his students, the religious worker in his private ministrations and his leadership of worship, the great multitude of those who love the Bible and grope for clearer understanding of its incomparable message: these are they who will say through the process of years whether or not the translators have served well their day and generation. That they have produced a version for centuries hence not one of them supposes or wishes; their one hope is that they may have contributed significantly toward a better realization in our time of the unrivaled beauty and greatness of the Bible.

Appendix

The Dead Sea Scrolls[1]

The scrolls merit more extended treatment than was possible within the logical balance of our chapter on the Hebrew Bible (Chap. I). Their story is one of scholarly uncertainty and keen debate over problems that seemed, as often happens in archaeological research, to grow more baffling with each new discovery. Yet slowly the facts have fallen into place and large outlines of the situation have emerged, although there still remains matter for argument for years to come. The major issues have been three, though each of these is complex, in some cases with subsidiary questions that approximate primary importance. The three are, the age of the scrolls, their origin (that is, to whom they belonged and who put them in the caves, and under what circumstances), and their bearing on problems of the text of the Old Testament and on the history of their period.

Even before the existence of the scrolls had become generally known, their date was disputed. Mar Samuel, the Syrian archbishop, has related the skepticism he encountered in his stubborn confidence that his acquisitions were ancient and of high value. Similar was the belief of Professor Sukenik of the Hebrew University, who acquired for the university the remainder of this first group; he too was convinced that they were unique manuscripts from an ancient and little known Jewish sect. Professor John Trever, the first Western scholar to deal with the archbishop's scrolls, when he was satisfied that they were old, was driven to the obvious question, How old? He had recourse to the first edition of the present work, where, he recalled, a picture of the Nash papyrus stood as frontispiece. (It is still one of the illustrations; see Fig. 2.) We have related above (page 30) that, when first published, this fragmentary page of Biblical Hebrew was assigned to the first or second century A.D. However, a few years prior to the discovery of the scrolls, Professor Albright of Johns Hopkins had set forth his argument that it should actually be carried back to the second century B.C. Trever's examination convinced him that the style of writing in the scrolls is comparable, hence they must be of a similar date. He sent some photographs to Professor Albright, who fully endorsed this view. Before formal

[1] See pp. 30-32.

publication came about, vigorous criticism had been expressed, so that other considerations, of a sort to be mentioned in a moment, came under review. But it was largely on the basis of orthographic similarities that the scrolls were at length presented to the reading public as documents of the second century B.C.

But in reality we then knew very little about ancient Jewish styles of writing, and were in no position to determine the history of Jewish orthography. We had a few inscriptions of varying purpose on stone, commonly dated shortly before or soon after the beginning of the Christian era; there was an Aramaic mosaic from somewhat later; earlier than either were a few Aramaic documents from Egypt, though too early to be relevant to the current problem was the considerable group of Aramaic papyri from Elephantine of the fifth century; and there was the Nash papyrus. But it is apparent that inscriptions on stone are dubious evidence for the development of the written hand. And how far was it justifiable to invoke Jewish writing from Egypt, that is, the Nash papyrus as well as the Aramaic documents, as determinative norms of Palestinian writing? Further the dating of the famed Nash papyrus was itself highly debatable. Presently a minute study of its orthographic features was made by Professor Lacheman and led him to reverse Albright's opinion; it ought to be attributed, he held, to about the end of the second century A.D. Notwithstanding much printer's ink and contradictory claims by different scholars, it became apparent that orthographic evidence was inconclusive; at the best, if we were limited to it, we could attain no more than some balance of probability, one way or the other.

One of the most vigorous opponents of the prevailing view was Professor Zeitlin of Dropsie College, editor of *The Jewish Quarterly Review*. In issue after issue of this journal he stoutly maintained that the ascribed dating was wrong; the scrolls were medieval, a claim which he explained as meaning that he was not concerned for the moment about an exact date; the important thing was that they were not pre-Christian and must not be invoked as in any sense valid evidence of that time. Reminding his readers of the famous Shapiro forgeries of a couple of generations before, he even charged that the scrolls were "a hoax." No scholar had interviewed the Arabs who allegedly "found" them, none had even seen these men, much less examined the reputed cave; and anyhow there were notable inconsistencies in the stories of persons who had seen the scrolls in the archbishop's palace.

The hoax charge did not stand, especially when in course of time the cave was visited by competent archaeologists, and when other manuscripts began to appear in Jerusalem offered for sale by Bedouin. But Zeitlin had effectively compelled broadening of the basis of investigation with other considerations which, it is true, had already been envisaged but had not received the attention they deserved. The skepticism of British and European scholars also contributed to the growing urgency of a broader research.

Jewish scribes normally did not date their manuscripts. Here was the crux of the scholarly predicament. Then it will be seen on a moment's consideration that in addition to the dubious quality of orthographic evidence, we were dependent on three lines of approach to the mystery, When in all the centuries are we to fix a group of Hebrew manuscripts that suddenly force themselves on our attention? These three are: the archaeological context, if any, of the finds; the manuscripts as material objects; and finally their contents. All three are highly complex, as we must now show; and they ramify afar.

Archaeologists have refined their methods to an approximation of scientific precision in the dating of their materials. In particular, the succeeding styles of pottery: its texture, shapes, manufacture, finish, and decoration, are known—to speak narrowly of our present concern—through four millennia. By associated potsherds—worthless rubbish as they seem from other points of view—the skilled archaeologist can tell, frequently within astonishingly narrow limits, the period of any ancient find. The results of investigation of this famous first cave, already mentioned, have never been disputed. Why should they? They were the considered opinion of competent archaeologists. But it is one thing to have a fact; it is a very different matter to tell what that fact means. The predominantly Hellenistic pottery of the cave with slight Roman intrusion gave rise to long and keen debate. The apparently obvious inference was at once accepted by many scholars; the cave was used and presumably sealed in the Hasmonean period (143-63 B.C.), but was entered by some unidentified person or persons in Roman times. Clearly the scrolls weree written and deposited in the cave some time before its ancient sealing, hence a second century B.C. dating for them seemed a cautious conclusion.

The apparent entrance of the cave in Roman times seized the imagination. The great church historian, Eusebius of Caesarea, was claimed to have related that Origen at some time during his work on the Haxapla (pages 74-78) had gone into a cave near Jericho and consulted manuscripts. Was this the very cave? Did he forget his lamp and leave it for us, by this means to come almost into arm's reach of him? It was a thought redolent of the romance with which archaeology is infused. But, alas! the rosy dream dissipated. Examination of Eusebius shows that he said nothing of the sort, but only that Origen had used a manuscript which had been "in a pot." The vogue of this method of preservation of documents in a world that knew nothing of fireproof buildings and safe-deposit boxes is attested as far back as the sixth century (Jeremiah 32:14). The story lacks significance for our purpose.

While repudiating this connection, Professor Driver of Oxford drew attention to an ancient account of how an Arab followed his dog into a cave somewhere near Jericho; there he saw "a small house" that contained many books. The matter was reported in Jerusalem, and Jews came in large numbers and found manuscripts of the Old Testament as well as other Hebrew books. Driver went on, "Although there are not a few caves in the hills of this district, there cannot have been many, possibly not even two, containing considerable libraries, and the possibility cannot be excluded that this is the very cave of the recent discoveries, and that the scrolls now found are the residue left by the Jews on that previous occasion." (*Jewish Quarterly Review*, April, 1950, page 368.) It is a view which Professor Rowley of Manchester also favored. Once again one fairly catches his breath with astonishment. How the event anticipated that of 1947 and following years! Did crowds of devout Jews from Jerusalem actually throng to *our* cave, then leave it to be undisturbed through another thousand years until we in our time joined hands with the ages gone, impelled by almost the same Biblical interest as they? The answer has already been given in the brief sketch of subsequent archaeological survey of this region. So many "library" caves were found that we may say this was a common feature. We cannot accept the tempting guess, but must look elsewhere for solution of the persisting mystery.

Over against theories of this sort, Professor Dupont-Sommer of the Sorbonne propounded and continued to defend a quite different interpretation of the archaeological evidence. The pots in which the manuscripts were preserved were common types. And why should Jewish potters have suddenly changed their styles just because Romans had come to the land? Instead we deal here with a slow cultural interpenetration, in which Jewish pottery continued side by side with the newer techniques introduced from the West. Instead of demonstrating that the lower terminus must be the arrival of the Romans, with then a later unidentified and unauthorized visit, the meaning of the pottery of this first cave is single and harmonious. And it points to about the beginning of the Christian era, probably the first century A.D. Then the cave was closed; and it remained undisturbed until 1947.

Whatever the cogency or the inadequacy of such variant deductions from the same archaeological facts, one thing became clear: these facts were insufficient to establish finality. That further archaeological evidence presently became available has already been pointed out; we must examine its import in a moment. But now we turn instead to the light provided by the content of the scrolls. And we do so with quickened anticipation, for surely they must make some allusion to events of their time which then can be identified through our knowledge of Jewish history. It is clear, however, that all this relates only to the non-canonical materials; for the Biblical manuscripts contained, apart from textual variants, only what had been familiar through all the centuries. The problem is highly complex, extensive, and intricate. Doubtless for many years debate will continue, and also scholars will succeed in uncovering fresh allusions or statements that reveal the date of the authors or of the scribes of the documents.

Professor Zeitlin, in his repudiation of a high dating invoked the manuscript of Habakkuk, which was freely admitted to be a commentary. But, he argued, such Biblical interpretation belongs exclusively to a later time. But this also is not a conclusive consideration; for it is apparent that if presently other evidence were to demonstrate that this document really is pre-Christian, then the implication is the reverse of Zeitlin's view; Jewish commentaries originated in a higher antiquity than was formerly supposed.

Many other considerations of a comparable sort were put forward—and rightly, for certainly all this is relevant evidence, though much of it subject to the reply just now proposed. The term "righteous teacher" is reminiscent of a famous document of the genizah finds (pages 27-28, 32) commonly known as "The Zadokite Fragment." Indeed in course of time the interrelations of the scrolls with this hitherto very strange work became more and more clear. The date and authorship of the Zadokite work were unknown; but some scholars claimed that it is not earlier than the Eighth century. A.D. The common words for God (YHWH and *'adonay*), while used normally through the second commonwealth, do not occur here, but instead the short Hebrew word, *'el.* The Jews are not called *yehudim* but *yisrael,* contrary to the usage of the second commonwealth. Hosts of such minor points, words, phrases, forms of expression, ideas, modes of thought, allusions, calling for a familiarity with extracanonical and rabbinic literature, are the basis of the charge attributed to some Jewish scholars that Christian scholars do not know enough to deal properly with the scrolls. It must, indeed, be granted that first-class Talmudic scholarship is extremely rare among Christians.

The argument proceeded: the documents are of mediocre quality without style or distinction; it is certain they do not belong to the pre-Christian period. "If the orthography . . . and errors in use of the Hebrew language . . . reflect a period when it had ceased to live on the lips of those who used it, if the Aramaisms . . . are not otherwise recorded before Targum and Talmud, if some grammatical forms cannot be explained except as due to Arabic influence, the terminus a quo must be the early part of the 7th century A.D."

Prominent also was the debate about the *kittim.* In the Old Testament "the isles of *kittim*" means Cyprus, although in Daniel 11:30 the word refers quite clearly to the Roman world. Now in "The War of the Sons of Light with the Sons of Darkness," one of the manuscripts which Professor Sukenik acquired, there is mention of the *kittim* of Ashur and the *kittim* of Egypt. But the Habakkuk commentary speaks simply of the *kittim.* Are these the same? And in any case who are the *kittim*, since patently they are not the Cypriotes? Some scholars argued that Jewish expectations aroused by the First Crusade indicate that these Christian armies are the *kittim*, and thus the literary compositions are not earlier than the eleventh century A.D. But many believe that the *kittim* of Egypt and of Ashur are the Ptolemaic and Seleucid dynasties which terminated, the Ptolemies of Egypt in 31 B.C., and the Seleucids of Syria in 64 B.C. Further, Dupont-Sommer argues vigorously that the *kittim* of the Habakkuk commentary are not at all the same; from their character and conduct as deduced from the references to them, notably that "they sacrifice to their standards, and their very weapons of war are the objects of their worship," they can be none other than the Romans. He seems to favor republican as against imperial Rome, a view that became explicit when he went on to identify the episode of "the Wicked Priest" and "the Teacher of Righteousness" with Pompey's capture of Jerusalem in 63 B.C. But Professor Rowley disputed this. For him, these figures and in addition "the house of Absalom," and the rest, can confidently be identified with familiar personages of the time of Antiochus Epiphanes and the Maccabean movement.

Appraise these views as one will, the fact is that the area was a battleground of scholarship, with a plethora of discordant views such as to defy present summary. From such uncertainty we go, with shaken hope, it is true, to the finds as physical objects—as archaeological materials, one might say. In the course of a thoughful and cautious discussion that was frankly skeptical of the high antiquity claimed for the scrolls, Professor Driver suggested that chemical analysis of the ink used on the documents might throw light on their origins, since older Jewish inks were composed of soot mixed with oil and balsam gum, but from about A.D. 100 ink from a metallic base was known, and by the Talmudic age it was in common use. Six months later he reported that the analysis had beeen conducted by a specialist in the British Museum; the ink was of the carbon variety, "unfortunately," he says, for such inks continued to be used even after the prevalence of metallic ink. The result was completely indecisive.

About the same time the famous "carbon 14" test was invoked. The principle entailed is that all living organisms secrete this form of radioactive carbon, but at death the radioactivity begins a slow but uniform decrease at a rate that has been scientifically determined. Thus measurement of residual radioactivity in organic matter is an index, not precise, yet dependable within reasonable limits, of the time elapsed since death occurred. Some pieces of linen from the first cave were thus examined at the University of Chicago; the test indicated that the flax had been pulled about 1917 years previously; this is, in A.D. 33, with a margin of uncertainty of some years one way or the other. Now it is probable that the linen was woven within a few months of the destruction of the flax stalks. But linen is sometimes kept in a home for a generation or more. And did the guardians of the manuscripts deliberately choose old, hence cheaper, linen in which to wrap them? So the most that may be deduced with safety is that the manuscripts, if all deposited at one time, were put in the cave at some uncertain point between, say, the beginning of the Christian era and, perhaps, the end of the first century A.D. Professor Dupont-Sommer welcomed the result as support of his position. He holds the view, independently advanced in the first printing of the second edition of this present work, that the manuscripts were hidden in the cave at the time of impending peril for the Jewish nation, specifically during the great revolt against Rome in A.D. 66-70. Then, he believes, the cave was sealed and not again opened until 1947. But on this matter again we find no scholarly agreement, but a confusing diversity of opinions.

So then we must invoke further archaeological evidence. Fortunately we possess some of very high relevance.

In the excavation of Khirbet Qumran, the ruins of the Essene monastery, there were found a couple of inscribed ostraca—more simply, potsherds. One of them contains nothing but the Hebrew alphabet, of which a few letters have been erased and rewritten. Clearly it is a pupil's trial copy, as he learned to write. In a rather awkward, elementary way it will then provide a model of the writing of the time. And its letters are just like those of the manuscripts of the nearby caves. However, Essene occupation of the site extended over two centuries; the result is still vague. But it is reasonable to assume that a worthless fragment of this sort, left behind when the building was abandoned by the sect, had been written not long before. If so, it provides a sample of Jewish writing of the third quarter of the first century A.D.

The Murabba'at caves also gave us something of importance. It has been mentioned that they were intermittently occupied from Chalcolithic times (approximately the fourth millennium B.C.) onward into the Christian era; indeed the latest remains are attributed to the thirteenth century. Materials from the Roman period are our present concern. Coins were discovered from the time of the procurators, from the reign of Agrippa I (A.D. 41-44), and from that of Hadrian (117-138). Among the Greek documents was a marriage contract of the seventh year of Hadrian. The occupation of the caves in the first and second centuries of our era is thus well attested. But it is the Hebrew documents that are especially notable and relevant. There were a number of copies of a single work that refers to "the deliverance of Israel through Simon ben Koseba, prince of Israel." This Simon is none other than Bar Kochba, the leader of the desperate revolt against Rome in A.D. 132-135; and it is believed that the documents are originals of his proclamation of independence; they were here preserved because this cave was apparently the center and stronghold of the movement. For with still more incredible bounty the cave gave us also two letters from Bar Kochba himself to his general Yeshua ben Golgola. A third letter to Yeshua, sent by two underlings, reports among other concerns the movements of "the *goyyim* who fight against us."

We need not now dilate upon the astonishing circumstance that has given us such correspondence, nor delay over the alluring fact that David in his outlaw days had likewise his stronghold in a cave in the wild country of Judah. Instead the significance of this correspondence for our quest demands attention.

The course of investigation has again and again compelled discrimination between a fact and its interpretation (though in reality we never deal with pure fact; always there is some greater or less admixture of interpretation). And archaeological facts are no more than that such and such objects were discovered at such a time and under stated circumstances. All the rest is interpretation. The first with which the archaeologist has to deal is the genuineness of the find and then its relation to its archaeological context. Other equally perplexing questions follow; and if the object is a document the problems are multiplied.

The Bar Kochba letters have strange features. Critics were quick to seize upon them; the charge of hoax was again heard. We repeat: all this was to the good; such possibilities must be examined. But scholarship in general was convinced of the genuineness. In that case, here at last we secured just what the entire investigation has needed and for lack of which it has bogged down in contradictory theories. Here were dependable samples of Hebrew writing in Judea in the years A.D. 132-135. Now we have a fixed point, in fact two of them; for this serves to verify the Qumran ostracon. And from these points, with caution and full realization of individual idiosyncrasies of penmanship, the whole body of our now-considerable group of Hebrew documents can be arranged in approximately final sequence, and to some extent assigned dating.

Now the pieces begin to fall into place; the large outlines of the picture become clear, although small pieces still defy placing and there remain many blanks. But already the massiveness of our new knowledge overwhelms. It calls for a complete reconstruction of our ideas about the immediate background and the environment of the Christian movement.

Khirbet Qumran was the Essene monastery, the great headquarters of the sect. The manuscripts found in the caves of the region are Essene documents. We have already spoken of the astounding result, that our sources for the text of the Old Testament are thus carried back about a thousand years closer to their remote originals. Whether the caves were actual library caves, or were used by the sect for safekeeping of their precious documents in time of trouble—and probably both theories possess truth—the great matter is that they have preserved for us pre-Christian copies of large sections of the Scriptures. Differing appraisals of the worth of these relevant to the accepted massoretic text have been expressed—and again we can afford to be tolerant of both views—still it is not too much to say that textual criticism of the Old Testament has been revolutionized.

But this is only one aspect of our good fortune. The non-Biblical manuscripts also are Essene. "The Habakkuk Commentary," the manuscript of psalms which Professor Sukenik reported, his "War of the Sons of Light with the Sons of Darkness," the justly famous "Manual of Discipline": they are all documents jealously guarded in antiquity, but now revealing to us the organization, the principles, and the religious meaning of Essenism; into them the accounts by Josephus, Philo, and Pliny now integrate, though overshadowed by these firsthand documents. The "Zadokite Fragment," so long a puzzle for scholars, is also Essene. And the nature of the sect, that emerges from these sources, is rich in astonishment. Instead of considering, as formerly, the Essene movement an interesting but minor phase of Judaism at the beginning of Christian times, we must now recognize it as only in degree of lesser significance than the official Judaism of Jerusalem and the Temple. It was a movement of deep and austere personal piety. But as well, the remarkable contents of these documents of Essene faith and practice have led some scholars to claim that the sect must be identified as Jewish-Christian, an heir of the mother church of Jerusalem. Some on the other hand have entertained the speculation that John the Baptist was an Essene; others would even say the same about Jesus. All three views and their like are extreme. But they illumine the real situation. There is a wealth of interrelations between these documents and the New Testament; there are similiarities in the history and faith of the two movement; there is a kinship of spirit between them. Yet one was indubitably Jewish, the other Christian. The final comment is apparent. Judaism in its deepest essence meant personal piety; witness the Book of Psalms which has stood through all these centuries as the great classic of the inner life. This essential urge gave birth to movements in which individuals found a ritual and way of life more congenial to their aspirations than the official cultus of Jerusalem. As one of these, and as heir of all that Judaism had created in this direction, Christianity came into being; and its literature likewise.

A FEW SUGGESTIONS FOR FURTHER READING

The articles by Burrows and Trever in *The Biblican Archaeologist* xi (1948) constitute in a sense the official announcement of the finds, although numerous brief notes had preceded. Succeeding issues of this journal should be consulted, as also of BASOR (*The Bulletin of the American Schools of Oriental Research*), *The Palestine Exploration Fund Quarterly, The Jewish Quarterly Review, The Expository Times, Vetus Testamentum.* A large number of other journals, scholarly or popular, have also published material of varying significance. The long article by Edmund Wilson in *The New Yorker* of May 14, 1955 (later published by Oxford) justly attracted wide interest.

Some complete texts were published in photographic reproduction, and transcription into familiar Hebrew, by Burrows, Trever, and Brownlee, *The Dear Sea Scrolls of St. Mark's Monastery I: The Isaiah Manuscript and the Habakkuk Commentary,* 1950; *II: Plates and Transcription of the Manual of Discipline,* 1951. New Haven. A translation of the latter was published the same year by Brownlee: *The Dead Sea Manual of Discipline.* BASOR Supplementary Studies 10-12.

The following books will prove useful both for their factual content and their argued conclusions, widely divergent, but consequently illuminating:

BIRNBAUM, S. A. *The Qumran (Dead Sea) Scrolls and Paleography.* BASOR Supplementary Studies 13-14. 1952.

DRIVER, G. R. *The Hebrew Scrolls from the Neighborhood of Jericho and the Dead Sea.* Oxford, 1950.

DUPONT-SOMMER, A. *The Jewish Sect of Qumran and the Essenes.* Translated by R. D. Barnett. London, 1954.

ROWLEY, H. H. *The Zadokite Fragments and the Dead Sea Scrolls.* New York, 1952.

Selected Bibliography

APART from texts of the Bible and its versions, this brief bibliography is limited, in the main, to works in English. A few foreign titles have been included where they are of special importance. Periodical literature is also restricted; it contains such an immense bulk of relevant material as to dictate the policy of admitting only a few articles that are peculiarly pertinent. The purpose is merely to offer a useful, introductory bibliography; comprehensiveness lies far beyond.

Within the four major sections of the bibliography a further grouping of titles by their subject matter will be observed; such groups are then arranged alphabetically, according to authors. It should be noted that several works are relevant to topics subsequent to that with which they are mentioned.

GENERAL WORKS

BAIKIE, J. *The Romance of the Bible*. London, 1931.

BENTZEN, A. *Introduction to the Old Testament*; vol. i. Copenhagen, 1948.

COLWELL, E. C. *The Study of the Bible*. Chicago, 1937.

COOK, A. S. *The Authorized Version of the Bible and Its Influence*. New York, 1910.

COPINGER, W. A. *The Bible and its Transmission*. London, 1897.

DEISSMANN, ADOLF. *Light from the Ancient East*. rev. ed., London, 1927.

DE RICCI, S. AND WILSON, W. J. *Census of Medieval and Renaissance Manuscripts in the United States and Canada*. 2 vols., New York, 1935-37; Index vol., 1940. Revision in process.

DOBSCHUTZ, E. VON. *The Influence of the Bible on Civilization*. New York, 1914.

ENCYCLOPAEDIAS AND BIBLE DICTIONARIES, articles on "Apocrypha," "Septuagint," "Versions," "Vulgate," etc.

ENCYCLOPAEDIA BRITANNICA, 14th ed., article, "Bible."

ENSLIN, M. S. *Christian Beginnings*. New York, 1938.

INNIS, K E. *The Bible as Literature*. London, 1930.

The Interpreter's Bible, vols. I, VII. Nashville, 1952, 1951.

KENYON, F. G. *Our Bible and the Ancient Manuscripts*. 4th ed., London, 1939.

MACDONALD, D. B. *The Hebrew Literary Genius*. Princeton, 1933.

MARGOLIS, M. L. *The Story of Bible Translations*. Philadelphia, 1917.

MOFFATT, JAMES. *An Introduction to the Literature of the New Testament*. 3rd ed., New York, 1918.

PFEIFFER, ROBERT H. *Introduction to the Old Testament*. New York, 1941.

ROBINSON, H. W. (ed.). *The Bible in its Ancient and English Versions*. 2nd ed. revised by W. D. McHardy. Oxford, 1954.

RYPINS, S. *The Book of Thirty Centuries*. New York, 1951.

WINTER, J. G. *Life and Letters in the Papyri*. Ann Arbor, 1933.

PART I *The Old Testament*

Chapter I

BAER, S. AND DELITZSCH, F. *Textum Masoreticum accuratissime expressit*. . . . Leipzig, 1869-95.

GINSBURG, C. D. *The Old Testament Diligently Revised according to the Massorah and the Early Editions*. . . . London, 1894, 1911; 3rd ed. completed by H. E. Holmes, 1926.

KITTEL, R. *Biblia Hebraica*. Leipzig, 1905-06, 1913; 3rd ed. with co-operation of P. E. Kahle, A. Alt, and O. Eissfeldt. Stuttgart, 1937.

GINSBURG, C. D. *Introduction to the Massoretico-Critical Edition of the Hebrew Bible*. London, 1897.

KAHLE, P. E. *The Cairo Genizah*. London, 1947.

PICK, B. "History of the Printed Editions of the Old Testament, together with a description of the Rabbinic and Polyglot Bibles." *Hebraica*, 9 (1892-93), 47-116.

WEIR, T. H. *A Short History of the Hebrew Text of the Old Testament*. 2nd ed., London, 1907.

DIRINGER, D. *Le Inscrizioni Antico-Ebraiche Palestinesi*. Firenze, 1934.

DUNAND, M. *Byblia Grammata; documents et recherches sur le dévelopement de l'écriture en Phénicie*. Beyrouth, 1945.

TORCZYNER, H. *The Lachish Letters*. Oxford, 1938.

Chapter II

GALL, A. VON. *Der Hebräische Pentateuch der Samaritaner*. Giessen, 1914-18.

LE JAY, G. M. *Biblia. 1. Hebraica. 2. Samaritana. 3. Chaldaica. 4. Graeca. 5. Syriaca. 6. Latina. 7. Arabica*. . . . Paris, 1629-45.

WALTON, B. *Biblia Sacra Polyglotta*. London, 1657

GASTER, M. *The Samaritans, Their History, Doctrines and Literature*. London, 1925.

GOLDBERG, L. *Das Samaritanische Pentateuchtargum, eine Untersuchung seiner handschriftlichen Quellen*. Stuttgart, 1935.

MONTGOMERY, J. A. *The Samaritans, the Earliest Jewish Sect*. Philadelphia, 1907.

ROBERTSON, E. *Catalogue of the Samaritan Manuscripts in the John Rylands Library, Manchester*. Manchester, 1938.

Chapters III-IV

BROOKE, A. E. AND MACLEAN, N. *The Old Testament according to the text of Codex Vaticanus, supplemented from other uncial manuscripts, with a critical apparatus.* Cambridge, 1906-.

FIELD, F. *Origenis Hexaplorum quae supersunt sive veterum interpretum graecorum fragmenta.* Oxford, 1875.

HATCH, EDWIN AND REDPATH, HENRY A. *A Concordance to the Septuagint and Other Greek Versions of the Old Testament.* Oxford, 1897.

JOHNSON, A. C., GEHMAN, H. S. AND KASE, E. H. *The John H. Scheide Biblical Papyri: Ezekiel.* Princeton, 1938.

KENYON, F. G. *The Chester Beatty Biblical Papyri.* London, 1932-37.

RAHLFS, A. *Septuaginta, id est Vetus Testamentum Graece iuxta LXX interpretes.* Stuttgart, 1935.

————. *Septuaginta.* Göttingen, 1922-.

SANDERS, H. A. *The Old Testament Manuscripts in the Freer Collection.* Part I, *The Washington Manuscript of Deuteronomy and Joshua.* New York, 1910. Part II, *The Washington Ms. of the Psalms.* New York, 1927.

SANDERS, H. A. AND SCHMIDT, C. *The Minor Prophets in the Freer Collection and the Berlin Fragment of Genesis.* New York, 1927.

SWETE, H. B. *The Old Testament in Greek according to the Septuagint.* Cambridge, 1887-94; later editions of parts to 1925.

BELL, H. I. *Recent Discoveries in Biblical Papyri.* Oxford, 1937.

KATZ, P. *Philo's Bible.* Cambridge, 1950.

KENYON, F. G. *Recent Developments in the Textual Criticism of the Greek Bible.* London, 1933.

ORLINSKY, H. "Current Progress and Problems in Septuagint Research." *The Study of the Bible Today and Tomorrow,* Harold R. Willoughby, ed. Chicago, 1947; pp. 144-61.

OTTLEY, R. R. *A Handbook to the Septuagint.* London, 1920.

RAHLFS, A. *Verzeichnis der griechischen Handschriften des Alten Testaments.* Berlin, 1914.

SWETE, H. B. *An Introduction to the Old Testament in Greek.* Cambridge, 1900.

Chapter V

FISCHER, B. *Vetus Latina. Die Reste der altlateinischen Bibel nach Petrus Sabatier.* Freiburg, 1949-.

GASQUET, A. *Biblia Sacra juxta Latinam Vulgatam versionem ad codicum fidem iussu Pii Pp. XI cura et studio . . . edita.* Rome, 1926-.

HETZENAUER, M. *Biblia Sacra Vulgatae Editionis ex ipsis exemplaribus Vaticanis inter se atque cum indice errorum corrigendum.* 2nd ed., Innsbruck, 1922.

Liber Psalmorum . . . cura Professorum Pontificii Instituti Biblici edita.

SABBATHIER, P. *Bibliorum Sacrum Latinae Versiones Antiquae seu Vetus Italica.* Rheims, 1743-49.

VERCELLONE, C. *Variae Lectiones Vulgatae Latinae Bibliorum Editionis.* Rome, 1860-64.

BERGER, S. *Histoire de la Vulgate pendant les premieres siécles du moyen âge.* Paris, 1893.

BILLEN, A. V. *The Old Latin Texts of the Heptateuch.* Cambridge, 1927.

BURKITT, F. C. *Old Latin and Itala.* Cambridge, 1896.

COPINGER, W. A. *Incunabula Biblica: the First Half Century of the Latin Bible.* London, 1892.

FREEMANTLE, W. H. *The Principal Works of St. Jerome.* New York, 1893.

GOODSPEED, E. J. *History of Early Christian Literature.* Chicago, 1942.

STUMMER, F. *Einführung in die lateinische Bibel.* Paderborn, 1928.

Chapter VI

BARNES, W. E. *The Peshitta Psalter according to the West Syrian Text.* Cambridge, 1904.

Biblia Sacra iuxta versionem simplicem quae dicitur Peshitta. Mosul, 1887-91.

LEE, S. *Vetus Testamentum Syriace et Neosyriace.* Urumia, 1852.

BLOCH, J. "The Printed Texts of the Peshitta Old Testament." *American Journal of Semitic Languages* 37 (1920-21), 136-44.

BARNES, W. E. *An Apparatus Criticus to Chronicles in the Peshitta Version.* Cambridge, 1897.

BROCKELMANN, C., LEIPOLDT, J., FINK, N., AND LITTMANN, E. *Geschichte der christlichen Literaturen des Orients.* Leipzig, 1930.

BURKITT, F. C. *Early Eastern Christianity: Lectures on Syriac-speaking Churches.* London, 1904.

SPRENGLING, M. AND GRAHAM, W. C. *Barhebraeus' Scholia on the Old Testament.* Part I. Chicago, 1931.

WRIGHT, W. A. *A Short History of Syriac Literature.* London, 1895.

Chapter VII

Mikra'oth Gedholoth. 2nd ed. New York, 1937-47.

BERLINER, A. *Targum Onkelos herausgegeben und erläutert.* Berlin, 1884.

GINSBURGER, M. *Das Fragmententhargum (Thargum Jerushalmi zum Pentateuch)* Berlin, 1899.

———. *Pseudo Jonathan (Thargum Jonathan ben Uzziel) zum Pentateuch nach der Londoner Handschrift.* Berlin, 1903.

CHURGIN, P. *Targum Jonathan to the Prophets.* New Haven, 1927.

———. *The Targum to the Hagiographa.* New York, 1945.

OESTERLEY, W. O. E. *A Short History of the Literature of Rabbinical and Mediaeval Judaism.* New York, 1920.

SILVERSTONE, A. E. *Aquila and Onkelos.* Manchester, 1931.

STENNING, J. F. *The Targum of Isaiah.* Oxford, 1950.

Chapter VIII

BUDGE, E. A. W. *Coptic Biblical Texts.* London, 1912.

———. *The Earliest Known Coptic Psalter.* London, 1898.

THOMPSON, H. *The Coptic (Sahidic) Version of Certain Books of the Old Testament from a Papyrus in the British Museum.* London, 1908.

———. *A Coptic Palimpsest Containing Joshua, Judges, Ruth, Judith and Esther in the Sahidic Dialect.* London, 1911.

———. *The New Biblical Papyrus; a Sahidic Version of Deuteronomy, Jonah, and Acts of the Apostles.* London, 1913.

WORRELL, W. H. *The Proverbs of Solomon in the Sahidic Coptic.* Chicago, 1931.

HALLOCK, F. N. "The Coptic Old Testament." *American Journal of Semitic Languages*, 49 (1933), 325-35.

HYVERNAT, H. "Etude sur les versions coptes de la Bible." *Revue Biblique Internationale*, 5 (1896), 427-33, 540-69; 6 (1897), 48-74.

O'LEARY, DE L. "The Egyptian Contribution to Christianity." *The Legacy of Egypt*, S. R. Glanville, ed. Oxford, 1942; pp. 300-331.

SCOTT-MONCRIEFF, P. D. *Paganism and Christianity in Egypt*. Cambridge, 1913.

WORRELL, W. H. *Coptic Sounds*. Ann Arbor, 1934.

BOYD, J. O. *The Octateuch in Ethiopic according to the Text of the Paris Codex, with Variants of Five other Manuscripts*. Princeton, 1909-11.

MERCER, S. A. B. *The Ethiopic Text of the Book of Ecclesiastes*. London, 1931.

STREITBERG, W. *Die Gotische Bibel*. Heidelberg, 1908.

BLAKE, R. P., "Ancient Georgian Versions of the Old Testament." *Harvard Theological Review*, XIX (1926). Pp. 271-97.

SPINKA, M. "Slavic Translations of the Scriptures." *Journal of Religion*, XIII (1933), 415-32.

Chapter IX

KENNEDY, J. *An Aid to the Textual Emendation of the Old Testament*. Edinburgh, 1928.

NYBERG, H. S. *Studien zum Hoseabuch; zugleich ein Beitrag zur Erklärung des Problems der alttestamentlichen Textkritik*. Uppsala, 1935.

REIDER, J. "The Present State of Textual Criticism of the Old Testament." *Hebrew Union College Annual* VII. Cincinnati, 1930, pp. 285-315.

VOLZ, P. "Ein Arbeitsplan für die Textkritik des Alten Testaments." *Zeitschrift für die Alttestamentliche Wissenschaft* 54 (1936), 100-113.

Chapter X

BACON, B. W. *The Making of the New Testament*. New York, 1912.

CHARLES, R. H. *The Apocrypha and Pseudepigrapha of the Old Testament*. Oxford, 1913.

GOODSPEED, E. J. *The Formation of the New Testament*. Chicago, 1926.

HARNACK, A. *The Origin of the New Testament*. Eng. tr., New York, 1925.

JAMES, M. R. *The Apocryphal New Testament*. Oxford, 1924.

LEWIS, F. G. *How the Bible Grew*. Chicago, 1919.

MARGOLIS, MAX L. *The Hebrew Scriptures in the Making*. Philadelphia, 1922.

PFEIFFER, R. H. *History of New Testament Times with an Introduction to the Apocrypha*. New York, 1949.

PART II *The New Testament*

Chapters XI-XII and General Treatments

BARDENHEWER, OTTO. *Geschichte der altkirchlichen Literatur*. 5 vols., Freiburg im Breisgau, 1913-32.

BARNARD, R. M. *The Biblical Text of Clement of Alexandria. Text and Studies*. vol. 5, Cambridge, 1899.

BELL, H. I. *Recent Discoveries of Biblical Papyri*. Oxford, 1937.

BREHIER, L. *L'Art chrétien*. 2nd ed., Paris, 1928.

CLARK, KENNETH W. *A Descriptive Catalogue of Greek New Testament Manuscripts in America*. Chicago, 1937.

———. *Eight American Praxapostoloi*. Chicago, 1941.

COLWELL, E. C. AND WILLOUGHBY, H. R. *The Four Gospels of Karahissar*. 2 vols., *History and Text; The Cycle of Text Illustrations*. Chicago, 1936.

———, AND RIDDLE, D. W. (eds.). *Prolegomena to the Study of the Lectionary Text of the Gospels*. Chicago, 1933.

DALTON, O. M. *Byzantine Art and Archeology*. Oxford, 1911.

GARDTHAUSEN, V. E. *Griechische Palaeographie*. Leipzig, 1911.

GOODSPEED, E. J. *Greek Gospel Texts in America*. Chicago, 1902-18.

———. RIDDLE, D. W. AND WILLOUGHBY, H. R. *The Rockefeller-McCormick New Testament*. Vol. I, *Introduction and Color Facsimile;* Vol. II, *The Text;* Vol. III, *The Miniatures*. Chicago, 1932.

GREGORY, C. R. *The Canon and Text of the New Testament*. New York, 1907.

———. *Textkritik des Neuen Testaments*. 3 vols., Leipzig, 1900-09.

Die Griechischen Christlichen Schriftsteller der Ersten Drei Jahrhunderte. Leipzig, 1897-.

HATCH, W. H. P. *Facsimiles and Descriptions of Minuscule Manuscripts of the New Testament*. Cambridge (Mass.), 1951.

———. *The Greek Manuscripts of the New Testament at Mt. Sinai*. Paris, 1932.

———. *The Principal Uncial Manuscripts of the New Testament*. Chicago, 1939.

HUTTON, E. A. *An Atlas of Textual Criticism*. Cambridge, 1911.

KENYON, F. G. *Books and Readers in Ancient Greece and Rome*. Oxford, 1932.

———. *Handbook to the Textual Criticism of the New Testament*. 2nd ed., London, 1926.

LAGRANGE, M.-J. *Introduction à l'étude du Nouveau Testament, Deuxième Partie, Critique textuelle:* II, *La critique rationelle*. Paris, 1935.

LAKE, K. *The Text of the New Testament*. 6th ed., revised by Silva Lake. London, 1928.

LAKE, K., AND LAKE, SILVA. *Dated Greek Minuscule Manuscripts to the Year 1200. Monumenta Palaeographica*. First Series, Fasc. I-x, Boston, 1934-39; Index, 1945.

MADAN, FALCONER. *Books in Manuscript*. New York, 1927.

MALDFELD, G. AND METZGER, B. "Detailed List of the Greek Papyri of the New Testament." *Journal of Biblical Literature* LXVIII (1949), 359-70.

METZGER, B. *Annotated Bibliography of the Textual Criticism of the New Testament. Studies and Documents* XVI. Copenhagen, 1955.

MILLET, M. GABRIEL. *Recherches sur l'iconographie de l'evangile*. Paris, 1916.

MILLIGAN, GEORGE. *The New Testament Documents*. London, 1913.

NESTLE, EBERHARD. *Einführing in das griechische Neue Testament*. 4th ed., fully revised by E. von Dobschütz, Göttingen, 1923.

OMONT, HENRI. *Minatures des plus anciens MSS grecs de la Bibliothèque Nationale*. Paris, 1929.

OXFORD SOCIETY OF HISTORICAL THEOLOGY. *The New Testament in the Apostolic Fathers.* Oxford, 1905.

PALEOGRAPHICAL SOCIETY. *Facsimiles of Manuscripts and Inscriptions.* London, 1873-94. New Paleological Society, *idem.* London, 1903-30.

PARVIS, M. AND WIKGREN, A. (eds.). *New Testament Manuscript Studies.* Chicago, 1950.

ROBERTSON, A. T. *An Introduction to the Textual Criticism of the New Testament.* New York, 1925.

SANDAY, W. AND TURNER, C. A. *Novum Testamentum Sancti Irenaei.* . . . Oxford, 1923.

SCRIVENER, F. H. A. *A Plain Introduction to the Criticism of the New Testament.* 4th ed., rev. by E. Miller, London, 1894.

SOUTER, ALEXANDER. *The Text and Canon of the New Testament.* New York, 1913 (2nd ed., by S. C. S. Williams, 1954.)

THOMPSON, E. MAUNDE. *Greek and Latin Palaeography.* 4th ed., augmented by G. Bascape, Milan, 1940.

VAGANAY, LEO. *An Introduction to the Textual Criticism of the New Testament.* Eng. tr., London, 1937.

VOGELS, H. J. *Handbuch der neutestamentlichen Textkritik.* Münster, 1923.

VON GRONINGEN, B. A. *Short Manual of Greek Paleography.* Leyden, 1940.

Chapter XIII

Corpus Scriptorum Ecclesiasticorum Latinorum. Vienna, 1866.

CHAPMAN, J. *Notes on the Early History of the Vulgate Gospels.* Oxford, 1908.

CORSSEN, P. *Bericht über die lateinischen Bibelübersetzungen.* Leipzig, 1899.

HARNACK, ADOLF. *Zur Revision der Prinzipien der neutestamentlichen Textkritik.* Leipzig, 1916.

JÜLICHER, ADOLF AND MATZKOW, WALTER. *Itala, das Neue Testament in altlateinischer Überlieferung* . . . ; I, *Matthäus Evangelium.* Berlin, 1938; II, *Marcus Evangelium,* 1940; *Lucas Evangelium,* 1954 (Ed. by Kurt Aland).

NESTLE, E. (ed.). *Novum Testamentum Latine.* 7th ed., Stuttgart, 1952.

PLATER, V. E. AND WHITE, H. J. *A Grammar of the Vulgate* . . . Oxford, 1926.

QUENTIN, HENRI. *Mémoire sur l'établissement du texte de la Vulgate. Collectanea biblica latina* VI. Rome and Paris, 1922.

———. *Essais de critique textuelle, Ecdotique.* Paris, 1926.

VON SODEN, HANS. *Das lateinische Neue Testament in Afrika zur Zeit Cyprians.* . . . Leipzig, 1909.

VOGELS, H. J. *Vulgatastudien.* . . . Münster, 1928.

WORDSWORTH, J. AND WHITE, H. J. *Novum Testamentum Domini Jesu Christi Latine secundum editionem Sancti Hieronymi.* (Oxford, 1889-   ); *Gospels* (1889-98); *Acts* (1905); *Romans* (1913); *I Corinthians* (1922); *II Corinthians* (1926); *Galatians and Ephesians* (1934); *Philippians, Colossians, I and II Thessalonians* (1937) ed. by H. F. D. Sparks; *I and II Timothy, Titus* (1939) ed. by Sparks and Claude Jenkins; *Hebrews* (1941) ed. by Sparks. *Catholic Epistles* (1949), ed. by Sparks and A. W. Adams; *Apocalypse* (1954), ed. by Sparks.

WORDSWORTH, WHITE, SANDAY, *et al. Old Latin Biblical Texts.* Oxford, 1883-.

WHITE, H. J. *Novum Testamentum* . . . *latine* ε . . . , *editio minor.* Oxford, 1911.

Chapter XIV

BRITISH AND FOREIGN BIBLE SOCIETY. *The New Testament in Syriac.* London, 1905-20.

BENSLY, B. L., HARRIS, J. R., AND BURKITT, F. C. *The Four Gospels in Syriac, transcribed from the Sinaitic Palimpsest.* Cambridge, 1894.

BURKITT, F. C. *Evangelion da-Mepharreshe, The Curetonian Version of the Four Gospels.* . . . 2 vols., Cambridge, 1904.

GWYNN, J. *Remnants of the Later Syriac Versions of the Bible.* London, 1909.

———. *The Apocalypse of St. John in a Syriac Version Hitherto Unknown.* Dublin, 1897.

HARRIS, J. RENDEL. *Fragments of the Commentary of Ephraem Syrus upon the Diatessaron.* London, 1895.

HATCH, W. H. P. *Album of Dated Syriac Manuscripts.* Boston, 1946.

HJELT, ARTHUR. *Syrus Sinaiticus.* Helsingfors, 1930.

KRAELING, CARL H. *A Greek Fragment of Tatian's Diatessaron from Dura. Studies and Documents,* Vol. III, London, 1935.

LEWIS, AGNES S. AND GIBSON, MARGARET D. *The Palestinian Syriac Lectionary of the Gospels.* . . . London, 1899.

LEWIS, AGNES S. *The Old Syriac Gospels, or the Evangelion da-Mepharreshe.* . . . London, 1910.

MARMARDJI, A. S. *Diatessaron de Tatien.* Beyrouth, 1935.

PETERS, CURT. *Das Diatessaron Tatians. Orientalia christiana analecta.* Rome, 1939.

PLOOIJ, D. *A primitive text of the Diatessaron.* Leyden, 1923.

PUSEY, P. E. AND GWILLIAM, G. H. *Tetraevangelium sanctum, iuxta simplicem syrorum versionem.* . . . Oxford, 1901.

VÖÖBUS, A. *Early Versions of the New Testament.* Stockholm, 1954.

WHITE, JOSEPH. *Sacrorum evangeliorum versio syriaca Philoxeniana.* . . . Oxford, 1778; *Actum apostolorum et epistolorum.* . . . 2 vols., Oxford, 1799, 1803.

HORNER, GEORGE. *The Coptic Version of the New Testament in the Northern Dialect otherwise called Memphitic and Bohairic.* 4 vols., Oxford, 1895-1905.

———. *The Coptic Version of the New Testament in the Southern Dialect otherwise called Sahidic and Thebaic.* 7 vols., Oxford, 1911-1924.

KOOLE, JAN LEUNIS. "Studien zum koptischen Bibeltext. Kollationen und Untersuchungen zum Text der Paulusbriefe in der unter- und oberägyptischen Überlieferung." *Beihefte zur Zeitschrift f. d. Neutestamentliche Wissenschaft, 17.* Berlin, 1936.

THOMPSON, HERBERT. *The Coptic Version of the Acts of the Apostles and the Pauline Epistles in the Sahidic Dialect.* Cambridge, 1932.

———. *The Gospel of St. John according to the earliest Coptic Manuscript.* London, 1924.

SIMON, S. J. "Repertoire des Bibliothèques Publiques et Privées Contenant des Manuscrits Coptes," *Le Muséon,* 43-46 (1930-33).

HOSKIER, H. C. *The Date of the Bohairic Version of the New Testament: an Examination of the Text of the Apocalypse.* London, 1911.

VASCHALDE, A. "Ce qui a été pubileé des Versions Coptes de la Bible," *Revue Biblique*, 16-19 (1919-22).

SIMON, JEAN. "Note sur le dossier des Textes Akhmimiques," *Mémorial Lagrange*, Paris, 1940, pp. 197-201.

————. "Quelques publications recéntes de textes coptes (1938-1941)," *Orientalia christiana*, 11 (1942), 367-384.

CONYBEARE, F. C. *The Armenian Version of Revelation*. London, 1907.

LYONNET, S. *Les Origenes de la arménienne et le Diatessaron*. Rome, 1950.

MACLER, F. *Le texte arménien . . . d'après Matthieu et Marc*. Paris, 1919.

ZOHRAB, JOHANNES. *The Holy Bible* (Armenian). Venice, 1805.

BENEŠEVIČ, VLADIMIR. *Quattuor evangeliorum versio georgiana vetus, e duobus codicibus. . . .* Fasc. I, *Ev. sec. Matthaeum*. St. Petersburg, 1909. Fasc. II, *Ev. sec. Marcum*. St. Petersburg, 1911.

BLAKE, R. P. "The Old Georgian Version of the Gospel of Mark from the Adysh Gospels with the Variants of the Opiza and Tbet' Gospels," *Patrologia Orientalis* XX, 3 (Paris, 1928). ". . . Matthew . . . ," *Ibid.*, XXIV, 1 (Paris, 1933). ". . . John . . . ," *Ibid.* XXVI, 4 (Paris, 1950).

FRIEDRICHSEN, G. *The Gothic Version of the Gospels*. Oxford, 1926.

————. *The Gothic Version of the Epistles*. Oxford, 1939.

DA BASSANO, F. *New Testament in Ethiopic*. Asmara, 1920-26. (2nd ed., 1934.)

PLATT, T. P. *Novum Testamentum . . . aethiopice*. London, 1826-30.

DE LAGARDE, PAUL. *Die vier Evangelien arabisch*. Leipzig, 1864.

CASEY, R. P. AND LAKE, SILVA. "A New Edition of the Old Slavic Gospels," *Journal of Biblical Literature*, LV (1936), 195-209.

VAJS, JOSEF. *Evangelium sv. Matouše . . . Marka . . . Lukáše . . . Jana. Kritické studie staroslavanského textu biblického*, III-VI, Prague, 1935-36.

VOSKRESENSKI, G. N. *The Gospel of St. Mark* . . . (in Russian). Moscow, 1894.

————. *The Epistles of St. Paul. . . .* Part I, *The Epistle to the Romans* (in Russian). Moscow, 1892.

SKEAT, WALTER W. *The Holy Gospels in Anglo-Saxon, Northumbrian and Old Mercian Versions. . . .* Cambridge, 1871-87.

Chapters XV-XVI

BOVER, J. M. *Novum Testamentum Graece et Latine*. Matriti, 1943 (2nd ed., 1950).

LEGG, S. C. E. (ed.). *Novum Testamentum Graece, Secundum Textum Westcotto-Hortianum, Evangelium Secundum Marcum*. Oxford, 1935.

————. . . . . . . , *Evangelium Secundum Matthaeum*. Oxford, 1940.

MERK, A. *Novum Testamentum Graece et Latine*. . . . 6th ed by S. Lyonnet, Rome, 1948. (7th ed., 1951.)

NESTLE, EBERHARD. *Novum Testamentum Graece*. 20th ed., Stuttgart, 1950.

VON SODEN, HERMANN. *Die Schriften des Neuen Testaments in ihrer ältesten erreichbaren Textgestalt*. Vol. I, Berlin, 1902-10; II Göttingen, 1913.

SOUTER, ALEXANDER. *The Revisers Greek Text*. 2nd ed., Oxford, 1947.

TISCHENDORF, CONSTANTINUS. *Novum Testamentum Graece . . . Editio octava critica maior*. 2 vols., Leipzig, 1869-72.

TREGELLES, S. P. *An Account of the Printed Text of the Greek New Testament*. London, 1854.

VOGELS, H. J. *Novum Testamentum Graece. . . .* 2nd ed., Düsseldorf, 1922; Graeco-Latin text, 3rd ed., Düsseldorf, 1949.

WEISS, BERNHARD. *Das Neue Testament.* 3 vols., Leipzig, 1894-1900.

WESTCOTT, B. F. AND HORT, F. J. A. *The New Testament in the Original Greek.* 2 vols., Cambridge and London, 1881.

WEYMOUTH, R. F. *The Resultant Greek Testament.* London, 1886.

CLARK, A. C. *The Descent of Manuscripts.* Oxford, 1918.

———. *The Acts of the Apostles.* Oxford and New York, 1933.

COLLOMP, P. *La Critique des textes.* Paris, 1931.

HARRIS, RENDEL. *Four Lectures on the Western Text.* London, 1894.

———. *On the Origin of the Ferrar Group.* New York, 1925.

HOSKIER, H. J. *An Indictment of the Codex B and Its Allies.* London, 1914.

———. *Concerning the Text of the Apocalypse.* 2 vols., London, 1929.

KENYON, F. G. *The Western Text in the Gospels and Acts.* London, 1938.

KLIJN, A. F. J. *A Survey of the Researches into the Western Text of the Gospels and Acts.* Utrecht, 1949.

KÜMMEL, W. G. "*Textkritik und Textgeschichte des Neuen Testaments 1914-1937.*" *Theologische Rundschau.* Neue Folge X (1938), XI (1939).

LAKE, KIRSOPP. *Codex 1 of the Gospels and Its Allies. Texts and Studies.* Vol. vii, Cambridge, 1902.

——— AND NEW, SILVA. "The Caesarean Text of the Gospel of Mark," *Harvard Theological Review* XXI, No. 4 (1928).

——— AND LAKE, SILVA. *Family 13 (The Ferrar Group). The Text According to Mark. Studies and Documents XI.* London, 1941.

LAKE, SILVA. *Family II and the Codex Alexandrinus. Studies and Documents V.* London, 1937.

LIETZMANN, HANS. *Einführung in die Textgeschichte des Paulusbriefe an die Römer.* Tübingen, 1933.

METZGER, BRUCE. "The Caesarean Text of the Gospels," *Journal of Biblical Literature, LIV* (1945), 457-489.

POTT, A. *Der Text des Neuen Testaments nach seiner geschichtlichen entwickelung.* Berlin, 1919.

ROPES, J. H. *The Text of Acts. The Beginnings of Christianity.* ed. by F. J. Foakes-Jackson and K. Lake, Part I, *The Acts of the Apostles.* Vol. III, London, 1926.

SCHMID, JOSEF. *Untersuchungen zur Geschichte des griechischen Apokalypsetextes.* Athens, 1936.

STREETER, B. H. *The Four Gospels.* New York, 1925.

VINCENT, M. R. *A History of the Textual Criticism of the New Testament.* New York, 1890.

ZUNTZ, G. *The Text of the Epistles . . . Corpus Paulinum.* Oxford, 1953.

PART III   *The English Versions of the Bible*

GENERAL WORKS

ANDERSON, C. *Annals of the English Bible.* 2 vols., London, 1845; Vol. I rev., 1862.

BAGSTER, SAMUEL (ed.). *The English Hexapla.* London, 1841.

BAIKIE, JAMES. *The English Bible and Its Story.* London, 1928.

BARKER, HENRY. *English Bible Versions, with special reference to the Vulgate, the Douay Bible, and the Authorized and Revised Versions.* New York, 1907.

BROWN, J. *The History of the English Bible.* Cambridge, 1911.

CROOK, MARGARET B. (ed.). *The Bible and Its Literary Associations.* New York, 1937.

DARLOW, J. H. AND MOULE, H. F. *Historical Catalogue of the Printed Editions of Holy Scripture in the Library of the British and Foreign Bible Society.* 4 vols., London, 1903-11.

EADIE, JOHN. *The English Bible.* 2 vols., London, 1876.

FOXE, JOHN. *The Acts and Monuments of the Church.* ed. by M. Hobart Seymour. New York, 1855.

GOODSPEED, E. J. *The Making of the English New Testament.* Chicago, 1925.

———. *New Chapters in New Testament Study.* New York, 1937.

———. *Problems of New Testament Translation.* Chicago, 1945.

GUPPY, HENRY A. *A Brief Sketch of the History of the Transmission of the Bible down to the Revised English Version of 1881-95.* Manchester, 1936.

HOARE, H. W. *The Evolution of the English Bible.* New York and London, 1901.

HUNTING, H. B. *The Story of Our Bible.* New York, 1915.

INGE, W. R., *et al. Our English Bible.* London, 1938.

LENHART, JOHN M. "The Printed Bible: A Study in Bibliography." *American Ecclesiastical Review,* 110 (1944), 286-294.

LOVETT, ROBERT. *The Printed English Bible,* 1525-1885. London, 1894.

MADISON, J. V. "The English Versions of the New Testament," *Journal of Biblical Literature,* XLIV (1925), 261-288.

MCAFEE, CLELAND B. *The Greatest English Classic, a study of the King James Version of the Bible and its influence on life and literature.* New York and London, 1912.

MILLIGAN, G. *The English Bible: a sketch of its history.* London, 1895.

MOMBERT, J. I. *A Hand-book of the English Versions of the Bible.* New York, 2nd ed., 1890.

MOULTON, W. F. *The History of the English Bible.* 5th ed., London, 1911.

PATTISON, T. H. *The History of the English Bible.* Philadelphia, 1894.

PENNIMAN, JOSIAH H. *A Book About the English Bible.* New York, 1919.

POLLARD, ALFRED W. *Records of the English Bible: The Documents Relating to the Translation and Publication of the Bible in English,* 1525-1611. London, 1911.

ROBINSON, GEORGE L. *Where Did We Get Our Bible?* New York and London, 1928.

RUMBALL-PETRE, EDWIN A. R. *Rare Bibles.* New York, 1938.

SCHAFF, PHILIP. *A Companion to the Greek Testament and English Version.* 4th ed., New York, 1894.

SIMMS, P. MARION. *The Bible from the Beginning.* New York, 1929.

———. *The Bible in America.* New York, 1936.

SMYTH, J. PATTERSON. *How We Got Our Bible.* New York, 1915.

STOUGHTON, JOHN. *Our English Bible: Its Translation and Translators.* London, 1878.

Variorum Edition of the Holy Bible. London, 1880.

WESTCOTT, B. F. *A General View of the History of the English Bible.* 3rd ed., rev. by W. A. Wright, New York, 1905.

WILD, LAURA H. *The Romance of the English Bible.* Garden City, N. Y., 1929.

WHITLEY, W. T. *The English Bible under the Tudor Sovereigns.* London, 1938.

Chapter XVII

BRIGHT, J. W. *The Gospels in West Saxon.* Boston and London, 1905-10.

COOK, A. S. *Biblical Quotations in Old English Prose Writers.* London, 1898.

DUCKETT, ELEANOR S. *Anglo-Saxon Saints and Scholars.* New York, 1947.

MILLAR, E. G. *The Lindisfarne Gospels.* Paris, 1923.

WARDALE, E. E. *Chapters on Old English Literature.* London, 1935.

WATSON, R. S. *Caedmon the First English Poet.* London, 1875.

WHITE, R. M. *The Ormulum.* 2nd ed., Oxford, 1878.

WRIGHT, THOMAS (ed.). *The Religious Poems of William de Shoreham.* London, 1849.

BRAMLEY, H. R. (ed.). *The Psalter, or Psalms of David, and Certain Canticles . . .* by Richard of Hampole. Oxford, 1884.

HORSTMANN, CARL (ed.). *Richard Rolle of Hampole and his Followers.* New York, 1896.

PAUES, ANNA C. (ed.). *A Fourteenth Century English Biblical Version.* Cambridge, 1904.

Chapter XVIII

CAMMACK, M. M. *John Wyclif and the English Bible.* New York, 1938.

DEANESLY, MARGARET. *The Lollard Bible and Other Medieval Versions.* Cambridge, 1920.

FORSHALL, J., AND MADDEN, F. *The Holy Bible, containing the Old and New Testaments, with the Apocryphal books, in the earliest English versions, made from the Latin Vulgate by John Wycliffe and his followers.* 4 volumes, Oxford, 1850.

WORKMAN, H. B. *John Wyclif, a Study of the English Medieval Church.* 2 volumes, Oxford, 1926.

Chapter XIX

The Beginning of the New Testament Translated by William Tyndale, 1525. Facsimile of the Unique Fragment of the Uncompleted Cologne Edition. Oxford, 1926.

ARBER, E. *The First Printed English New Testament. Fragment of the quarto edition (Matt. 1:1-22:12) . . .* London, 1871.

DEMAUS, ROBERT. *William Tindale: A Biography. Revised by R. Lovett,* London, 1886.

FRY, FRANCIS. *A Bibliographical Description of the Editions of the New Testament: Tindale's Versions in English, 1525-1566.* London, 1878.

GREENSLADE, S. L. *The Work of William Tindale, with an Essay on Tindale and the English Language by G. D. Bone.* London, 1938.

GRUBER, L. F. *The First English New Testament and Luther.* Burlington, Iowa, 1928.

GUPPY, HENRY. *William Tindale and the Earlier Translators of the Bible into English.* Manchester, 1925.

MOMBERT, J. I. *William Tyndale's Five Books of Moses . . . a verbatim reprint of the edition of 1530. . . .* New York, 1884.

MOZLEY, J. F. *William Tyndale.* London, 1937.

Chapter XX

BAGSTER, SAMUEL. *Memorials of Myles Coverdale.* London, 1839.

FRY, FRANCIS. *The Bible by Coverdale.* London, 1867.

GUPPY, HENRY. *The Royal Injunctions of 1535 and 1538, and the Great Bible, 1539 to 1541.* Manchester, 1938.

————. *Myles Coverdale and the English Bible.* Manchester, 1935.

HUTSON, HAROLD H. AND WILLOUGHBY, H. R. "The Ignored Taverner Bible," *Crozer Quarterly,* XVI (1939), 161-176.

PEARSON, GEORGE (ed.). *Remains of Myles Coverdale.* Cambridge, 1846.

MOZLEY, J. F. *Coverdale and His Bibles.* London, 1954.

WILLOUGHBY, H. R. *The Coverdale Psalter and the Quatrocentenary of the Printed English Bible.* Chicago, 1935.

————. *The First Authorized English Bible and the Cramner Preface.* Chicago, 1942.

Chapter XXI

EASON, CHARLES. *The Genevan Bible, Notes on its Production and Distribution.* Dublin and London, 1937.

CARLETON, J. G. *The Part of Rheims in the Making of the English Bible.* Oxford, 1902.

Chapter XXII

BUTTERWORTH, C. C. *The Literary Lineage of the King James Bible.* Philadelphia, 1941.

DAICHES, DAVID. *The King James Version of the English Bible.* Chicago, 1941.

GOODSPEED, E. J. *The Translators to the Reader. Preface to the King James Version of 1611.* Chicago, 1935.

SCRIVENER, F. H. *The Authorized Version of the English Bible, 1611.* Cambridge, 1884.

SCRIVENER, F. H. (ed.). *The Cambridge Paragraph Bible of the Authorized Version.* 3 vols., Cambridge, 1870-73.

WRIGHT, W. A. (ed.), *The Authorized Version of the Bible. Reprint in Octavo Form of the First Edition of 1611.* 5 vols., Cambridge, 1909.

Chapter XXIII

AMERICAN COMMITTEE. *Anglo-American Bible Revision.* 2nd ed., New York, 1879.

————. *Documentary History of the American Committee on Revision.* New York, 1885.

AMERICAN NEW TESTAMENT COMPANY. *The New Revision and Its Study*. Philadelphia, 1881.

BURGON, J. W. *The Revision Revised*. London, 1883.

CHAMBERS, T. W. *A Companion to the Revised Old Testament*. London and New York, 1885.

FIELD, F. *Notes on the Translation of the New Testament*. Cambridge, 1899.

LIGHTFOOT, J. B. *On a Fresh Revision of the English New Testament*. 3rd ed., London, 1891.

LIGHTFOOT, J. B., TRENCH, R. C., AND ELLICOTT, C. J. *The Revision of the English Version of the New Testament*. New York, 1873.

MOULTON, R. G. *The Modern Reader's Bible*. New York, 1897.

RIDDLE, M. B. *The Story of the Revised New Testament*. Philadelphia, 1908.

WHITNEY, S. W. *The Reviser's Greek Text*. Boston, 1892.

Chapter XXIV

GOODSPEED, E. J. *New Chapters in New Testament Study*, chaps. IV-V. New York, 1937.

KNOX, RONALD. *The Trials of a Translator*. New York, 1949.

Chapter XXV

ALLIS, O. T. *Revision or New Translation*. Philadelphia, 1948.

AMERICAN REVISION COMMITTEE. *An Introduction to the Revised Standard Version of the New Testament* (1946), and to the *Old Testament* (1952). Div. of Christian Ed., National Council of the Churches of Christ in the U. S. A.

GROBEL, KENDRICK. "The Revision of the New Testament," *Journal of Biblical Literature*, LXVI (1947), 361-384.

JOHNSON, SHERMAN E. "The Revised Standard Version," *Anglican Theological Review*, XXX (1948), 81-90.

WEIGLE, LUTHER A. *The English New Testament from Tyndale to the Revised Standard Version*. Nashville. 1949.

WIKGREN, ALLEN. "A Critique of the Revised Standard Version of the New Testament," *The Study of the Bible Today and Tomorrow*, Harold R. Willoughby (ed.), chap. XXII; Chicago, 1947.

SUPPLEMENTARY

MAY, H. G. *The English Bible in the Making*. Philadelphia, 1952.

POPE, HUGH. *English Versions of the Bible; revised and amplified by Sebastian Bullough*. St. Louis, 1952.

ROBERTS, B. J. *The Old Testament Text and Versions; the Hebrew Text in Transmission and the History of the Ancient Versions*. Cardiff, 1951.

FISHEL, W. J. *The Bible in Persian Transmission*. London, 1952.

GLEAVE, H. C. *The Ethiopic Version of the Song of Songs*. London, 1951.

Index of Names and Subjects

Peshitta—(*Continued*)
  dependence of on the Septuagint,
    97
  origin of, 94
Peshitta project, 100
Petermann, 46
Philips, Henry, 249
Phillips, J. B., 304
Philo, 329
Philocrates, 51
Philostorgius, 117
Philoxenus, 193
Pinkerton, John, 99
Pius X, Pope, 91
Platt, T. P., 200
Pococke, Edward, 193
Poetry
  Canaanite, 13-14
  Hebrew, American Standard Rendi-
    tion of, 290-91
  of Israel, 1
  of Old Testament, 24
Polyglot
  the Antwerp, 274
  Complutensian, 35, 59, 68, 185, 203,
    256, 274
  London, 36, 46, 59, 98, 116, 204, 275
  Paris, 36, 45, 46, 98, 193
potsherd, 14, 15, 327
Praxapostolos, 172
Price, Ira Maurice, 172
Primasius, 181
Princeton Corpus of Septuagint Illus-
  trations, 175
Princeton Index of Christian Art, the,
  175
printing
  art of, 35, 155, 185
  beginning of in England, 243
  speedy growth of, 242-43
Prophets
  Earlier, 17
  Latter, 33
Psalter, 35
  of Aldhelm, 226
Psalmists, 1
Pseudepigrapha, the, 141, 144
Ptolemy Philadelphus, 51, 110

Puritans, 269
Purvey, John, 236

Quentel, 245, 247
Quentin, Dom H., 91, 213
Qumran, 32, 327, 328

rabbinic Bible, 20, 38, 107
Rabbula, Bishop of Edessa, 94, 191
Rahlfs, Alfred, 69-70
Rashi, 35
Ras Shamra, 14
Reformation, the Protestant, 187, 243
Regnault, 256
Renaissance, the, 240-43
Repetitions by Hebrew scribes, 22
Revised English Bible, 279
Revised Standard Version, 305-320
  *Companion to the Revised Standard
    Version,* 315
  *Revised Standard Version of the New
    Testament,* 158, 314-15
Revised Standard Version of this Bible,
  4, 316-320
Revised Version, 4, 5, 203, 211, 262,
  278-91
  annotated edition of, 287
  commendable qualities of, 286
  completion of, 284
  differences from King James Ver-
    sion, 285
  inclusion of American scholars in
    making, 282
  New Testament, 283
  objections to, 287
  Old Testament, 284-85
  organization of scholars for, 281
  Preface of, 281
  principles of procedure, 281-82
Reynolds, John, 269-70
Rheims-Douai, 140, 301
Rheims New Testament, 266, 268
Riddle, D. W., 173, 174
Rieu, E. V., 304

Index of Scriptural References